Ecological Ethics
An Introduction

Patrick Curry

polity

First published in 2011 by Polity Press

Polity Press
65 Bridge Street
Cambridge CB2 1UR, UK

Polity Press
350 Main Street
Malden, MA 02148, USA

ISBN-13: 978-0-7456-5125-5
ISBN-13: 978-0-7456-5126-2(pb)

A catalogue record for this book is available from the British Library.

Typeset in 11 on 13 pt Bembo
by Servis Filmsetting Ltd, Stockport, Cheshire
Printed and bound in Great Britain by MPG Books Group Limited, Bodmin, Cornwall

The publisher has used its best endeavours to ensure that the URLs for external websites referred to in this book are correct and active at the time of going to press. However, the publisher has no responsibility for the websites and can make no guarantee that a site will remain live or that the content is or will remain appropriate.

Every effort has been made to trace all copyright holders, but if any have been inadvertently overlooked the publisher will be pleased to include any necessary credits in any subsequent reprint or edition.

For further information on Polity, visit our website: www.politybooks.com

Ecological Ethics

This book is dedicated to the memory and example of

Stan Rowe (1918–2004)
John Livingston (1923–2006)
and Val Plumwood (1939–2008)

Contents

15 Postscript 267

Acknowledgements

This edition has grown considerably since the first, but I retain some important debts, especially to David Orton, Ian Whyte, Ted Mosquin, Victor Postnikov, Stuart Hertzog, Jack Stillwell, Suzanne Duarte, Ron Huber, Douglas Woodward and Dave Greenfield. All are present or former members of Left Bio, the online discussion group whose ethos is integral to the spirit of this book, and whose wisdom it is a privilege to be able to tap. (Left Bio is very much a collective project, however, and I do not speak for it.) For extremely helpful comments and suggestions, in some cases for both editions, I remain grateful to Michael and Penny Novack (also of Left Bio), Sandy Irvine, Nigel Cooper, Ariel Salleh, Val Stevens and the late Stan Rowe. Harry Cripps, Clay Ramsay, Kigen-san Licha and, as ever, Michael Winship also made valuable suggestions for some chapters, as did Martin Desvaux and Edmund Davey for the revised overpopulation chapter, and five anonymous readers for the new edition as a whole.

This book began life six years ago as a short essay for the website of ECO, a British online group which flew the flag for ecocentrism as long as personal resources permitted, so I would like to thank Sue Birley, Val Stevens and Barbara Droop, along with Harry Cripps, for their support.

I am very much beholden to John B. Thompson, Andrea Drugan,

Sarah Dancy and, for the new edition, Emma Hutchinson, all of Polity Press, who made this book possible and with whom it has been a pleasure to work. I also thank Joseph Bruchac for permission to include his poem 'Birdfoot's Grandpa', first published in his *Entering Onondaga* (Austin: Cold Mountain Press, 1978).

Among my other personal debts, in addition to some people already mentioned, I would like to thank the following: for her staunch support throughout, Susan Peters; for accommodating a father sometimes doubling as a writer, my daughter Sylva, as well as her mother, Suzanna Saumarez; my own late mother, Noreen Curry, who loved wild places, animals and books, and introduced me to many; my late father, Peter Curry, for his quiet environmentalism; for walking the talk, Anne Carpenter, Vincent Chambers, Jo Dubiel, Tom Martin, Yannis Mitzelos, Tim Robinson, John Sleep, Tim Winship and Fr. Guglielmo Spirito. In addition to most of the above people, other friends whose encouragement is appreciated include David Abram, Francesco Barravechia, Deborah Bird Rose, Tom Bristow, Margarita Carrereto Gonzalez, Peter Case, Sheryl Cotleur, Laurence Coupe, Mark Dickinson, Stephen Fitzpatrick, Leslie van Gelder, Graham Harvey, Patrick Joyce, Sean Kane, Ray Keenoy, Brian Kennedy, Vito de Lucia, Fabrizio Manco, Garey Mills, Garry Phillipson, Chrissie Philp, Neil Platts, Kate Rigby, Martine Sandor, Ruth Thomas-Pellicer, Bron Taylor, Wendy Wheeler and the Imaginals. I am also grateful to Howard and Annette Preston for their hospitality at a key point in my getting to grips with the first edition; for their personal and practical support, my sons Xavier and Simon, my sister Kathy and, notwithstanding any differences of opinion, my brothers Steele and Mark; for helping to keep the mind–body show on the road, my teachers and friends Dwyer Evelyn of Physical Arts and Barry McGinlay of Tai Chi Life; and, for enabling me to experience an ethic of care arising from compassionate reverence for life, the late Kobun Chino Otagawa, his dharma heir Vanja Palmers (himself active on behalf of animals), Pepi Sinnegger, and all the members of the sangha whose spiritual home is Puregg. This is not to say, of course, that all or even any of these people would necessarily agree with everything I have said here.

The three people to whom this book is dedicated have had a big influence on my thinking, and life. Two of them (Rowe and Plumwood) I knew personally, if not well or for nearly long enough.

I would also like to acknowledge the influence of Gregory Bateson, whose final classes at the University of California at Santa Cruz I was lucky enough to attend. For me, he will always be an honoured elder.

Finally, I want to thank all the green places and persons, human and otherwise, who have so enriched my life, and to whom I hope hereby to give something back. I hope this book will aid not only scholars but the unsung activists who are struggling – against the odds and always at the cost of an easy life – to protect the natural world we all share from its many enemies. They are not thereby misanthropes, but (as Stan Rowe once described himself) defenders of the Earth against the excesses of anthropes: Earthlings worthy of the name.

P.S. David Orton became terminally ill as this book was going to press. His name therefore belongs, with the greatest possible honour, among this book's other dedicatees.

Birdfoot's Grandpa

Joseph Bruchac

The old man
must have stopped our car
two dozen times to climb out
and gather into his hands
the small toads blinded
by our lights and leaping,
live drops of rain.

The rain was falling,
a mist about his white hair
and I kept saying
you can't save them all,
accept it, get back in, we've got places to go.

But, leathery hands full
of wet brown life,
knee deep in the summer
roadside grass,
he just smiled and said,
they have places to go
too.

1

Introduction

This Book

This book is intended to introduce the reader, clearly and critically, to the subject of ecological ethics. It is not meant to provide an in-depth analysis of any one school or thinker, nor to arrive at detailed philosophical conclusions that are irrefutable. Rather, my goal is to suggest a promising and reasonably coherent set of ethical ideas and practices, based on ecocentric values, which I believe are now urgently needed. Why so? Because to treat the natural world ethically means loving and respecting it for its own sake, not just ours; and unless more of us do so more often, not only will we suffer more but we will destroy many more others who are themselves blameless. Indeed, both things are already happening.

Let us take an initial look at ethics. Put at its simplest, ethics is the question of how one should best live and act. Even in the context of the Western philosophical tradition, that is a very old question. *Ecological* ethics, however – the view that ethical questions can no longer be restricted to how to treat other human beings, or even other animals, but must embrace the entire natural world – is a very recent phenomenon indeed. (The idea itself is not new, but taking it seriously is.) It has only come to the fore in the past 30 or so years, in exact parallel with increasing awareness of the worsening global ecological crisis. And that crisis is the ultimate context for this book. My hope and intention is that the notion of ecological ethics will make a positive difference, however small, not only in university departments but also outside them, in the wider world. We are therefore not concerned here with scholarship for its own sake, fine and important though that is, but with scholarship for the world's sake. So I will try to concentrate on those ideas or books related to ecological ethics which have the most to offer in that respect, and I will give less attention to any others.

Of course, enough time has passed for several good textbooks on the subject to appear, as well as some excellent anthologies.[1] What is distinctive about this one, however, is its emphasis on ecological ethics in the fullest and deepest sense. There are three basic strands: light green or environmentalism; mid-green, mainly concerned with (other) animals; and dark or deep green, or ecocentric. The last, which includes but exceeds the other two, is fully ecological.

Unlike, it seems, most other authors, I take the view that there is nothing inherently difficult, obscure or problematic about this view, even if it does require leaving the usual human comfort zone. So I spend longer on the deep or dark green ethics of Deep Ecology, Gaia Theory and so on, and on related ethics such as ecofeminism, than you will probably find in otherwise similar books, for the simple but valid reason that they have been comparatively neglected, even by 'environmentalists' and 'environmental philosophers' (for reasons and in ways we shall examine). And I shall try to stay focused on the distinctive perspective of ecological and especially ecocentric ethics, not least in order not to become lost in the many other subjects we have to consider.

This book therefore does not advocate ethics by 'extension' from human beings through other animals (mostly those lucky enough to resemble people in some way that is valued) to, perhaps, and only after much agonizing, trees.[2] Rather, I *start* from the belief, or perception, that nature – which certainly includes humanity – is the ultimate source of all value. This 'more-than-human' nature, as Abram (1996a) aptly calls it, is not simply a set of 'resources' for us to use as we will. Not only does it have intrinsic value (something we shall discuss further below), but agency, intention, emotion: attributes which some arrogantly claim as solely human, but which result from, and are properties of, the entire web of life.[3] And relationships between subjects entail ethics. (Even if you can do whatever you want with or to an object without any ethical implications, you cannot do so to another subject.) As Richard Sylvan and David Bennett put it, 'the ecological community forms the ethical community' (1994: 91).

This move resituates humans in ecological terms and nonhumans in ethical terms (Plumwood 2006b: 64). Along with the promise of a more just, stable and fulfilling life for all come some novel, even (for most people) startling, implications. One, as we shall see, is that in order to be truly ecocentric an ethic must recognize that, in certain situations, the needs or rights of the Earth or its nonhuman inhabitants must take precedence over purely or narrowly human ones.

Why do we need an ecological ethic as distinct from one based, say, on enlightened human self-interest?[4] One reason is that the record of the latter, which has provided the basis for all our ethical philosophies until now, is not encouraging. The current and ongoing ecocrisis clearly implies that 'environmentally at least, *all established ethics are inadequate*' (Sylvan and Bennett 1994: 26; emphasis in original). Although we shall have to qualify what is meant by 'established ethics', the broad truth of this statement stands: our ethics needs to change, because our behaviour, as influenced by ethics, needs to change.

Relatedly, the problem with self-interest is that it is, as Mary Midgley (1997: 94) says, 'by its nature rather unenlightened and hard to enlighten'. Ethics that is only concerned with humans encourages our powerful susceptibility to limited sympathies, short-termism and greed, rather than checking it. It also denies any responsibility for the effects of our behaviour on the millions of other species and many millions of living individuals with whom we share the Earth: not exactly an ethically impressive position.

An Initial Example

Suppose a company, with official blessing, wants to cut down a forest of old-growth hardwood trees and convert them into paper products. Some environmentalists strongly oppose this, arguing that the trees are more valuable, even useful, as they are. Local people are largely split between those whom the company employs (or lays off) and their supporters, and others for whom the most important thing is preserving the natural environment.

Is one side ethical and the other not? No: they are informed by *different* ethics, based on different values. Simply put, the values of those supporting the cut are anthropocentric (mainly or only concerned with human beings) and instrumentalist (the value of the forest is what it can be used for); the values of those opposing it are ecocentric (concerned with nonhuman nature as well as humans) and intrinsic (the forest has value in itself, regardless of its usefulness to us). We shall flesh out all these terms later.

Those in favour of logging might argue that local jobs depend on it, that the (human) public needs such products, that the old-growth trees can be replaced by purpose-grown ones which (in terms of timber) are just as good, and so on. Against this, there is an argument from enlightened self-interest that these particular trees are more 'useful' to us left alone because of their contribution to stabilizing the climate, air and soil upon which we ultimately depend. However, that point, although important and almost self-evidently true, can appear vague and abstract; more urgent considerations in 'our' interest are always close to hand. But add the arguments that old-growth forest is vastly richer (in terms of biodiversity) than a planted monoculture and can never, as such, be replaced; that it has value in and for itself regardless of its use-value to us, which can never be measured in units of square yards or dollars; that the conversion of an irreplacable living place and home to so many others into, say, cardboard and toilet-paper would be despicable or even mad – and so on. Now we are approaching a level playing-field, at least, for such disputes.

Of course, the points just mentioned are 'value-judgements' – just as the arguments on the other side are, notwithstanding their sometimes 'rational' language. Value-judgements are unavoidable for humans. (Even if all considerations were somehow quantified and fed into a computer for an 'objective answer', the outcome would simply reflect the value placed by its supporters on quantification, something called 'objectivity', and machines.) As one of the founders of Deep Ecology said, 'The strength of the Deep Ecology movement depends upon the willingness and ability of its supporters to force fact-dependent experts who underpin environmental decisions into discussions in terms of values and priorities' (Naess 1989: 72).

When it comes to ecocentric values and ethics, Stephen Jay Gould (1993: 40) has observed that 'we cannot win this battle to save species and environments without forging an emotional bond between ourselves and nature as well – for we will not fight to save what we do not love'. In other words, an emotional and even religious apprehension of nature's intrinsic value is not necessarily a problem; it is an important *part* of an ecological ethic.[5] (Conversely, the classical economists' image of human beings as purely rational individuals seeking to maximize their own self-interest *is* a problem.) And however paradoxical it may appear, concern for nonhuman nature greatly increases the likelihood of our own survival.

The trouble is (and herein lies many of our woes) people often don't value what is valuable. But what is valued is what ultimately determines ethics in practice. People will treat properly whoever or whatever they care about, and whatever they don't, they probably won't. So there is also an irreducible political, social and cultural dimension to ecological ethics: how to encourage enough people to behave in a sufficiently eco-ethical way, and discourage them from acting otherwise; and sooner rather than later.

People lead busy lives, dominated mostly by urgent personal concerns. Does it seem far-fetched that those lives become ones of more, if not absolute, ecological virtue? Perhaps, but as Sylvan and Bennett point out, 'Part of the task of implementing environmental ethics consists in imagining and aiming for what lies entirely beyond the bounds of present practice, thinking the unthinkable' (1994: 182). We could start by considering this: is not everything humanity has ever done, in the broadest possible sense, a development, no matter how refined, of the Earth out of which we have evolved, and of which we are still composed? More: take away the Earth and its so-called support-systems, and all life-forms, including you and me, would vanish without a trace. Is it then something of which we need take no serious heed?

Looked at in this way, an ecological ethic surely amounts to profound common sense. Indeed, the longer one spends thinking about these matters, the more today's so-called hard-nosed, single-minded and ruthless realists – corporate directors, political leaders, media moguls and other opinion-formers – appear to be the ultimate dreamers. Some of the most disastrous fantasies in human history have been espoused and pursued by 'realists'.[6] (As for professional economists, it beggars belief what some will believe: that growth can continue forever in a finite world, say, not to mention Credit Default Swaps and increasing debt as a way to get rich.)

Even the kind of realism that is called 'enlightened self-interest' is not enough. For one thing, the nonhuman nature with which we share the Earth deserves as serious moral consideration as do humans. For another, unless nature gets such consideration, its richest and most wonderful places and the greater part of our fellow Earthlings are unlikely, as a direct result of our self-centredness, to survive this century – at least as great a crime as any we have committed against each other – and many, if not most of us are likely to follow.

Notwithstanding our usual intense entanglements with ourselves and those in our immediate circle, however, even we modern human beings have not entirely lost touch with an awareness of our profound involvement in, and dependence on, the natural world. Many people, perhaps a surprising number, still 'feel they live within a vast whole – nature – which is in some sense the source of all value, and whose workings are quite generally entitled to respect' (Midgley 1997: 95–6). This is a hopeful sign.

Looking Ahead

In what follows in this chapter, I shall briefly review the nature and scale of the problem for which a good short word is **ecocide**: the wholesale destruction of life and the source of life, including ours – an Earth able to provide a livable home.[7] Then I shall sketch out ethics as such, two modern kinds and one ancient but recently revived. The last, known as 'virtue ethics', I shall suggest offers the most hope for developing a widespread, lasting and flexible ecological ethic. The book then turns to three kinds of specifically ecological ethics: light green (environmental), mid-green (especially animal libera-tion/rights/welfare), and dark or deep green (ecocentric), which last includes Aldo Leopold's Land Ethic, James Lovelock's Gaia Theory, Arne Naess's Deep Ecology, Richard Sylvan's Deep Green Theory, Left Biocentrism, and the Earth Manifesto and Earth Charter.

After that, in what is essentially the second part of the book, we shall consider various dimensions of what goes to make up ecocentrically virtuous character (being) and behaviour (doing), both individually and collectively. That includes the contributions of ecofeminism; pluralism and pragmatism; religion and/or spirituality, with special emphasis on Christianity, Buddhism and animism; developing green citizenship, on the model of civic republicanism, together with eco-education and traditional ecological knowledge; and ecologically sustainable economies/societies, including the food system, energy and climate change. There follows a chapter on the eco-ethical problem of human-overpopulation, before I conclude with some final thoughts.

This new edition has seen much of the first one revised or augmented, but most of the new material is in the sections on religious ethics, virtue ethics, animals (including meat-eating), green ethics as post-secular, and green citizenship and eco-education, with the chapter on 'grounding an ecological ethic' (including sustainability, ecosocialism, business, the commons, climate change, wind power and green movements) entirely new.

Value and Nature

There is a spectrum of what is valued, proceeding from the anthropocentric (human-centred), which is entirely restricted to humanity, through to the thoroughly ecocentric (Earth-centred). We shall increasingly concentrate on the latter kind as we move through the spectrum, looking at the strengths of each major position on it, but also limitations that point to the need for a more ecocentric alternative. However, ecological ethics is not intended to replace traditional human-centred ethics, which has a legitimate and important role in intra-human relationships. The point is, rather, that adding something new will enable an ethical behaviour that a more anthropocentric ethics cannot, on its own, accomplish. (I would add that once we arrive at a fully deep or dark green ethic, there will also be no attempt to judge between the several different kinds as to which is the 'most ecocentric'; here too, each has its strengths and weaknesses.)

The same reasoning explains why I have not called the subject, as it is more commonly known, 'environmental ethics'.[8] While there is

no point in trying to ban the term, 'environment' is widely understood in its literal meaning, namely that which surrounds. It thus
denotes a passive setting which is really of secondary interest to the
supposed stars. In recent years, the term has acquired a more abstract
and scientific dimension, designating the biological processes and
systems that sustain – again, so far as most people are concerned – us.[9]
In either case, the term lends itself far too readily to two assumptions
that contribute massively to ecological crisis: that ultimately, only
'we' matter (which, in practice, is usually restricted to only a few
humans at that); and that the value, and indeed reality, of everything
else only matters to the extent that it enables us to get on with our
own show. It thus tends to support the ongoing collective cult of
human narcissism or self-celebrity-worship, while the wide world –
the only one we have – goes to hell in the proverbial handcart (or
Hummer, perhaps).

  To be sure, 'ecological' is not without its problems. The word was
coined in 1866 by the German natural philosopher Ernst Haeckel,
who borrowed the Greek word *oikos*, meaning 'home' or 'household', to describe the scientific study of the relationships among
organisms and between them and their environments. In recent
years, however, almost any subject or its study which emphasizes
interrelationships has come to be described as ecological: the ecology
of cities, family ecology, etc. In this way a whole range of meanings has now evolved, and confusion can arise if the kind of ecology
intended is not made clear. But there is no reason to allow biologists
proprietary rights over the word. 'Ecological' is now also commonly
understood, quite legitimately, to describe a metaphysical and/or
political philosophy centred on nature. And an ecological understanding of nature itself is as the extraordinarily complex and subtle
web of organic and non-organic life which is entirely *relational* – so
the entities related are constituted by those relations – and *reflexive*,
so that it is impossible to stand outside and observe or manipulate it,
either as a whole or in part, without affecting it or its other parts, or
without being affected by it. Needless to say, I hope, human beings
are part of nature so conceived; but they are only a part, and in many
ways far from the most important.

Ethics and Grub

It might be asked, why do we need ethics at all and thus, by implication, a book such as this? We shall look more closely at ethics in Chapter 3, but its basic questions are: What is good? And what (if anything) is the ultimate good? What is the best way to live? Or the right way to be, or at least to act? Of course, these can be troubling questions and for many people, both as individuals and collectively, in any kind of organization, it often seems easier to avoid them. This has led to the convenient assumption (for some) that ethics is at most some kind of special subject which is separate from, and therefore ultimately an optional add-on to, the rest of life. To put it crudely, as Bertold Brecht once did, 'Grub first, then ethics.' But all human societies have values and ethics; and far from being optional considerations, they are among the strongest factors that determine our actual behaviour on the ground. Brecht's statement reflects a particular kind of ethics, not an absence of any. And once having adopted such a view, grub – particularly when it is not actually an urgent issue – is often followed by a long list of other concerns which apparently also take precedence over ethics. (When these extend to personal security, comfort and glamour, a single person purchasing a four-wheel SUV for use in the city, for example, can apparently make perfect sense.)

We are also in real trouble when we allow questions of efficiency or technical 'sweetness' to shut out ethics altogether. There is massive institutionalized and career pressure to do so in most modern professions, especially the most richly rewarded. An SS doctor from the Auschwitz–Birkenau death camp told his interviewer, Robert Jay Lifton: 'Ethics was not a word used in Auschwitz. Doctors and others spoke only about how to do things most efficiently, about what worked best' (1987: 91). Of course, this is an extreme example, but I don't doubt that most readers will readily recognize the sentiment from their own or others' experience. As Feyerabend (1987: 313) comments: 'Auschwitz is a manifestation of an attitude that still thrives in our midst.' (Even – especially – if it feels wrong, keep your head down, don't ask awkward questions, just do it.)

The view of ethics as optional is thus not only nonsense – as if anyone lived or acted without any idea of what is good, and therefore right (however perverted from another ethical point of view) – but dangerous. The consequences affect us all; and when I say 'all', I don't just mean human beings. With the possible exception of those living in extreme poverty where simple physical survival is an issue, there are always choices available regarding how to acquire one's grub, to say nothing of other goods, and some will be distinctly more ethically defensible than others. To pretend otherwise simply allows the values that do guide our choices to go unexamined and undiscussed, often under a cloak of a 'sensible consensus'.

Lately, when pressed, some committees have taken to hiring an 'ethicist'. But ethics, properly understood, is a dimension of every human experience and enterprise; it cannot safely be left to others to take care of. As Joseph R. Des Jardins says, 'Leaving environmental decisions to the "experts" in science and technology does not mean that these decisions will be objective and value neutral. It means only that the values and philosophical assumptions that do decide the issue will be those that these experts hold' (2001: 7).

This point applies as much to ecology as to any other subject. The human-driven processes causing the present destruction of the natural world – unprecedented, if not in scale, in being largely the result of the activities of a single species – are not unethical in the sense that ethics is missing. On the contrary, they are saturated with a particular kind of ethics: one which is not only ecologically pathological, but largely unconscious. At that point, as someone once remarked, 'we do not have the idea; it has us' (quoted in Wenz 2001: 238). So ethics matters, ecological ethics in particular, and it is urgently important to raise its public profile.

A related point is that ethics is not, and never can be, like mathematics or the so-called exact sciences. It cannot provide a watertight set of rules, to be applied mechanically, that will save anyone the time and trouble of some hard thinking, and feeling, when confronted with a real, specific and unique situation that presents an ethical dilemma. As we shall see, there is not necessarily always just one right thing to do. Life is complicated and messy, and values can and do conflict. Whether personally or socially, ethics grows out of the ongoing interaction between one's ideas and values and the world, each affecting the other; and that does not happen without you being there, so to speak.

I should point out, though, that to say so is already to take sides in an argument within ethics. It is between, on the one hand, those who think (and feel) that ethics is essentially about selecting and applying rationally grounded principles or rules, and those who, on the other, hold that ethics grows out of lived life as a whole, not just as a portable head, and is ultimately answerable to experience rather than a theory, however fine. In ways and for reasons we shall consider, the latter approach – where 'Ethics is closer to wisdom than to reason, closer to understanding what is good than to correctly adjudicating particular situations' (Varela 1992: 3) – is not only itself more ecological, it is much the more hopeful direction for an ecological ethics to take.

What's New?

A specifically *ecological* ethic is one which values nonhuman as well as (not instead of) human nature. It recognizes that we are only a part of life on Earth; that we need the rest of it vastly more than it needs us; and that there is an ethical dimension to all our relationships with it. In other words, as I have said, a fully ecological ethic is *ecocentric* (perceiving and protecting value in all of nature), not *anthropocentric* (restricting value to humanity alone). It therefore encourages ways of living and acting which, as much as possible, allow both human and nonhuman nature – that is, more-than-human nature – to flourish.

Is an ecological ethic in this sense something new? Richard Routley first suggested in 1973 that there was now a need for 'a new, an environmental, ethic'. (Writing later as Richard Sylvan, he has been one of the principal influences on this book.) His suggestion led to a flurry of rearguard action by philosophers on behalf of the status quo. It was led by a fellow Australian, John Passmore, who maintained that what was needed was 'not so much a "new ethic" as a more general adherence to a perfectly familiar ethic' (1974: 186). According to that ethic, we are responsible only to fellow human beings; thus, it could include responsibilities *for* nature, insofar as that affects us, but not *to* nature.

Passmore's further point that 'A new ethic will arise out of existing attitudes, or not at all' (1974: 56) is well taken, but it doesn't follow that another ethic – in its composition and intention, new – is impossible. 'New' always means relatively new. I would add that, in this instance, there is something ancient about an ecological ethic; it is more something we have forgotten than something we have never known. Indeed, its fundamental intuition concerning the Earth and our fellow creatures therein is still present in the culture of the vast majority of indigenous people, where they have not been colonized by modern commerce (or simply exterminated). An awareness of the intimate relatedness and co-dependency of humans with plants, other animals and the places of the Earth therefore still exists, I suggest, in our collective cultural memory. Deep Ecologists Bill Devall and George Sessions are right: the change that is needed involves a 'reawakening of something very old' (1985: ix).

As to whether such a 'new' ethic is actually needed, surely the answer is 'yes'; and now more then ever. The continuing conservatism of many philosophers begs the question: if the ethics we already have is indeed adequate, why are we in such an ongoing, and worsening, mess? Presumably they would reject one possible answer, as I would, which is that ethics as such has no significant impact on what happens in the world. That would seem to leave the strong possibility, at least, that what we have (and may have been good enough in its time) is no longer up to the job.

In any case, the current human impact on nature is driven by institutionalized ideas and values which embody a very familiar ethic, according to which the consequences of this impact simply do not matter. So a new ecological ethic, albeit one with old roots, is urgently needed. And as Sylvan and Bennett say, 'Changing to respectful approaches to the environment and supplanting the place of humans in the world and their ethical systems may seem excessive and extreme. Yet what is now seen as unthinkable, as the voice of extremism, will in a decade or two be seen as necessity' (1994: 184).

Transparency and Responsibility

I make every effort to be comprehensive, fair and evenhandedly critical. However, let me point out that the author of every book, without exception, also holds certain positions; but in keeping with certain academic conventions, they are usually relatively covert – and therefore, ironically, harder to perceive, analyse or discuss.

The same point can be understood another way. We are used to a firm distinction between description (of what 'is') and prescription (of what we should do), the latter kind of statement also being called 'normative'. But that distinction is founded more on intellectual habit than anything else. A particular description is only one way out of a theoretically unlimited number of ways the world, and any part thereof, could be described; it therefore also prescribes a particular way of looking at it. Equally, a prescriptive or normative statement also involves a particular description of the world, i.e. an assertion that it is one way and not another. It follows, then, that there is no point in pretending that it is possible to describe anything in a completely neutral or detached way. That still leaves the attempt at fairness, comprehensiveness and so on as an ideal that can, in certain situations, be healthy and helpful; but it must not be confused with the actuality, or even an ultimate ideal. We are all (intellectuals included) participating *in* the world, even when we are commenting *on* it. Observation is always a kind of intervention. To pretend otherwise simply amounts to trying to avoid acknowledging and taking responsibility for one's own perspective.[10]

For this reason, I have decided to be open about my own assumptions, values and priorities. Thus, this guide to ecological ethics is (openly) committed to a global ecological ethic and, by extension, to its realization in practice. That commitment means that I unapologetically concentrate on and try to bring out the ecocentric dimension – so often ignored in mainstream and even environmental discourse – of all the issues discussed here. For that reason, its treatment of properly ecological ethics is, I believe, more thorough than those of other introductory books. By the same token, I hope it will be of interest, use and maybe even inspiration not only to fellow members of the academy, whether teachers or students, but also to activists (who may be the same people).

This book is therefore not concerned with academic debates *as such*. Our primary concern here is **anthropogenic** (human-caused) ecocrisis and its possible resolution, or at least mitigation. Scholarly contributions are very important in this context, of course; but they are only aired to the extent they can contribute, through an intelligent and well-informed understanding of the relevant issues, to a better (stronger, richer, deeper) understanding of ecocentrism, what it has to offer, and its practice in the world at large. (Understanding and practice are never radically separate anyway; 'theory' is itself just another kind of practice.) I share the goal described by van Wensveen: to find 'a middle ground between death by analysis and death by lack of critical awareness' (2000: 162).

Finally, let me be clear that I am not suggesting that ecocentric ethics is 'the answer', in the sense that it alone can win through and turn things around. Purism is not a serious option, because an ecological ethic stands no chance of being realized without many other things which are not themselves, or not necessarily, ecocentric; and since my approach is ultimately pragmatic, we shall have to address them too. On the other hand, I shall also argue strongly that no real turning can succeed without ecocentric ethics at its heart. Anthropocentric ethics alone – ethically, a form of business as usual – is simply not a serious option. And being 'progressive' or 'left' does not make it one, either. As long as human needs are our *only* concern, we shall fail both ourselves and the rest of life.

2

The Earth in Crisis

The Signs

This is not the place to spell out the current ecocrisis or its context in detail,[1] but since it is a primary reason why an ecological ethic is needed, it must at least be pointed out. Of course, the human propensity for denial and wishful thinking should never be underestimated. In the ecological field, it even has a high end in the form of well-publicized commentators reassuring us that, overall, everything is fine, even getting better.[2] Given the preponderance of otherwise bad news, these individuals have received media attention out of all proportion to their merit. But the remarkable thing about the global ecological crisis is that even though most analysts say it is serious, it really *is* serious – and getting worse. This is true on any major kind of indicator, such as the following.[3]

Climate change

Despite recent controversies, which we shall return to later, the overwhelming consensus among scientists remains that so-called global warming – almost certainly (i.e., with as much certainty as the subject permits) largely as a direct result of human overproduction of

CO_2 – is now well under way.[4] Carbon dioxide levels are now the highest they have been for at least 440,000 years, and the effects may already be entering a stage of runaway positive feedback. Yet the prospect of serious measures addressing anthrogenic causes of climate change currently seem unlikely, even (or especially) in the case of the two countries that are the greatest sources of greenhouse gases, China and the USA.[5] So despite the probable consequences of extreme weather conditions for all forms of life on the planet, ranging from stress to disaster, this enormous and wildly irresponsible experiment on our common and only home continues. As Madeleine Bunting writes: 'With a kind of savage justice, climate change is an issue which exposes the weakest link in the cultural mindset of Western market capitalism: the collective capacity for self-restraint in pursuit of a common good.'[6] (This is something which will be discussed in Chapter 13.) But climate change is far from the only serious crisis.

Biodiversity

There was a 31 per cent decline in terrestrial biodiversity between 1970 and 2003 alone. At the present rate of extinction, 12 per cent of bird species and 25 per cent of mammal species are likely to disappear within the next 30 years.[7] A recent report (Butchart et al. 2010) concludes that although, in 2002, governments promised to act (none yet has), the decline and *rate* of decline in global biodiversity continues to accelerate. The day I write this, the secretary-general of the UN Convention on Biological Diversity pleads for those governments to realize that 'What we are seeing today is a total disaster . . . We are losing biodiversity at an unprecedented rate. If current levels go on we will reach a tipping point very soon.' And what he points out should be blindingly obvious: *if ecosystems collapse, so will economies and cultures.* (Where is the 'reason', one wonders, of which human beings are so proud?) But the losses continue to mount, and it is factually uncontroversial among biologists that we are now in the midst of the sixth great extinction in the Earth's history: at least 1,000 times faster than the normal 'background rate' of the preceding 60 million years.[8] The word 'massacre' naturally comes to mind, especially since this one, unlike all the others, results overwhelmingly from the actions of a single species.

It is instructive to compare the number of human beings – currently nearing 6.9 billion, with about 250,000 more arriving every day – with the number of our fellow 'higher' mammals that still remain. Virtually all those that are large, dangerous, edible and/or profitable enough to attract our attention (or, almost as unlucky, unprofitable enough to be regarded as dispensable) now number in the tens of thousands at very most. There remain perhaps 414,000 great apes, all species combined, in the wild (the population of a town: Lyons, France, for example); about 3,200 tigers; guesses for African lions centre on 20,000; and in the case of most whale species, a few hundred thousand.[9] The last four remaining white rhinos in the wild were killed in Kenya by poachers in 2008. Considering a world of 11 billion people by 2150 (the 'medium-fertility' prediction), 'all of whom will continue to occupy space, drink water, burn energy, consume solid resources, produce wastes, aspire to material comfort and safety for themselves and 2.0 children, and eat', it is very hard to disagree with David Quammen: 'Call me a pessimist, but when I look into that future, I don't see any lions, tigers, or bears' (2003: 413–14). Nor, by any means, does the toll stop there.

Habitat

Directly implicated in crashing biodiversity is the fact that the number and area of wild places – that is, those relatively unaffected by human activity – continue to decline rapidly, as 'development' continues apace. Wild, that is, not in the unrealistically purist sense of places where there are or have been no people, but in the sense rightly suggested by David Wiggins: 'not as that which is free of all trace of our interventions . . . but as that which has not been entirely instrumentalized by human artifice, and as something to be cherished . . . in ways that outrun all considerations of profit' (2000: 10). This decline includes (but is by no means limited to) the still accelerating destruction of rainforests and coral reefs, the most biodiverse places on the planet. In fact, the situation is worse the biologically richer the habitat concerned, and thus the more species it supports. About 50 per cent of the Earth's forests have already been cleared, and the annual net loss of forests is now about 130 square miles.[10] Up to 25 per cent of coral reefs, atolls and cays have now been destroyed, and over half of the remainder are in danger of degradation beyond recovery in the next 30 years.[11] Of the Earth's ecosystems, 605 are already estimated to be degraded.[12]

By the 1990s, only one-third of the Earth's continental surface was left for the use of other life-forms, and by far the greater part of that was in relatively impoverished or stressed ecosystems.[13] Such conversion is virtually always accompanied by gross biotic simplification towards an unsustainable monoculture. Furthermore, biologists estimate that at least 40 per cent of the Earth's ecosystems need to be protected from significant human impact in order for them to remain viable; yet only about 10 per cent are currently in a protected area (and even then, significant problems of enforcement remain).[14] Human beings – again, one species – now use some 50 per cent of the world's fresh water and around 42 per cent of its plant growth. It should also be noted that consumer demand for seafood has almost doubled in the past 20 years – just as wild fish stocks are crashing.[15]

Pollution

In addition to pollution driving climate change, tens of thousands of synthetic chemicals – potentially, at the very least, toxic: most are untested – have now been introduced into the environment, especially in the overdeveloped world. (Industrial dumping, however, favours the less developed world, where controls are laxer and an official blind eye is often easier, or at least cheaper, to buy.) These are substances known to disrupt the immune, endocrine and hormone systems of virtually all organisms. At the same time, the incidence of cancers among the same human population also continues to rise, along with reports of disruption to normal biological development among individuals of other species. Everywhere, fresh-water rivers are becoming polluted by fertilizer and slurry run-off, or degraded by large-scale dams. Plastic waste, on land and sea, is out of control. Another instance, and sign of the times, is the Great Pacific Garbage Patch (or Trash Vortex): a floating mass of plastic rubbish in the North Pacific, the smallest estimate of whose size is roughly that of Texas.

These crises are all connected, of course. For example, it is estimated that on average, *one-quarter* of all land animals and plants, or more than one million species, could well become extinct by 2050 as a direct result of climate change.[16] The biggest danger to coral reefs is from increasing seawater acidity, also resulting from global warming; and so on. Nor does this summary exhaust the problems. For example, there is the staggering (and largely unremarked) loss of topsoil: more than 25 million acres degraded or lost annually. As Jared Diamond has said, 'There are about a dozen major environmental problems, all of them sufficiently serious that if we solved eleven of them and didn't solve the twelfth, whatever that twelfth is, any could potentially do us in.'[17]

Yet there are few signs that enough people – especially, but by no means only, among the powerful – have noticed, or really care. Gregory Bateson used to point out to his students that a frog, placed in a pan of hot water, would immediately jump out; but in water that was very gradually heated, it would boil to death. He applied this story, with grim relish, to the inability of humans to notice what was happening to the environment. My only reservation is a weak but important one: not to *try* to act differently, at least, is to participate in a self-fulfilling prophecy. And let me add, once again, 'we' (humans) are not the only ones whose lives and well-being are at stake, even though 'we' (humans, but some decidedly more than others) are endangering them.

Analysing Ecocrisis

As I have suggested, behind the processes driving these human-caused changes is pathological ethics, not an absence of ethics. But there is also a dimension of truth or knowledge involved here. That includes scientific knowledge, certainly, but extends well beyond it. For the ecological crisis will not begin to change for the better unless enough people face up to the realities I have just mentioned, both personally and collectively. There is definitely an emotional dimension to such work,[18] which is too often ignored; but clear thinking is also required.

Before taking up ethics directly, therefore, I would like briefly to suggest a framework for understanding the basic dynamics at work in ecocrisis, because these make up the principal areas requiring eco-ethical renewal. Erazim Kohák sums them up well: we are too 'numerous, demanding, and powerful' (2000: 10–11). There is a widely accepted equation for these factors: **I=PLT**.[19] That is, our ecological **I***mpact* is a function of:

> **P***opulation size* (the number of humans), times **L***ifestyle* (affluence or consumption, the per capita use of resources), times **T***echnology* (the per capita effect of technologies either more or less energy-consuming and polluting).

(David Willey suggested adding another factor, namely 'O' for the effects of the way human societies, whether micro- or macro-, are organized, both institutionally and ideologically; hence, I=PLOT.)[20]

We shall look very briefly at these in turn, but first it is necessary to stress that (1) *each* of the components is fundamental, and (2) they are *interactive*. In fact, virtually every major ecological problem is a result of their interaction; one or another factor may predominate, but the others can and must not be neglected, because they can wipe out any gains made by addressing solely the dominant cause. As we shall see, there are other more subtle implications, too. For example, we have (in principle) a choice between high population and low-impact lifestyle *or* low population and higher-impact lifestyle – at whatever level of technology (and organization) human wit, constrained by the laws of physics, among other things, can achieve.

Population

Since it is the subject of a chapter below, I won't say much about this here, except to note that global human population makes at least as significant a contribution to ecocrisis as any of the other factors. Recently, the rate of *growth* has slowed, but the increase of *numbers* of new people being born has not. At a time when the Earth's eco-systemic ability to produce food and absorb wastes is already under severe strain – even for most of us, the ruling species – the seven billionth person is expected (as I write) towards the end of 2010, and a conservative estimate for 2050 is around 9 billion.[21]

Lifestyle

Affluent overconsumption – that is, well beyond what is necessary for a mentally, physically, emotionally and spiritually healthy life – is a problem overwhelmingly present in the so-called developed world. (Although that is not to say the developing world would necessarily behave with any more restraint if given the opportunity.) It is part of the dynamic, both a result and a cause, of global corporate capitalism. It is not even necessary to oppose capitalism as a whole – let alone markets, which are not the same thing – to realize that the extreme form that now dominates the world through its chief financial institutions (the World Trade Organization, G8, the World Bank) is having equally extreme effects: in this case, a deliberate programme to encourage consumption beyond what is desirable, let alone necessary, in human terms, or remotely sustainable in ecological ones.

Part of this process is a cult of material consumption, now spread by the billion-dollar advertising and entertainment media industries worldwide, so that more people than ever now desire an 'American lifestyle'. The result includes some bitter ironies. It seems universally true that after a certain level of income, further increases do not lead to any more happiness. What does create discontent is a wide gap between the relatively poor and the rich, as perceived by the former. As a result of neoliberal economic globalization, that is exactly what is happening: the income gap between the wealthy (who are getting even richer) and the poor (who are getting poorer) is steadily increasing too. So the world is dividing into the self-indulgent wealthy few, who can afford to consume irresponsibly, and do, and the many others who are unhappy because they would like to – and who, we are driven to hope, will not be able to.

Why 'irresponsibly'? Because those who abuse the Earth's resources by using far more than they need make up a relatively tiny minority of all people. As is well known, Americans, for example – 5 per cent of the world's people – not only co-emit the largest national proportion of greenhouse gases, but consume nearly 40 per cent of the Earth's natural resources (excluding those several million Americans living below the poverty line). This situation, to put it mildly, hardly seems fair. So what requires us to hope that there will be no global upgrade for everyone to the same lifestyle? Because *the Earth and its resources are finite*; so it would take at least another three planet Earths for everyone else to join the privileged few (Rees 1996: 210). This, to state the obvious, is not possible without destroying the one we actually have – not exactly an ethically defensible option.

Of course, neither is trying to keep the roughly 2+ billion people now living in poverty in that condition. Clearly, the most ethical option (to quote the Deep Ecologist philosopher Arne Naess) is that 'We must live at a level that we seriously can wish others to attain, not at a level that requires the bulk of humanity NOT to reach' (quoted in Witoszek and Brennan 1999: 224). In principle, there would be no need to choose between social injustice and ecological suicide if the wealthy minority were to reduce their consumption – and only to a level which would still enable a reasonably comfortable 'European' lifestyle (at the modest end of the spectrum) – while the majority increase theirs enough to permit the same. (Nor would it be necessary for the majority to live at low consumption levels if the total number of people was smaller, however.)

These eventualities are surely at least *possible*. So, however madly optimistic it may sound at the moment, let us hope that sufficient integrity, will and intelligence, on the part of both political and other leaders and the public, can still be found to institute a programme of reduced consumption in time for it to matter. That is an enormous challenge, some aspects of which will be discussed below.

All this said, there is a tendency for environmentalists on the left to grant transnational companies even more power than they actually have (and thereby neglect other aspects of the I=PLOT equation). They are a huge part, but ultimately only part, of the problem, and therefore only part of the challenge. Companies are driven by, as well as drive, many aspects of the economic and social environment in which they work. They are a symptom of the problem as well as a cause, being importantly products of, for example, the economic environment, government fiscal policy, trade regulation or lack thereof and (not least) both the greed and the ignorance of many of their customers as well as of their directors and shareholders. Since we are not going to get very far unless we tackle the causes of eco-crisis, these too are things which must be faced up to. Just appealing to the ecological conscience of corporate producers and consumers and instituting purely voluntary controls, for example, will certainly fail; but for tougher measures to succeed, there has to be at least some degree of general cultural understanding and support for them.

We shall consider these issues in more detail in Chapters 12 and 13 below.

Technology

Let me remind you of the interactivity of these factors. So, for example, even in the decidedly optimistic scenario just described, unless overall consumption declines markedly (and stays that way), the issues of technology and population cannot simply be ignored. And if the number of people on the planet increases sufficiently, then *no* amount of progress in reducing consumption *or* instituting green technology will suffice.

Many people, including those in most governments, place their faith in new technologies as the solution to every present and indeed future ecological problem. And it is true that appropriate, clean and affordable technology has an important role to play in resolving the ecocrisis; but it cannot bear the weight of cornucopian dreams. Technology is vanishingly unlikely to be able to compensate for uncontrolled expansion of either population or consumption. For example, it tends to become increasingly expensive and/or specialized, and technological 'solutions' notoriously tend to create new problems, which then seem to require more technological intervention, and so on. Still more fundamentally, such 'solutions' to ecological problems ignore the urgent need actually to reduce consumption (thereby, of course, spending less) and lock us into a collective mindset – run by technoscience, financed by capital, and protected by state power – which is a principal *cause* of the problems. Then more of that cause can only be perceived, with increasingly desperate denial, as the only solution.

Let us assume that cheap and efficient non-polluting technologies were in fact developed and made widely available. If they were simply used to license massive increases in consumption – i.e., if they were not accompanied by a (successful) attempt to control and reduce *demand*, and thus consumption – then the end result would just be the same. Indeed, abundant cheap energy could well be an absolute disaster from an ecocentric point of view, if it were used to advance even further human domination and exploitation of the planet – even if the profits were fairly divided up among the conquerors.

(Which seems more unlikely? That they would be so divided, or that such a discovery wouldn't be used for that end? Hard to say!)

It is also worth pointing out, against the more optimistic exponents of future techno-fixes, that 'sooner or later, all technologies attain their optimum. Thereafter, the law of diminishing returns comes into operation.'[22] And while technology develops with certain advances in scientific knowledge, it is still constrained by the laws of physics. Doubtless, our understanding of physics will continue to grow, but it seems unreasonable to rely on developing technology which requires what we know of the underlying behaviour of the physical universe to change as well.

In short, as Kohák writes, 'the Earth cannot be saved by even the most perfect technocratic scheme if ordinary citizens do not themselves realize the need for a basic change in the way we dwell upon this Earth, confront the apostle of consumption and find the will to live in sustainable ways' (2000: xxvi).

Science and Technology

Belief in technological fixes is symptomatic of a wider faith in modern technoscience. (The term is justified: it is becoming ever-increasingly difficult to distinguish between science and technology.)[23] Actually, in recent decades that faith has been shaken by nuclear accidents and BSE ('mad cow disease')/vCJD (its human version), as the cool public response to GM foods, in Europe at least, seems to have shown. Even so, technoscience is now integral to both industry and government, with those two also becoming ever closer.[24] In the global North, it has now become so powerful and dogmatic as to constitute, in effect, a secular religion with its own powerful and democratically unaccountable elite.[25] And as with other major institutionalized religions, this social, political and economic power involves a self-justifying ideology that can and must be questioned.

For example, the belief that science arrives at the final or complete truth of anything – including such refinements as 'eventually', or 'as close to it as we can ever get' – is ultimately nothing more nor less than an article of faith, requiring sweeping prior assumptions that cannot themselves be scientifically tested. (Not, that is, without already assuming the truth of science.)[26] More specific tenets of the scientific faith can also be questioned: that there is such a thing as *the* scientific method, for example;[27] or that repeating experiments, or replication, guarantees the truth of their outcome.

Nonetheless, the idea that science offers unique access to the truth has widespread rhetorical plausibility, even among those whose interests are damaged by its exercise. (The word for such a phenomenon, incidentally, is **hegemony**.) When this plausibility is embodied in official institutions and the general culture it lends technoscience great political, social and cultural power. And to these points can be added the corruption of science by the politics and especially capital investment with which it is now so entangled.[28]

Yet none of this is to deny that science can supply us with very important *truths* (lower-case 't' and plural), nor that it has a rightful place in our ongoing cultural conversation. These criticisms, I must stress, are not 'anti-science'. They are anti-*scientism*: the modern cult of science, according to which science is not one way of being among many but the *only* valid or true one.[29] (Pluralism has important implications for any project to bring about a more ecological society, as we shall see in Chapter 11.)

For several reasons, the situation presents a particular problem for ecological ethics. One is that the science of ecology was, of course, a major inspiration for metaphysical and political ecology. Another is that science plays an important part in our awareness of the fact of ecocrisis; it supplies many indicators that supplement and support direct personal experience, and virtually all of the quantifiable and statistical ones. Furthermore, it is needed to underpin the limited but important role of green technology in alleviating that crisis. So its importance is clear.

Yet there are also cogent reasons why technoscience does not itself offer a solution to the ecocrisis. Indeed, paradoxically, the value that proponents of science place on 'objectivity' can contribute to the ecocrisis as much as, in another way, it can help by gathering, analysing and presenting evidence. Why? One reason is that an overemphasis in this respect, and a corresponding devaluation of the value of the Earth in its sensuous particulars and emotional meanings – 'things' which do not survive being quantified, or commodified – is itself implicated in that crisis. J. Baird Callicott says: 'If it weren't for ecology we would not be aware that we have an "ecologic crisis." If it weren't for the theory of evolution we would be both blind and indifferent to the reduction in global biodiversity' (quoted in Bron Taylor 2010: 211). With respect to a distinguished environmental philosopher, this is highly doubtful. To coin a phrase, you don't need a weatherman to know which way the wind is blowing, nor do you need science to tell you something is seriously amiss if you can no longer walk safely on the pack-ice, if there are no longer any birds in your garden, if your crops are failing again, etc. And if such voices are disregarded – the ones at the sharp end of climate change – it is not for scientific reasons, but for political ones.

Nor can science on its own (let alone the theory of evolution as such) make us care about the Earth. Relatedly, it is highly doubtful that reason alone, scientific or otherwise, will suffice to turn the situation around. As I have already pointed out, we fight to save who and what we *love*. That will take emotion as well as intellect – and probably also, as we shall see, spirituality (of a particular kind).

Still another reason for caution is that in a society dominated by financial, commercial and fiscal imperatives, science is no more immune than any other human enterprise to the corruption entailed by selling your services to the highest bidder. Not only are the subjects of research largely dictated by their potential profits, but experimental results are themselves increasingly influenced by the interests of corporate funding.[30] The last effect is most evident in medical research, where pharmaceutical companies have a direct stake in the outcome of published trials, but the same general point also applies to apparently disinterested science. Compared to commercialization, the idea that the greatest threat to science is 'postmodern relativism' (itself largely a media creation) is laughable.

Even research questions are now frequently led by the available technology itself, not the other way around, and, to a massive extent, support for scientific research is based on the assumption of profitable hi-tech spin-offs for the communications, defence, pharmaceutical and other industries.[31] Ultimately, it feeds into what Plumwood (2006b: 62) called 'the scientific fantasy of mastery', in which the task is 'that of remoulding nature to conform to the dictates of reason to achieve salvation . . . as freedom from death and bodily limitation'. Appraising the extraordinary clouds of salvific rhetoric surrounding biotechnology and bioengineering, Midgley agrees: such a way of looking at nature 'is not scientific . . . [but] an exuberant power fantasy' (2000: 12–13). A more anti-ecological mode would be difficult to conceive.

More subtly, an apparently purely scientific approach lends itself too readily to a 'sensible consensus' in which those interests are concealed and made difficult to question because such questions are deemed to be unscientific and therefore, conveniently, illegitimate. But this is precisely the most serious problem with technoscience. It cannot supply answers to the kinds of question that most urgently need asking, questions of meaning, value and justice: in short, of ethics. Its strength is also necessarily its weakness, because in order to be 'objective' science must set aside as 'subjective' precisely such questions. Science can tell us (subject to the appropriate qualifications) what is currently considered 'true', but it cannot tell us what is *good*, or *right* or *fair*. These are not, and cannot be, scientific questions; nor are they questions that should be left to scientists or other 'experts' to decide. They are existential ethical decisions we must make for ourselves.[32]

Even in science's own terms, it should never be forgotten that our ignorance – as Wes Jackson (2008) has reminded us – always far outstrips our knowledge. Paradoxically, one feels more confidence in scientists' always-provisional conclusions to the extent that they show awareness of this point and the humility it entails. There is no view from nowhere, or everywhere; humans and everything about them is ultimately limited, because we are parts of a much, perhaps infinitely, greater whole; so our knowledge too is necessarily limited, and open, in principle, to correction. This conclusion sounds severe, but it only does so because of the extent to which science has allowed itself to become a swollen ideology and a partner, together with capital and the state, in ecological destruction. (It is significant that the so-called sceptics who have recently attacked climate science remain uncritical partisans of unrestrained business.) So this discussion does not call for abandoning science, but for qualifying and recontextualizing it. I believe, with Bruno Latour, that 'The critical mind, if it is to be relevant again, must devote itself to the cultivation of a stubborn realism, but a realism dealing with . . . matters of concern, not matters of fact.'[33] And what more deserving matter of concern is there, calling for just such a stubborn realism, than the fate of the Earth and its inhabitants?

3

Ethics

What is Ethics?

'Ethics' comes from the Greek word *ethos*, meaning custom, but in its proper philosophical usage it now refers not to how people actually *do* behave in their dealings with each other, but to how they *ought* to live and act.[1] It is a complex and controversial subject, both as a branch of philosophy and in its various 'applications' (such as in medicine, law and now 'the environment'). The fundamental ethical question, which I have mentioned Socrates as posing, is how should one best live, or what should one best do? At least three points follow:

1 Questions of value – whose study is called **axiology** – are unavoidable. Ethics concerns the realization of values (both in the sense of 'realizing what they are' and of 'making them real'). For example, philosophers argue about what sort of entities qualify as *morally considerable* – that is, have moral standing. Some characteristic (or set of characteristics) is required to confer this status. It is usually one they agree is possessed by humans, such as sentience or self-consciousness. And the qualifying characteristic is only relevant because it is deemed to have special value.

2 Particular instances of individual right and wrong behaviour

– which are often described as instances of morality – are important, but they are only a subset of ethics as a whole.

3 Ultimately, private ethics is secondary to public, for three reasons. First, what finally matters, insofar as it has direct effects upon the world (including other beings), is not private states of being but public behaviour. Second, human beings are highly, perhaps even necessarily, social animals; so private ethics is crucially affected by public. And third, much of ethics necessarily concerns constraints on the activities of individuals for the common good of the communities of which they are a part, and upon which they depend. (But, to anticipate a point made below, those communities should no longer be restricted to purely human ones.)[2]

Finally, ethics also overlaps with questions of knowledge, such as how we actually know – or at least, decide – what has value and what is good behaviour, the study of which is called **epistemology**. So we now turn to the epistemological issues that impact upon ethics.[3]

Realism vs. Relativism

Simply put, **realism** is basically the view that there are things, values or ways of behaving that exist independently of whether anyone knows them (in any way) – often put as being 'really there', or 'out there' – which are therefore real; the accuracy of our knowledge of them, as representations of realities, can therefore be judged – in principle, at least – the way one would compare copies with an original. Therefore, a representation which matches its original reality in every relevant respect is the truth. Science is usually held to be the best exemplar of this process, which is also therefore described as 'objective'. Realists are therefore almost always also **objectivists** (and are happy to call themselves such).

Relativism is basically the counter-view that, whether or not there are 'things in themselves', some things (and arguably all things) can never actually be known in themselves, because they can never be separated from our knowledge of them (perception, conception, etc.); therefore, 'representations' can only ever be compared with other 'representations', never with an unrepresented reality; there are, therefore, and can be, only truths which are relative in the sense that they are not final, complete or absolute. This view, sometimes described as 'subjective', has a strong affinity with the humanities and arts. Relativists are therefore often called **subjectivists**. (However, since this tends to be used as a term of abuse in a society which places great value on 'objectivity', it is a label many relativists resist.)

It is important to understand that both positions are open to abuse; indeed, both are widely misunderstood, sometimes even by those who seem to advocate them.

Realism – the *effort* to see things 'as they are', regardless of our own or others' biases and personal desires – certainly has its place as a valid and valuable *ideal*, and the experience of closing in on the truth, so to speak, is an integral part of it.[4] But the relativists have a valid point, at least respecting loose talk about objective truth and/or reality. As one of them puts it, 'the "truth", factual or otherwise, about the being of objects is constituted within a theoretical and discursive context, and the idea of a truth outside all context is simply nonsensical' (Laclau 1991: 105). This is because neither objects nor facts – let alone concepts or values – exist *for* us except insofar as they are apprehended *by* us, and that apprehension is necessarily inseparable from the processes of learning (such as what qualifies as a thing or a fact, and all further gradations) that have made it possible. Furthermore, no one has a 'view from nowhere' (Nagel 1986); everyone's apprehension is necessarily from, and constituted by, a particular biologically embodied and socially embedded perspective.

However, relativism is commonly portrayed (by realists) as suggesting that (a) since absolute truth is impossible, (b) there is no such thing as truth *at all*, and that any representation or statement therefore has as much or little truth as any other. This is indeed absurd, but it is hard to find anyone who actually holds such a view. In any case, (b) does not follow from (a) unless one *assumes* an absolutist definition of truth.[5] More broadly, truth results from ongoing processes of perceiving and conceiving animals in continuous interaction with the world. Even in its most stable forms truth therefore cannot be taken to be complete or final; but that certainly does not mean there is no such thing at all. Indeed, we cannot live our daily lives without some notion of what is true and what isn't, let alone practise a higher cultural form such as science (or, for that matter, art).

In short, everything we can know, think about or discuss – including ethics – is a function *both* of the 'objective' world *and* of our 'subjective' apprehension of it. And the resulting knowledge is converted, through the same processes of awareness, reflection and interaction, into decisions (both individual and collective) for action.

We may therefore legitimately speak of facts, understood as truths at the present time and in relation to particular, not universal, circumstances; but claims by scientific spokespersons of objectivity (held to be superior to subjectivity) and realism (as superior to relativism) should be rejected, and viewed as essentially rhetorical and political interventions. Equally unacceptable, however, are the interventions of vulgar relativists along the lines of, 'Well that's just your opinion. Mine is different and that's all there is to it.' Such a move kills off debate (reasons, arguments, etc.) just at the point when it is most needed. It is, of course, an argument itself, and a bad one.[6]

The Naturalistic Fallacy

This term refers to the point that no single ethical position about what should be logically follows from any set of facts about what is. Or, as philosophers tend to put it, you cannot legitimately derive an 'ought' from an 'is'.[7] Indeed, it is hard enough to derive an 'is' (general conclusion) from an 'is' (as a set of empirical data). Not only is it impossible to collect data without criteria that embody assumptions that are not themselves subject to 'testing', but it is always possible to interpret the same set of facts in more than one way, and thereby arrive at very different conclusions.[8] Furthermore, in daily practice there is no clear-cut distinction between what we consider a fact and what we value; the two constantly interact in both directions.[9]

In relation to the naturalistic fallacy, however, the fundamental point is that ethics and facts are two different orders of discourse. There is no (good) reason to think that just because a behaviour is 'natural' – say, the persecution of an outsider by a group – it is therefore ethically correct. The latter is another and, for ethics, more important question, and it should be decided on other grounds.

True, it is valuable to have an idea of our so-called natures: how we tend to respond to certain situations, what we tend to value, and so on. This sort of attention to our biological 'hard-wiring' is especially the province of sociobiology and evolutionary psychology. But (as I suggested earlier) such knowledge cannot answer the hard ethical questions we face, and thereby replace ethics. Even if subordinating everything to professional status, or producing 10 children or eating a high-meat diet are indeed 'natural' behaviours, are they good or right?[10] That, once again, is a necessary but very different question.

This is not to say (as a dogmatic realist might) that no sound ethical conclusions at all are possible, or (as a dogmatic relativist might) that any ethical position has as much or little validity as any other. The fallacy is the attempt to use facts about what is 'natural' (such as evolutionary theory) to justify a *particular* ethic as 'good'. But it does not invalidate all attempts to arrive at a defensible ethic; it just means that the attempt must proceed on other grounds, such as arguments as to what is needed, desirable, and so on.

Religious Ethics

Virtually all ethics began, and for most of human history has persisted, as *religious* codes of behaviour. There is wide variation, of course, but such codes are derived from interacting with either local spirits (animism), a pantheon of deities (polytheism), the sacred nature of reality itself (Buddhist nontheism), or God through the words of His prophets and/or incarnation (Judaic, Christian and Islamic theism). In the 'West' – and much of the rest of the globe, as a result of colonialism, including globalization, during the past 300 or so years – the most influential kind of religious ethics has been Christianity. We shall therefore discuss that here and defer other kinds of spiritual/religious ethics until Chapter 10.

It is worth mentioning that philosophically speaking, ethics itself cannot validly be derived directly from a deity, no matter how apparently authoritative or comprehensive. The reason is that 'Should I obey the commands of this deity?' is a valid ethical question, and arguably an unavoidable one.[11] However, perhaps not surprisingly, this point has not received much encouragement among religious adherents.

Ecologically speaking, the legacy and continuing influence of Christianity is highly mixed. Textually, according to the New Testament, Jesus praised the lilies of the field (Matthew 7: 28–9); but he also blasted a fig tree for failing to feed him (Mark 11: 12–14, 20–1), and his use of a herd of pigs to dispose of two demons (Matthew 8: 28–32) was disturbingly casual at best. In any case, the foundational text in this context has always been Genesis 1: 26, 28, which states what has come to be known as the **dominion thesis**:

> And God said unto them, Let us make man in our image, after our likeness, and let them have dominion over the fish of the sea, and over the fowl of the air, and over the cattle, and over all the earth, and over every creeping thing that creepeth upon the earth. . . . And God said unto them, Be fruitful, and multiply, and replenish the earth, and subdue it: and have dominion over the fish of the sea, and over the fowl of the air, and over every living thing that moveth upon the earth.

In 1967, Lynn White Jr. wrote a short article pointing out that this passage had been overwhelmingly, and understandably, interpreted as giving humans the right to do whatever they want to the Earth and all its nonhuman inhabitants, subject only to God's approval – in practice, it seems, rarely a stringent test. He also pointed out – again, correctly – that with the insistence on a single, transcendent and universal God, Christianity in its dominant form (and, by implication, Islam) had removed the sacred focus from the Earth and its creatures. For pagan animists, nature itself had been sacred; a transcendent and thus essentially off-planet deity, in contrast, amounted to a potential licence to plunder. White went on to suggest that Christianity is therefore the primary historical cause of ecological crisis.

However plausible, this suggestion has been criticized on the grounds that (1) other very different interpretations of the Bible are possible; (2) pre-Christian humanity also engaged in many bouts of ecological destructiveness (mass felling of forests, the hunting of some megafauna to extinction, etc.); (3) non-Christian people have done the same; and (4) the ecocrisis didn't really gather pace until the Industrial Revolution in the nineteenth century. However, such points, while true, have tended to obscure another one: that whether or not the 'real' message of Christianity is ecologically despotic or not (something that could be debated indefinitely), that is in fact how it has so far been *commonly and influentially understood*.[12]

There is an alternative interpretation of the Bible known as the **stewardship thesis**, based on Genesis 1: 24 and 2: 15:[13]

> And God made the beast of the earth after his kind, and the cattle after their kind, and every thing that creepeth upon the earth after their kind: and God saw that it was good. . . . And the Lord took the man [i.e., Adam], and put him into the garden of Eden to dress it and to keep it.

According to this benevolent reading, humanity can use the natural world but only with due regard for the fact that God created it and gave us responsibility for its well-being: something which provides an opportunity for Christian environmentalists to try to put ecology onto the churches' agenda. And that is indeed a good thing, which should be wished every success. Not surprisingly, when it comes to caring for Creation, the Franciscan order, in particular, starts from a position of strength. Although the ultimate authority remains God the Creator (a potentially serious point of difference with ecocentrics such as some pagans), there can be no mistaking the deeply ecological sensibility of St Francis's teaching, as reflected in his famous 'Canticle of the Sun'.[14]

Since his election, Pope Benedict XVI has given a high priority to the environment, calling its wanton destruction a new sin. Orthodox Patriarch Bartholomeos I strongly condemned crimes against nature and campaigned against them. The current Archbishop of Canterbury, Rowan Williams, is personally highly supportive of environmental ethics. The Church of England has a pioneering and intelligent national environment programme centred on reducing carbon emissions ('Shrinking the Footprint'), and there are many related regional and local initiatives around dioceses and parishes.[15] In America, there are several recent currents of faith-based environmentalism: the National Religious Partnership for the Environment, an alliance of several groups, Christian and Jewish; and initiatives by the National Council of Churches and the US Catholic Conference. The Evangelical Climate Initiative, launched by the National Association of Evangelicals in 2006, remains controversial within the evangelical movement. Pre-millennials (as opposed to the more liberal, or at least neutral, a-millennials) are likely to interpret environmental disaster as a sign of the approaching divine millennium and, as such, of course, a good thing.

Of course, the bulk of the Christian agenda overall remains strongly anthropocentric, compared to which ecological Christianity remains a minority and controversial concern with a long way to go. But that is certainly not a reason not to try to develop it further, and the green shoots just mentioned are encouraging.

Stewardship has a problem of substance, however: it is distinctly paternalistic. While there are things we can do to help nature, does it actually *need* us to guide or manage it? Surely we need the Earth much more than it needs us. And that weakness makes it a cousin (perhaps ancestor?) to one of the curses of our time: **managerialism**, or the belief that human beings have not only the 'right' but the ability, even if only potentially, to successfully manage the natural world. Given the overall historical record for successfully managing even ourselves, plus our all-too-human susceptibility to narrow and short-term self-interest, this prospect is open to serious doubt. It might just be possible – but only if the managers accept that no amount of knowledge will ever suffice without the wisdom to recognize its limits, and ours. But this is a point with which the great majority of ecotheologians (perhaps all) would agree.[16]

In any case, as Ronald Sandler reminds us, 'the majority of the world's population subscribes to some religious tradition, so to be relevant to the actual world an environmental ethic must be able to engage those traditions' (2005: 10). And there is certainly more to say on the subject, so we shall return to it in Chapter 11.

Secular Ethics

With the modern world – beginning, for most intents and purposes, in the mid-seventeenth century – *secular* (i.e. non-religious) ethics became increasingly important. (There were earlier precedents; Michel de Montaigne suggested in the late sixteenth century that while the most serious Christian sins were offences against God, our worst crimes were actually against each other – and animals.)[17]

The process of secularization has been slow, uneven and notably incomplete, even in the 'West', but very broadly speaking it took place like this. With the rise of the philosophy known as **humanism** in and soon after the Renaissance in the sixteenth century, man (although not, until much later, woman) increasingly began to replace divinity as the central focus of life. At the same time, secular natural truth took the place of God as the ultimate goal, and human reason played the part once given to divine revelation as the means to attain it. Originally itself religious, in the eighteenth-century Enlightenment, humanism became increasingly, and more openly, secular, and God an increasingly hands-off figure who no longer interfered in the universe He had set, like a clock, to working. Public atheism finally became possible in the nineteenth century.

Note, however, the profound continuities with monotheism, namely the monist logic: there is still only one legitimate source of meaning ('truth'), with only one legitimate caste of interpreters. As reason itself became steadily replaced by scientific and technical reason, in the course of the Scientific Revolution (which really was revolutionary),[18] that caste eventually became the authorities in white coats we still, however uneasily, recognize today. Here the distinction must be repeated between genuine science itself and scientism – science as a faith in, or even cult of, reason.[19] The latter is yet another example of how much secularism still functions as a crypto-religion; true scepticism is also *self*-critical.[20]

The original Renaissance philosophy about the importance of human initiative within divine and natural limits thus mutated into an arrogant techno-humanism which now recognizes none.[21] Its followers, sometimes called **cornucopians**, believe that there is no serious problem which does not have a scientific/technological solution, and no end to human progress and growth. The latter tends, it seems, to merge with economics and so-called economic reason (hence, **economism**). According to this faith, what matters most is literally business as usual, only ever more so, according to the logic of the cancer cell: growth without limits.[22]

It may be argued that philosophers such as Descartes, Newton and Kant, who helped create the modern world and were, in turn, created by it, had no such intention. Perhaps not, but as with the Bible, what has mattered more is the dominant (mis)understanding and (ab)use of their ideas. In relation to much the greater part of humanity's existence, for which nature was also subject and agent, the changes they initiated are very recent and drastic. The result was to supercharge a powerfully held view of the nonhuman natural world as a set of inert raw resources to be mastered and exploited by human reason – in other words, ethically negligible.

Nor was this purely a matter of misunderstood good intentions; the campaign, beginning in the mid-seventeenth century, is quite unmistakable. Hear the fathers of modern science (there are no mothers in this story) proclaim the new dispensation, perhaps most influentially, René Descartes: 'There exist no occult forces in stones or plants. There are no amazing and marvellous sympathies and antipathies, in fact there exists nothing in the whole of nature which cannot be explained in terms of purely corporeal causes totally devoid of mind and thought.' Not much ambiguity there; nor in Francis Bacon, who notoriously advised us that to 'conquer and subdue Nature with all her children, bind her to your service and make her your slave', she must be 'pierced', 'vanquished' and 'put to the question' (in other words, interrogated under torture); the new science that results will 'extend the bounds of human empire, as far as God Almighty in his goodness shall permit'. Nor in Robert Boyle: reverence of nature is 'a discouraging impediment to the empire of man over the inferior creatures of God'.[23]

In the course of this process, ethics as a subject was transformed from a branch of theology into a secular philosophical discourse, with the focus not on divinity but on purely human relations. The price, however, was that ethics itself became increasingly a matter of mere technical intellectual expertise, confined to university departments: one speciality among many.

If ethics was no longer predominantly religious, how did it connect with the so-called real world? Or, to put it another way, what world(s) did it now take in? Modern secular ethics divides largely into two concerns, which we shall examine more closely next: the individual rights of liberal democracy, and the collective rights of social/socialist democracy. But both, note, are anthropocentric. And in both cases, the guarantor of rights is the state, with which individuals and/or groups supposedly have a contract: they cede the state its power in return for its protection of them and their rights. (The dominant philosopher of this *statism* was Thomas Hobbes.)[24]

Despite the control over it that democracy is supposed to exert, the state itself is increasingly run, and its ethics determined, by the power of capital and its principal representatives, transnational companies, together with the technoscience from which both states and capital are increasingly inseparable. The best name for this entire process is **modernism**. The term does not refer here to a school of artistic, architectural or other such thought, but to the nexus of ideas and values – centred on the interlocking institutions of capital, technoscience and the nation-state – that drive the project of modernity.[25] Socially and historically speaking, then, this is the 'environment' which gave birth to modern ethics. To question the latter, as increasing numbers of people are now doing, and as we are doing here, is therefore also to question that project.

4

Three Schools of Ethics

Broadly speaking, there are three approaches to ethics in philosophy. One could also call them 'traditions', except that two are modern. It is important for our purposes to know something of them, since they provide much of the intellectual part of any contemporary context for discussing ethics. It is equally important, however, to realize their limitations, particularly ecological. The following discussion is therefore framed by ecological ethics; it is not meant to be an exhaustive treatment of each school in itself. We shall start with the two most recent kinds before turning to the oldest and potentially most ecological kind.

Deontology ('Rights')

Deontological ethics takes its name from the Greek *to deon*, meaning duty, or 'that which must be done', rather than 'is simply an option'. To put it simply, in this view actions fulfilling duty are morally right regardless of their consequences. Its founder was Immanuel Kant (1724–1804), a complex and difficult philosopher whose work does not lend itself to ready summary except to say that it is supremely rationalist.[1]

Where Aristotle (to whom we shall return) had found the goal of ethics to be happiness or fulfilment, Kant concluded it was duty. But more immediately, he was reacting against the earlier assertion by David Hume that ethical behaviour is, in the end, not a matter of reasons, or even reason as such, but of people's sympathy and emotion, or what he called 'passions', respecting the individual cases which they encounter. (Hume reserved reason for logic and mathematics.) Kant was determined to come up with a rational definition of ethics, whose principles would be *categorical* (unconditional and, as such, binding for any rational being) and *universal* (apply without any exceptions). Such principles would therefore compel the agreement of every rational being.

Kant's solution to this challenge was to propose a 'categorical imperative', the two principal aspects or formulations of which are as follows: (i) act only on a maxim that you can will, at the same time, to be or become a universal law; and such maxims can only, he thought, be discovered by autonomous agents who are both the agents and source of value; (ii) treat all people as ends or subjects in their own right and never merely as means or objects only.[2] These injunctions were meant to be followed regardless of the specific consequences (for oneself or others).

One implication is that good intentions are all-important. Another is that so too is duty, including specific duties, as infallible guides (in principle) to how to behave and what to do. And from both principles together follows the idea of universal individual human rights. Duties and rights are ultimately inseparable, because your duty to treat the other person as you would wish to be treated is his or her right to be treated thus, and vice versa. The name 'contractarianism' comes from the idea that the only role of the state, as a limited if legitimate collectivity, is to guarantee and enforce people's rights. But note that both rights and duties are, at least in Kant's intention, limited to human beings as supposedly the only rational animals, and are purely individual. Therefore, since only individual human beings are rational, only they are directly morally considerable.

Not surprisingly, given its rationalism, deontological ethics has come to dominate academic ethical philosophy, especially as developed by the work of John Rawls, together with legal philosophy. More broadly, its focus on duties, in a culture increasingly dominated by rights alone, is welcome, and it embodies some important truths with an intellectually satisfying elegance. But its weaknesses result from the same emphases, and are at least equally serious in an ecological context.

To begin with, it is questionable to what extent Kant's answer to Hume's challenge was successful. The 'passions' play as large a role in our lives as ever, and reason is by no means necessarily the most important or even distinctive human attribute; it is certainly not an absolute attribute. (Reasoning is, finally, increasingly admitted to be present in other species as well.) Similarly, people have many other values and reference points than reason, or rights. Again, in practice – notwithstanding 'universal reason' – both rights and rules can and do conflict, and it is merely an assertion of faith that there is always a higher principle to appeal to which will resolve the conflict. We might also remark that neither reason nor duty is proof against the fact that 'people's consciences can be as perverted as anything else' (Blackburn 2001: 19). In fact, as Schopenhauer observed, not only can 'reasonable' and 'vicious' be mutually consistent but 'only through their union are great and far-reaching crimes possible'.[3]

Much of the substance of these problems stems from the underlying fact that rationality, in this theory, is extraordinarily abstract. Even the beings concerned are abstract ones, insofar as deontological ethics is entirely non-empirical and supposedly rests on a priori principles, i.e. ones not derived from personal experience. Radically isolated from the embodied and substantive ways actual persons live and experience their lives, 'rational' easily becomes circular: those who agree to these rational principles are therefore rational people, and the principles are rational because those people agree that they are. Meanwhile, in practice, it tends to end up referring to an elite restricted not only to humans but also mainly males, whites, members of the professional middle class, and Westerners.

It is true that one's categorical duty might well be to protect nature, for example. But nature here is understood as a passive and inferior recipient of any such protection; it is not an agent and thus an equal, because it is not 'rational'. As a believer in rationalism, Kant was unable to supply any substantive reason as to why, as supposedly non-rational beings, even animals, let alone the rest of nature, should be treated well – except as practice for treating humans well! (Schopenhauer was rightly scathing on this point too.)[4] In this important sense, deontology is decidedly anthropocentric. Rawls confirms it: the 'status of the natural world and our proper relation to it is not a constitutional essential or a basic question of justice', and any beliefs pertaining to the nonhuman world, no matter how 'considered', are 'outside the scope of the theory of justice' (Rawls 1993: 246, 448). Justice, it seems, is reserved for humanity alone.

Rationalist deontology, as developed by Rawls and his peers, has also become academic in the unflattering sense. However influential within the academy, from a more broadly and deeply engaged perspective it appears largely divorced from life in practice: scholastic, hyper-abstract, and with correspondingly little to show in positive political influence.[5] Deontology has achieved considerable social and political influence with the idea of rights or, at least, the common understanding thereof. (Hitherto, at least, these have been very largely human rights.) It is possible to value such rights while also being aware of the limitations. In relation to ecological ethics, there are at least three.

One is the troubling tendency to disassociate rights from corresponding duties and responsibilities. (This is a result of the triumph of the modern liberal version of rights over the older republican version; as we shall see, the latter, significantly, is closely related to Aristotelian virtue ethics.)[6] The second is individualism, which leaves questions of the common good − not exactly unimportant − dangerously unattended. The third flaw was well put by the radical ecologist John Livingston (1994: 161): 'One need not invoke rights . . . when a relationship rests on mutual trust, respect, and (especially) affection.'

Some philosophers, notably Tom Regan, have extended deontology to animals, arguing that as beings with interests they too qualify for treatment as ends in themselves, not just as means to human ends. This has resulted in the influential **animal rights movement**. As we shall see later, others, such as Paul Taylor, have tried to extend the same theory even to (individual) plants. But this attempt suffers from the same defects just noted. In any case, for the reasons just listed, it is difficult to see how a fully ecological ethics could be developed while still remaining within the deontological fold.

Consequentialism ('Effects')

The chief competing school of modern ethics is *consequentialism*, according to which 'the value of an action' – and thence its ethical character – 'derives entirely from the value of its consequences' (Blackburn 1994: 77). This view is the opposite of what deontologists assert. Its dominant form, founded by Jeremy Bentham (1748–1832) and further developed by John Stuart Mill (1806–73), holds that the highest good, and therefore the ultimate ethical criterion, is the greatest happiness – itself defined as pleasure – of the greatest number of people. In other words, the decisive ethical question about an action is whether or not it is useful in advancing the general happiness of humanity. For that reason, the principal school of consequentialism is known as *utilitarianism*.

There are two kinds of utilitarian ethics: *hedonistic*, in which a general definition of happiness (decided, in practice, by the relevant 'experts') is applied; and *preference*, in which the goal is to maximize not pleasure but the satisfaction of preferences which people are permitted to define for themselves. The last kind is certainly more democratic; however, it should also be noted that such utilitarians make it difficult to criticize what those preferences actually are.[7] No matter how heinous what makes someone happy may be, this school has little to say about it as such. Note too that preferences often conflict, and are therefore not susceptible to a final ordering without one particular kind being imposed (ultimately, arbitrarily) as the highest or best kind.

Some important general points follow. One is that for consequentialists/utilitarians – and this sharply marks them out from the preceding school – the subjective motivations of objective actions are irrelevant; it doesn't matter if the right thing is done for the 'wrong' reason, or vice versa. This results in a tendency to dismiss motivation as irrelevant – something that does not follow from the plausible belief that results are ultimately more important. And that belief is attractive. If taken to be in any way absolute, however, it is vulnerable to the reply the late twentieth-century Chinese politician Chou En-lai gave when asked what he thought of the consequences of the French Revolution: 'It's too soon to tell.' There is a serious point behind the quip: since utilitarianism can only judge the correctness of actions after the fact, in order for it to help make decisions an assumption is necessary along the lines of 'based on predicted outcomes' or 'given past occurrences it is probable that . . . '.[8]

Also in contrast to the deontologists, consequentialism is ultimately collective. True, individual experiences matter – but only, in the end, to enable totting up a final tally of general happiness; if the latter clearly outweighs a few of the former, it is too bad for them. Social well-being trumps individual rights. Consequentialism thus has a potential political affinity with collectivist politics, whether of the 'right' (authoritarian/fascist) or 'left' (collectivist-socialist).

Notice too that happiness has to be susceptible to being 'objectively' measured; otherwise, it cannot be calculated, or outcomes compared. For the same reason, it must be 'universal'; if there are substantively different happinesses, they may be incommensurable (i.e., incapable of being compared), and then the system would break down. As a result, utilitarians tend to measure that which can be measured and ignore that which cannot; or, relatedly, they redefine something that cannot be measured as something that can, and then use that (without changing its name) to replace the awkward original. This problem is further compounded by its vulnerability to a few powerful people deciding what 'general happiness' consists of, and giving the result a spurious air of objective and universal truth. (Indeed, happiness is not even necessarily everyone's overriding goal.)

Putting these points together, it is hardly surprising that utilitarianism is probably the most powerful single philosophy in social and economic policy in the modern 'Western' world. Step forward, the ubiquitous 'Cost Benefit Analysis' (CBA). Thus utilitarianism's emphasis on objectivity, on collectivity and on measurement is a fundamental part of the modern project; and so too, sadly and even tragically, are its flaws.[9]

As we shall see, utilitarianism has been influentially extended to animals by Peter Singer, following on from Bentham's famous assertion that 'The question is not, can they *reason*? Nor, can they *talk*? But can they *suffer*?' (1907: ch. 17, sec. 1, fn. to para 4). This point is very well taken, but Singer's programme does not entirely escape the problems just mentioned. Together with the animal rights school, the resulting **animal liberation movement** (largely inspired by Singer) is achieving admirably practical results in improving animal welfare;

and it has helped that he has largely dropped the illusion that what matters most can be measured. But it remains vulnerable to anyone claiming that the collective human happiness resulting from, say, factory farming outweighs the suffering of the animals themselves.

Its greatest ecological weakness, however, results from the unavoidable utilitarian position that 'actions are right or wrong, good or bad, according to how they affect the experiences of beings capable of experience' (Wenz 2001: 85). In other words, utilitarianism requires, and is limited to, *sentience*; or rather, *sentient beings*. (This doesn't contradict the collectivist emphasis just noted; sentience is simply a prerequisite for it.) A being without sentience cannot (apparently) suffer, or experience pleasure, or have preferences; so about a non-sentient being – a species, for example, or an ecosystem, or a place – utilitarians have, again, little to say. Furthermore, it cannot prevent the possibility, otherwise absurd at best, of someone successfully arguing that the suffering of a number of 'less sentient' animals may be justified by the pleasure or satisfaction it gives 'more sentient' ones – i.e., naturally, us. (Just how good does that steak taste? Well, that's alright then.)

Virtue Ethics

Virtue ethics is by far the oldest of the three kinds of ethics, stemming largely from the philosophy of Aristotle (384–322 BCE). Its central focus is on *developing a virtuous character*, such that good or right actions result naturally from its dispositions. Conversely, the exercise of virtue is what produces a good person. Such a character is marked by its possession of the four classical virtues: temperance, justice, courage and (practical) wisdom. (It is interesting to contrast these with the later and rather different Christian virtues: faith, hope and charity.) These attributes characterize what Aristotle called *eudaimonia*, which is often translated as 'happiness'. A better rendition, however, would be 'well-being', including not only living well but doing good.

The emphasis on character is not as individualistic as it sounds to us, for a number of reasons. In this tradition, humans are seen as inherently social and political animals; thus, *eudaimonia* cannot be developed in isolation. Furthermore, by the same token, a person who embodies it will also promote it in relation to others. Also (and this is a point of potential ecological importance), although Aristotle and his successors clearly had other human beings in mind, there is nothing in the theory itself limiting who or what can be the object of virtuous behaviour.

Virtue ethics has been criticized as being potentially circular – a character is defined in terms of the virtues, which are in turn defined by that character – and **teleological**. That means having or being defined by a predetermined goal (*telos* in Greek), which Aristotle called a 'final cause'. The two aspects are related: behaviour is taken as determined by goals, which are inferred from behaviours. Teleology has been distinctly out of philosophical favour for the past 350 years; much of the knowledge resulting from modern science (especially biology) was, in part, the result of abandoning whatever had already been decided was the purpose of, say, an organism, in favour of examining what Aristotle would have called its 'efficient cause'(s): what is 'driving' or 'pushing' rather than 'pulling' it into its particular existence. Typically, however, this movement went too far and tried to banish consideration of purpose altogether. Now it is difficult (some philosophers think impossible) to give a causal account of how 'subjective' purposes result in 'objective' behaviour; but that does not mean organisms do not have goals, or that they do not matter. In short, this criticism of virtue ethics is not difficult to overcome with a less ambitious and more limited, but still real, version of purpose.

Be that as it may, virtue ethics was almost completely eclipsed with the rise of modern ethics in the form of deontology and consequentialism. Those warring twins agreed that in addition to bearing the taint of prescientific teleology, virtue ethics was much too vague – it couldn't be expressed neatly in a set of (supposedly) incontrovertible principles or (purportedly) comprehensive rules – and impractical, giving no precise guidance as to how to deal with concrete ethical challenges beyond saying, it seems, that the right thing to do would be whatever a good person would do in that situation. Such complaints, however, reveal the Achilles heel of modernist ethics: what basis is there to suppose that there can ever be a principle (such as Kant's imperative) that is *universally* true (always, everywhere and regardless of who is involved), let alone practically helpful? And how can anyone defensibly purport that there is, or ever could be, a set of rules that are (in the same way) universally applicable without further ethical reflection that is not covered in the rules?[10] In addition, more problematically still, such blithe rationalism, especially when it takes the form of neoliberal economics, is deeply implicated in the ecological destruction and damage that I have termed ecocrisis. In that weakness, then, also lies the potential challenge that a renewed virtue ethics offers, appearing as it does in a time of widespread disillusionment with modernity.[11]

Of course, ethics being what it is (or life being what it is), there is some overlap between the two modern schools and the revived older one. Indeed, in practice it is hard to see how they could be completely separated. For example, it is plausible to see 'maximizing the good of the greatest number' as a universal rule-of-thumb and duty; motives for actions (especially insofar as they influence the choice of means) usually have a significant effect on their outcomes; and the successful realization of rules for realizing the good requires, and results in, a kind of virtue, just as the accumulation of virtues (or vices) results in a certain kind of character. In fact, *all* the considerations characteristically emphasized by each school – motivations for actions as well as their effects, rules for behaviour but also their inculcation as virtue – are important.

Nonetheless, where the emphasis is put does matter. In assuming that ethics is entirely about following rules or principles, or engaging in complex calculations (from a genuinely mathematical point of view, pseudo-calculations), deontology and consequentialism share a fundamental rationalist assumption: the belief, in the words of the great theorist of modern disenchantment Max Weber (1991: 139), 'that one can, in principle, master all things by calculation'. (How appropriate, then, is the motto of the giant management company McKinsey: 'Everything can be measured, and what gets measured gets managed.')

That is just what virtue ethics throws into doubt. It argues instead, in the words of Francisco Varela, that ethics 'is closer to wisdom than to reason, closer to understanding what is good than to correctly adjudicating particular situations. . . . [A] wise (or virtuous) person is *one who knows what is good and spontaneously does it*' (1992: 3, 4; emphasis in original). Compared to the abstract hypothetical models used by professional ethicists, this approach brings us significantly

closer to the actual ethical situations, the challenges and dilemmas
that confront us in lived life, daily as well as extraordinary. It is also
more ecological than its competitors, because the virtuous person
'knows what is good' as part of a lifelong process of learning that
depends upon, and contributes to, social participation in a community; or rather, a number of overlapping communities, both human
and nonhuman. Virtue ethical behaviour is not about knowing *what*,
but know-*how*, and we learn that through the lived experience of
finding ourselves in concrete situations of ethical challenge guided
by, and guiding as, exemplars: education, in its broadest lifelong
sense. (We shall develop this point further in Chapter 12.)

It might be argued, as Sylvan and Bennett do, that since they
are overwhelmingly concerned with human beings and their interrelationships, 'environmentally at least, all established ethics are
inadequate' (1994: 26). As I have said, the inadequacy of deontological and consequentialist ethics is inseparable from their modern
origins and modes – not because ecological problems began with
modernity, but because they became drastically worse in modernity,
in ways which those ethics reproduce: chiefly, anthropocentrism and
rationalism. Louke van Wensveen (2005: 27–8) notes that virtue
ethics 'has premodern roots, and although it comes to us sifted
through the mazes of modernity, its internal consistency and com-
prehensibility are not dependent on the worldview that came into
power with the scientific and industrial revolutions'. Insofar as it is
complicit, at least, with the ecological crisis, we should therefore be
glad 'to have access to a form of moral discourse that is not too much
in cahoots with this worldview'.

The inadequacy is arguably worse with deontology, as we saw with
Kant and Rawls. Rights, while they offer some practical purchase in
contemporary political culture, suffer from the same deficiencies
respecting both human and nonhuman life as that culture itself. As
Livingston (1994: 175) put it: 'Rights must be seen and understood
for what they are: artificially institutionalized technical surrogates for
naturally evolved mutualistic, participatory compliance and reciproc-
ity. Even in human affairs, rights are prostheses for "rightness."'

At least consequentialism such as Singer's isn't necessarily biased
towards human sentience and therefore suffering. It is, however,
biased towards sentience as such, and that introduces all the licence
that human chauvinism usually needs to justify itself: for are we not,

it claims, the most if not the only sentient animal? (The fact that it would be extremely difficult actually to support such a claim without circular thinking should not delude us into thinking that, in common practice, even among scientists and philosophers, it is therefore in any great danger.) Thus both approaches – deontology directly, by making a fetish of reason (itself understood to be solely human reason), and consequentialism indirectly, by inviting the fetishization of human reason as the ultimate form of sentience (because it is supposedly *self*-conscious) – support the anthropocentrism which supports them in turn.

If we include virtue ethics among those that are 'established', however, Sylvan and Bennett's statement may be doubted. In addition to the 'ecological' character of its provenance and exercise, there is the point, mentioned earlier, that the object of virtuous behaviour need not be restricted to other humans. As Cooper and James point out, the fact that virtue ethics centres on the question of one's own (human) life 'does not imply that it is egoistic in any substantive and pejorative sense. For what ethical reflection leads to is a recognition that genuinely *other*-regarding virtuous behaviour, engaged *for its own sake*, partly constitutes the agent's own good' (2005: 16; my emphases). As some environmental philosophers have noticed, virtue ethics is the most fully ecologically promising kind, with the potential to contribute to understanding and developing the virtues, both individually and collectively, which constitute a deep green way of life.[12] Nor is this a purely optional luxury. As Ronald Sandler (2007: 2) says: 'Attempts to improve society, including its relations with the natural environment, will amount to mere moonshine if its citizens lack the character and commitment to make them work.'

A Green Virtue Ethic

Let us sketch out what a green virtue ethic (GVE) would look like, a sketch that will be filled out a bit more in Chapter 12. I say 'would', but in important ways, which we shall come to later, it already exists in at least two forms: an ecofeminist ethics of care – 'world protection, world-preservation, world repair' (Ruddick 1989: 79, quoting Adrienne Rich) – and indigenous culture-natures which haven't been entirely colonized by modernity. There are also countless ordinary unsung acts and habits that qualify whose performers would be surprised to hear were anything special. (I say this, by the way, without discounting the equally countless ordinary destructive acts of ignorance, greed and hate.) So all we are trying to do here is to begin to theorize a specifically *green* virtue ethic.

Minimally, it seems to me, a GVE is developed and practised in the course of a lifelong process of learning in communities (so far, so standard) which include, on a broadly equal footing of value and importance, *non*humans. In that process, human exemplars of virtue are such because of their virtue, to an important and valued extent, in relation to nonhuman nature.

Surprisingly, this point does not appear in what Sandler (2005: 3–6) specifies for a GVE. His requirements, all of them implicitly or explicitly anthropocentric, leaves it as environmental or light green at best, and a long way from fully ecological. Or perhaps it isn't surprising, since Sandler also thinks that natural phenomena which appear to be agentic ('goal-directed'), let alone cooperative, are 'only a by-product of the behaviour of the individuals [involved] pursuing their own good': a neat encapsulation of Darwinian classical economics! But that is alright, it seems, because 'species, ecosystems, and other environmental collectives are *often* morally considerable, even though they lack inherent worth'. Nonetheless, 'this means that conduciveness to promoting their good is not among the considerations that make a character trait a virtue'. At which point, Sandler produces the tired anthropocentric objection to holism and the moral considerability of ecological entities, namely that 'the biotic community and the individuals that comprise it do not have (with rare exception [*sic*]) the capacities to participate in cooperative arrangements and deliberative discourse, which are *often* considered distinctive of moral communities' (2005: 79–81; my emphases: 'often' does a lot of work here).

However we might get to a GVE, it won't be this way. It does not even permit a virtue ethic of the kind developed by Rebecca Walker, in which 'animal good lives are of a kind with our own good lives' (2007: 187). So it seems that a truly ecological virtue ethic would be a radical departure for many, even within the field of environmental virtue ethics. Let us not exaggerate its radicality, however. To grasp that such a thing is possible, all that is needed is to realize the truth of Rowe's observation that 'We are Earthlings first, humans second' (2006: 21). (Calvin Luther Martin [1992: 18] puts it more strongly: 'Only a fool would imagine himself as somehow exclusively a human being.') That is, we are beings not only *on* but *of* the Earth, who happen to be *human* beings. Then both virtues and vices no longer need be considered, inadequately and damagingly, as solely human, when they are in fact more-than-human.

To put it another way, virtue ethics can only be reserved for humans alone by assuming just what is in question: (a) that there is an ethically significant foundational difference between humans and all the rest of nature; (b) that that difference outweighs all commonalities; and (c) that it confers a unique privilege and/or responsibility. Not only are none of these steps axiomatic or self-evident; they are, I argue throughout this book, wrong, and destructively so.

Once that point is grasped, ethical virtues to be emulated and learned and vices to be avoided and discouraged can take their proper place as what this particular 'plain citizen' of the biotic community (as Aldo Leopold called us) needs to learn to do, in order to become who, at our best, we are. Conversely, nature takes its proper place at the heart of *all* beings, not merely an add-on extra to make us better humans. As Wensveen shows, this is a task to which an ecological virtue ethic, including sensibility and language, 'directed not simply at human happiness but at the good of the entire Earth community', has a lot to contribute (2000: 161).

5

Value

Some Issues

I have already said that there can be no ethics without value, the study of which is called 'axiology'. In this section, therefore, we are going to look more closely at the nature of value, especially as it concerns the natural world.

Value can be held to inhere in either single, discrete items, in which case it is *individualist*, or in sets of such items, in which case it is *holist*. The usual example of the former is an individual person, animal or living being; the latter may include species or biotic places, comprising (at a minimum) two or more individuals who are connected in some non-arbitrary way – with species, genetically, or with places, ecosystemically.

Another important distinction is between **instrumental value** and **intrinsic value**. The first kind is the value someone or something has as a means to something else, where that something else constitutes, in effect, a good in itself (or at least, is more valued than the means). In contrast, when someone or something has value as an end in itself, for its own sake, it has intrinsic value. (A variant of the latter is **inherent value**, meaning that in order to exist, intrinsic value, while still inhering in the person or thing concerned, also requires one or more valuers.)[1]

There has been a great deal of confusion around this issue, so let us try to clear it up. In the first place, the distinction between instrumental and intrinsic value is necessary. Why? For one thing, each such term depends for its meaning on the contrasting one it is defined against. Furthermore, if there were only instrumental value, then *everything* would only have value as a means to something else; but for something to have value as a means, that something else must, at least in practice and relative to the means, have value in itself. In other words, it must have intrinsic value. But if there was only intrinsic value, it is not at all clear how it would actually be possible to live, i.e., without using anything or anyone.

Second – and this confusion relates closely to the subject of the earlier discussion of realism and relativism – there is the vexed question (among environmental philosophers) of whether intrinsic value is 'objective' or 'subjective'. Much ink has been spilled in debates between realists or objectivists, who assert that value is 'really there', 'actually there' or even 'out there', and relativists or subjectivists, who argue that we 'project', 'create' or 'construct' it. Some of the former use their assertion to argue for the pre-eminence of science among all the ways of knowing. For their part, the subjectivists, who also believe that there is such a thing as True Knowledge but that we cannot have it, hold that any agreement is therefore arbitrary.

The problem is that both sides, or rather dogmatic proponents of both these views, tend to talk past each other. The resulting stalemate is unnecessary for the same sort of reasons mentioned earlier in the section on epistemology.[2] On the one hand, there can be no value that is objective *in the sense of* being 'out there' whether we know it or not. Any such value (like anything else) has no reality, let alone meaning, for us; to put it bluntly, reality just *is* reality-for-us (whoever 'us' might be; it need not be just human). On the other hand, neither is value created willy-nilly, conjured by us out of nothing, and as whatever we wish. Nor is it subjective *in the sense of* being purely our personal creation; we only exist in, and not apart from, a world of others which exercises constant constraints.

We should therefore abandon the untenably extreme views according to which value must either be completely independent of human apprehension, in order to qualify as objectively real, or else 'merely' subjective, meaning arbitrary or trivial, and therefore (in another variation) in need of some kind of other support, usually scientific.[3] That is a false choice. Value requires both a world *and* participation by valuers to be real. It is both objective – 'really there . . .' – *and* subjective: '. . . for us'.

In short, instances of intrinsic value are *valued for their own sake*, without any reference to their usefulness in realizing some other goal. Now it may be too strong to maintain, with John Fowles, that 'We shall never understand nature (or ourselves), and certainly never respect it, until we dissociate the wild from the notion of usability – however innocent or harmless the use' (1979: 43–4). But there are certainly good grounds for holding that nature must not be seen as *only* of instrumental value. With this in mind, we can turn to the next major distinction: between anthropocentrism, which limits most if not all intrinsic value to humans, and ecocentrism, which finds intrinsic value in nature. (That can mean nonhuman nature, but properly speaking, as we shall see, it should also include humans.)

Anthropocentrism

Anthropocentrism – literally, human-centredness – is one of the most contentious concepts in ecological ethics. There have been several attempts to replace it, but none has been particularly convincing, and since some such concept is definitely needed, it would probably be better to stick with this one, while being careful about exactly what we mean by it.

One objection to the term can be cleared up right away. It goes something like this: 'For us, everything is necessarily human-centred. Therefore there is no alternative to being anthropocentric, and the term is meaningless.' This point (already overstretched) is then used to argue that all value is human, and that ethics should therefore have human beings as its principal or even sole focus: '"Man" never left centre stage, nature *never has been, and never will be*, recognized as autonomous' (Jordanova 1987).[4]

The premise here is true as far as it goes. All value, for us, is *anthropogenic*: generated by human experience (although always co-created with, and in, worlds). But because value is generated *by* human beings, it does not follow that humans must be the main or only repository or concern *of* value. Similarly, recognition of the intrinsic value of the natural world may require a human valuer. (Although, are we the only animals to value it? I doubt it!) Again, it does not follow that such value is therefore *itself* purely human. As Wiggins put it, 'In thinking about ecological things we ought not to pretend (and we do not need to pretend) that we have any alternative, as human beings, but to bring to bear upon ecological questions the human scale of values. . . . [But] The human scale of values is by no means exclusively a scale of human values' (2000: 7–8).[5]

Notwithstanding these points, however, there are those who maintain that as a matter of existential or metaphysical fact, humanity is the principal or sole thing of value, and that the only appropriate scale of value for humans is a scale of human values. We therefore still need a word signifying this position. Now, the use of 'anthropocentrism' has been criticized, not without reason, as being too sweeping. After all, there is nothing wrong with a concern for human beings as such, nor is it necessarily inconsistent with a concern for nonhuman nature.[6] For this reason, alternative terms have been suggested such as *human chauvinism*, *speciesism* and *human racism*.[7] These all have some merit, although the first term is awkward, the second a clumsy neologism and the third involves too narrow an analogy. More important still, however, the term 'anthropocentrism' is pretty well established by now. Also, there is already a reasonably good word for a healthy and non–exclusive appreciation of human value, namely humanism.[8]

For these reasons, I think we should retain 'anthropocentrism' to refer to *the unjustified privileging of human beings, as such, at the expense of other forms of life*, analogous to such prejudices as racism or sexism. John Muir, a prophet of Deep Ecology long before the term was coined, put it this way:

No dogma taught by the present civilization seems to form so insuperable an obstacle in the way of a right understanding of the relations which culture sustains to wildness as that which regards the world as made especially for the uses of man. Every animal, plant, and crystal controverts it in the plainest terms. Yet it is taught from century to century as something ever new and precious, and in the resulting darkness the enormous conceit is allowed to go unchallenged.[9]

It is important to recognize how dominant the anthropocentric mindset is, whether in politics, economics, science or culture. Neil Evernden calls it **resourcism**: 'a kind of modern religion which casts all of creation into categories of utility' to humans, whereby there is literally nothing in the natural (and human) world which cannot be transformed into a resource. 'By describing something as a resource,' he points out, 'we seem to have cause to protect it. But all we really have is a licence to exploit it' (1985: 23). This is the ideology *par excellence* of modernity, and thus of ecocrisis.[10]

I cannot summarize the problem better than Rowe (although his preferred term for anthropocentrism was 'homocentrism'): 'The ultimate crimes against the environment, crimes that also threaten the human enterprise, are fecundity and exploitative economic growth, both encouraged by the homocentric philosophy' (2002: 120). And its dominant expression vis-à-vis the natural world is in various forms of **managerial environmentalism**.[11]

Extraordinary as it may seem, but as we shall repeatedly find, anthropocentrism prevails even among those on the side of nature, so to speak. It may not be 'inevitable' (Katz 2000), but it is common. And however subtly, it prevents them from contesting the dominant cause of ecological destruction and restricts them to fighting its effects. David R. Keller's recent anthology, to pick just one example, is a fine one, and I recommend it. But his opening affirmation that 'Environmental ethics constitutes critiques of anthropocentrism' is then undone by one of his conclusions: 'We are unique and deserve some sort of moral consideration above and beyond that accorded to other life' (2010: 1, 19): a statement of unvarnished anthropocentrism.[12] To be sure, we are, in certain respects, unique; but so is virtually every other species. As Andy McLaughlin puts it: 'The human capacity for reason is no more a justification for a value hierarchy among all life than is the cheetah's speed or the eagle's vision' (1993b: 156). So the question is, does our particular uniqueness entail *ethical* uniqueness, a uniquely privileged position in the more-than-human world? The anthropocentric answer is, yes; the ecocentric one, no.

Ecocentrism

Here we come to the contrary position: a very important one, both in itself and as a counterpole. There are intermediate varieties, of course. One might be called *zoocentrism*, according to which the principal locus of value is animals: in practice, nonhuman animals. (It is neither impossible nor unknown, nor for that matter indefensible, to prefer at least some nonhuman animals to other humans.) Another, less limited and arbitrary, is *biocentrism*: life itself as value, in all its forms, i.e. organisms. Why is this still an intermediate position? Because, simply put, life is itself dependent on components aptly summarized in the ancient symbolic elements of earth, air, water and fire (sunlight). Ecosystems thus comprise a complex ongoing dance of interrelationships not only with other organisms but with the non-organic. For this reason, although 'biocentrism' is sometimes used to mean the same thing, properly speaking *ecocentrism* is the more inclusive concept and value.[13]

Ecocentrism is equally as contentious and delicate a matter as anthropocentrism. At first sight, it seems, its meaning should be simple: placing, or rather finding, *ultimate value in the natural world*. But a crucial question is, does, or should, that include human beings? It would certainly seem so – albeit in a way that root-and-branch anthropocentrics would find very difficult to accept – from Rowe's (1994) majestic summary: 'The ecocentric argument is grounded in the belief that compared to the undoubted importance of the human part, the whole Ecosphere is even more significant and consequential: more inclusive, more complex, more integrated, more creative, more beautiful, more mysterious, and older than time.'

Nonetheless, some critics of ecocentrism have charged it with a simple inversion of anthropocentrism which is not only potentially misanthropic (and strategically counterproductive), but preserves the radical split between the human and natural worlds that we inherited from Platonism, Christianity and Cartesianism.[14] That split is one which ecologists in general rightly see as an integral part of the problem. And the accusation of misanthropy is not always without justification, as far as a few populist Deep Ecologists are concerned. But, as Tom Athanasiou points out, their despair is often mistaken for malevolence. Dave Foreman and Nancy Morton, for example, anticipate an imminent ecological (and therefore social) crash; having said so, they feel impelled by bitter media experience to add: 'We do not think that believing this means one is racist, fascist, imperialist, sexist or misanthropic, even if it is politically incorrect for cornucopians of the Left, Right or Middle' (quoted in Athanasiou 1997: 101).

In any case, evidence of 'ecocentric' misanthropy on any significant scale is extremely thin, and its actual harmful effects in the world, compared to those of toxic anthropocentrism, are a birdbath compared to an ocean.[15] As Bron Taylor remarks, 'Far more dangerous is the present course' (2010: 219). Nor will you find any in the work of its leading exemplars such as Arne Naess, David Orton or Stan Rowe. Indeed, the passage just quoted by the last comes from an essay entitled 'Ecocentrism: The Chord that Harmonizes Humans and the Earth' (1994).

It is more reasonable to see compassion for human beings and compassion for nonhuman animals and nature as integrally related. Logically speaking, if humans are a part of nature, then they share, at least in part and/or potentially, in nature's intrinsic value. And in practice, the two kinds of compassion are likely to *reinforce* each other. (It is also significant that, as is well attested, those who are cruel to animals are more likely to abuse other humans, and vice versa.) Therefore ecocentrism does not necessarily exclude humanity, and there are powerful reasons, both substantive and strategic, why it should not. Warwick Fox is right that 'being opposed to human-centredness is logically distinct from being opposed to humans per se' (1995: 19). And misanthropy is as unjustifiable as it is unattractive. As Robyn Eckersley writes, respecting the Earth's bounty: 'The principle of common entitlement makes it clear that humans are not expected to subvert their own *basic* needs in order to enable other life-forms to flourish' (1998: 177).

Humanity does pose something of a conundrum, being plainly part of the natural world and, at the same time, distinct from other animals in the degree to which individual reflective consciousness, and its socialization as culture, affects to a relatively unique extent how otherwise 'purely' natural factors play themselves out. Note that no superiority or special privileges necessarily follow from this relative uniqueness. But it does mean that ethically, as Ken Jones puts it in an excellent discussion, '[h]umankind does have a unique responsibility for the wellbeing of other creatures and the whole ecosystem, yet is at the same time a dependent and integral part of that system' (1993: 97). So neither exclusive anthropocentrism nor an exclusive ecocentrism is a defensible, or desirable, option.

However, it is vital to recognize that even with an inclusive ecocentrism, there can be serious conflicts between humans and nonhuman nature; and an arrangement in which the former *cannot lose*, if and when there are such conflicts, cannot be called ecocentric. Some people – most social ecologists, for example – maintain that the 'liberation' of nature (a rather anthropocentrically patronizing idea in any case) *necessarily* follows from the liberation of oppressed humans.[16] But this wishful thinking obscures the real conflicts and hard choices that can occur between what are at least perceived as humans' and nature's interests, and makes it harder to evaluate and decide between them. There are many possible examples: should DDT be banned on ecological grounds, even though that would jeopardize the eradication of malaria in the Third World? In a world of rapidly shrinking wild enclaves and widespread species decline, should aboriginal people be permitted to hunt and trap within the few remaining protected areas? Indeed, even within the broad movement to protect the nonhuman world, there are clashes between proponents of animal liberation/rights (trying to protect individual animals) and ecologists/environmentalists (trying to protect species and/or ecosystems).[17] Alliances between different progressive and emancipatory movements do not come ready-made; the hard work of forging them is unavoidable. And it should be recognized that in many, perhaps even most, situations, a strategic appeal to anthropocentric value (human self-interest) may be an unavoidable part of the argument for an ecocentric outcome.

It follows that an ecocentric ethic alone will probably not suffice to save an Earth fit for life as we know it; but that also won't happen without one. As Frederic Bender says: 'It takes extraordinary forbearance to refrain from exploiting nature. To find nature important enough to justify the changes necessary to preserve and restore it, first we must experience it as intrinsically valuable (or sacred)' (2003: 348). In our unprecedented circumstances, the dominant philosophy of the last two millennia, both in religious and secular forms, is now in drastic need of change. Ecocentrism recognizes, as anthropocentrism does not, that human beings live in a more-than-human world.

Anthropocentrism's denial of such a fundamental point cannot be corrected by 'enlightened self-interest' through limited add-ons. That cannot place the perception of uselessness *to us* (especially economically) in the contexts which draw its poison: the extraordinary complexity of the natural world, on the one hand, and the extent of our ignorance and our greed, on the other. The problem with 'enlightened anthropocentrism' is exactly the same as with 'enlightened egoism'; to repeat Midgley, 'egoism is by its nature rather *un*enlightened and hard to enlighten' (1997: 94). Here is the trap into which modern environmentalism has fallen: 'By basing all arguments on enlightened self-interest the environmentalists have ensured their own failure whenever self-interest can be perceived as lying elsewhere' (Evernden 1985: 10).

As Kenneth Anderson says about calls – often from so-called greens – for ecologism to meet the demands of anthropocentric 'progressivism' (also sometimes called 'realism'): 'It is not hard to see how [such] arguments seek in the end to draw radical ecology into the "conversation" of bureaucracy and managerialism, from which, once drawn in, it will go nowhere that "progress" does not approve that it should go.'[18] This has happened time and again, and it remains a trap.

At the moment, of course, such anthropocentrism rules, even inside the environmental movement. The results, jeopardizing both humanity and nonhuman nature, are all too evident. An ecocentric 'horizon' to our concerns, in contrast, would help avert (or at least mitigate) ecological disaster, and do so in a way that also furthers anthropocentric interests: '[I]f humans do learn to care about what happens to other species and ecosystems – that is, to treat nature as if it mattered – then the repercussions [of ecological destruction] to humans will be lessened.' The vital thing, therefore, is to 'set anthropocentric concerns within ecocentric concerns' (Sylvan and Bennett 1994: 6, 90). But note: this only works to the extent that we really *do* care about nonhuman nature and beings for their own sakes (intrinsic value); pretending to care because it might save us (instrumental value), and basing a programme on that pretence, won't change a thing. Why? Because being anthropocentric and instrumentalist, it remains wholly within the mode which – especially in its most intensely organized and institutionalized form, industrial capitalism – is causing the problems that the move is supposed to relieve.

6

Light Green or Shallow (Anthropocentric) Ethics

We have now arrived, via value, at ecological ethics as such: that is, principles (incorporating values) concerning how human beings should best behave in relation to nonhuman nature. Here, too, there is a spectrum. However, we shall content ourselves here with three broad kinds. At one end, corresponding to instrumental value, consideration for the nonhuman is only indirect, insofar as the well-being of humans is affected. In the middle, there is consideration for nonhuman individuals. At the other end, we find consideration for the well-being of nonhuman places and ecosystems. We shall consider several different kinds of each of these three principal positions, especially the last.[1]

What is a Light Green Ethic?

Its chief characteristic is that of limiting direct value to human beings. In other words, it is anthropocentric. Nonhuman beings of any kind have no independent moral status or considerability and only merit consideration insofar as they matter to humans; consequently, any parts of nonhuman nature that have no use-value for humans are fair game to be exploited, and any parts which apparently have no value can be disposed of. Likewise, an ecological problem is defined here as one that poses difficulties for humans, regardless of its effects on the rest of nature.

Despite the criticisms made so far of anthropocentrism, I am not assuming that an ecologically sound programme based on light green ethics is necessarily impossible. But it would have to include, for example:

- a very strong *precautionary principle* – that is, acting cautiously, on the assumption that our knowledge of the effects of our actions is always exceeded by our ignorance;
- a definition of 'sustainability' that rules out all practices except those that are, in principle, *indefinitely* sustainable; and
- a conviction that as much rather than as little as possible of nature should be preserved intact.

The result, in effect, would favour the survival and possibly flourishing of nonhuman nature, even if the reason was still human survival and flourishing, and that (from a consequentialist point of view, which in this case seems appropriate) would be fine.[2]

Of course, the unlikeliness of this degree of enlightened self-interest, on any significant scale, should be virtually self-evident. Given that the well-being of human beings is so intimately tied to the well-being of the natural world, however, a considerable amount of ecologically sound regulation and legislation can be defended in terms of human interests. That includes a great deal of what is within the current range of political possibility. The problem, as I have suggested, lies with the serious limitations of human beings when it comes to perceiving, let alone acting on, that dependency. Both individually and collectively, we tend to self-interest narrowly construed, in such a way and to such an extent that our dependence on the natural world is very difficult to notice; and that weakness is literally capitalized on by those with the equally narrow but powerful motive of profit. Many would argue that this existential fact makes an ecocentric ethic unrealistic or even impossible. Another possible conclusion, however, is that it makes one even more necessary and urgent.

In any case, light green or shallow ethics and its accompany-ing **ethos** (way of behaving) does not even attempt to break out of anthropocentrism. Not surprisingly, then, this least ecological ethic is also the ruling one. Its roots lie in the dominion thesis discussed earlier, but now secularized. This is the dominant philosophy, where nature is concerned, in government departments and ministries, corporations, research laboratories and institutes of all kinds. Its followers see nonhuman nature as a resource to be exploited for human ends, and that view is encapsulated in resource management and conservation, human welfare ecology and a great deal of what is called environmentalism. A light green ethic doesn't preclude precautionary arguments, but its concern is still human well-being. The furthest it can reach in an ecological direction without becoming something else is the version of 'sustainability' which asks, 'How long can we continue to exploit this natural resource without destroying it altogether, and thus not be able to exploit it any longer?'

'Sustainable growth', as an ecological gesture, is thus empty. Given that nothing is sustainable without limits, which are just what development and growth resist recognizing, these terms translate as: 'How can we go on living unsustainably for as long as possible?' As Rudolf Bahro pointedly observed: 'Almost everywhere in the world people still want a megamachine which nevertheless doesn't destroy anything, and they don't want to know they can't have one' (1994: 56).[3] 'Sustainable development' is somewhat more complex. Insofar as there *will be* so-called development, it is of course better if there is an attempt to keep ecological constraints in mind. It all depends on where the emphasis is put: on the 'sustainable', or on the 'development'? If the former doesn't take priority, sustainable development becomes simply another green fig-leaf.[4] (We shall go into these questions in more detail in Chapter 13.)

The light green view has recently found new and more sophisticated expression among techno-optimists, who use the ever-increasing impact of humans on global ecosystems to advocate what Rowe (1995) called 'managing profligacy more efficiently': basically, a more scientific plundering of 'resources' and further attempted evasion of natural limits on human desires.[5] A related project is to put a price on almost everything, thus allowing ecological 'costing' – something that has now been joined by 'ecosystem services'.[6] (The last euphemism reminds me unavoidably of another, also covering a set of exploitative power relationships: 'sexual services'.) The anthropocentric bias of this programme, as well as its ruthlessness, is exposed by the fact that while there is some recognition of the abuse of nature by humans as well as its use, there is none for its non-use by us, or its use by nonhumans. The title of a book by James Trefil says it all: *Human Nature: A Blueprint for Managing the Earth – by People, for People* (2004).

The underlying assumption of this philosophy seems to be that having done such a good job of managing itself and the world to date, the duty of humanity is now to take charge of evolution and, principally through genetic engineering, direct it: a kind of 'intelligent species' burden', as Fox aptly puts it (1995: 195).[7] The fine print specifies that it is, of course, scientists (the brain of collective humanity, perhaps?) whom we should allow to lead, and morally, politically and financially support, in this adventure.[8]

Such advocacy, common among sociobiologists and evolutionary psychologists, is often identified as politically right-wing. If so, then it is instructive to consider for a moment a movement which characterizes itself as on the left (albeit as much anarchist as socialist): **social ecology**. In this view, human–nature relations depend completely upon human–human relations, so that improving the former depends entirely on resolving the latter; any serious ethical consideration of nonhuman nature is therefore superceded by intra-human politics. Furthermore, in its founder Murray Bookchin's words, it is 'the responsibility of the most conscious life-form – humanity – to be the "voice" of a mute nature' (Bookchin 1990: 44).[9] This seems patronizing at best, and at worst an invitation to the kind of self-serving anthropocentrism and utilitarianism we have just been discussing. Bookchin's advocacy of evolutionary stewardship could legitimate the wildest current aspirations of biotechnology. At their best, social ecologists perform valuable political and social service, both theoretical and practical, in the form of municipal and community development; but these, while valuable in themselves, leave the heart of the ecological crisis untouched.[10]

Such basic agreement across the usual political spectrum, from right to left, is significant. It reveals that the differences between such political opponents are frequently, at least in this context, superficial; both subscribe to a shallow ecological ethic. Still on the political 'left', the extent to which green political parties at large have abandoned their radical origins is striking. ('Radical' here means existing outside the anthropocentric stronghold. Disagreements within it, no matter how sharp, are not fundamental.) Everywhere in the global North – and not least in Germany, where the Green Party once showed such promise – they have paid the price that is demanded to join the club of political power: deny that nature has any meaning or value independent of human beings (ecocentrism), and that there are any limits in principle to our ability and right to exploit nature (limits to growth).[11] In anthropocentric terms, I don't doubt that the Greens' accession to real power would be an improvement on what we have, but no one should fool themselves that that would be anything other than an improved version of business-as-usual. And it is business-as-usual that is destroying the natural world, and us with it.

Of course, the very dominance of the light green ethic – not only among those in positions of authority, but also among members of the public – means that in many actual situations a direct connection to human interests may be the only practically available argument for ecologists to fall back on. And it may well serve for a while, or in an immediate crisis, as long as a human use-value for the natural item (plant or animal, species or place) can be found. It may even be possible to stretch the concept of 'use' beyond its normal boundaries: for example, to argue that an item's 'use' is that it meets our aesthetic or spiritual needs.

Ultimately, though, for the reasons I have mentioned, shallow ecological ethics as a way to defend nature is inadequate. As Livingston says, 'This is not to deprecate what some environmentalism does, but to emphasize what it does not do' (1994: 186). But what it does not do is precisely what most needs doing. In theory, anthropocentric ethics alone could perhaps suffice to restore sanity to humanity's relationships with the rest of the natural world, *if* it were sufficiently enlightened; and, in practice, it can sometimes take us part of the way. But the rub is in that 'if '. The evidence that self-interest can ever be that enlightened, on sufficiently widespread, deep and long-lasting a scale, is vanishingly small. Facing up to that uncomfortable fact obliges us to recognize that, ecologically, 'enlightened self-interest' is ultimately an oxymoron.

By the way, it is worth remarking on a curious paradox at work in light green ethics. Anthropocentric apologists for human superiority frequently argue that (in the words of one defender of animal experiments), '[a]ll animals put their own survival first, and we should do the same'.[12] This attitude assumes a human nature that is ethically

identical with that of other animals. The only difference lies in our
superior power, resulting from the contingent success of our evolutionary position: in short, might makes right. Political ecologists, on
the other hand – who otherwise tend to emphasize our continuity
with the rest of the natural world – argue that human beings can, and
should, choose not to exploit our species-dominance and expand in
every way possible. This assumes that we are significantly *different*
from all other animals, which are presumably incapable of practising
quasi-voluntary restraint (and probably do not need to).

The question for the latter group then becomes, how can you
argue for ecocentrism without thereby encouraging human exceptionalism? The answer is, you can't, and that is all right – as long as
difference does not slip into superiority, and our participation in and
dependence upon nature is given its due weight. The capacity to be
moral is not, as such, a sign of superiority, and in any case, whatever
privilege it entails would seem to be a demanding one of care, service
and even sacrifice.

Environmentalism

The fact that even much environmentalism falls into the light green
category is disturbing, because, as a few lone voices have pointed out,
with 'resourcism' the terms of the debate are already loaded in favour
of human interests, themselves almost always construed in relatively
narrow and immediate economic terms:

> The basic attitude towards the non-human has not even been
> challenged in the rush to embrace utilitarian conservation. By
> basing all arguments on enlightened self-interest the environ-
> mentalists have ensured their own failure whenever self-interest
> can be perceived as lying elsewhere. . . . The industrialist and the
> environmentalist are brothers under the skin; they differ merely as
> to the best use the natural world ought to be put to. (Evernden
> 1985: 10)[13]

Livingston similarly concludes that '[t]he overwhelming thrust of
the "environmental" movement is dedicated not to the interest of

Nature, but to the security and sustainability of the advancement of the human enterprise' (1994: 214). Regrettably, the truth of these words has been amply confirmed since they were originally published. As we shall see in Chapter 13, the largest and most influential environmental non-governmental organizations (NGOs), in a way that parallels political green parties, have almost all been seduced into collaborating with business and its anthropocentric ethos. As Christine MacDonald (2008) reports: 'Not only do the largest conservation groups take money from companies deeply implicated in environmental crimes; they have become something like satellite PR offices for the corporations that support them' (quoted in Hari 2010; for chapter and verse, see both MacDonald's book and Hari's article). With the words 'environment', 'sustainable development' and 'natural capital' on all political and business leaders' lips, '[t]he success of environmentalism', as Paul Kingsnorth says, 'has been total – at the price of its soul' (2010: 52).

It was not always so. Rachel Carson, who practically launched modern environmentalism with *Silent Spring* (1962) – and was vituperatively attacked by industrialists and the mainstream media for doing so – criticized our 'habit of killing . . . any creature that may annoy or inconvenience us', arguing that we had to find 'new, imaginative and creative approaches to the problem of sharing our earth with other creatures'.[14] (This is a mid-green ethic; see Chapter 7.) The environmentalism of the early 1970s around Greenpeace, Friends of the Earth and Earth Day included a large measure of respect for, and love of, nonhuman nature. The radical resistance in Britain in the 1990s to the stupid and destructive building of new motorways was deeply ecocentric, defending wild places, trees and fellow creatures alike with passion and imagination.[15] Both are now rare in contemporary environmentalism, which is terrified of being branded as 'romantic', 'nostalgic', 'Luddite' or 'NIMBY' (not in my back yard), as opposed to 'realistic' or 'progressive'. But such language should alert us to the strong possibility that the critic is a proponent of the dangerous and reactionary fantasy that humans own the Earth and its life, and can do what they want and 'need' to do to it. In other words, toxic anthropocentrism.

Kingsnorth's 'Confessions of a Recovering Environmentalist' appeared just as I was writing this new edition. With bitter eloquence, he concludes that '[t]oday's environmentalism is as much a victim of the contemporary cult of utility as every other aspect of our lives, from science to education'. Its new banner, 'sustainability', is an entirely human-centred piece of politicking, disguised as concern for 'the planet', and the imposition of large-scale industrial 'renewable' development on formerly relatively wild places amounts to more 'business-as-usual: the expansive, colonising, progressive human narrative, shorn only of the carbon' (2010: 51–3).

The fact that this is taking place in the name of 'environmentalism' means, I believe, that the term has now been successfully colonized by the anthropocentrism it was originally meant to counter, and can be abandoned by anyone who still holds to that ideal. Sadly, that belief is confirmed by a response to Kingsnorth from Andrew Dobson, the author of *Green Political Thought* (2007).[16] If someone as intelligent and well intentioned as he can nonetheless maintain that '[i]t's not about nature's intrinsic value but about the human species adapting to the long era of low-energy living', then the game for environmentalism is probably up. It *is* about that, but crucially, not *only* about that, and certainly not – as Dobson's dismissal of nature's intrinsic value conveys – only about the human species.

Lifeboat Ethics

I would like to turn now to a particular kind of shallow ethics known as 'lifeboat ethics'. Its originator, Garrett Hardin, pointed out that natural resources are necessarily limited, and that the human population is now well past what those resources can support without measures, such as the 'Green Revolution' and now biotechnology, that will simply result in further population increases, and thus more strain on resources, etc., making an uncontrolled crash likelier than ever. (For saying this, Hardin was widely accused of callousness!) He therefore suggested that the most appropriate metaphor for the situation facing humanity is that of a lifeboat: the wealthier societies live in a relatively (but not, note, infinitely) capacious boat, with room for some but certainly not all of the remaining and more numerous human victims in the sea. The most just solution, to pick them all up, would simply sink the boat. The only real questions, then, are how many and whom to allow on board?

This metaphor captures some of the dilemmas which some people and their societies face, and to accuse Hardin of cruelty is simply to shoot the messenger. A lifeboat ethic is applicable to situations, which do sometimes occur, where there are no good ethical solutions, only a choice, initially, of whether to choose between various horrors or refuse to do so. Assuming the first course is taken, one can only hope further choices are less evil than the alternatives. (This is similar to, but not quite identical with, triage, where there is a more-or-less rational set of criteria for determining which two, of any three, should be saved.)

A more serious limitation of lifeboat ethics, in an ecological context, is that if, as Mary Midgley has remarked, it is actually the entire human lifeboat that is sinking, it doesn't make much sense to respond, 'Not at my end!' (1997: 93). It is true that the poor and defenceless will be hit hardest, but ultimately, if the scale of the crisis is sufficiently serious, no one will be exempt.

Hardin's most influential work (1968), and metaphor, is **the tragedy of the commons**. In this view, briefly, any common good that is communally owned invites abuse by free-riders taking advantage of unlimited access; combined with its limited resources, that will result in its destruction. His argument has been widely interpreted as a right-wing one for privatization as the best way to protect nature, but Hardin himself was not so simple-minded. Pointing out that limited resources cannot meet unlimited demands, and, in a commons, freedom (a frequent right-wing/libertarian byword) therefore brings ruin to all, he called for 'mutual coercion, mutually agreed upon by the majority of the people affected' – not a bad description of, simply, regulation. Hardin also pointed out that '[t]rouble comes when man steps into the system of nature and tries to increase productivity *without limit*'. That is not exactly a neoliberal point. Nor is his central insight that individual consumer choice, the mantra of the market, can produce disaster.[17]

The main problem with Hardin's idea is that it assumes a capitalist kind of common, which approaches a contradiction in terms. Or rather, the commons or community it describes is one in which regulation by custom has *already* broken down; and historically, overwhelmingly, that has happened under the impact of capitalism, allied with imperialism.[18] As E. P. Thompson wrote of Hardin's theory: 'Despite its commonsense air, what it overlooks is that the commoners themselves were not without commonsense. Over time and over space the users of commons have developed a rich variety of institutions and community sanctions which have effected restraints and stints upon use' (1991: 107).[19] Hardin's criticism is therefore not really so much of commons as of capitalism, or rather the kind of 'commons', in such respects as scale and organization, that results from capitalism. Subsequently, the important work of Elinor Ostrom (1990) has shown that the tragedy of the commons is a special case, not a necessary one. Effective long-term self-governing commons are possible when they are designed and controlled by those most directly involved; they are least likely to be so when those in charge are 'higher' and made up of more external state or private interests.

Hardin has faced a great deal of rather pious political criticism from the *bien pensant*.[20] Most of it is an exercise in denial, demonstrating that anthropocentric faith in progress-without-limits can be found as much on the left as on the right. As Kohák recognizes: 'Hardin's greatest and most unpopular contribution may be his willingness to face the reality that some solution must be found even when none is acceptable. . . . Our possibilities are limited, our demands unlimited: if we are to survive, we must limit them ourselves' (2000: 96–7). And although Hardin's work remains within light green ethics – it is really only concerned with the fate of humans – his insights transcend that boundary.

7

Mid-Green or Intermediate Ethics

There are two ways of defining this kind of ethics. In Sylvan and Bennett's terms, it denies the Sole Value Assumption – that humans alone have any intrinsic value – but subscribes to a modified version, the Greater Value Assumption, according to which natural items have some intrinsic value, but wherever they conflict with human interests the latter must take precedence. (There is, however, a range of opinion regarding whether those interests must be 'vital' ones, and what exactly constitutes them.) It follows here that ecological problems are not defined solely in terms of problems they cause to humans; but there are sharp limits to this advance. Wilderness preservation, for example, is defensible in these terms as the preservation of something that does indeed have some intrinsic value which also meets some human (aesthetic, etc.) needs; where oil, minerals and other apparently vital needs are concerned, however, the former must give way.

The other and ultimately more useful way of defining mid-range ecological ethics (which is not necessarily consistent with the first) is as non-anthropocentric but not fully ecocentric. That is, value is not restricted to human beings, but it also does not extend all the way to ecosystems. As we shall see, this is the position of biocentrism. Its main way of proceeding is to build on anthropocentrism by arguing that what has been thought of as a solely human value is also true of nonhumans. Called **moral extensionism**, it extends moral considerability to (primarily) animals, which are therefore perceived as possessing independent moral status, and therefore as deserving protection for their own sakes, regardless of whether they matter to human beings. So most of mid-green ethics concerns our relationships with other animals and, virtually always, individual animals.

Some defenders of human chauvinism (e.g., Passmore 1974) have argued that qualification for such membership depends on also being a responsible moral agent. But if so, as Midgley (1992) has pointed out, one would also have to exclude from ethical consideration all children, the senile, the temporarily and the permanently insane, defectives, embryos (human and otherwise), sentient animals, non-sentient animals, plants, artefacts (including art), inanimate objects, groups of all kinds, ecosystems, landscapes and places, countries, the biosphere and potentially oneself – in other words, the majority of entities with whom we have to deal. In fact, Andrew Linzey (2009) has argued that, along with some of these, such as infants and young children, other animals should be accorded *special* moral status and protection. In other words, their very inability to grant or withhold consent, to argue their case and to defend their interests as such, rather than marking their deficiency as moral agents or patients, are grounds for protecting them.

Extensionism remains human-centred, however; it retains the assumption that humans come with rights which can in certain cases be extended to (in effect) honorary humans, but which otherwise trump all other considerations. Such a position is vulnerable to 'rights' that have been transmogrified into straightforwardly non-vital wants, usually with the help of an economic system whose considerable resources are dedicated to creating and exploiting just that process. As Rowe (1994) says, ethics by extension 'only strengthens anthropocentrism, making it certain that land, air, water and other organisms will always in the crunch take second place to the [perceived] welfare of self, family and friends'.

This kind of ethics can best be considered in terms of its leading schools. We have already examined some of the problems with each in Chapter 4, so I shall be brief. Then we shall look at the fundamental problem – the human treatment of other animals – that mid-green ethics tries to address.

Animal Liberation

The movement that bears its name began with the book *Animal Liberation* (1977) by Peter Singer, mentioned in Chapter 4 in the section on utilitarianism. Using as a starting point Bentham's famous assertion already quoted there (see page 44), Singer has bravely tackled the horrendous suffering, and its sheer scale, that we directly inflict on other animals – mainly through factory farming for meat and dairy foods (in the billions), but also through medical and pharmaceutical experiments (in the millions) and hunting (ditto). This is the moral basis of the case for vegetarianism and, ultimately, veganism – or, at the very least, for not eating factory-farmed animals – and for working towards banning all experiments on animals.

Carried forward by various campaigning organizations, Singer's arguments have already had a significant effect on animal welfare, if still regrettably small in relation to the problem. They have gone far in establishing the ethical point that the literally vital interests of nonhuman beings should not be violated for relatively trivial human reasons. The key to this advance is *sentience* – especially the ability to *suffer* – together with basic logical consistency. Since we grant moral considerability on that basis to young children and mentally handicapped adults – rather than requiring, say, the ability to reason – it is fundamentally inconsistent and arbitrary to deny it to nonhuman animals that (or, we should say, who)[1] are also clearly sentient: pigs, chickens, monkeys, sheep, etc., not to mention wild animals.

The only reason for doing so is therefore what Singer calls **speciesism**: 'a prejudice or attitude of bias in favour of the interests of members of one's own species and against those of members of other species' (1977: 26).[2] Not many people would openly admit to such prejudice, although more, perhaps, than would to racism or sexism. The potential for shaming bad practice – especially when it threatens to erupt in bad corporate publicity – is thus significant. And there are other advantages; one is that there are simple things one can do (such as buy free-range eggs instead of factory-farmed ones). Another is that, as Sylvan and Bennett remark, 'It is easier to empathise with the deer in the field, than the field the deer is in' (1994: 85).

However, as they also point out, that is also the animal liberation movement's weakness: Singer has 'traded human chauvinism for *sentient* chauvinism' (1994: 87; emphasis in original). That is, only sentient beings are deemed worthy of ethical consideration; living but non-sentient ones, such as (so far as we know) plants, let alone ecosystems, are not. The criterion is thus seriously impoverished, and the programme based on it, stopping well short of ecocentrism, cannot protect anything apparently non-sentient. For that, it has to fall back on the relatively weak (because shallow) argument that rainforests, say, should be protected insofar as they are of use to people and animals. The next question would almost certainly be, 'Which bits?'

Closely related to the problem with sentience, and equally serious, is Singer's irreducible individualism, which means that only individual animals deserve direct moral consideration. Once again, collectivities of any sort are left dangerously exposed. Of course, it would be possible to get from individual animals to collections of them, and even ecosystems, if it was admitted that the welfare of individual wild animals required others of its kind, and other interrelated kinds, flourishing in an undamaged environment. There is little evidence, however, of mid-green animal liberationists being willing or able to take this further step. (And to be fair, they have their hands more than full with what they have set themselves to do.)

Animal Rights

Also influential is the animals *rights* movement inspired by Tom Regan (1983). Although both its ultimate concerns and its practical upshot are much the same as that of animal liberation – which therefore need not be repeated – its philosophical basis is different. Regan bases his programme squarely on human individual rights extended to animals, which takes us back to the different emphases of utilitarian and deontological ethics that we looked at earlier. He argues that all adult mammals, at least, are self-aware. As 'subjects-of-a-life' (i.e. their own), they therefore have a *right* to life, including a certain quality of life.

As with Singer, we are compelled to grant that right, almost universally recognized for humans, to other mammals, on pain of either inconsistency or ugly and irrational prejudice. Regan can thus take advantage of modern Western (and especially American) 'rights culture' to alleviate the suffering of animals. Yet the animal rights approach shares the same weaknesses, just noted, as animal liberation. Only individual animals – and 'higher' ones, such as primates, at that – are granted direct moral considerability. But, as Holmes Rolston III rightly says, 'Every organism has a good-of-its-kind; it defends its own kind as a good kind' (1988: 105). In that case, ethical argument does not begin or end with self-awareness.

In short, the intermediate ethics of both Singer and Regan have succeeded in extending ethical consideration to (some) animals only by using a criterion that excludes most of the natural world 'as surely as the most narrowly human speciesism' (Benson 2000: 87). The point made by John Rodman in 1977 still stands: 'I need only to stand in the midst of a clear-cut forest, a strip-mined hillside, a defoliated jungle, or a dammed canyon to feel uneasy with assumptions that could yield the conclusion that no human action can make any difference to the welfare of anything but sentient animals' (1977: 89).

Biocentrism

In ecological ethics, biocentrism – literally, life-centredness – is associated almost entirely with the work of Paul Taylor and his book *Respect for Nature* (1986). The central focus here is on what Taylor calls 'an attitude of respect for nature'. To have this attitude, he writes, 'is to regard the wild plants and animals of the Earth's natural ecosystems as possessing inherent worth. That such creatures have inherent worth may be considered the fundamental value presupposition of the attitude of respect' (1986: 71). And in order to possess inherent worth, a being only has to have 'a good of its own', that is to say, it can be benefited or harmed in relation to its potential biological development (1986: 199). (Sentience, self-consciousness or conscious interest are therefore not required for moral considerability.)

There are four related aspects to this biocentric outlook:

1 Humans are members of the community of life in the same sense, and on the same terms, as other living things.
2 That community, of which humans are a part, consists of a

system of interdependence comprising not only physical conditions, but also relations with other members.

3 Every such organism is a teleological centre of life, i.e., an
   individual pursuing its own kind of good (Greek *telos* = goal or
   end).

4 Humans are not inherently superior to other organisms. (1986:
   99ff.)

From these points, Taylor infers that respect should be accorded
to all organisms, human or otherwise, alike: that is, *unconditionally*.
Furthermore, since the flourishing of each is a good thing, it should
be promoted; in other words, that is its right and our duty. Finally,
since this result applies *universally* (i.e., in theory, without exception),
it is a rational 'foundation' for the biocentric position – by implication, the only kind of foundation worth having – and, as such, merits
(without any other substantive reasons) the support of all *rational*
beings.

Such reasoning and its implicit values, together with the firm
emphasis on rights and duties, ought to remind the reader of the
earlier section on deontological ethics. Although Taylor extends
Kant's human-centred system to other animals and into the arena of
mid-green ethics, which is a definite advance, his work – like that
of the arch-Kantian John Rawls – suffers from an arcane rationalism
which is unlikely to leave much of a mark outside the intellectual
and legal academy. (This, of course, is a broadly consequentialist
criticism.)

The other problem with biocentrism is its individualism. Like
other kinds of mid-green or intermediate ethics, Taylor's 'respect
for nature' is indeed non-anthropocentric, but it really denotes
respect for *individual living things*. In this perspective, an individual of
a common species has exactly the same value as one of a species on
the verge of extinction. Such an ethic therefore cannot handle a non-
random collection of individuals such as a species, and the challenge
of the point well made by Rolston that 'Every extinction is a kind of
super-killing. . . . It kills birth as well as death' (1992: 141). Nor can
it directly address – as our current ecocrisis urgently requires – the
non-random collection of individuals that is an embedded ecological community (or series of overlapping communities); individuals
always trump the interests of ecosystems, because the latter are not

morally considerable. But these points have already been discussed as limitations of a deontological ethics, so let us turn to a deeper kind of ethics which does recognize such 'things' as deserving direct moral consideration.

Animals and Us

First, however, we need to address the issue of anthropogenic animal suffering more directly. To begin with, I would like to make it clear that what I call a fully ecological ethic – an ecocentric one, of the kind we shall be discussing in the next chapter – is not at all insensible to animal suffering, and does not inhibit action on that front. Far from it. As Callicott (1989) argued in his defence of Aldo Leopold's 'Land Ethic', in a wild biotic community, the importance of ecosystems and species overrides the interests of individual animals *when they conflict*, such as in natural predation. (Ecological ethics has no place for bizarre fantasies about eliminating predation in nature.)

Domestic animals, on the other hand, are our direct responsibility; after all, humans domesticated them! Here, individual animal welfare is legitimately the overriding concern – especially when there is no ecological need for us to eat them (i.e., nearly all the time). So with domesticates, there is a lot for ecological ethics to do. But even regarding wild animals, note that most 'predation' *by humans* (hunting, trapping, etc.) is not ecologically justified: how much of it do humans really need to do, and how much ecosystemic good does it accomplish? Hence, where humans are involved, the welfare of the individual wild animals also becomes an ecologically ethical issue of paramount importance.[3]

There is another fundamental point involved. As with all basics, it is difficult to state without sounding banal, but let us risk it, because, in the modern world, it is one that many people seem to have forgotten. Abram (1996a: ix) puts it this way: '[W]e are human only in contact, and conviviality, with what is not human.' After all, for the overwhelmingly greater part of their time, humans have lived with, in relationships with, nonhuman nature, of which other animals are such an integral and spectacular part. Thus, more specifically, to quote Midgley (1983: 109–10), 'Man does not naturally exist in species isolation.' And *where there are relationships between subjects, there is ethics*. Apropos this point, Milan Kundera observed:

> True human goodness, in all its purity and freedom, can come to the fore only when its recipient has no power. Humanity's true moral test, its fundamental test (which lies deeply buried from view), consists of its attitude towards those who are at its mercy: animals. And in this respect humankind has suffered a fundamental débâcle. (1984: 289)

Looking at the ongoing ethical history of humans and other animals, it is hard to disagree.[4]

Part of that history, which is an integral part of modern medicine and science (and therefore modernity as a whole), is experimentation on animals. Integral in turn has been Cartesianism, the campaign to portray animals as merely objects or, rather, quasi-machines, without genuine sentience or significant agency – attributes which, building on anthropocentric Christian theology and still earlier, Greek philosophy, humans reserved for human souls alone. Such a move was, of course, an attempt to eliminate ethics altogether from the issue, in order to combine complete human domination and exploitation of animals with a clear conscience.

Few scientists take Descartes's concepts seriously any more, but Cartesian values have proved far too useful to be easily eradicated; even the potentially levelling spirit of Darwinianism (according to which we are all animals of one kind or another) has had little effect on it. As Livingston points out, respecting experiments on animals in biomedical research, there are certainly 'guidelines' prohibiting 'unnecessary' suffering. But as for the research itself, no matter what it is – crashing pigs in cars, infecting chimpanzees with AIDS, or a hundred other ingenious experiments by sado-dispassionately 'objective' men – 'necessity itself – as an idea or principle – is not open to discussion . . . If it is in the human interest, it is necessary' (1994: 146). Livingston also has rightly little time for the *tu quoque* ('you too') argument, invariably trotted out, that 'You too have benefited from such research.' As he says, 'past cruelties do not justify present or future cruelties. That would be neither ethical nor logical' (1994: 149).

Scientific experiments on animals constitute a kind of litmus test for where anthropocentrism ends and mid-green ethics begins. A compromise might be possible along these lines: 'I only support medical experiments on animals where nothing less than human lives are at stake and there is no known substitute for such experiments, and I shall encourage the development of other procedures as fully and as quickly as possible.' That position would seem defensible to most people, but it is far from ethically impregnable. A fully mid-green perspective, such as Livingston's here, would deem it a dangerous if not contemptible fudge, and in terms of ecocentric ethics I do not think there is any room for compromise. In the words of Bahro, a visionary ecocentric and founding member of the German Green Party, when he resigned after it voted to approve experimentation on animals:

> Yesterday, on the subject of animal experiments, it clearly came down in favour of the position taken by the speaker who said: 'If even one human life can be saved, the torture of animals is permissible.' This sentence expresses the basic principle by which human beings are exterminating plants, animals, and finally themselves. (1986: 210)

Wild Animals

I have already mentioned that a mass extinction of other animals, including whole species, is now under way. It has happened five times before in the billion-year-old history of the Earth, but this one, unlike all the others, is anthropogenic. A great deal of it is indirect: humans appropriating natural habitats and remaking them for their own purposes alone, thus destroying the homes and livelihoods of the others who had lived there. Much of it is also direct, however: hunting and poaching, and trapping. And most of that is not for survival but for (a) commercial gain and (b) fun, or 'sport'. ('A sportsman,' as the Canadian writer Stephen Leacock remarked, 'is a man who, every now and then, simply has to get out and kill something.')

What examples should I mention, with so many to choose from? The bushmeat trade in Africa, now a thriving business that is emptying that continent of wild animals – including the few remaining great apes – while supplying jaded or nostalgic palates with exotic meats in Europe? The annual indiscriminate slaughter of millions of birds – warblers, shrikes, cuckoos, bee-eaters, hoopoes, golden orioles, shearwaters, storks, herons, hawks – in Malta, Cyprus and Italy?[5] Another annual massacre, that of dolphins and whales in Japan and the Faroes, and by Japanese whalers, as well as Norwegian and Icelandic, on the high seas? Of almost everything that moves, in China? Of wolves in America? (Coleman [2004] recounts how wolves in North America in the past centuries were not just killed but tortured with deliberate and extravagant cruelty. He asks, but cannot really answer, why even death was not enough.)

Note that many of those acts are committed *not* in order to survive, nor even 'for the pot', but by relatively well-off people. One of the most egregious instances of mass cruelty today, ethically utterly unjustifiable, is the annual Canadian seal kill. Depressingly, it includes the collaboration of the democratically elected government of a wealthy and relatively well-educated nation with the most barbaric tendencies of industrial capitalism, as well as people willing (as there always are) to act as hired killers. There is some national and (more) international resistance, but it takes place against a background of public as well as official indifference to a speciesism every bit as ugly as sexism or racism.

Or take tigers: only 3,200 left in the wild, but commercial poaching continues. And, of course, the rarer the tiger becomes, the more valuable its skin and parts become, thereby increasing the incentive to kill as many as possible. (Ah, the wonder of 'market solutions'!) Protecting tigers from poachers and actually enforcing the illegality of tiger parts could work – if combined with uncompromising core and cross-boundary protected areas – but governments themselves are apparently too compromised by market values to care enough to make it happen.[6]

Now the ethically preferable way to tackle animal abuse and exploitation is through a combination of policy initiatives resulting in legislation (political and legal) and campaigning: publicity and education to raise public awareness and, when necessary, agitation and confrontation through non-violent direct action (NVDA). Perhaps it would help too if, as with female genital mutilation, we called these activities what they are: not 'hunting', but 'recreational killing'; not 'harvesting', but 'slaughtering'; and for that matter, not 'bull-fight-ing', but 'bull-torture'.

In certain circumstances, however – such as cruelty on a massive scale (e.g., the seals), or where the animals involved are ones whose sentience and therefore susceptibility to extreme pain and suffer-ing cannot be doubted (e.g., whales), or when an entire species is in danger (e.g., gorillas, tigers, etc.) – that may not be enough, and more direct measures are needed. Even here, NVDA is highly preferable on both ethical and strategic grounds. If, however, in such circumstances, the killers attack and endanger the lives of those animals' human defenders, then I believe that vigorous self-defence – on behalf of both themselves and the animals – is ethically licit. As Mahatma Gandhi himself noted, 'Merely taking life is not always *himsa* [harm]; one may even say that there is sometimes more *himsa* in not taking life' (1969: 525).

Indirect measures are also permissible. In South Africa – where poachers are now using helicopters to shoot the few remaining rhinos for their horns, to be sold on for supposedly medicinal prop-erties – some people are starting to inject the horns of living rhinos with chemicals which do not affect the animals but would make a consumer of the horn very ill. In addition to its justice, which seems incontestable, it might just work, since the possibility alone might suffice to put off buyers. (Apparently this suggestion has caused 'international outrage'.[7] Presumably when there are no wild rhinos left, there will be no more cause for such outrage.)

I can already hear the sharp intake of moral breath, so three things should be carefully noted.

(1) *The kind of people we are talking about, and with whom animals' defenders are dealing.* That is, people who are quite willing to club and skin completely helpless young seals, sometimes while they are still alive and conscious; to machine-gun entire families of elephants, while the elders desperately try to defend their children; to set count-less snares which result in agonizing and lingering deaths for the animals caught; to fire exploding projectiles into the living bodies of marine mammals at least as sensitive as you or I; to capture bears in agonising leg-hold traps before putting them in cages no bigger than their bodies, and extracting their bile through infected catheters or simply holes, until they die.

(2) *The rarity of such a situation.* Paul Watson is the founder of the

Sea Shepherd Conservation Society, which leads much of the resistance to both the Canadian seal hunt and almost all of it to Japanese whaling, and the violent actions of those sealers and whalers regularly place him and his colleagues in extreme physical danger. Yet, showing extraordinary restraint, they have never reciprocated in like terms. Watson is, in fact, an excellent example of someone tirelessly active on behalf of animals who is motivated not only by their rights, nor even their ability to suffer, but also by ecocentricism. Does this (reverting to the question raised above) mean that he is 'against people'? Once again, the answer is 'no'. Watson has recorded that one day in 1975, looking into the eye of a dying sperm whale whose harpooning he had been unable to prevent, he realized 'that my allegiance lay with the whales first and foremost, over the interests of those humans who would kill them' (quoted in Bron Taylor 2010: 98). Note that he does *not* say, or mean, 'all or any humans', but specifically whale-killers. His position is therefore not misanthropic. It amounts rather to maintaining that in certain relatively well-defined situations, other animals can be more important than humans. To maintain that that is *never* the case is simply a religious version of anthropomorphism, namely **anthropolatry**: the unconditional and uncritical worship of humanity as such.

(3) *The importance of the precise circumstances.* The situation with African wildlife, say, is different: the gangs are heavily armed, often willing to inflict lethal violence on those trying to stop them, and events are rarely played-out in public (not that that would trouble the poachers in any case: another difference from the whalers, who have some residual nationalistic aversion to unduly bad publicity). Mark and Delia Owens, working in rural Zambia with desperately unsupported government game scouts and local residents, succeeded in stopping the murder by criminal gangs of scores of thousands of elephants and rhinos, and in weaning the local economy off commercial poaching into one of improved agriculture, small business and micro-development, including improved education and healthcare, that continues to flourish. Let me be plain: however 'understandable' it might be, there is no ethical excuse whatsoever for commercial poaching; and there is a prima facie case, at the least, for taking as vigorous measures as are necessary to end it.[8]

After all, the poachers/hunters here do have other options, especially since they are almost never driven by simple survival or subsistence needs, but by profit. It is true that they may have been pushed in the direction of what they do by the actions of others – wealthy capitalists together with their local despotic allies, say – over which they have no control, and for which they are not responsible. But they do still have some control over how they respond, and some responsibility for their own choices. Starving is not an ecocentric requirement! The other side of the coin, however, is that when pure survival is not the issue, nothing absolves individuals and communities of the ethical responsibility, when choice is still possible, to choose less rather than more destructive means. Those looking for profits from killing have been able to choose, and they have chosen ill. The result is the intense suffering and death of fellow-Earthlings, some of them whole kinds; and while the poacher, and certainly the whaler, could turn to another way to make a living, what is at stake for the elephant or the whale is the only life they have.

In this situation, *an ecocentric must take, or at least support, action to defend the victims.* Perhaps a fairer economic system, more and better education and so on would remove some of their motivation, although that doesn't automatically follow either; neither Southern European songbird shooters and trappers nor insecurely masculine middle-class American bear-hunters are exactly peasants or subsistence farmers. In any case, where the three kinds of extreme circumstances just mentioned apply – mass cruelty, highly sentient animals and endangered species – the killers must first be stopped.[9]

Not surprisingly, I suppose, deep (ecocentric) ecologists have been attacked for saying things that threaten automatic human superiority. Ramachandra Guha, for example, has described their primary concern as 'unspoiled wilderness', which is apparently 'uniquely American' – something that would have surprised Arne Naess, among others. Regarding the imminent extinction of the tiger (population: 3,200 and declining) in the remaining wilds of India (human population: over one billion and rising), Guha attacks 'tiger-lovers' (a phrase presumably chosen to resonate with the equally contemptuous 'tree-huggers') for putting the lives of people at risk from tigers by defending the latter's 'lebensraum' (a word that can only have been chosen to tar the tigers' defenders by association with the military programme of the Nazis).[10]

At the other end of the spectrum, let's hear Val Plumwood on the ethical ideal:

In terms of virtue ethics, the existence of free communities of animals that can prey on humans indicates our preparedness to share and to coexist with the otherness of the earth, to reject the colonizer identity and the stance of assimilation, which aims to make the Other over into a form that eliminates all friction, challenge, or consequence. (1999: 90)

Domestic Animals

Although they are inextricable in practice, I am going to discuss here humans' treatment of domestic animals they eat and perform experiments on, while reserving analysis of such treatment as part of the modern industrial food system as a business for Chapter 13. And I should mention the important cultural/natural place of pets, in their millions. Alongside horrific instances of abuse and neglect, most people try to take good care of their pets (and spend a total of several billion dollars every year doing so). As usual, it is not a simple issue. On the one hand, this concern evidences genuinely loving relationships between persons human and nonhuman.[11] On the other, it also coexists with the enormous suffering humans – very often, the same individuals – indirectly inflict on the animals they eat, in a way that reminds me of a shrewd observation by Carl Jung that sentimentality and brutality are two sides of the same coin. In any case, we turn now to the domestic animals most of us (including pet-lovers) eat.

On better authority and with considerably more reason than Guha, the Nazis have appeared elsewhere in discussions of human–animal relations. A character in a short story by Isaac Bashevis Singer, the 1978 Nobel Prize winner, says simply, 'for the animals, it is an eternal Treblinka' (1982: 271).[12] This was Singer's own belief as an ethical vegetarian for the last 35 years of his life. (When asked whether he had stopped eating chicken for health reasons, he replied that he had stopped for the health of the chickens.)

In 2002, Charles Patterson borrowed Singer's words for the title of his extraordinary book, *Eternal Treblinka: Our Treatment of Animals and the Holocaust*, which shows in detail the intimate links between the Nazi death-camps and the immense mechanized slaughterhouses of Chicago at the turn of the last century. (Interestingly, the latter also partly inspired Henry Ford, a rabid anti-Semite, and both personally and professionally a big supporter of Hitler, to develop the production-line factory for his motorcar.) Patterson also discusses the depersonalization that permits brutality. (A nice bit of cunning, that: the most violently destructive animal names his worst behaviour after the other animals – the 'brutes' – who are its foremost victim!)[13] In the same vein, Livingston (1994: 145) points out that Josef Mengele 'need not have hated Jews to do what he did. . . . By perceiving a taxonomic gulf between himself and Jews, he could view as necessary their role in a particular program, and their fear, pain, and suffering as an externality. He need only have seen them as animals' – and therefore, for anthropocentrics, morally inconsiderable for their own sakes.

More recently, hear Elizabeth Costello, a character created by another Nobel Prize winner, J. M Coetzee:

> Let me say it openly: we are surrounded by an enterprise of degradation, cruelty, and killing which rivals anything the Third Reich was capable of, indeed dwarfs it, in that ours is an enterprise without end, self-regenerating, bringing rabbits, rats, poultry, livestock ceaselessly into the world for the purpose of killing them. (1999: 21)[14]

Now, as Arthur Koestler once remarked, 'Statistics don't bleed; it is the detail which counts',[15] which is why the enormous effort to communicate and educate, as well as legislate, is always needed. And narratives, which must be skilful as well as well-informed, have pride of place in that process; as I shall argue in Chapter 12, stories and examples are how people learn best. But numbers too have some role to play, so let us now consider just a few. Currently, every year, throughout the world, between 45 and 50 *billion* farmed animals are killed for food, plus at least as many marine animals. (Either the meaning of the word 'farm' should be formally altered to reflect what they have now largely become, or we should use the more accurate term, 'factory'.) In the US alone, more than 10 billion animals are killed each year for food consumption – *27 million each day; nearly 19,000 per minute*. In addition, 100 million other animals die in laboratories, and 50 million for their fur (more 'farms').[16] And while we are on the subject, every year sharks kill about ten people, while humans kill roughly 73 million sharks. Which makes us approximately seven million times more dangerous to them than they are for us.

As for the sheer depth and scale of suffering all this entails, do I need to mention the short lives spent in misery or in pain from forced breeding characteristics, from having beaks or tails docked, given highly unnatural food to eat, their offspring immediately removed, and crammed into cramped indoor cells that they never leave except to be slaughtered, often while still conscious? As Michael Pollen[17] puts it, to visit a Concentrated Animal Feeding Operation, or CAFO (and note the clean, efficient, Orwellian terminology):

> is to enter a world that for all its technological sophistication is still designed on seventeenth-century Cartesian principles: animals are treated as machines – 'production units' – incapable of feeling pain. Since no thinking person can possibly believe this anymore, industrial animal agriculture depends on a suspension of disbelief on the part of the people who operate it and a willingness to avert one's eyes on the part of everyone else. (2006: 317)

If one has succeeded in not averting one's eyes, then the next item on the ethical menu is the food one eats, and thence how one participates in and contributes to, or not, such a system.

On (Not) Eating Animals: The Options

It seems to me there are four possible responses to the situation just outlined, at least for most people in the global North and many in the South now too. They do not apply to indigenous people, such as those in the circumpolar regions, who are genuinely hunting wild animals for meat and skins, etc., in order to live. As I have said, an ecological ethics does not demand starvation. Nor would it be fair to expect it of people for whom the absence of meat would pose real problems, even though their diet does not entirely depend on it. Furthermore, such hunters normally have a spiritual-cultural ethic respectful of the animals that prevents overexploitation. (Although as a friend once pointed out, if you could ask the respectfully and sustainably hunted animal whether it minded being killed, it would almost certainly say, 'Yes!')

Option one: *carry on eating industrially produced meat*. If one 'must' eat meat but can afford not to, then at the very least one has an ethical responsibility to ensure that the animal lives well while it lives and doesn't die for any trivial reason, such as 'I fancy a hamburger'. Clearly, then, to carry on consuming industrial meat is only ethically defensible if it is absolutely unavoidable. And it could only be unavoidable for very poor people whose eating options are therefore extremely limited. Even so, I would question whether it is *absolutely* unavoidable for everyone in circumstances of poverty. Even McFood offers some choices which include vegetarian options; furthermore, if nutrition is an issue, avoiding industrial meat would be better for one's health on a wide range of indicators. And the fact is, meat *should not be* cheap. We shall see the enormous price that the world pays for such false economy (not only by the animals but ecologically, as well as in terms of human health) in Chapter 13.

The specifically ecological basis for refusing to participate in and support the system of industrial meat was well put by Plumwood:

> This concept of human identity positions humans outside and above the food chain, not as part of the feast in a chain of reciprocity but as external manipulators and masters of it: Animals can be our food, but we can never be their food. . . . We act as if we live in a separate realm of culture in which we are never food, while other animals inhabit a different world of nature in which they are no more than food, and their lives can be utterly distorted in the service of this end. (2000a: 294)[18]

Option two: *eat only meat that is not industrially produced*. In other words: meat from animals who have been well cared for and (insofar as it is possible) humanely killed. Being necessarily farmed on a smaller scale, it would, of course, be more expensive, and almost certainly be eaten less often – not only for that reason, but in recognition that the animal had given up his or her life so that the humans could have a special meal. This is surely the mimimally ethical position. And I concede that in mid-green terms, there is a genuine difference between meat from such a source, and treated in such a way, and cheap fast meat entailing appalling suffering in order to maintain the profit margin of a transnational company. Meat consumed infrequently, on special occasions and with some awareness of what that animal's sacrifice actually involved (which, by the way, should be a non-negotiable and universal educational requirement), would clearly be a significant ethical advance on the current typical Western meal.

On the other hand, the fact cannot be evaded that that animal did not agree to die so you could eat him or her. (Meat companies would love to figure out a way for animals to sign, say, voluntary termination forms [VTFs]. Maybe they're working on it.) Jonathan Safran Foer (2009) recently put his finger on the problem: a 'painless' death for animals we want to eat is ultimately self-serving rationalization, especially when no one (with the rare aboriginal exceptions already noted) physically *needs* to eat meat.

Is it alright to kill an animal to eat, even if you don't need it as food, so long as you take responsibility for doing so? Returning to Michael Pollan's otherwise excellent *Omnivore's Dilemma*, what about his wild pig meal: hunted, shot, prepared and cooked by the author? I don't think this is acceptable. The stubborn fact remains that, as the Greek philosopher Bion remarked in the second century BCE, 'Though boys throw stones at frogs in sport, yet the frogs do not die in sport but in earnest.' To judge (as is entirely reasonable) by its efforts to avoid being shot, that wild pig died against its will, and in a way that we would not find acceptable even for our pets, unless they were already dying, let alone other humans. And the pig died only to provide a tasty meal, for which there were many alternatives: Professor Pollan and his friends were not starving.

Option three: *vegetarianism*. That is, eating no dead animals (mammals, birds, fish, etc.), although 'dairy' products which are not themselves biologically alive (milk and thence cheese, unfertilized eggs, etc.) are permitted. This next step becomes ethically unavoidable if one accepts, as I have argued one should, that it is wrong to kill animals that have as much interest in staying alive as we do, and make that interest quite plain when they come to be killed, just for our non-essential desires.

It should be admitted, as Foer does, that for many people, 'Vegetarianism requires the renunciation of real and irreplaceable pleasures' (2009: 78). But shall we demand of ethics, 'Never ask me to do anything difficult'? And there is a pleasure involved which perhaps does not get discussed much, so cynical have we become: the quiet pleasure of a clean conscience. Only relatively clean, of course, but none the less pleasant for that. This is not to deny that some vegetarians manifest something different, namely sanctimonious superiority. But the two should not be confused, as meat-eaters, not always by sincere error, are wont to do.

Before vegetarians are tempted into complacency, however, there are unresolved ethical issues that come attached to both milk (and thence cheese) and eggs. Consuming milk means supporting the system in which cows are kept in an unnatural cycle of pregnancy and lactation, and their calves are quickly taken away (causing emotional pain for both) in order for us to have their milk instead. Furthermore, most cows are kept permanently indoors in order for them to be milked frequently. (Most organic dairies only remove calves after they have been weaned, and cows are milked less intensively.) Eating eggs is less problematic, as long as one ensures that the eggs are laid by genuinely free-ranging hens; otherwise, one is supporting the system which condemns those chickens to the horrific conditions of a battery 'farm'.

Those who eat fish but no other kinds of meat – 'fishetarians', 'piscetarians' or even 'liberal vegetarians', as I have also heard them called – can take some comfort, perhaps, from ascribing an ethical dimension to the difference between warm-blooded animals (mammals and birds) and cold-blooded creatures. On the other hand, unless they are sure of only eating fish that (who?) are 'sustainably' managed, line-caught, etc., they are contributing to the industrial decimation of fish stocks via the marine equivalent of clear-cutting: purse-seining or bottom-trawling, echo-sonar, and 'fish aggregating devices' or FADs – note the coolly abstract language hiding brutality, as usual. (And what is the main source of food for farmed fish? Wild fish, of course.) In *Do Fish Feel Pain?* (2010), Victoria Braithwaite, reviewing all the scientific evidence to date, has definitively answered that question. Yes, they do.

Option four: *veganism*. Logically, then, the most ethical step to take is to become fully vegan, eating no animal or animal-derived foods at all. We have discussed all the important relevant ethical issues by now, so there isn't much left to say about veganism. Without any doubt, it is the ethically most irreproachable position in relation to food and thence the major impact of humanity on other animals.

But, as ever, there are no simple or complete answers, and veganism is no exception. Let us see why.

One reason is simple, deceptively so: eating, especially in the usual form of meals, is not only a basic need, it is also strongly social and cultural. And there is no denying that veganism is a very unusual and, in that sense, extreme position which therefore separates its practitioner from most of the larger human community as presently constituted. That can result in alienation for the vegan and offence for others, which, ironically, could reduce the chances of them moving in a more ethical direction. The *way* in which one is a vegan, then, could make a big difference. Just as importantly, though, there is room for other positions which are ethical in different ways and to different extents. Total purity is impossible, and I'm not sure it is desirable either. In this context, a potential problem for veganism is implicitly recognized by a recent campaign by one of the largest and most effective charities lobbying for improved animal welfare, Compassion in World Farming (CIWF): not to become a vegetarian, let alone a vegan, but simply to 'Eat Less Meat'.

Veganism can also result in health problems unless it is intelligently undertaken: something which suggests that it might be an easier option for the relatively better-educated and better-off. In other words, veganism *could* be seen as a function, to some extent, of privilege.

A characteristically perceptive analysis by Plumwood challenges feminist veganism as offering a very incomplete challenge to the gulf between humans and nonhumans, because it brings animals into ethics by enlarging the human/nature dualism to animal/nature dualism, rather than rejecting that damaging dualism altogether. The result preserves an enlarged human privilege, still kept 'beyond ecology and beyond use, especially in the food chain'. Plumwood argues: 'An ecological consciousness gives a more thorough disruption of the dominant narrative which sets humans beyond ecology.' This position returns us 'semi-vegetarianism'; it entails 'an end to factory farming and great reductions in first-world meat-eating, but could still see a place for respectful and mutual forms of use in the food chain' (2006b: 56, 57).

In conclusion, I hope to have shown that our relationships with other animals is a valid and urgent issue for ecological ethics. It is true that mid-green ethics cannot accommodate the ethical dimension of ecosystems or species. So a way of life that neither directly nor indirectly harms animals is not in itself fully ecological (ecocentric); nor does it rule out other activities which are ecologically harmful. But it is a major ethical good in itself, and it coheres with and supports an ecocentrically ethical life – a fully-fledged green virtue ethic – much more readily than not. More: unless one is living where no alternatives are available, an ecocentric life must *include* vegetarianism, if not veganism. The alternative is not just inconsistency, but hypocrisy.

8

Dark Green or Deep (Ecocentric) Ethics

A Suggested Definition

Ecocentric (literally, Earth-centred) ethics, like biocentrism, is
non-anthropocentric. However, it differs from biocentrism in that
ecocentric or dark green ethics takes as objects of ethical concern
holistic entities (although that can and usually does include individuals); and those entities include integral components that are
non-living as well as animate.

An ecocentric, dark green or deep ecological ethics must, I
suggest, be able to satisfy at least these criteria:

1 It must be able to recognize the value, and therefore support
  the ethical defence, of the integrity of species and of ecosystemic places, as well as human and nonhuman organisms. So it
  is holistic, although not in the sense of excluding considerations
  of individual value.
2 Within nature–as–value, it must (a) allow for conflicts between
  the interests of human and nonhuman nature; (b) allow purely
  human interests, on occasion, to lose. (It is hardly a level
  playing-field otherwise.)

Thus, dark green ethics rejects both the Sole and the Greater Value
Assumptions in favour of the idea that some or all natural beings, in

the broadest sense, have independent moral status.[1] Ecological problems are not solely defined by reference to human beings (although
they can be so defined), other natural entities deserve protection
regardless of their use or value to humans, and nature has intrinsic
value (although there is room for differences about exactly what that
means) which may, in specific instances, predominate over human
value. All deep or dark green ethics subscribes to the position that
'the ecological community forms the ethical community' (Sylvan
and Bennett 1994: 91), and although we shall look at Sylvan's Deep
Green Theory separately later on, it is fair to borrow his description
of it for ecocentric ethics as such: it 'find[s] all standard ethics mired
in heavy prejudice, a prejudice in favour of things human and against
things nonhuman' (1994: 139–40). Note, however, that the truth of
that observation depends on what sorts of ethics are considered to
be standard; standard modern ethics is, certainly, but not necessarily
virtue ethics.

Of the possible objections to the points above, let me briefly
address three. One is that the concept of ecological integrity (or
a natural or healthy condition) is now considered to be more
complex and contingent than when it was assumed that every ecosystem naturally arrived at a 'climax state'. That is true, but it does
not invalidate the sense of integrity 'in terms of the capacity of the
Earth's ecosystems to continue functioning so that the environmental
services are maintained upon which the wellbeing of humans and all
life depend' (Mackey 2004: 79).[2] (Note, however, the inaptness of
the term 'environmental services' when what is serving and what is
being served are, in actuality, inseparable; and the danger of a narrow
definition of 'well-being' by those for whom a broad one would be
inconvenient.)

The second possible objection can be disposed of quickly: 'Who
sides with nonhuman nature if not people? So how can an ethic
be ecocentric?' Of course this is an ethic *for* humans; but that does
not mean humans can or must side only *with* humans. (The parallel
with the confusion between anthropocentric and anthropogenic is
precise.)

The third is the pious and highly convenient opinion that 'everything green that matters can be taken care of by looking out for our
own human interests'. I hope no one who has got this far can still
take such wishful thinking seriously. And if 'saving' what can still

be saved, including ourselves, requires measures protecting nature's interests as such, ask yourself this: to what extent do we see each of the following kinds of measures enacted: ones which (i) solely benefit humans, (ii) benefit humans in ways which could indirectly benefit others as well, (iii) directly benefit both humans and nonhumans, or (iv) solely benefit nonhumans. To grasp the extent to which the things we do are skewed in favour of our self-interest, as we usually see it, ask yourself what the ratio is between measures of the first kind and of the fourth. A thousand to one? A million to one? Let us just say that moving towards more measures of the last three kinds, at least, would be a very good thing.

Ecocentric ethics is our principal concern in this book, partly because the perspective it offers cannot be replaced by the light or mid-green kinds. It is a deep green ethic that helps us realize the enormity of the crime when an old-growth forest is razed for pulp, a mountain-top is levelled for coal, a seabed is covered in oily slime, or the very last few members of a species die – obscure, perhaps, but unique and irreplaceable, and not insignificant to themselves – as a result of human greed or selfishness.

The other reason for giving ecocentrism pride of place is that the urgency of its contemporary relevance seems matched only by the extent to which it has been ignored or disparaged.[3] So let us turn, in more detail and depth, to its principal varieties.

The Land Ethic

The Land Ethic was formulated by the wildlife biologist and conservationist Aldo Leopold (1887–1948) in *A Sand County Almanac with Essays on Conservation from Round River* (1949). More a work of mature reflection than academic philosophy, this became perhaps the single most influential statement (certainly so in America) of ecocentric ethics. That has been assisted by its further development by J. Baird Callicott (1987, 1989).

A number of Leopold's pithier maxims have, with good reason, taken root in green ethical discourse. Let us review them, with some comments. One is that 'A thing is right when it tends to preserve the integrity, stability and beauty of the biotic community. It is wrong when it tends otherwise' (1949: 224–5). The 'biotic community' is potentially misleading here; it is not, like biocentrism, limited to biota or organisms. As Leopold also wrote: 'The land ethic simply enlarges the boundaries of the community to include soils, waters, plants, and animals, or collectively: the land' (1949: 204). It does not require much of a leap of imagination to extend this idea to include an *ocean ethic*, as of course it should.[4] The logical conclusion would then be an *Earth ethic*.

The virtues of this formulation are considerable. First, it is fully ethical in the sense of specifying what is good/bad and right/wrong, and (in its intention) consequentially so. As Leopold realized, an essential part of an ethic is limiting what can and cannot be done – in this case, ecologically. Note that a limitation on human freedom is the very thing most often and bitterly rejected by adherents of anthropocentric ethics and instrumental value, for whom nature is, and must be kept as, an ethically inconsiderable resource for humans to do with whatever they wish. Such defensive hostility is a back-handed compliment to the merits of Leopold's suggestion.

Second, its focus is an unambiguously ecocentric one which does not restrict ethical consideration to either the animate (thus excluding ecosystemic places) or individuals (thus excluding wholes and relations). Leopold recognized the Earth itself as possessing 'a certain kind and degree of life' (1991: 95), and infers from his grasp of ecology how it is not only context but creator. Unlike any of the ethics we have so far discussed, the Land Ethic thus qualifies as a dark green or deep one.[5] Third, its clarity and simplicity are also very helpful in getting the message across – no small matter.

To 'enlarge' the community in such a way reframes all ethical discourse. As Leopold noted, 'a land ethic changes the role of *Homo sapiens* from conquerer of the land-community to *plain member and citizen of it*' (1949: 204; although 'peculiar member' might be more apt; my emphasis). What a radical change that is, or would be!

No ethical position is without its problems, of course. A potentially serious one here arises from Leopold's holism, namely that individual interests could be unduly overridden in the interest of (someone's particular version of) the collective whole. This has invited the somewhat overheated charge of 'environmental fascism' from Tom Regan, the defender of individual animal rights (1983: 362).[6] It is certainly true that there is a clear difference (axiological and ethical) between the emphases of the Land Ethic on the one hand and animal liberation and/or rights on the other. Indeed, that difference is one reason why the former qualifies more straightforwardly as dark green.

As Callicott has rightly pointed out, any distinction between 'inner' and 'outer' or 'self' and 'other' is strictly relative and never ultimate, except as a modernist fantasy: '[I]t is impossible to find a clear demarcation between oneself and one's environment. . . . The world is, indeed, one's extended body' (1989: 113).[7] But such holism is not necessarily collectivist in an authoritarian (let alone fascist) way. As Callicott also suggests, there is nothing in Leopold's work to suggest that the Land Ethic was intended to replace all other ethics; instead, it was to be added to the others, and to contextualize them in a new way. Conflicts between the ecological good and that of any individual human where the latter must give way thus cannot be ruled out (we sometimes have that already, where the common good is restricted to its social version), but they do not necessarily follow from the Land Ethic as such.[8]

Another potential problem, more narrowly philosophical, is the one discussed earlier of trying to infer an ethical 'ought' from a factual 'is' – in this case, the injunction to value and protect nature from knowledge produced by the science of ecology. And it is true that Leopold often seems to be doing just this. But his goal was, and surely ours still is, not the hopeless enterprise of arriving at a philosophically (or scientifically) impeccable theory which will command the assent of all rational beings, etc. Rather, it is to articulate a reasonably coherent, consistent and clear set of ethical principles, informed by and conveying ecocentric values, which will lend themselves to incorporation into people's attitudes and ways of life.

This is a political, social and cultural programme, not a purely logical one. Nor should it try to be all-encompassing, dominating or replacing all other considerations. A normative ecological imperative such as the Land Ethic – or any of the others discussed here – can only hope to acquire sufficient influence in the world to *check* anthropocentrism, instrumentalism and utilitarianism; not to eliminate greed, stupidity and hate in relation to our home and fellow creatures, but to significantly reduce their scope.[9]

Who, it might also be objected, is to say what a particular biotic community's 'integrity, beauty and stability' consist of? This is not self-evident, especially given (as earlier mentioned) that contemporary ecological science has changed since Leopold's day and no longer perceives 'climax' states, for example, but more complex successions. But the answer to this fear is implicit in the question. The Land Ethic introduces no new demands or problems here. Decisions about what matters most in any given situation are already taken everywhere, all the time. And such decisions are always axiological and political; they have never been purely scientific. Science requires judgement as much as any other human enterprise, and that judgement necessarily involves values, emotions and ideas that have not themselves been arrived at 'scientifically'.[10] We may update Leopold's definition of an ecosystem which, 'now meaning something more akin to a locale, has integrity and stability to the degree that it is capable of sustaining biological processes' (Des Jardins 2001: 201) and that is indeed helpful, but such refinements cannot ever relieve us of the responsibility of making decisions on ethical grounds.

It is also to the point that Leopold's own understanding of ecology involved grasping (unlike so many of the techno-managerial 'ecologists' of today) that the immense complexity of ecosystems is matched by our own relative ignorance. The upshot is the advice, when dealing with the natural world, to proceed with respect, caution and, whenever possible, a light touch – what we earlier identified as the precautionary principle (see page 62). Working with rather than overruling evolutionary changes, encouraging native species, and preferring biological to artefactual (engineering) solutions would be good examples (Des Jardins 2001: 198). Cross-species gene transfers, before releasing the resulting organisms to interact with those in the wild, would definitely not; nor would 'relocating' habitats.[11]

Such an emphasis is part of what Leopold had in mind when he recommended that we learn to '*think like a mountain*' (1970: 129–33): that is, to see things from (say) a mountain's perspective, with its time-scale and, indeed, priorities. This metaphor has been adopted by Deep Ecologists, who have given it a flavour at once mystical and literal-minded. But they have a point; it is anthropocentrism (especially in its Cartesian modernist form) that has restricted subjectivity and agency to human beings. Indeed, its extreme scientific expression has long been trying to eliminate this last stronghold, in a programme of perfect, if suicidal, consistency. Ecocentrism must counter that attempt with many subjectivities and perspectives, including nonhuman ones.[12]

Gaia Theory

Gaia Theory is the name that has replaced its original tag, 'the Gaia Hypothesis'.[13] It was suggested 35 years ago and subsequently developed, primarily by the independent scientist James Lovelock, although Lynn Margulis has also made important contributions.[14] The basic idea is that the Earth is more like a living organism than an inanimate machine, which is made up of highly complex inter-acting ecosystems binding together not only the continents, oceans and atmosphere, but also its living inhabitants; and, like an organism, it is (within limits) self-renewing, adjusting to changing conditions through feedback loops in order to maintain relative stability, espe-cially of the atmosphere and temperature. Gaia and its inhabitants co-evolve together in a web of relationships of which symbiosis (not, as in most evolutionary theory, competition) is the dominant kind.

'Gaia' is the name of the ancient Greek goddess of the Earth, which Lovelock adopted following a suggestion by the novel-ist William Golding. It has aroused a great deal of hostility among scientists who, significantly, seem to feel that animism (the world, and/or its parts, as alive) is still the Enemy; on the other hand, it has also conferred on the theory an accessible and, to others, attrac-tive handle. And the description of the Earth as a super-organism is controversial even among its supporters, some of whom prefer an emphasis on systems theory, with its stress on physical states chang-ing over time, weather patterns, etc.[15] The basic objection seems to be that Gaia Theory merely offers a new (or old) metaphor without specifying any 'mechanisms'. However, the basis of the objection is itself metaphorical, despite assuming its own 'objective' validity: namely the *metaphor*, beginning in the mid-seventeenth century, of the world and all its parts as a machine.[16]

Gaia Theory started out as a scientific theory, but it has had, and will continue to have, a significant impact in other contexts; so it is fair, and important, to ask what kind of *ethics* follows from it.[17] The inclusion of inanimate elements, integral to animate life – or rather, as at least equally integral to the life of the Earth as its organisms – points towards ecocentrism. So too does the holist emphasis, which is perhaps stronger in this ethic than in any other considered here. But as with the Land Ethic, that emphasis is double-edged. Positively, there are urgent ecological problems which at first seem difficult to bring under the umbrella (so clearly vital in most other respects) of place, specific ecosystems and localism. Although they will not succeed without local, regional and national participation, the issues of fluorocarbons and the ozone layer, and carbon dioxide emissions and global warming, require international scientific cooperation in order to collect and evaluate evidence, and demand international political cooperation for their resolution.[18] They also present a kind of quasi-universal challenge to much of life as such. Note too the salutary point that humans constitute only one player, albeit currently a major one, in the Gaian drama; even if we succeed in making the planet uninhabitable for ourselves, we will undoubtedly be survived by other forms of life, and by Gaia herself. A likelier scenario is that humanity will survive, but in extremely difficult circumstances in a biotically degraded world.

In bringing the situation about, we would destroy many other forms of life as well, entirely non-voluntarily, and cause unimaginable suffering to them as well as to other humans. And nothing in Gaia Theory actually specifies − as I believe a fully ecocentric theory should − that this matters ethically. In fact, rather like Hardin's lifeboat ethics (with which it shares a certain sensibility), the theory could be interpreted entirely within an anthropocentric and shallow ethical frame: we should stop destabilizing Gaia simply because that is dangerous to us. Of course, to the extent that we succeeded in stopping or sufficiently slowing that process, many species would thereby also be saved. But it is quite possible to imagine a world that is stable for most humans, in Gaian terms, but is highly impoverished in terms of 'biodiversity', dominated by a few hardy 'weedy species'.[19] It is also true that Gaia Theory *could* be interpreted ecocentrically with respect to other life-forms and specific, unique places; but the fact that that would seem to be optional is a weakness.

Gaian holism also presents, it seems to me, a danger of collectivist political authoritarianism. For example, the leap to the Gaian level is sometimes taken without much evident ethical concern for the mere organisms, including human, 'down here'. That level, as far as most personal experience is concerned, is highly abstract; like 'God', 'the nation', 'the people', etc., it therefore leaves an uncomfortable amount of leeway for it to be appropriated for very different political purposes, and taken in some highly questionable directions. And the fact that such abstraction is 'scientific' (at least as far as its principal advocates are concerned), far from undercutting the point just made, simply adds another dimension to its potential rhetorical power.

Finally, Lovelock has rightly condemned 'the three C's' – cars, cows and chainsaws – on account of their direct contribution to potentially ruinous climate change; but he cavalierly countenances nuclear energy as no threat; indeed, as a solution. Fastening single-mindedly on Gaian criteria, however, overlooks the ethical significance of other considerations: the potential for nuclear accidents or terrorist strikes resulting in massive long-term environmental pollution and ecological damage (by the standards of organic life) together with lingering deaths and disease (both human and otherwise); the corrosive political effects of the dangerous hypertechnology, enormous expense, unaccountability and secrecy that nuclear power always entails, and so on. These are not ethically neglible considerations, but they find no firm foothold here.

Oddly, Lovelock also overlooks the probability that, in addition to these problems, a resurgent nuclear industry would almost certainly continue to be used as an excuse to avoid the energy conservation and efficiency measures, on the demand side, and cheaper, more efficient renewable technologies (wind, wave and solar power), on the supply side, that really do offer a non-life-threatening solution.

I have already praised holism elsewhere and described the individualism of intermediate ecological ethics (for example, animal liberation/rights) as a limitation. Is it therefore inconsistent to criticize Gaia Theory for ignoring the importance of individuals? No. Ecological holism *is* needed; but it is only safe, so to speak, in the hands of those who understand that when it is necessary to wrong certain individuals (that is, overrule their self-perceived interests) in order to defend the common good (upon which *all* depend), it *is* necessary, but that does not 'justify' it as unproblematically ethical.[20] In short, ethically speaking, Gaia Theory certainly has powerfully positive ecocentric potential, not least for an ethic of 'global medicine' (although it will take more than a science of 'planetary biology' to realize that goal).[21] Its current limitations, however, seem to indicate that it would need supplementing.

Deep Ecology

Deep Ecology is both a metaphysical philosophy and a social/cultural movement with political implications. It began as essentially an attempt to work out the principles of ecological activism, rather than as a strictly academic theory. Within the world of contemporary ecological discourse generally, it remains one of the most influential approaches, particularly in America. It was inspired by the work of the Norwegian philosopher Arne Naess, beginning with his paper of 1973, 'The Shallow and the Deep, Long-Range Ecology Movements'. Bill Devall and George Sessions (1985) have also contributed importantly to its development.[22] The formal basis of Deep Ecology are the *eight Platform Principles* formulated by Naess and Sessions:

1. The flourishing of human and nonhuman life on Earth has intrinsic value. The value of nonhuman life-forms is independent of the usefulness these may have for narrow human purposes.
2. Richness and diversity of life-forms are values in themselves and contribute to the flourishing of human and nonhuman life on Earth.
3. Humans have no right to reduce this richness and diversity except to satisfy vital human needs.
4. Present human interference with the nonhuman world is excessive, and the situation is rapidly worsening.
5. The flourishing of human life and cultures is compatible with a substantial decrease of the human population. The flourishing of nonhuman life requires such a decrease.
6. Significant change of life conditions for the better requires change in policies. These affect basic economic, technological and ideological structures.
7. The ideological change is mainly that of appreciating life quality (dwelling in situations of intrinsic value) rather than adhering to a high standard of living. There will be a profound awareness of the difference between big and great.
8. Those who subscribe to the foregoing points have an obligation directly or indirectly to participate in the attempt to implement the necessary changes.[23]

Some of this ground we have discussed in other but related contexts: the distinction between Shallow Ecology or 'environmentalism' and Deep Ecology (which, indeed, derives from Naess); ecological holism; and the idea of intrinsic value. Subject to what has already been discussed, these important aspects of Deep Ecology need no further comment. One peculiarity, however, is that the Platform Principles make no explicit reference to the Earth as such, emphasizing instead life-forms. That means Deep Ecology could well be identified as a biocentric mid-green or intermediate ethic. However, I am going to argue that the import of Deep Ecology is ecocentric nonetheless, both in the intentions of its founders and (more importantly) how it has been commonly understood. Within the Deep Ecology movement, the terms 'biocentric' and 'ecocentric' tend to be used interchangeably, and it is significant that the main activist movement inspired by Deep Ecology was called 'Earth First!' The common adoption by Deep Ecologists of Leopold's injunction to 'think like a mountain' points to the same conclusion.

Another complication is more serious. Together with Sessions, Naess has outlined a particular instance of a Deep Ecological theory, Ecosophy T, which emphasizes two further principles.[24] In theory, these do not replace the original eight, and remain optional for supporters of Deep Ecology. (As we shall see, the Left Bio group, for example, accept the eight but tend to reject Ecosophy T.) However, Naess himself and others have laid considerable stress on them, and as Kohák perceptively notes, that stress has been accompanied by a perceptible drift in Naess's work since 1973 from a 'Deep Ecology' to a 'Depth Ecology' – as in, depth psychology – that has contributed to the importance of these two principles for the Deep Ecology movement (Kohák 2000: 117).[25] Yet they are also, as we shall see, its most problematic elements. The two principles concerned are as follows.

Self-realization (with an upper-case S). The idea here is that the nature of entities is *constituted* by the relations between them, rather than entities being preformed and then establishing relations, or such relations being simply one-way: in Naess's words, a 'relational, total-field image' rather than a 'man-in-the-environment' image. So far so good, but this total field is then conceptualized as one's real Self, as distinct from one's illusory ego-self, and a normative imperative derived: to realize one's Self, i.e., to perceive that that is one's true nature, and to identify with it. (This is a psycho-spiritual process that can be ongoing and take place by degrees.) The hope is that since one's own nature is identical with nature's nature, so to speak, then one would no more harm the natural world unnecessarily than one would harm oneself; and ethics, at least as any kind of rules or imperatives, becomes redundant.

Biocentric egalitarianism. Naess paraphrases this idea as 'the equal right' of life-forms 'to live and blossom'. (It turns out this means ecospherical, or simply ecocentric, egalitarianism.) This seems to be a particular development of ecocentrism which emphasizes not only the value of nature, both human and nonhuman, but the equality of entities – analogous to human equality despite social class – as instances of such value.

Now some of the criticisms levelled against Deep Ecology do not pass muster. This applies particularly to the vitriolic attacks of Murray Bookchin.[26] For example, Deep Ecology is certainly not necessarily misanthropic (let alone fascist); it simply denies that humans alone have intrinsic value. A more ambiguous question is whether it is inherently quietist, that is, passively anti-political, insofar as an emphasis on states of consciousness (to which we shall return) is a dominant theme; however, as the Platform Principles make clear, political action is, at least in principle, also encouraged.

Together with the work of the writer Edward Abbey, who coined the term 'monkey-wrenching' (i.e. throwing what we in the UK call a 'spanner' in the ecocidal works), Deep Ecology has also inspired some engaged and effective direct activism in defence of nature. Earth First! itself, as far as I know, no longer exists, and the extent to which the direct action with which it was associated has been effective is debatable. However, it very effectively enlarged the debate about what was, and is, really valuable. It also succeeded in revealing the values of some of its critics, like the President of the American Wildlife Federation, who apparently stated in 1987 that he saw 'no fundamental difference between destroying a river and destroying a bulldozer'.

In any case, let's be clear (as Abbey was): sabotage – the destruction of inanimate objects or property – is not identical to terrorism, which is violence against living beings. The same applies to *ecotage* as against *ecoterrorism*.[27] Bron Taylor describes Deep Ecologists as adherents of 'dark green religion' (something we shall take up in Chapter 11). His considered conclusion is that 'the main themes of dark green religion – which include the idea that all living things have intrinsic value – do not easily lend themselves to indifference toward human suffering, let alone to virulent streams of religious, ethnic, or territory-based hatred' (2010: 218).

Some social ecologists and ecofeminists have charged Deep Ecologists with failing to recognize that contributions of people to ecological destruction are not the same, but wildly unequal (e.g., that of an oil corporation president versus that of an impoverished child in the global South), and likewise those who suffer its consequences. This point is certainly valid and we should not lose sight of it. But it is also true that there is a common hierarchy of value, which is the essence of anthropocentrism, in which any human being, *simply as such*, has more value than any nonhuman being. This is the sense in which 'human chauvinism' or 'speciesism' is as much a vice as racism or sexism.

There has also been intellectual criticism such as that of John Benson, who maintains that the identification with Self demanded by Deep Ecology has three possible senses, all of them unsatisfactory (2000: 126). One is empathy, but this is apparently limited in its objects to other intelligent and/or sentient animals, since it 'cannot carry over to plants and mountains'. Here Benson simply assumes, without feeling the need for argument, an individualistic sentience-chauvinism. Second, 'the [natural] object is thought of as partly constitutive of who one is', giving rise to the same kind of concern one feels for oneself. However, '[i]t is of the essence of such relationships that they are to particular places and beings', and such empathy will therefore not 'take us as far in concern for natural beings as Naess wishes to go'. Here Benson has touched on something important, for it may be that (as I shall argue later) that is as far as anyone *needs* to go, or *can* go, in any kind of ecological context; in which case, Deep Ecologists' calls for a cosmic or cosmological consciousness are mistaken. Third, he points to close human relationships, such that the other person's good is felt to be one's own good. Once again, however – and characteristically of writers even on environmental ethics – Benson dares not venture very far from the modernist anthropocentric redoubt: such empathy, it seems, cannot extend to 'mountains and rivers'. Why not? The work of Anthony Weston (1994) and David Abram (1996a) is evidence to the contrary. (Or rather, one kind of evidence, namely convincing arguments. The other kind, equally necessary and usually more vivid, is sympathetic personal experience of the natural world beyond the confines of any book, no matter how good.)

Nonetheless, the problems with Ecosophy T that remain are severe. I shall take the two 'basic principles' above in reverse order. Biocentric egalitarianism can be dealt with quickly. Ecocentrism is both possible and needed, or so I maintain; but this particular version of it is neither.[28] It is both intellectually and metaphysically implausible – why should value in nature be distributed equally or evenly? (Ironically, there is a mechanistic quality to that very assumption.)

It is also hopelessly impracticable as a guide to action: you cannot ask anyone (let alone everyone) to live as if literally every life-form – a lethal virus, say – has equal value to all others, including her- or himself; and it offers no guidance, indeed it allows no way, to resolve inevitable conflicts. Perhaps this is why Naess, under pressure, retreated to the assertion that it was intended 'simply as a statement of non-anthropocentrism', and added the words 'in principle' to its formulation (1989: 28).[29] But in thus trying to correct what was badly formulated from the start, this simply relieves the point of any force at all. What is needed is a coherent and defensible ecocentrism.

Self-realization

This idea fares still worse.[30] Naess frequently stated that he has been influenced by Buddhism, but talk of a Big Self and its 'realization' flatly contradicts the fundamental Buddhist denial of any ultimate reality to a self, whether big or little; it is much more in keeping with the very different metaphysics of Advaita Vedanta or neo-Platonism.[31] Furthermore, metaphysical enlightenment and spiritual purity as a supreme value may offer individual salvation, but only at the price of abandoning the rest of the natural world: not exactly the Bodhisattva ideal![32] As Deane Curtin shows, a much more promising (and valid) Buddhist approach than 'Self-realization' is '*co*-realization', based on the thirteenth-century Zen master Dōgen-zenji: 'If the Self simply extends itself to new realms of identification, values appear to be created relative to the state of the Self. But when we *and* the "myriad beings" go forth to corealize, this is a way of *being in the world*, not a mental construction' (2000: 263). Indeed, although

Curtin is too tactful to say so, keeping realization as a mental or spiritual process is itself anthropocentric. As Plumwood (2006a) has convincingly showed, an emphasis on cognition, mind and/or spirit in a way that presupposes their superior status (as Naess and Sessions do; otherwise why proclaim its central importance?) is part-and-parcel of the programme to reserve these attributes, and attached privileges, for humanity alone. The emphasis on Self-realization as the 'real work' courts idealism and dangerously neglects 'external' consequences and effects. Nature, after all, is just as much 'outer' as it is 'inner'.[33]

Ecosophy T holds that people will 'naturally' do the right thing(s) when their apprehension of the natural world is correct, as a result of ever-wider identification of oneself with that world and its fellow inhabitants. This is to ask too much of metaphysics or spirituality. There is no one 'solution' to a problem as complex and deep as ecocide; nothing follows automatically from anything else, and at no point are there any guarantees, as some Deep Ecologists seem to imply.

Significantly, Naess maintains that 'If Deep Ecology is deep it must relate to our fundamental beliefs, not just to ethics' (1989: 20). This simply assumes that ethics cannot be deep or fundamental, because it consists only of following rules or applying principles. But as we have seen, those are neither the only nor the most promising kinds of ethics. Unaware of virtue ethics, it seems, some Deep Ecologists confuse moral*ity* with moral*ism*, and see ethics as a kind of optional add-on at best. They fail to see that Deep Ecological insights *and* rules alike can only succeed to the extent that they become an integral part of the political, social and cultural processes of 'being in the world' as active – and in this case, green – citizens.[34] When Naess asserts that 'Ethics follow from how we experience the world', and David Rothenberg asks, 'But just how should we experience the world?', that question is as ethical as it is unavoidable (see Naess 1989: 20).

In sharp contrast, the pure identity via a Big Self that Ecosophists seek terminates in solipcism (absolute egoism and subjective idealism). It also contradicts Naess's own stress elsewhere on relations and pluralism. In practice, too, otherness – recognizing, respecting and valuing differences – is as valid and integral to our relationship with nature as commonality.[35] As we saw in the earlier discussion of ecocentrism, human beings have certain distinctive characteristics vis-à-vis nonhuman nature, even though these confer no special privileges or superiority (or should not), and are ultimately themselves the work of nature too. To deny difference as such in favour of 'oneness' is dangerous, because that is to deny relations and therefore ethics. It is also to invite a misanthropic ecocentrism which either demands the sacrifice of human distinctiveness as the price of entry to an abstract and collectivized nature, or tries to exclude a demonized humanity from nature. Either way, that programme would amount to an ethical disaster (if it 'succeeded'), or a political disaster (if it failed), opening the door to a reactionary reassertion of anthropocentrism.

'Self-realization' also falsifies an important part of our lives as natural beings who experience themselves as distinct from other natural beings and vice versa. To quote Evernden, 'Wildness is not "ours" – indeed it is the one thing that can never be ours. It is self-willed, independent, and indifferent to our dictates and judgements' (1992: 120). Bill McKibben (1990) has suggested that nature is coming to an end, with the effects of human meddling, if not exactly control, becoming unavoidable everywhere on the planet. His definition of nature may be questioned, but the undeniable poignancy involved draws its force from deep regret at the passing of what is *not* 'us'.

This point is also perceptible in other, more mundane, ways. Was it delightful watching two foxes play, as I did recently, because they were somehow my Self? No. It was delightful because they had nothing to do with me, in any meaningful sense of the word. They were quite unconcerned with me, my will or my desires; they were, in fact, much more important to each other.

Actually, 'Self-realization' is covertly anthropocentric, thus undermining Deep Ecology's own ecocentrism. As Plumwood has shown, it entails a kind of chauvinism in favour of those beings evidently capable of Self-realization, for which humans are (in their own opinion) the obvious candidates. It denies the agency and autonomy of nonhuman beings and places – hardly an ecological move! – while opening the door to 'an enlargement and extension of egoism' (1995: 160). The New Age version of spiritual Self-realization, selling ancient wisdom to the middle classes, has proven to be highly compatible with the commodification and market capitalism that form one of the chief motors of ecocide.[36]

Plumwood points out that Deep Ecologists have suggested 'that once one has realised that one is indistinguishable from the rainforest, its needs would become one's own. But there is nothing to guarantee this – one could equally well take one's own needs for its' (1995: 160). Indeed, where there is a strong cultural tradition of conflating the social and natural worlds, as with Confucianism, that seems to be exactly what happens: human self-improvement 'cannot' conflict with what is regarded as the good of nature.[37] (I would add that, as a matter of fact, people *do* harm themselves, to varying extents, not infrequently. So even if the metaphysics worked, so to speak, it would not necessarily deliver the desired result.)

In short, Ecosophy T's unity within an enlarged Self 'implies reduction to the personal, a dismissal of ethics, and a limitation of the political to the intra-human. . . . [T]he key concept for understanding why people become active on behalf of nonhuman nature is not identification or unity but *solidarity*, the most fundamental of political relationships' (Plumwood 2006b: 65, 70; my emphasis). Sylvan too was right: 'The very pedigree of the directive' – to maximize Self-realization – 'should have alerted suspicion. It emerges direct from the humanistic Enlightenment; it is linked to the modern celebration of the individual human, freed from service to higher demands, and also typically from ecological constraints' (Sylvan and Bennett 1994: 154).

An ambitious version of Deep Ecology has been developed by Fox (1995) under the name of **transpersonal ecology**, with the intention of improving the original while meeting, or undercutting, the criticisms of feminism and socialism. Unfortunately, his emphasis on replacing a sense of personal self with an 'ontologically' or 'cosmologically' based Self suffers from the defects just noted. Here, too, ecofeminists have been astute critics. Ariel Salleh (1993) notes that Fox's attitude is totalizing in a way that resonates with the anthropocentrism it is supposed to be correcting – and with the androcentrism (male-centredness), including its own, that it fails to address.[38] Plumwood (1995, 1993) points out that such a degree of bloodless abstraction ('Being', 'the cosmos', etc.) is an integral part of the anthropocentric, rationalist and masculinist ideology of power over nature. By the same token, it is hostile to just the kind of intimate daily relationship with sensuous natural particulars, and the value of them, that is so important to recover.[39] It is passionate attachments to *particular* places, things and nonhumans that move people, and motivate people to defend them. As Plumwood says: 'It is a short step from the accounts of the ecological [S]elf as the overcoming of "selfish" attachment and particularity . . . to demanding detachment from epistemological location' (2002: 255, n.19). That step in turn opens the way to the poisoned chalice of technoscientific 'solutions' to ecological problems; and at least one influential Deep Ecologist, George Sessions (1995b), has apparently taken it, sanctioning genetic bioengineering.

Fox argues: 'We can make no firm ontological divide in the field of existence . . . there is no bifurcation in reality between the human and the non-human realms . . . to the extent that we perceive boundaries, we fall short of deep ecological consciousness' (1984: 196). But this is to overstate, and thus distort, the case. The point is not there are *no* boundaries, limits or distinctions (we experience these all the time, and they are a part of life it is futile to try to deny). It is rather that they are only *relatively*, not absolutely, real. This is actually another Buddhist point: not the absolute denial of ego, any more than the assertion of its absolute reality, but a Middle Way: the relative, contingent, impermanent nature of Self. (To say that there is a cosmic spirituality superior to mere things – or indeed, ultimately even different from messy mundane reality – is to assert that there is an 'emptiness' different or apart from 'form', which is about as close to Buddhist 'theological' heresy as is possible.)[40]

This critique overlaps with the one by ecofeminists. We have already reviewed the problems highlighted by Plumwood, and in the course of a long-running debate between Fox (1989) and Salleh (1984, 1992), the latter severely (and in my view, rightly) criticized transpersonal ecology for its supervaluation of an abstract and wholly spiritual Being, so to speak, as distinct from particular beings. Salleh pointed out that such a practice has a long androcentric as well as anthropocentric pedigree, preserving and extending both masculine privilege and ecological destruction (in a way we shall examine further in the next chapter).

Like Naess, Fox also presents transpersonal ecology as a way of bypassing the axiological issue of value-in-nature and rendering ethics superfluous. He quotes John Seed approvingly: '*It is only by identification with the whole process that correct values will emerge. Otherwise we see it as self-sacrifice or effort*' (Fox 1986: 63; emphasis in original). I have already indicated how such a position depends on ignoring green virtue ethics, but in any case I am not sure why self-sacrifice, let alone effort, should be so problematic (as distinct from merely unfashionable); they surely have a part to play. Rules and duties do have their limitations. But such Deep/Transpersonal Ecologists are vulnerable to Gandhi's pointed remark about trying to devise 'a system so perfect that no one will have to be good.'[41] I'm afraid people will always have to try to be good, or at least not to do bad, as well as be actively encouraged to do good, and discouraged from doing bad.

I have spent some time trying to show exactly why, in terms of what the world needs and what Deep Ecology has to offer, Ecosophy T (that is, Naess and Sessions's own version of a Deep Ecological theory) is a bad idea, a distraction at very best. But the ethical heart of Deep Ecology itself, so to speak, is in the right place, and in a world so saturated with anthropocentrism, justifying the domination and exploitation of nature, it continues to offer a lifeline to those seeking an ecocentric alternative. This could perhaps be strengthened by a renewed emphasis on the Platform Principles.

These were condensed and reformulated by Stan Rowe in a way which avoids some of the drawbacks just described and is well worth mentioning:

1 The well-being and flourishing of the living Earth and its many organic/inorganic parts have value in themselves. . . . These values are independent of the usefulness of the non-human world for human purposes.
2 Richness and diversity of Earth's ecosystems, as well as the organic forms that they nurture and support, contribute to the realization of these values and are also values in themselves.
3 Humans have no right to reduce the diversity of Earth's ecosystems and their vital constituents, organic and inorganic.
4 The flourishing of human life and culture is compatible with a substantial decrease of human population. The creative flourishing of Earth and its multitudinous parts, organic and inorganic, requires such a decrease. (1997: 151)

However, even this version, excellent in what it does say, neglects to mention the critical importance of structural social and political change, as well as reducing consumption, and of becoming actively involved in bringing about such changes.

Deep Green Theory

Richard Sylvan (*né* Routley) developed a version of Deep Ecology called 'Deep Green Theory' (DGT), which is perhaps one of the most promising yet.[42] DGT shares the key value-orientation of Deep Ecology: '"thinking like a mountain" instead of thinking like a cash register' (Sylvan and Bennett 1994: 182). It is a fully ecocentric ethic, as defined earlier, in which (as already mentioned) the ecological community is identical with the ethical community (1994: 91). Its holism is benign, not that of a forced collectivity, and its emphasis is on the common good of communities, including that of individuals – up to the point where their activities threaten the former, upon which *all* depend. DGT also shares the more specific import of Rowe's four reformulated points of Deep Ecology just quoted. Unlike Naess and Session's version of Deep Ecology, however, it is a fully and overtly *ethical* theory, with these characteristics:

- All established or traditional ethics are recognized as inadequate, ecologically speaking. (We have already qualified this point, however, on account of virtue ethics.)
- The human chauvinism of both the Sole Value Assumption and the Greater Value Assumption is rejected, so the intrinsic value of natural items can, in particular situations, override strictly human interests.
- The human/nonhuman distinction is not ethically significant; in fact, no single species, class or characteristic (whether sentience, life or whatever) serves either to justify special ethical treatment, or to deny it. This eco-impartiality, however, does not entail trying to adhere to equal value or treatment in specific situations. Nor does it try to rule out human use of the environment – 'only too much use and use of too much' (Sylvan and Bennett 1994: 147). It follows, for example, that sustainable indigenous inhabitation and use of remaining wildernesses is perfectly acceptable, and indeed potentially a key to

their preservation; but indigenous industrial development and/ or commercial exploitation, unrestrained by ecological consid- erations, is not.[43] Similarly, broadly sustainable hunting for the pot is one thing; the 'bushmeat' trade in Africa, which is now threatening whole species, largely for profit, is something very different. (The ecological effects of development/exploitation are not affected by who its agents are, and, to that important extent, charges of elitism or ethnocentrism are therefore beside the point.[44] But an ecocentric perspective, such as that of DGT, is required in order to recognize this fact.)

- 'What is required now is that reasons be given for interfering with the environment, rather than reasons for not doing so' (Sylvan and Bennett 1994: 147) – a point that becomes more urgently true with every passing year. Or, as Midgley puts it, from an ecocentric point of view, 'the burden of proof is not on someone who wants to preserve mahogany trees from extinc- tion. It is on the person who proposes to destroy them' (1997: 96).

- 'The implementation of environmental ethics is a top-down and bottom-up and inside out issue. . . . Achieving individual change . . . is a start, but it is not enough. Institutional change is also required. It is not enough that individuals may want to change practices in their own lives. The community in which they live must meet their needs by offering environmentally sound alternatives' (Sylvan and Bennett 1994: 180).

These points have specific and important economic and fiscal impli- cations, such as replacing profit maximization with *satisization* (i.e., sufficiency) and so-called free markets with *fair*. Sylvan and Bennett's political analysis, including an ecocentric programme for change, is wide-ranging and astute. Here the contrast with Naess and Session's Ecosophy T is striking. Nonetheless, Sylvan, accepting the eight-point Platform, viewed DGT as part of the Deep Ecology movement.

There is considerable detail in Sylvan and Bennett's work about the political, cultural and educational ways in which DGT could – and to become influential, must – be realized as ethical virtue in the practices of green citizenship. They recognize, rightly, that you should not have to be a saint to be ecologically virtuous, but that an ecological society in which such virtue is normal will only come about through a great deal of hard individual and collective work. It will not result from metaphysical enlightenment alone, although a spiritual practice can certainly be part of such work. But this is not the place to go into detail, so I urge readers to seek out their book.

They also point out that, as I have already implied, there are circumstances in which arguments of a shallow and intermediate type may well be appropriate to invoke; deep green ethics is not meant to cancel these out or replace them, but to reach the places they cannot. The same applies to individual and rights-based approaches. Conversely, however, the absence of deep green ethics makes the current vogue for largely cosmetic measures like 'environmental modernization' – what Bahro aptly called 'cleaning the teeth of the dragon' – all too easy.[45]

There is one major point about which I think Sylvan was mistaken, and that is his rejection of reverence for nature in favour of mere 'respect'. For the reasons mentioned earlier in connection with Plumwood's criticism of transpersonal ecology, ecocentrism cannot afford to sacrifice emotional, spiritual and cultural valuing of specific wild places, or, even more importantly, the wild *in* places. As a philosopher (and, perhaps, as a male philosopher), Sylvan's own attachment to rationalism is understandable; but here, ironically, it weakens his own case. We shall return to this point later.

It is puzzling why, given that Sylvan's work is of high quality, original and uncompromising, he is so neglected in ethical-ecological discourse. Perhaps the problem is that last point. In any case, the little criticism he has received so far (such as that of Grey 2000) has been thin and unconvincing. The 'weaknesses' Grey identifies will arguably be true of *any* normative ethical discourse, and, ironically, Grey's own narrowly academic rationalism rules out one serious criticism that could be made of Sylvan: that his own severely intellectual style of writing limited, even contradicted, the import of his message.

Left Biocentrism

This is a green philosophy and activist movement (both are equally emphasized) which initially grew out of the work of an activist and writer in Canada, David Orton. His website 'The Green Web',[46] led to an internet discussion group, now the 'Left Bio' list, whose members agreed a primer of points in collective discussions culminating in March 1998. Now, general agreement is the basis for membership, and there is considerable and lively discussion of the problems facing those trying to build an ecocentric movement. (The 'Bio' of the name is ambiguous, often being used to mean 'eco'.)

This collective character is one of the distinctive aspects of Left Biocentrism, both internally, as a group, and as a movement that explicitly identifies itself as working within the larger Deep Ecology movement, accepts both its ecocentric values and the eight-point Platform, and speaks respectfully of Naess. At the same time, the Left Bio emphasis is quite distinct. Its other main inspiration, the 'Left' part, is that of social justice, political radicalism (both socialist and anarchist) and revolutionary idealism, and its other influences include the ecocentric philosopher-activists Judy Davis, Richard Sylvan, Rudolf Bahro and Andrew McLaughlin.

Rather than believing an ecological society can come entirely from individual change, psycho-spiritual or otherwise, Left Bios recognize that our problems – and therefore any real solution to them – are structural or systemic. Without diminishing the necessity of personal responsibility and initiative, they see that our current collective addiction to overconsumption, overpopulation and technical fixes is a context of irresponsibility that undercuts individual efforts.[47] A truly sustainable society requires social and political structures that actively encourage ecologically virtuous practices by enough individuals, and discourage the contrary, to make a real difference.

As to whether such a society could be achieved 'within' a capitalist framework, there are obviously large questions attached to what is defined as capitalist; but even so, this remains a difficult question.[48] In any case, from a Left Bio perspective, capitalism and socialism are two sides of the same coin: two different aspects of, and responses to, the same process, whose proper name is **industrialism**.[49] The properly socialist end of the spectrum is the more humane and intelligent (potentially, at least!), and is therefore to that extent preferable, but both are anthropocentric, sharing the same blind spot regarding nature. Adherents of Left Bio retain that preference but no longer believe that all 'our' problems are resolvable within an anthropocentric ambit – or that human problems are the only ones that matter.

A Left Bio perspective is also aware that saving biotic systems will result in harm to humans that is unequally distributed, those with the least resources suffering most. It therefore urges that the latter be actively considered in any transition to an ecologically steady-state society. That point, however, must not be used as an excuse to duck the whole issue.[50] (We shall return to this and related matters in more detail in Chapter 13.)

By the same token – and this is another significant departure from its other main source, the traditions of social democracy, socialism and anarchism – Left Biocentrism is keenly aware of the ecological limits of anthropocentric social justice. It is certainly not that questions of social justice are unimportant or irrelevant, just that they 'are not the *whole* answer, and probably not the primary reason we humans are so far out of balance with what might be sustainable'.[51] (After all, some human societies destroyed their own and others' environments long before capitalism did so.) Concerns with class, gender and race, while urgent, are therefore viewed in the context of *ecological* justice. The goal, as Orton puts it, is 'solidarity with all life, not just human life'. In this view, nature, not labour power, is the principal source of wealth, and that wealth is shared with other life-forms. It is a true commons – even, as such, sacred – and therefore 'not to be privatized': NOT FOR SALE.[52]

As that last point implies, most Left Bios also reject the secularism and/or atheism of traditional leftism. But they are also critical of both traditional religions, on the one hand, and fully privatized spirituality on the other. Instead, Left Biocentrism affirms a 'collective spirituality' based on the ultimate value of the Earth and its life-forms. The connection with politics is the power of such a perception, both individually and shared, to inspire and sustain a defence of the Earth and its life. It is fair to say, however, that this subject remains one of occasional heated exchanges on the list. (We shall return to it in Chapter 10.)

The Left Biocentrism Primer

Here is the text which Left Bios have agreed:

1 Left biocentrism is a left focus or theoretical tendency within the Deep Ecology movement, which is subversive of the

existing industrial society. It accepts and promotes the eight-point Deep Ecology Platform drawn up by Arne Naess and George Sessions. Left biocentrism holds up as an ideal, identification, solidarity and compassion with all life. 'Left' as used in Left Biocentrism, means anti-industrial and anti-capitalist, but not necessarily socialist. The expressions 'Left Biocentrism' or 'Left Ecocentrism' are used interchangeably.

2 Left Biocentrism accepts the view that the Earth belongs to no one. While raising a number of criticisms, Left Biocentrism is meant to strengthen, not undermine, the Deep Ecology movement which identifies with all life.

3 Left Biocentrism says that individuals must take responsibility for their actions and be socially accountable. Part of being individually responsible is to practise voluntary simplicity, so as to minimize one's own impact upon the Earth.

4 Left Biocentrists are concerned with social justice and class issues, but within a context of ecology. To move to a Deep Ecology world, the human species must be mobilized, and a concern for social justice is a necessary part of this mobilization. Left Biocentrism is for the redistribution of wealth, nationally and internationally.

5 Left Biocentrism opposes economic growth and consumerism. Human societies must live within ecological limits so that all other species may continue to flourish. We believe that bio-regionalism, not globalism, is necessary for sustainability. The perspective of the German green philosopher Rudolf Bahro is accepted that, for worldwide sustainability, industrialized countries need to reduce their impact upon the Earth to about one-tenth of what it is at the present time. It is also incumbent upon non-industrialized nations to become sustainable and it is necessary for industrialized nations to help on this path.

6 Left Biocentrism holds that individual and collective spiritual transformation is important to bring about major social change, and to break with industrial society. We need inward transformation, so that the interests of all species override the short-term self-interest of the individual, the family, the community and the nation.

7 Left Biocentrism believes that Deep Ecology must be applied to actual environmental issues and struggles, no matter how

socially sensitive, e.g., population reduction, aboriginal issues, workers' struggles, etc.

8 Social ecology, ecofeminism and eco-Marxism, while raising important questions, are all human-centred and consider human-to-human relations within society to be more important and, in the final analysis, determine society's relationship to the natural world. Left Biocentrism believes that an egalitarian, non-sexist, non-discriminating society, a highly desirable goal, can nevertheless still exploit the Earth.

9 Left Biocentrists are 'movement greens' in basic orientation. They are critical of existing green political parties, which have come to an accommodation with industrial society and have no accountability to the Deep Ecology movement.

10 To be politically relevant, Deep Ecology needs to incorporate the perspective advanced by Left Biocentrism.

Ecocentrism and the Left

The explicitly ethical, social and political focus of Left Biocentrism corrects perhaps the single most serious blind spot of other and hitherto better-known versions of the Deep Ecology movement. Left Biocentrism is also well placed, by virtue of its dual ancestry, to put ecology onto the progressive political agenda, where it is now glaringly absent. Extraordinary as it may seem, feminists, anti-racists and socialists are almost as likely as those on the neoliberal and anti-democratic right to ignore the claims of even mid-range ecological ethics, let alone a fully ecocentric one.

This fact is sadly evident in the programmes of many, probably most, of today's green parties, where the green values are strictly shallow: that is, advocated insofar as they further human interests, and not when they conflict with them. Recall, in this connection, Bahro's words quoted above when he resigned from the German Greens (see page 79). That was the moment, by the same token, when the Greens gained a certain political world in exchange for their soul. Not so many years later, the Green minister Joschka Fischer could say, with a straight face: 'A politics of ecological reconstruction is dependent on the mobilisation of enormous sums of money, [which] requires, therefore, a flourishing economy and a financially strong state' (quoted in Sarkar 1999: 161). He said nothing about the unsustainable impact of those things on the ecosystems that they depend on, which, even in purely anthropocentric terms, is self-defeating.

I am generalizing, of course, and there are individuals who are honourable exceptions. The general rule, however, is further confirmed by the apparently enlightened and progressive government of Brazil, under 'Lula' da Silva, under whose leftist government the destruction of the Amazonian rainforest has advanced apace (2003 was one of the worst years ever, although 2009 saw the lowest rate of increase in two decades: something we are apparently supposed to celebrate, although the deforestation itself grinds on). The main driver is forced conversion to cattle-ranching for meat and agricultural production, mainly soya, including GM soya, for foreign markets. The Amazonian forest produces more than 20 per cent of the world's oxygen, but apparently global lungs are optional for ambitious socialists in power. Lula has also personally pushed through the giant Belo Monte Dam, which is poised to drown about 500 square kilometers of rainforest, not only terminating all its life-forms but jeopardizing the lives and livelihoods of tens of thousands of indigenous people there.

Perhaps none of this should be surprising, considering the anthropocentric and modernist (both statist and technological) lineage of Marxism and the socialism it has influenced.[53] To say so is to stray into an often bitter debate between a very few people. The implications are important enough to detain us, however. To begin with, it must be said that advocates of a 'green' Marx − as distinct from green*ing* socialism − indulge in an awful lot of special pleading. The dominance of the Promethean anthropocentric strain in Marxism must be admitted in exactly the same way as the exploitation licensed by the dominant Christian reading of Genesis must: they may be formally 'wrong', but they are the ones that have made the running, and that (especially for a 'materialist' analysis!) is the main point.

Nor is it entirely wrong even in formal terms. Marx's concern was entirely for human beings, and both his analysis and prescription were intra-human. So too is the rhetoric: for example, Engels's assurance (in *Anti-Dühring*) that under communism, 'man for the first time becomes the real conscious master of Nature'. Ecologically speaking, that is an unappealing prospect. ('Conscious' is merely an empty promise, while 'mastery' is deeply worrying.) As Teresa Brennan points out, 'from the traditional Marxist standpoint, the centralization of production was the necessary if not sufficient condition of revolution: accordingly, any revolutionary program and any revolutionary party had to advocate both industrial development and centralization.' She adds, in a point we shall take up below, that '[t]his advocacy is directly at odds with Gandhi's view that "industrial centralization" is precisely what is destructive to true human progress' (2003: 153).

Even the few Marxist thinkers who have engaged with the ecological challenge show limited ability to adapt.[54] Joel Kovel, for example, says that 'Marx sees no need to differentiate use-value from any notion of intrinsic value to nature. In other words, a term belonging to economic discourse suffices to embrace the entirety of what nature means' (2007: 306, n.28) – something with which Kovel apparently has no problem. A generous interpretation would be that by accepting natural limits to growth, he is greening Marxism. But the limits to growth thesis, being solely concerned with human well-being, is not itself ecocentric; and by collapsing the independent intrinsic value of nature into its use-value for humans, full-blown anthropocentrism has been readmitted by the back door.[55]

Other signs for ecocentric politics to be wary of include an overriding concern with capturing state power (have we learned nothing from the seeds of Stalinism in Leninist vanguardism, to say nothing of the Cambodian and Iranian bloodbaths?), and with hanging onto a reformed, kinder, greener industrialism. These are ambitions which the Marxist left seemingly cannot give up, despite the rather obvious lesson of history that by the time you have your hands on the levers of direct power, you will have become the people you were trying to replace.[56]

In short, 'The ecocentric Left' – of which Left Bio is the best example I know – 'is not anti-Marxist but accepts the limitations of Marx and Marxism from an ecological perspective'.[57] It also accepts that Marxist concerns and insights are often not only valid but urgent. Nor does it deny that sexism and racism need combating along with economic injustice. But these issues must be placed *within an ecocentric context*. Ultimately, as Rowe says: 'Neither philosophical liberalism championing liberty nor philosophical socialism championing equality will save us from ourselves. Human history will end in ecology, or nothing' (2002: 7).

Here are a few additional points to consider, especially for those who still think the left's traditional concern with ethics and justice in particular can or should be kept within a purely human ambit. First, at present, it is estimated that humans – roughly 0.5 per cent of the total biomass of the Earth – are consuming, directly or indirectly, between 24 and 39 per cent of the total net product of its terrestrial and aquatic photosynthetic energy (along with about 50 per cent of the accessible runoff of fresh water).[58] This is truly anthropocentrism in action: a single species has already appropriated for its sole use at least a quarter of the planet's energy, upon which *all* life depends. In other words, humanity is behaving just like the biological equivalent – and *ethical* equivalent, assuming humans have any choice (which most of us, including those on the left, would like to think) – of a capitalist upper class, master race or patriarchy. Is there nothing here for a progressive political agenda to address?

Second, it is possible to imagine a world devoid of most species which do not directly or indirectly serve human interests, and of any places which qualify as wild, but in which (although this is harder to imagine) any significant degrees of racism, sexism and inequality also do not exist; a world, in other words, in which the progressive anthropocentric agenda has largely been realized but is nonetheless ecologically severely impoverished at best, and a disaster at worst. But that outcome would (will?) take down any politically progressive agenda with it – not only ultimately, because of our dependence as organisms on ecological dynamics, but well before then, because of the social and political effects of the social stress and disorder, to outright war, resulting from competition, within as well as between countries, for increasingly scarce resources.

Third, when there are direct conflicts between jobs and the economy on the one hand and threatened nonhuman nature (e.g., old-growth forest) on the other, we know from historical experience how rarely the latter wins, and how tenuous those few victories are: 'the long defeat', indeed.[59] And in this context, the perceived interests of unionized or collectivized labour put it on the same side as capital.[60]

Finally, the unpalatable fact remains (as Sandy Irvine [2001] once put it) that from the Earth's point of view, the effects of an armoured personnel carrier and an ambulance are indistinguishable. However preferable the latter may be – and it *is* – both remain with an anthropocentric ambit that urgently needs an additional, wider and deeper perspective. Orwell touched on that perspective in the homely, ordinary and egalitarian sort of way that is available to most of us, in his 'Some Thoughts on the Common Toad', written in 1946:

> Is it wicked to take a pleasure in spring and other seasonal changes? To put it more precisely, is it politically reprehensible, while we are all groaning, or at any rate ought to be groaning, under the shackles of the capitalist system, to point out that life is frequently more worth living because of a blackbird's song, a yellow elm tree in October, or some other natural phenomenon which does not cost money and does not have what the editors of left-wing newspapers call a class angle? There is no doubt that many people think so.

But Orwell's point is not a right-wing one, either. He concludes:

> [S]pring is here, even in London N1, and they can't stop you enjoying it. . . . The atom bombs are piling up in the factories, the police are prowling through the cities, the lies are streaming from the loudspeakers, but the earth is still going round the sun, and neither the dictators nor the bureaucrats, deeply as they disapprove of the process, are able to prevent it.

I will suggest in Chapter 13 that ecocentrism, to become successfully realized, does require anti- (or non-)capitalism; an ecocentric society would be an egalitarian one. The reverse, however, does not follow. As Orton says, 'Implicit in the anti-capitalist view is that it is the ownership of wealth which is the main problem. But the natural world can be destroyed individually and communally, or by the capitalist or socialist state.'[61] The common good, upon which everything depends, includes but vastly exceeds humanity, and what Orton calls 'ecological honesty', as well as ethics, requires that we recognize that fact.

The Earth Manifesto

Two Canadian ecologists/naturalists loosely associated with the Left Bio network have recently produced another deep green manifesto with an even more explicitly ecocentric emphasis. They are Ted Mosquin[62] and Stan Rowe. 'A Manifesto For Earth' was published in 2004. It sets out a worldview, with its corresponding ethic and broadly sketched programme, that shifts the focus 'from humanity to the Ecosphere', identified as that 'life-giving matrix' (including its nonorganic components) that is the source of *all* its organisms, sustains them, and to which they ultimately return.

Mosquin and Rowe characterize the dominant contrary view as homocentric (i.e., anthropocentric), and point out that '[h]umanity's 10,000-year-old experiment in mode-of-living at the expense of Nature, culminating in economic globalization, is failing. A primary reason is that we have placed the importance of our species above all else.' But like the other dark green ethics discussed here, this one is critical of human chauvinism, not humans as such.

There is a vital place for wonder here, and a sense of the sacred, but not for the off-planet spirituality that characterizes most theistic (and New Age) religions. Similarly, this Earth is not an abstract concept to be wilfully manipulated and 'managed', but a profoundly complex and intricate affair, whose local and regional particularities are of the essence. One can only work *with* them. 'The goal is restoration of Earth's diversity and beauty, with our prodigal species once again a cooperative, responsible, ethical member.' (The resonances with Gaia Theory, Land Ethic and Deep Ecology need no emphasis.)

The principles of the Earth Manifesto cannot be quoted in full here, but what follows is a basic outline, with excerpts and a few comments.

Core principles

1 *The Ecosphere is the Centre of Value for Humanity*. 'Comprehension of the ecological reality that people are Earthlings shifts the center of values away from the homocentric to the ecocentric, from *Homo sapiens* to Planet Earth.' As the authors rightly point

out, 'Without attention to the priority of Earth-as-context, biocentrism easily reverts to a chauvinistic homocentrism, for who among all animals is commonly assumed to be the wisest and best?'

2 *The Creativity and Productivity of Earth's Ecosystems Depend on their Integrity.* 'The evolutionary creativity and continued productivity of Earth and its regional ecosystems require the continuance of their key structures and ecological processes.'

3 *The Earth-centred Worldview is supported by Natural History.* (It is good to see natural history, as distinct from modern biology, restored to prominence.)

4 *Ecocentric Ethics is Grounded in Awareness of our Place in Nature,* which brings with it 'a sense of connectedness and reverence for the abundance and vitality of sustaining Nature'.

5 *An Ecocentric Worldview Values Diversity of Ecosystems and Cultures.* 'An ecocentric worldview values Earth's diversity in all its forms, the non-human as well as the human.' The corresponding ethic 'challenges today's economic globalization that ignores the ecological wisdom embedded in diverse cultures, and for short-term profit destroys them.'

6 *Ecocentric Ethics Supports Social Justice.* Social ecologists rightly attack inequalities that hurt relatively powerless humans but fail to consider 'the current rapid degradation of Earth's eco-systems that increases inter-human tensions while foreclosing possibilities for sustainable living and for the elimination of poverty'.

Action principles

7 *Defend and Preserve Earth's Creative Potential.* Barring cosmic collisions, 'Earth's evolving inventiveness will continue for millions of years, hampered only where humans have destroyed whole ecosystems by exterminating species or by toxifying sediments, water and air'. Therefore activities that do so – especially lethal technologies and industries, 'enriching special corporate interests, and satisfying human wants rather than needs' – 'need to be identified and publicly condemned'.

8 *Reduce Human Population Size.* 'A primary cause of ecosystem

destruction and species extinctions is the burgeoning human population that already far exceeds ecologically sustainable levels.' Every additional human adds to the immense pressure on inherently limited resources (renewable as well as nonrenewable), especially in the overdeveloped world where consumption is highest.

9 *Reduce Human Consumption of Earth's Parts.* 'The chief threat to the Ecosphere's diversity, beauty and stability is the ever-increasing appropriation of the planet's goods for exclusive human uses. Such appropriation and over-use, often justified by population overgrowth, steals the livelihood of other organisms.' Our vital needs do not amount to a 'license to plunder and exterminate'.

10 *Promote Ecocentric Governance.* 'In present centers of power, who speaks for wolf? and who speaks for temperate rain forest? Such questions have more than metaphorical significance; they reveal the necessity of legally safeguarding the many vital nonhuman components of the Ecosphere.' New bodies of law, policy, and administration are required as 'embodiments of the ecocentric philosophy, ushering in ecocentric methods of governance'.

11 *Spread the Message.* 'Those who agree with the preceding principles have a duty to spread the word by education and leadership. The initial urgent task is to awaken all people to their functional dependence on Earth's ecosystems as well as their bonds to all other species.'

The Earth Charter

Completely independently, 'The Earth Charter' appeared in 2000.[63] It was a statement of 16 ethical principles 'for building a just, sustainable and peaceful global society in the 21st Century'. These principles are intended to be widely (although not necessarily universally) shared, in order to provide a basis for 'defining sustainable development in terms of global ethics' (Lynn 2004: 2, 3). The Charter has been recognized by UNESCO and adopted by the IUCN/World Conservation Union. Its offshoots, which give the idea some legs, include Earth Charter Community Summits and initiatives, sustainable business awards and the Earth Scouts.

The Charter begins with an ecocentric recognition of the Earth as our home, and therefore the protection of its vitality, diversity and beauty as 'a sacred trust'. It also points to the deteriorating global situation respecting both natural and human communities. It names the primary challenge of our times as forming a 'global partnership' to bring about '[f]undamental changes . . . in our values, institutions, and ways of living'. Finally, it calls for 'a sense of universal responsibility, identifying ourselves with the whole Earth community as well as our local communities'.

The principles, too lengthy for quotation here, are organised under four headings: (1) Respect and Care for the Community of Life, (2) Ecological Integrity, (3) Social and Economic Justice, and (4) Democracy, Nonviolence, and Peace.[64] It can hardly be doubted that they specify admirable and desirable ends in a comprehensive way; nor that the recommended means are appropriate. And such documents involve a lot of painstaking work which should be recognized and applauded. But there is a problem here which grows out of the very comprehensiveness and generality that the goal of 'widespread agreement' requires. It is difficult to believe that what approaches being a progressive wish-list which includes nature *and* social justice *and* peace *and* democracy *and* diversity will have much real impact in and on the world of concrete particulars. (Genuine world-government – and even that assumes a benign and competent world-government – might provide the conditions in which it could acquire such influence, including some teeth, but we remain very far from that.)

This problem has another serious aspect, which is that the Earth Charter fails to admit the possibility of conflict in actual cases – always possible, and virtually inevitable – between these various ideals, especially between the interests of human and nonhuman nature. It thus falls short of an ecocentric ethic as I have defined it above, and as compared with the Earth Manifesto. And the overwhelmingly dominant ethical consensus is anthropocentric and/or light green at best: an imbalance that urgently needs redressing. So Mosquin and Rowe's more uncompromising stance, which firmly places human concerns within an ecocentric context, is preferable. This is not just a strategic point; we do all live on (or rather in, since it includes the breathable atmosphere), and depend on, the Earth. Despite its virtues, that is a truth which the Charter makes it too easy to ignore or fudge in practice; whereas the Manifesto, quite rightly, makes it that much harder.

9

Ecofeminism

Perhaps even more than the other schools of ecological thought and action, ecofeminism is rich and complex in ways – including disagreements, or at least different emphases (not necessarily a weakness) – that are difficult to encompass within the necessary simplifications of an introductory text. In addition, placing it in this company is bound to be controversial, for it is not necessarily ecocentric (nor would all ecofeminists want it to be seen as such). Nonetheless, there is a strong case for including it.[1] One reason is that as the prefix suggests, ecofeminism is in important part ecological. Another is that its effects are powerfully ecocentric. And a third is that insofar as **patriarchy** identifies women with nature and dominates both, they are internally linked, so a struggle to resist or overturn *either* must address both. As Salleh puts it, 'You can't address the oppression of nature by men without simultaneously addressing the oppression of women by men' (2010: 188).

Rather like Left Biocentrism, ecofeminism is a meeting of two strands. One is feminism itself: the awareness of the pathological effects of dominant patriarchal or (to use a more recent term) *masculinist* structures, both 'inner' and 'outer' – particularly, of course, on women but also, ultimately, on their oppressors – and the attempt to replace them with ones that *also* value the feminine. ('Masculinist' bears the same relationship to 'masculine' as 'rationalist', for example, does to 'rational'; that is, it takes a natural or normal human attribute and turns it into the supervalued centrepiece of an ideology.) Another way to put it would be that such structures and attitudes are **androcentric** (male-centred).[2] In this central respect, feminism is an anthropocentric concern and ethic; at least, there is nothing necessarily ecological about it.

The other element is a recognition of, and deep concern about, the equally masculinist domination and exploitation of nature through the very same habitual structures of thought, feeling and action that devalue and harm women. This is the ecocentric dimension, and, in combining them, ecofeminism brings to the critique of that pathology, and suggestions for renewing our relationships with nature, a dimension which is missing from all the others we have so far encountered: sex-gender. As Mary Mellor points out, the most ecologically destructive people tend to be privileged males in the global North, who are able to get away with it 'by putting the burdens of human embodiment and embeddedness on to other peoples' – overwhelmingly women, especially but by no means only in the global South – 'other species, and the planet'. These also bear most directly 'the destructive ecological consequences of high levels of production, consumption and mobility' (1997: vii–viii).

Ecofeminists have performed an invaluable service in bringing to our attention the way sex-gender, often unconsciously, is deeply implicated in the ecological crisis – not only in the macro-level pathologies of ecological devastation, but also in the minute practices and assumptions of daily life. The connections with industrial capitalism, in both ways, are also clear. And they have much to offer positively, in terms of a green virtue ethic.

There is something of a division of labour in this respect, with some authors (like Val Plumwood and, allowing for other differences, Karren J. Warren) tending to more philosophical and cultural analyses, and others (such as Ariel Salleh, Maria Mies and Mary Mellor) working in a more politically and economically materialist vein. But this is only a question of emphasis, and in both respects the case for combining an ecofeminist perspective with ecocentrism is strong – not as replacing the concern with anthropocentrism, but as partly a refinement of it and partly as an additional dynamic.

A Master Mentality

One way of understanding the key role of gender in generating eco-crisis is through the concept of a ***master mentality***. Present throughout human history, it was given an enormous boost by the advent of modernity – that is, by the same processes, at the same time (beginning in the mid-seventeenth century), that licensed the capitalist and technoscientific exploitation of nature. So of what does this mentality, including its powerful acculturated and institutionalized forms, consist?

Basically, it draws on some ways of thinking and valuing, which Warren (1993) has analysed as:

- dualism, whereby all life is ordered into two opposing categories;
- value-laden hierarchies, whereby such dualism is not neutral, but what is 'up' has more value than what is 'down'; and
- the role of what is 'lower' is to serve the needs of what is 'higher'.[3]

But what of the specific content? The relevant dualisms, with the 'superior' first, are: humanity versus nature; male versus female; and reason versus emotion. These constellate a set of refinements such as abstract intellect versus the body, rationality versus irrationality, etc. These value-laden hierarchies draw heavily on old sources, especially informed by Greek philosophy and Christianity – or the cultural, social and political formations which they articulated – but it was most effectively formulated (as I have already argued) by the fathers of the Scientific Revolution such as Bacon, Descartes and Galileo. And while reason is taken as the 'highest' aspect of being human – thus implicitly but firmly excluding women – scientific rationality presents itself in turn as the ultimate expression of reason. It would indeed be extraordinary, then, if the ideology of modern techno-science was not deeply prejudiced against both women and nature. (There is a strong body of feminist analysis of science which I cannot describe here, but do recommend.)[4]

This, then, is the damaging ideological upshot:

Humanity = male = reason
over and against
nature = female = emotion & 'the body'

In short, the domination and exploitation of nature and women proceed by the same *logic*, the same *processes* and, by and large, the same *people*. As Plumwood says:

> What is taken to be authentically and characteristically human, defining of the human, as well as the ideal for which humans should strive, is not to be found in what is shared with the natural and animal (e.g., the body, sexuality, reproduction, emotionality, the senses, agency) but in what is thought to separate and distinguish them – especially reason and its offshoots. (1995; quoted in Benson 2000: 122)

Here, let us note three additional points. First, the actual processes of gender are messier and more complicated than the logic, and the people even more so; for example, men certainly dominate, but those dominating also include a few women. But the fact remains that even when women do get to be represented, and indeed do some of the representing, the structural terms of how society is organized and run tend to remain masculinist. And as Ynestra King asked, 'What is the point of partaking equally in a system that is killing us all?' (Compare Sandy Irvine and Alec Ponton's pointed description of orthodox socialism: 'fair shares in extinction'.)[5]

Second, the role of gender, including the structures and sensibilities that entail a masculinist bias, is indeed fundamental to ongoing ecocrisis. It is very difficult to imagine the latter being able to proceed without the kind of attitude, institutionalized and normalized, that Brennan (2000) brilliantly termed 'sadodispassionate'. The only qualification is that gender should not be considered the *only* cause, and in any given actual situation, the extent to which it is directly implicated – even if it is almost always present – will vary. (There are no a priori guarantees here, any more than with respect to other dynamics.)

Third, however close the connection between women and nature may be, and therefore their joint suppression, it is best viewed as ultimately contingent. To see it as essential or 'necessary' (whether on mystical, biological or other grounds) would be problematic, for two reasons. One, that is the very argument long used by male chauvinists to justify dominating women. And two, to exalt women-as-nature rather than despising them, while preferable, merely *inv*erts the dominant values attached to male/female essentialism; it preserves the same destructive logic, when the point is to *sub*vert it wholesale. (This is what Plumwood [1993: 31–4] calls the 'feminism of uncritical reversal'.) Any populist version of ecofeminism that inflated the feminine and demonized the masculine, while it would be a refreshing change for many, would not be much of an ethical advance on what we have. Nor would leaving women still supposedly less 'rational' than men, and men less 'emotional' than women. The point is that 'both men and women reside in both nature and culture' (Plumwood 2006b: 55).

Ecofeminism in Action

More promising, therefore, is the work of finding ways to extend and strengthen generally ways of perceiving, valuing and treating the natural world that have long been characterized as feminine, without subscribing to an essentialist determinism which would deny men the ability to change their ways or share in such a process. As a key part of that, women's experience and insights can be appreciated as special and important without being therefore morally superior. To quote Salleh: 'It is nonsense to assume that women are any closer to nature than men. The point is that women's reproductive labour and such patriarchally assigned work roles as cooking and cleaning bridge men and nature in a very obvious way, and one that is denigrated by patriarchal culture' (1992: 208).

As well as important writers and activists, there are several examples of influential ecofeminist movements. One is the Chipko Movement of the Garwhal Himalayas, which began in the 1970s with tribal women – both more directly affected by deforestation and more active in trying to stop it – surrounding and hugging trees in order to stop them from being felled. It spread, bringing tribal societies as well as 'environmental' issues to widespread attention in India and elsewhere. The movement also inspired Vandana Shiva, who has become a leading ecofeminist voice in defence of nature and women, especially in the global South, against the violence of 'maldevelopment' driven by commercial production and trade for profit, as well as the resulting monoculture, at once ecological, social and cultural.

Another instance is the Green Belt Movement in Kenya – led by Wangari Maathai, who was awarded the Nobel Peace Prize in 2004 – which started in 1977 with a grassroots tree-planting movement. By now, many millions of trees have been planted across Africa, not only nurturing soil, water and other life-forms, but rooting campaigns for sustainable economics and political reforms. It places the well-being of the local natural world where it belongs – at the heart of healthy human communities – and emphasizes the vital role of women in, and linking, both. But such grassroots movements have not been restricted to the global South. Local resistance to toxic waste pollution in the community of Love Canal, New York, led by Lois Gibbs, resulted in the Citizens' Clearinghouse for Hazardous Waste (CCHW).

The case for combining an ecofeminist critique of androcentrism (as the male-centred domination of women and nature) with an ecocentric critique of anthropocentrism (as the human-centred domination of nature) is strong. The former does not replace the concern that Deep Ecologists and other ecocentrics have with anthropocentrism; it refines and arguably deepens that concern. In practice, androcentrism and anthropocentrism are, unsurprisingly, mutually reinforcing; and so are their contraries. But I agree with Salleh (1992) that no attempt should be made to merge ecofeminism with ecocentrism or subsume it; it is a distinct perspective with a distinct contribution to make. Although both approaches are committed to nature as independent, alive and agentic, only ecofeminism brings a critical awareness of the extent and ways in which the subordination of women and ecological destruction are integrally linked.[6]

As I mentioned at the outset, the effects of ecofeminist experience and insights are potentially deeply ecocentric. They include ways of being and behaving in the world without which, I believe, ecocentrism must fail: an appreciation and reassertion, against modernist abstract universalism, the value of life as embodied and embedded, situated and engaged, local and particular; and against an inflated rationalism, the value of intuition and feelings; and finally, the potential importance and value of what cannot be rationally calculated, economically or otherwise.[7] The importance of these perspectives and values for an ecological ethic cannot be overemphasized.

Ecofeminism and Ethics

Non-exclusive and non-essentialist ecofeminism thus has powerfully positive resonances with the other ecocentric schools/movements analysed here. It also relates closely to the kind of ethics I have described as having the greenest potential: virtue ethics. (Not coincidentally, this is a kind that predates modernity and promises, by the same token, to survive it best.) Under the term an *ethics of care*, some feminists have moved away from the abstract universalism of both deontology and utilitarianism, and articulated instead the kind of ethical relationships that connect people, especially, but not only, women, to the world in situated and contextual ways.[8] This opens the way to recognize that valuing, caring for and protecting the natural world proceed best from particular, sensuous, emotional and (in a related, materialist sense) spiritual involvements with it. The attitude of 'holding', to use Sara Ruddick's term, that maintains a household, nurtures a child and sustains a network of mutually supportive relationships is equally suited to 'world protection, world-preservation, world repair' (Ruddick 1989: 79, quoting Adrienne Rich). As Plumwood writes:

> There is no good reason to think that the particularistic kinds of ethical relations feminists have discussed are any less relevant to interspecies ethics than to intra-human ethics, that these inter-species relationships are of necessity any less multidimensional, complex, rich and varied than our relationships with humans, or any more reducible to single parameters like rights. (2002: 187)

There is much food for thought here – and for action – with an ecofeminist ethic of care, on the one hand, potentially converging with the character orientation of virtue ethics, notwithstanding its more masculine origins in civic republicanism. But it is important to realize that, as Salleh (1997) reminds us, such work is presently being undertaken and performed by women worldwide, although it is relatively undervalued, unrecognized and untheorized. This labour not only makes such women indispensable in a global struggle to realize ecocentric values; it means that a vital basis for an ecocentric virtue ethic – not of laws, nor of calculations, but of character – *already* exists. And in a world littered with the wrecks and casualties of grand abstract schemes, that may be the most promising as well as most realistic place to start.[9]

10

Deep Green Ethics as Post-Secular

Dogmatic Secularism

As I mentioned earlier, Sylvan's Deep Green Theory rejects 'reverence' for nature in favour of less demanding 'respect'. Given the serious problems with the established religions, including their poor ecological record, one can see why, but Sylvan's move seems nonetheless a mistake. The problem is twofold. Strategically, secular 'respect' is much weaker and therefore potentially less effective. I have already quoted Stephen Jay Gould in my Introduction, who points out that the effort to save species and environments cannot succeed without 'an emotional bond between ourselves and nature as well – for we will not fight to save what we do not love' (1993: 40). And there is a religious or spiritual dimension to that emotion (we shall come to the difference in a moment), as there is to all love. Second, substantively, that dimension is present everywhere in both ecological and anti-ecological discourse, and trying to deny its presence only makes it harder to recognize and encourage or criticize it as required. Paradoxically, dogmatic secular rationalists thus make the very thing they want – the exercise of critical reason – harder to do when it matters most.

One thing secularism obscures is that the ideology accompanying most of modernity's onslaught on nature – 'progress', meaning strictly human progress (and in practice, only for some humans) – is, for most of its most influential adherents, a crypto-religion. Listen to the leaders and acolytes of the G8, World Trade Organization or the World Bank, for example, and it is quite clear that they are fuelled by what David Ehrenfeld defines as 'a supreme faith in human reason' (1981: 5). This *is* a faith, just as is its variant scientism, and for the same reason: the kind of evidence it cites cannot provide conclusive support without assuming what is in question, namely its superiority.

Conversely, and equally importantly, when people value nature strongly enough to act to protect it, they do so in a way that is *in effect* religious and, as such, this is stronger than respect. It has to be, in order to resist the all-too-available blandishments of utilitarian appeals to 'rational' self-interest. That is why advocates of the latter call their green opponents 'sentimental', 'nostalgic', 'emotional', 'subjective' and so on: in short, 'irrational'. (And the neurotic fear of many environmentalists of being called that, by conceding the ground of the argument, plays right into their opponents' hands.) Note too the way this mindset and strategy are powerfully gendered, with every term of opprobrium an implicitly feminine one, and thus – given the 'problems' posed by embodiment – also anti-Earth.

But secularism has a powerful grip on the modern mindset, including those on the political left, even when they are trying to oppose the industrial megamachine. Kate Soper's book *What Is Nature?*, for example, argues a socialist case for protecting nature, but it culminates in a rant against 'irrational forms of superstition': 'We cannot seek to protect nature by pretending to forms of belief that have been exploded by the march of science and technology.' Monsanto and Exxon could ask for no more. Typical of most 'progressive' secular intellectuals, Soper concludes with the fallacious assumption that reverence for nature is *necessarily* misanthropic (1995: 274–5, 277).

Similarly, Murray Bookchin (1995), the founder of social ecology, has inveighed against such reverence, charging it with everything from superstition, mystification, authoritarianism and fascism to (inevitably) Nazism.[1] Bookchin long ago identified market commodity capitalism as the single biggest enemy of both nature and humanity, yet somehow he failed to notice that it acts hand-in-glove with rationalist-realist scientism (which we discussed briefly earlier, in the section on 'Secular Ethics' in Chapter 3). His argument thus becomes indistinguishable from the attacks on ecocentrism by

neoliberals like Anna Bramwell (1989) and conservative anthropo-
centrists like Luc Ferry (1995).

Something that reveals how pervasive a secularist ideology is
among intellectuals is the fact that even Robyn Eckersley, one of
Bookchin's most acute critics, apparently shares the same blind spot.
She realizes that '[c]onforming to the requirements and modes of
rationality of the dominant culture has rarely served the interests
of diverse minority cultures' (1998: 171), to say nothing of nonhuman natures. Yet almost in the same breath, she rejects any spiritual
defence of nature, since 'it would seem more appropriate nowadays
to find a secular (and scientifically informed), public justification for
government action to protect the environment' (1998: 178) – as
if secular scientific discourse has played no part in the hegemonic
rationality of today's dominant culture!

Benson, in his book on environmental ethics, takes an apparently
sensible, balanced position on this question. He supports a ***naturalistic***
view of nature, which he defines as 'a view that is agnostic about the
existence of supernatural beings of any kind and is broadly consistent
with current scientific theory'. 'Nature' is then defined as 'the whole
material universe', in which case '[t]he only possible beings outside
of nature in this sense are supernatural beings, such as gods, which
are defined negatively as non-spatial and non-temporal' (2000: 120).
This sounds reasonable enough until you stop to consider what is
smuggled into the argument as assumption. Even if it is granted that
nature is material or physical in the modern sense – devoid of agency,
subjectivity or indeed life as such – why should it be *only* material (in
the sense Benson gives it)? No reason is given.

Nor can a scientific answer be given, for either science has
nothing to say about what it cannot detect and measure; or it does,
but then its pronouncements are no longer scientific ones, because
they depend on a wide range of assumptions and values that cannot
themselves be supported scientifically without already assuming the
truth or value of science.[2] As Feyerabend pointed out, 'the choice
of science over other forms of life is not a scientific choice' (1987:
31). In that case, why should the only possible spiritual beings be
'supernatural' ones, that is, outside nature and therefore non-spatial
and non-temporal? And in any case, if we want to avoid enlisting in
the modernist campaign for a disenchanted 'reality' and inanimate
'nature', then, as Feyerabend continued, '[t]here is no other way out:

we either call gods and quarks equally real, but tied to different sets
of circumstances, or we altogether cease talking about the 'reality' of
things and use more complex ordering schemes instead' (1987: 89).

In fact, the idea of nature as purely material, and secondarily
mechanistic, is by no means self-evident or axiomatic. It only gained
power, and then common currency, as a result of a long and complex
intellectual, social and political power struggle beginning in the mid-
seventeenth century, and resulting in what we now call 'modernity'.
(This history is one that Toulmin tells very well in his *Cosmopolis*
[1990].) Previously, for the vastly longer part of human history and
for many if not most people, nature had a spiritual dimension that
was, and to some still is, as obvious as its materiality. That materiality,
as Plumwood writes, 'is already full of form, spirit, story, agency, and
glory' (2002: 226).

But the fundamental flaw with any discussion such as Benson's
(which is the usual kind) is its uncritical acceptance of a firm distinction between 'material' and 'spiritual'. That assumption, inherited
from Platonism, Christianity and modern science almost unchanged,
is just the problem. (The fact that religion exalts one side of the
opposition and science the other is secondary to the split itself.) We
shall never be able to understand and appreciate nature until we re-
learn to see it as *both* 'spiritual' subject *and* 'natural' object.[3]

An Ecocentric Spirituality

It is true (as I noted in Chapter 3) that the world's major religions all
fall short, in their traditional and, for the most part, present forms,
of anything resembling an ecological ethic. Or more accurately, they
have just not been especially concerned with the issue. Furthermore,
most of them − especially the theistic ones − have lent themselves
to a ruthlessly anthropocentric exploitation of nature. At the same
time, however, religions also act as significant cultural repositories
of human wisdom, and therefore resources with which to meet new
(such as ecological) demands − a paradox we have already considered
in the case of Christianity.[4] The point I want to emphasize here is
that, as Kaebnick (2000: 22) puts it, there is a 'religious version of
the sacred', but it is not the only one. In other words, religions do

not exhaust the spiritual, or its importance.[5] And that importance has direct relevance, both substantively and strategically, to an ecological ethic.

First, though, let us agree a rough-and-ready distinction: 'religion' is a particular institutionalized instance of 'spirituality', which latter is therefore the more comprehensive phenomenon. Defining those two terms in the context of our concerns here, however, is especially difficult. Most definitions of 'religion' specify belief in one or more supernatural entities, which is not only parochial (the emphasis on belief, as distinct from practices and a way of life, is a particularly monotheistic one, and there is no God in Buddhism), but prejudices matters against nature from the start, since whatever this being or power is, it cannot be in or of nature, since it is *super*natural. The condition of 'spirituality' is equally bad, since 'spirit', in keeping with Western theism, is commonly defined as that which is *not* matter: another inherently anti-ecological assumption. So for religion, let us just stick with the point about institutionalization, with all that that implies about its involvement in issues of political, social and cultural power. For spirituality, let us think of it as a concern, sufficiently serious to make a difference in how one actually lives, and either personal or collective, with the **sacred**: that which is beyond human control, intrinsically valuable, wondrous and (as I said above) not for sale. As Kaebnick says, discussing the sanctity of nature: 'Something that is sacred has a value that transcends human affairs in the straight-forward sense that it is experienced as having value independent of humn decisions and preferences.' In other words, 'plainly, to say that something is sacred is to say that it has intrinsic value' (2000: 17, 20).

Beyond this, we could say that when either religion (relatively more organized) or spirituality (relatively more diffuse) is collective, it can be thought of as an attempt, together with others, to place and maintain ourselves in a healthy or correct relationship with the ultimate source of value, meaning and perhaps life itself; and as the ways(s) of life that follow. It is therefore inherently ethical, as it entails relationships with both that source and with others who are in the same existential position. It is also intellectual ('correct') in an engaged way that is more than technical or purely 'cognitive'. Such a working definition is undeniably broad but sufficiently meaningful, I hope, to enable us to proceed.

Now as we have already seen, there is good reason to be suspicious of attempts to convince us that nature is strictly or merely 'natural'. Disenchanting the world, so that nature and its places and fellow inhabitants can no longer be seen as sacred, is a fundamental prerequisite to exploiting, commodifying and selling it. If you see nature as essentially a passive and inanimate object with no intrinsic value, you will feel free to do with it whatever you will and you probably will. (That obviously includes, but is far from limited to, the treatment of animals.) And you will not feel sufficiently strongly moved to fight to protect it. In that case, a deep ecological ethic has no possible foothold. Indeed, for those powerful few and their many dependents who stand to profit from disenchantment, an attitude 'enchanted' and its corresponding ethic must be actively disparaged, usually as 'irrational' or simply 'ridiculous'. The result in the not-so-long run, as Bateson remarked, is that if you see the world as simply yours to exploit, '*and you have an advanced technology*, your likelihood of survival will be that of a snowball in hell' (1972: 462; italics in original).

Positively, the commitment to the intrinsic value of nature that is at the heart of a fully ecocentric ethic requires a recognition that its value cannot be exhausted by any use or understanding or even appreciation; it is *more*-than-human (and therefore – needless to add, I hope – includes the human). Such value is ultimately an inexhaustible mystery. It cannot be fully explained, analysed or justified in terms of other concepts or values; otherwise, it would not be intrinsic. In other words, the source, the 'goal' and the practice of an ecocentric ethic are all, in this sense, spiritual. A ***post-secular spirituality*** is therefore an inherent part of ecocentrism, and one which no ecocentric movement can afford to do without.[6] Nor is it by any means necessarily reactionary.

But, what kind of spirituality is it? That is a key question. Tom Cheetham put it well:

> The call for a 'resacralization' of nature as a necessary condition for the solution of global and local environmental problems has much to recommend it insofar as it emphasizes the local, the timely, and the particular. Nevertheless, insofar as such a move grounds environmentalism in 'Nature' conceived as an alternative absolute, it is misguided and dangerous for all the reasons that such claims to transcendent knowledge always are. (1993: 309)

We have discussed the dangers of a conception of nature that is overly abstract, universal or 'transcendental', thus inviting an authoritarian politics. By the same token, monism is also dangerous. Exalting One True Nature (whether in mystical or scientific terms is ultimately secondary) or Gaian Earth or, for that matter, a single Earth-mother goddess leaves the logic of abstract monism – so hostile to nature as a pluralist, perspectival, sensuous experience – fundamentally untouched. I have also argued against any view of nature that tries to exclude humanity entirely (as distinct from opposing human chauvinism and allowing room for human/nonhuman conflicts). So Cheetham's warning is quite in order, but it does not exclude spirituality as such.

In addition, I have criticized another spirituality in relation to Deep Ecology, namely the privatized kind of the New Age consumer. Purely personal and private religious belief lends itself too easily to an anthropocentric egoism that is itself vulnerable to being co-opted by 'lifestyle' consumer capitalism.

The understanding of the sacred that can make a positive and effective contribution to ecocentric ethics, then, is a valuing of the Earth which is:

- *pluralist* (while allowing commonalities, with other people in other places also valuing nature in other ways, to emerge);
- *local* (while allowing connections with those others elsewhere);
- deeply appreciative of, and involved in, the so-called material world in all its *sensuous particulars*, and which recognizes that being ultimately and fundamentally a mystery, it/they are not only or merely 'material'; and
- *social* as well as individual: if not exactly a religion, on account of the characteristics just mentioned, then a 'collective spirituality'.

The Land Ethic, Gaia Theory, Deep Ecology and Left Biocentrism all could contribute to and benefit from such a sense of the sacred, so different from the abstract universalism, both religious and secular, with which we are familiar. Ecofeminism too, in ways I have mentioned, entails and encourages a pluralist, embodied and locally engaged ecological spirituality, or what Plumwood calls 'a materialist spirituality of place' (2002: ch. 10).

I cannot emphasize too strongly that an ecological spirituality is not transcendentalism or supernaturalism, in which a supposedly purely spiritual dimension is added to the material world (or, for that matter, withheld from it by atheists). Nor is it 'mystical' in the sense of evoking or invoking such a force or being. It is a recognition and celebration of the spiritual, animated, agentic, mysterious and unmasterable *already in* nature.[7] Nor, finally, should it be thought of as a mere optional, feel-good add-on to the real business of politics. No less a politically and intellectually astute person than Teresa Brennan, in affirming what she called 'the prime directive' – to protect 'the continuity and specificity and endurance of biological and cultural diversity' – stated her belief that:

> [T]his affirmation, together with the real economic democracy it presupposes, can be accomplished only when a spiritual authority – and corresponding collective conviction – develops which is equivalent in force to the [present] centralized, global economic authority. . . . This spiritual authority does not require a new religion as such. It requires actualization, so to speak, of the prime directive, which can be found latent in the cardinal teachings of all religions. (2003: 166, 167)

Animism

Another potent source of inspiration comes from aboriginal sacrality. Sean Kane writes: 'As civilization feels its way forward to practices of living with the earth on the earth's terms, we are discovering the respect for nature demonstrated by archaic humanity' (1998: 14). Now, it is true that the way most surviving indigenous peoples live today is increasingly integrated into the global capitalist system, with the ecocidal consequences of its industrial dynamic; and no romanticism or cultural relativism should gloss over that fact. It is also true that the ancient aboriginal world included some ecological devastation (despite being restrained by the lack of modern technology).

Nonetheless, most indigenous peoples did manage, on balance, to coexist sustainably with the natural world considerably more successfully, and for a great deal longer, than moderns. And a key to their relative success has been an Earth-oriented spirituality with practical ethical implications which restrain, at least, destructive practices.[8] It must be added, however, that another reason for their success, in addition to relatively low-impact technology, was simply their much lower numbers; but this also was partly a result of the same ethic. But this is a discussion we shall have to continue in Chapter 12, in the section 'Traditional Ecological Knowledge'.

What is needed is to encourage and strengthen people's awareness and appreciation – which already exists, although it is rarely articulated – of the Earth and all its life as sacred: not an abstract Life, but one that is embodied and embedded in specific relationships, communities and places.[9] (There is a valid parallel here with what ecofeminists such as Salleh have pointed to: the nurturing labour, also already in place but too often unrecognized, that is another fundamental part of an effective ecocentrism.)

The best short term for such a spirituality is one which early anthropologists applied pejoratively to the religion of supposedly primitive people: **animism**.[10] But we in the West need, and should, no longer accept their assumption of 'our' cultural superiority. Far from it: as Kane writes, 'all the work that various peoples have done – all the work that peoples must do – to live with the Earth on the Earth's terms is pre-empted by the dream of transcendence' (1998: 255). That dream has turned toxic. It is also an aberration; for the vastly greater part of the time humanity has existed, its spiritual baseline was indigenous animism, and its displacement in and by modernity has closely coincided with the growing ecological holocaust. So let us consider animism more closely.

The best recent scholarly study, by Graham Harvey, describes animists as 'people who recognize that the world is full of persons, only some of whom are human, and that life is always lived in relationship with others' (2005: xi). It follows from the last point that ethics is integral to animism; and since the persons are not restricted to humans, *the ethics involved is ecological.* I hope the coherence between ecocentrism and post-secularism, and animism in particular, is therefore clear. In all its versions, value is found not in an abstract, objectified or commodified Nature, but in a more-than-human nature that is sensuous and alive, and which is always *potentially* a subject or set of subjects. (Not *necessarily*: that would simply reimpose an 'animist' abstract universalism.) It is embodied and embedded in specific relationships, communities and places, and realized in ongoing more-than-human relationships.

In the context of an ecocentric spirituality, especially important are particular *places* which, being sacred, serve to anchor the narratives which encode local ecological wisdom. In Kane's words: '[T]he notion of the sanctity of place is vital. . . . Once the power of the place is lost to memory, myth is uprooted; knowledge of the earth's processes becomes a different kind of knowledge, manipulated and applied by man' (1998: 50). I would add that the most compelling narratives are mythic: often anthropocentrically and androcentrically so, but not necessarily. As Kane skilfully shows, myth itself, at its most basic and powerful, concerns and expresses 'the ideas and emotions of the Earth' (1998: 34). That understanding opens the door to a wider cultural apprehension of the real drama: one in which we are not the stars but members ('plain citizens', in Leopold's words) of a much larger cast, with whom our destiny is inextricably linked.

A recent report compiled for the Gaia Foundation defined a sacred site as 'a place in the landscape . . . which is especially revered by a people, culture or cultural group as a focus for spiritual belief and practice or likely religious observance'. It concluded that such places, from the humble and obscure to the grand, have a major role to play in the contemporary 'rekindling of an ancient relationship with the land' that is by no means confined (indeed, must not be confined) to indigenous peoples (Thorley and Gunn 2008: 12, 34). An example from England, the first industrialized country and still one of the most overdeveloped (as well as overpopulated) in the world, is the way Neolithic sites such as Stonehenge have become sites of annual pilgrimage for hundreds of thousands of people as part of a process of 'touching base', reorienting their lives to the places and seasons of the natural world.

As Lovelock amusingly remarks, the quasi-religious valuation of nature is sufficiently popular that 'the churches of the monotheistic religions, and the recent heresies of humanism and Marxism, are faced with the unwelcome truth that some part of their old enemy, Wordsworth's Pagan, "suckled in a creed outworn", is alive within us' (1995: 206). And indeed, paganism – that is, the collective spirituality oriented to the natural world, the seasons, the feminine and what is known (or thought to be known) about local indigenous traditions – has an obvious place in this discussion. It is a fascinating phenomenon, but modern paganism is so various (embracing every-thing from Odinism to Wicca), and raises issues of such complexity,[11] that I am not going to attempt to summarize them here except to note that in overall ecocentric terms, it must surely be a good thing. At the same time, paganism is unlikely to sweep through the masses in such numbers and to such a depth as to usher in a new ecological era. But then, nothing is; it is enough to have something to contrib-ute.

The same could be said of other ancient spiritualities which might be fairly described as animistic. These include the whole rich family of native American traditions; the aboriginal Australian honouring the land by singing and walking its songlines; the Daoism of the *Daodejing* and the *Zhuangzi*; and the original 'religion' of Japan, Kami Nagari, later known as Shinto ('spirit way'). As we should by now expect, all have much to offer in supporting an ecocentric way of life; and, at the same time, without invalidating that truth, none has been able to prevent the anthropocentric ravaging of nature in either their native or new homes. Nonetheless, Bateson's remark applies in reverse, too: the animist re-enchantment of more-than-human nature is no fluffy optional extra. It has highly political and, ecologi-cally speaking, positive consequences. But a prerequisite is realizing that re-enchantment is not an act of will: that would simply be a reassertion of anthropocentric arrogance (as if it was really up to us whether or not to enchant the world!). Rather, it is an intention, a stance, a way of being in the world that is open, in a disciplined way, to *its* enchantment. As the Zen master Shunryu Suzuki remarked: 'The world is its own magic.'

Maybe we need a new religion. Watson says so: 'What we need if we are to survive is a new story, a new myth, and a new religion. We need to replace anthropocentrism with biocentrism. We need to construct a religion that incorporates all species and establishes nature as sacred and deserving of respect' (quoted in Bron Taylor 2010: 99). Taylor detects the stirrings of this 'terrapolitan' or 'dark green' reli-gion (2010: 196, 212).

I couldn't agree with Watson more, but it doesn't seem like that is going to happen any time soon; or at least, soon enough. And the fact is, as I quoted Sandler earlier saying, 'the majority of the world's population subscribes to some religious tradition, so to be relevant to the actual world an environmental ethic must be able to engage those traditions' (2005: 10). Furthermore, in both power and numbers, those traditions are led by the global ones of Christianity, Islam, Chinese traditional, Hinduism and Buddhism. So notwithstanding their profound ambivalence vis-à-vis the natural world – the three Abrahamic religions tend to locate ultimate value in a transcendent God and other-worldly heaven, and both Hinduism and Buddhism arguably emphasize the need to transcend this world – and despite their record of having long condoned (or at least not opposed) ecologically destructive development,[12] ecocentrics must be prepared to engage with them. In the case of Christianity, we have already seen (in Chapter 3) how it offers invaluable (albeit minority) resources for supporting ecological practices. The same could be shown of the others.

It's not only a matter of what religions have to offer ecocentrism. There is also the reverse to consider. The challenge to mainstream religion of the ecological crisis, and of ecocentrism as a direct and uncompromising response, was sounded in this mighty blast by Rowe (published, appropriately, in *The Trumpeter* [1994]): 'Blessed are those who make sacrifices to preserve and sustain the non-human, human-containing world. Cursed are those who wilfully destroy Earth's creativity and beauty. If religions cannot incorporate such ethics in their theologies, they too stand condemned.'

Green Buddhism?

Let us turn to a religion that many ecologically minded people in the West think shows unusual promise: Buddhism. There is a plethora of anthologies and edited collections whose titles speak for themselves: *Dharma Rain: Sources of Buddhist Environmentalism*, for example, and *Dharma Gaia: A Harvest of Essays in Buddhism and Ecology*.[13] Nor is this hope without evidence on the ground. Buddhism was for a long time a religion with a strong monastic base, albeit one that always extended to lay communities, so it is not surprising that activism remains a minority phenomenon. Nonetheless, there are influential Buddhist-inspired movements on behalf of social and environmental causes, including the Sarvodaya Shramadana movement in Sri Lanka; Sōka Gakkai International, based in Japan; the Sathirakoses-

Nagapradipa Foundation in Thailand, where monks have for many years been leading campaigns against deforestation; and the tireless work of the curent Dalai Lama, Thich Nhat Hanh, Sulak Sivaraksa and other eminent individual Buddhists. In America, the UK and elsewhere, there are now active a small but encouraging number of 'engaged Buddhist' groups.[14]

In fact, Western Buddhism – since the initial Japanese Zen pioneers in the 1960s, then a smaller wave of Theravadan teachers, but particularly since the Tibetan Buddhist diaspora began – has significantly changed under the impact of its new cultural environment, and those changes are gradually finding their way back East. There are three of particular significance, all (I would say) highly positive: the increasing importance and strength of lay practice, of women practitioners and teachers, and of ecological awareness.

If Buddhism is to contribute to an effective ecological ethic outside its traditional heartlands, it must be translated into, and become part of, local personal and cultural idioms in ways that do not sacrifice its integrity. Here, Gary Snyder's *The Practice of the Wild* (1990) still shows the way better than any. However, I am going to draw principally on a more recent book, David E. Cooper and Simon P. James's *Buddhism, Virtue and Environment* (2005), which is testament to the large body of excellent scholarly work that also now exists; but this one, as its title indicates, is particularly relevant.[15]

The authors are critical of much 'green' and 'ecological' Western Buddhism, accusing its proponents of pious and facile portrayals of Buddhism as straightforwardly ecocentric, and trying to align it with ideas of an all-embracing holistic 'unity' or monist 'Oneness similar to Advaita Vedānta's Absolute or Spinoza's God/Nature' (2005: 115). In this, there is no doubt they are right. Such ideas not only misrepresent Buddhism; as we have seen when considering 'Self-realization', because they downplay the vital importance of relationships, and therefore ethics, they are anti- (or at least non-) ecological: the antithesis of an ecological ethic, not its fulfilment.

Nonetheless, Buddhism has a lot to to offer, ecologically speaking. For example, the key doctrine of 'dependent origination' or 'conditioned arising' (*pratītya-samutpāda*, in Sanskrit) – according to which the nature of everything is constituted by everything else in a network of interdependent conditions which is always changing[16] – is surely powerfully ecological (more than these authors allow). It is also radically egalitarian, because every entity without exception, from (say) a micro-organism to (say) a god, is subject to the three 'marks' of existence: no transcendent self (*anatta*), impermanence (*anicca*), and suffering (*dukkha*). All are therefore equally deserving of compassion. This may not be exactly ecocentric – being more *a*centric – but it is certainly not anthropocentric.

The ethical nature of the Buddhist emphasis on loving-kindness (*mettā*) and compassion (*karuṇā*) is obvious, and it is worth adding that they are decidedly equivalent neither to sentimentality nor to total absorption in or identification with another, and must be combined wisdom or insight (*prajñā*) in action. (In Buddhism, action is what counts; beliefs and views only matter insofar as they help or hinder practice.) In Eastern Asian Mahayana Buddhism in particular – probably thanks to the cultural influence of indigenous Daoism in China and Shinto in Japan – the candidates for compassion gradually extended to plants, mountains, rivers and even soil, although a problem we encountered with Christianity arises here too: they may indeed need saving from developers, but do they need us to enlighten them? Isn't that rather anthropocentrically patronizing?

Cooper and James take their stand on somewhat different grounds. Convincingly and in detail, they argue that the place of ethics in Buddhism is 'central and integral' (2005: 57), and that Buddhist ethics is a virtue ethics which involves learning to do the right thing naturally and spontaneously. (This understanding accords, if you remember, with Varela's definition of ethics quoted in Chapter 4.)[17] Furthermore, Buddhist virtues should be exercised with respect to nonhuman life: 'on the Buddhist account, the virtue of compassion must be exercised in our relations with all sentient beings' – where 'sentient' can be defined far more widely than in the standard Western account – 'not just humans, so that someone who was compassionate in his dealings with other humans but not in his relations with non-human animals would not be regarded as compassionate at all' (2005: 128–9). After all, 'the desire to be free of suffering is common to all, and it is this desire that forms the basis for the sense of solidarity at the root of solicitude' (2005: 130). (Recall here Plumwood's emphasis on solidarity as 'the most fundamental of political relationships'.) There is thus enormous potential (which in various people and projects is, to at least some degree, already realized) for a specifically *ecological* Buddhist ethic.

Note 'other animals', however. Cooper and James insist that Buddhism concern is solely with individuals, so it cannot accommodate 'a moral concern for species' (2005: 141) or for ecosystems. Unlike them, I view this point (insofar as it is true, which I am not really in a position to judge) as a deficiency, one which potentially disqualifies this particular Buddhist ethic from being considered fully ecocentric. John Rodman's observation, already quoted above in Chapter 7, must be accommodated: 'I need only to stand in the midst of a clear-cut forest, a strip-mined hillside, a defoliated jungle, or a dammed canyon to feel uneasy with assumptions that could yield the conclusion that no human action can make any difference to the welfare of anything but sentient animals' (1977: 89).

Cooper and James are also quick to reject the idea of intrinsic value. They agree that other beings should not be treated only instrumentally, but why not? If it is only because of the ill-effects on humans of doing so (as per Kant), then the ethic is disablingly anthropocentric. They rightly reject that in favour of the answer: because for Buddhists, it is ethically wrong. But a principal reason it is wrong is surely because it violates others' flourishing, their 'good-of-a-kind', while not contributing to the common (ecological) good but instead the 'good', narrowly and unsustainably construed, of one species alone. Rather, we should value others for their own sake, not ours – which is intrinsic value in all but name. Neither of these points, however, means that a green Buddhist virtue ethic is anything other than important and even inspiring.

11

Moral Pluralism and Pragmatism

The Poverty of Monism

Moral pluralism is the view that our ethical life consists of a number of different principles or values which can conflict, and which cannot be boiled down to just one. They can be compared practically in the course of arriving at a decision; but in themselves, to a greater or lesser extent, they are 'incommensurable', so any agreement (which is relative) must be negotiated and agreed, and any such decision, in taking one principle as its guide, always runs the risk of (so to speak) offending one or more of the others.

Such a view has been taken by some great thinkers: from Machiavelli and Nietzsche to William James, Max Weber and Isaiah Berlin.[1] In the latter's words:

> The notion that there must exist final objective answers to normative questions, truths that can be demonstrated or directly intuited, that it is in principle possible to discover a harmonious pattern in which all values are reconciled, and that it is towards this unique goal that we must make; that we can uncover some single central principle that shapes this vision, a principle which, once found, will govern our lives – this ancient and almost universal belief . . . seems to me invalid, and at times to have led (and still to lead)

to absurdities in theory and barbarous consequences in practice. (1969: lv–lvi)

Nonetheless, pluralism remains a distinctly minority view. The reason is simple, if deep: the dominant kind of ethics in the West – from Greek philosophical and Christian religious to modernist/ humanist – is profoundly monist. Its fundamental premise is that there is *a single reference point*, whereby, to quote Weber, 'one can, in principle, master all things by calculation' (1991: 139).[2] In terms of the logic of this belief, whether this single principle or value is spiritual (God) or material (scientific truth) is secondary, although not unimportant: the former, as the ultimate mystery, ultimately cannot be mastered, whereas the latter does hold out the promise of ultimate mastery. Such monism is necessarily also universalist, since if there is only one such principle it must, by definition, apply every- where without exception. Of course, to ensure that the one truth is correctly perceived and promulgated, a cast of approved interpreters is also needed. The result, as Barbara Herrnstein Smith trenchantly notes, is 'intellectual/political totalitarianism (the effort to identify the presumptively universally compelling Truth and Way and to compel it universally)' (1997: 179).

This worldview, and its operation, is one of the primary causes of our current ecological crisis, because, as Weber famously put it, the belief (note: the *belief*, sufficiently socialized and institutionalized, is all it takes) that everything can, at least in principle, be mastered by calculation results in 'the disenchantment of the world' (1991: 155). Now, as I mentioned earlier, the disenchantment of nature began with Greek philosophical monism (especially Plato) and monothe- ism, and in particular their combination in Christianity and, later, Islam. But it was sharply intensified by modern science. And we have seen that such disenchantment is a prerequisite to the physical desacration of nature by unrestrained exploitation.

It is also significant that it is virtually impossible to subscribe to a monist universalism without rejecting limits (since universal truth is, by definition, without any limits); and that rejection is another key element of anti-ecological modernity. Such monism is also deeply anthropocentric: it is humans alone who are licensed by God, or Truth, to work their will on nature without, in principle, any natural limits. Finally, it overrules our experience – perhaps particularly of nature – as worlds (plural) of effectively endless sensuous particulars.[3] In short, as William James demanded, 'Why should we envelop our many with the "one" that brings so much poison in its train?' (1977: 141).

As we have also seen, any ecological fundamentalism would merely replace the one true and universal God with Nature. (It matters little whether the 'Nature' here is mystical or scientific.) Such a move would not only leave the destructive logic untouched, but ecocentrism, albeit of a pathological kind, would thereby become the enemy of nature. That would be a disaster.

Perhaps I should add that a commitment to intrinsic value is not necessarily a monism either, although it could be interpreted that way. There is no need to, for two reasons (which are not mutually exclusive). First, there are different kinds of intrinsic value, such as that of an individual and that of a species or place. This is only a crippling flaw if you assume, as Platonists and 'realists' do, that a single universal truth is the only kind that will do.[4] But there are no convincing grounds for such an assumption; quite the contrary, it is highly implausible, outside perhaps higher mathematics (and even then). Which leads to the second point: in lived practice, even if a single kind of intrinsic value was agreed, the very act of such agreement would require papering over disagreements, and any application of the ideal would instantly bring out the differences – and thence, the pluralism – inherent in life as it is lived by the variously embodied and embedded beings we are.

It follows that the only way to resist and ultimately replace the inherently anti-ecological logic of monism is through pluralism. And that means a *moral* as well as epistemological pluralism.[5] To quote Weber again: 'We are placed into various life-spheres, each of which is governed by different laws.' And being various, 'the ultimately possible attitudes toward life are irreconcilable, and hence their struggle can never be brought to a final conclusion' (1991: 123, 152). Furthermore, as I have already argued, in this situation science cannot make ethical choices for us. It 'presupposes that what is yielded by scientific work is important in the sense that it is worth being known. . . . [But] this presupposition cannot be proved by scientific means. It can only be *interpreted* with reference to its ultimate meaning, which we must reject or accept according to our ultimate position towards life' (1991: 143).

It follows that different considerations can *validly* apply in different cases, and that each case can *properly* be viewed in different ways.[6] Connections must then be made, and decisions taken, on grounds to be argued and established contingently in each case, which is to say (in the broad sense), politically. And those taking the decisions must therefore take responsibility for them, rather than hiding behind supposedly transcendental truths: a real advance.[7]

Abandoning what the philosopher Bernard Williams called 'a rationalistic conception of rationality' (1993: 18) – which asks reason (including scientific reason) to do what it cannot – does not make choice arbitrary, any more than does dispensing with the notion that truth must be singular. (There is a strong parallel here with what we saw earlier about how realists view the consequences of *what they think of* as relativism.) Neither confused nor dishonest, moral pluralism is, in Midgley's words, 'simply a recognition of the complexity of life'.[8]

Nor is it an ethical disaster. On the contrary, as Christopher Stone writes: 'It is by the choices we affirm in this zone of ultimate uncertainty that we have our highest opportunity to exercise our freedoms and define our characters' (1995: 525).[9] In other words, it is essential to the process of developing an ethically virtuous character – including ecologically virtuous – both individually and socially.[10]

The Consequences of Pluralism

We began this book by noting the gravity of the current ecological crisis. The subject of moral pluralism provides an opportunity to ask: what follows from this crisis as such? The short and perhaps unwelcome answer is that nothing *necessarily* follows from it, no matter how serious it is or may become. The reason is that any perception, assertion, valuation and meaning of ecocrisis is unavoidably only one among others, none of which is self-evidently true, let alone their implications. All of them are unavoidably contingent (partial, local, unstable) – which is *not* to say merely subjective – and competing in a complex rhetorical economy of claims and counterclaims, values and counter-values, all of them with actual or potential winners and losers (relatively speaking, of course). As Smith puts it, 'There is no way to give a final reckoning that is simultaneously total and final. There is no Judgement Day. There is no *bottom* line anywhere, for anyone or for "man"' (1988: 149). Indeed, when the end of the world for human beings comes, the last two will probably be arguing about what it means (assuming, of course, that they notice in time). And if they aren't, the reason won't be because its meaning is 'obvious'; it will be because they decided, and managed, to agree on something.

This is bound to be deeply frustrating for ecocentric ethicists. You can almost hear them saying, 'Everything – human rights, health, the lot – depends on ecosystems. No Earth, no nothing! There is no justice on a dead planet!' But I'm afraid that even this truth, unavoidably, is a claim and a value competing in an economy of many others; and as such it is not, even so baldly put as that, self-evident. Nothing that could happen, not even severe ecosystemic breakdown or ecological collapse, would *in itself* make ecocentrism universally accepted; people would, and will, always be able to come up with other explanations. ('God's will' is a perennial favourite.) So illusions of 'self-evident objective truths' only make the ecocentric work that needs to be done – mainly, that of facilitating a green virtue ethic – still harder.

Actually, exasperation at people's inability or refusal to recognize ecological reality and do what is rational reveals a subtle anthropocentrism. The assumption, just like that of economists, is that the special if not the unique mark of humanity is reason – so why aren't we using it? But living by reason alone, or even giving reason automatic pride of place among the whole range of human and Earthian possibilities, is an anthropocentric pathology, and ultimately impossible. The idea of an ideally disembodied, non-emotional, analytical, calculative reason in the service of self-interest terminates in an ideology, invented and spread to justify exploiting some other men, nearly all women, virtually all nonhuman animals, and the Earth itself: most recently and 'successfully' through industrial capitalism. It doesn't actually describe human beings as such (apart from those few who have succeeded, asymptotically, in turning themselves into quasi-machines), so it also can't be used to distinguish us from other animals.

The upshot of a pluralist world for ecocentrism is this: ecocentrics realize that since everything on this Earth depends on it and its vital constituent parts – the true common good – where purely human good, values or interests clearly conflict with the well-being of the Earth, *the former must give way*. Nonetheless, that truth can never be taken for granted. As much as possible, and wherever and whenever possible, it must be *argued, publicized, fought for* and *lived*.

There is a silver lining to this conundrum, for pluralism helps relieve ecocentric ethicists of at least three burdens they are better off without:

1   A tendency to moral self-righteousness which is counterproductive in terms of its effect on members of the public whom they are trying to influence. However paradoxical it may seem, the intrinsic value of nature is something that must be established. And to proceed as if it was obvious (i.e., to everyone who isn't a fool or a knave) is not the most promising way to do so.

2   A tendency to despair when they dramatically fail to change the public and/or offcial mindset, partly because of the first problem, combined with underestimating just how hard it is to do so. Any positive change will be incremental, partial, uneven and contested, and a grasp of pluralism would make this clearer from the outset.

3   The potential, at least, to entertain a green version of 'intellectual/political totalitarianism', which in this case takes the form of dogmatic misanthropy. It is usually nothing more than a side effect of the personal despair just mentioned, which is a more serious occupational hazard for ecocentrics. As I noted when discussing Deep Ecology, full-blooded and dangerous green misanthropy is actually strikingly rare, especially compared with how common lethal anthropocentrism is.

The case for moral/ethical pluralism overlaps closely with that for **pragmatism**. That word commonly refers to a mindset primarily concerned with what works in practice as distinct from theory, and the philosophical version is not radically different; it simply fleshes out such concern theoretically and philosophically. Oversimplifying, practice, or *praxis*, in the relevant context, is both the starting point and terminus of theory, or what is considered to be true.[11]

Pluralists are not necessarily pragmatists, nor vice-versa, but the consequences of pragmatism for ecocentric ethics are practically identical with those of pluralism, with perhaps a slightly different emphasis. What follows is that ecocentrics must be able to work together with those who are committed to mid-green or intermediate, light green or shallow, and even outright anthropocentric, ethics when there is real potential common ground on a particular issue. An ecocentric point of view is one among many, not a revealed Truth, and allies are not exactly thick on the ground, so when the opportunity arises to do so without sacrificing ecocentric principles, alliances must be forged.

As Bryan Norton (1991) has pointed out, agreement on principles can *follow* agreement on practice, i.e., what to do in or about a concrete situation or problem. (I have already criticized the crippling concession to anthropocentrism, however, in assuming convergence between the interest of people and nonhuman nature, and privileging so-called enlightened self-interest in order to remove any possible conflicts.) This is another aspect of the kind of labour-intensive, hands-on democracy-in-action just mentioned which ecocentric ethics requires in order to make a difference. Such agreement, however, is not a matter of necessity, and assurances of certain win–win solutions are pure pie-in-the-sky. There are absolutely no guarantees that policies in the interest of humanity and those in the interest of nonhuman nature will converge; all we can say is that, in certain instances, they may.[12]

Multicentrism

In a very interesting discussion, Anthony Weston advocates 'multi-centrism': something that is very close to pluralism as I have outlined it here. For example, it shares admiration for William James's pluralism and 'radical empiricism', and for the emphasis on relationality (respect, negotiation, solidarity), rather than 'unity', that is common to so many voices of eco-ethical sanity.[13] As Weston says, we cannot have an adequate idea of another being 'until we *already* have approached them ethically: that is, until we have offered them the space and time and occasion to enter into relationship. Ethics both implies and is implied by etiquette, in this sense, itself.' It follows that, as against monocentrism, '[o]nce other centers are acknowledged, always somewhat opaque to us as we are to them, there is no alternative but to work things out together, as far as is possible, when all are affected by the decisions taken' (2004: 19). Such an attitude is very close, not coincidentally, to an animist way of living.

Weston is critical of ecocentrism, arguing that it is 'too big' to be a (proper) centre, being 'not nodes of a matrix but the matrix itself' (2004: 35). He also suggests that its real point is to function as 'a form of resistance or refusal of the usual anthropocentrism'. His conclusion is that 'To "go beyond" anthropocentrism, on a multicentric view, what we must really challenge is not the "anthropo-" part but the implicit (con)*centrism*' (2004: 35, 37).[14]

There is a complex and subtle nest of issues here, and Weston's points are well taken as far as they go. To begin with, ecocentrism is a name for an *ethos* ('particular character and disposition, moral significance') or *habitus* ('system of durable, transposable dispositions') which is open to finding ultimate value in all life as such, including its inorganic parts; and that entails a particular way of living (individually or collectively) and a certain quality of relationships with others.[15] It is indeed arrayed against another ethos/habitus: anthropocentrism. But that is not a problem or even avoidable, since all terms depend for their meaning on *not* including something else. (Crudely put, 'cup' is only usable if it only refers to what we generally agree is, or could act as, a cup, as distinct from what isn't or couldn't.)

The multicentrism Weston advocates, however, is of a different order to that of ecocentrism, and the two should not be confused. Multicentrism is more of the same order as pluralism, including the kind that animism implies. It actually coheres very well with ecocentrism, because it encourages the awareness that life consists of many centres and therefore relations, not only human ones. (Indeed, in some construals – Buddhist, animist and Jamesian, for example – 'relations are fundamentals, relata are abstractions'.)[16] And it certainly does not disqualify ecocentrism as a stance which is indeed as 'big', or as open, as possible, as long as that openness or bigness is understood in *lived* terms – experience, or 'phenomenology', rooted in a way of living, or 'ontology' – rather than as an abstract universal truth to be enforced along the lines of, 'It really *is* this way, whether you know it or not.' Furthermore, within that way of living (first-order ecocentrism), you certainly can 'centre on the Earth' (one instance of second-order multicentrism). I'm sure Weston himself has experienced *geophany*: a showing forth of the Earth.[17]

Weston's own conclusion is therefore an important half-truth. It remains fundamental that '[a]nthropocentrism, properly interpreted, is a very useful concept for both the activist and the theorist and should be a major conceptual focus of environmental critique' (Plumwood 2002: 124). And we need to challenge both parts: the 'anthro' part – an unhealthy kind or degree of human-centredness – *and* centrism: an unhealthy attachment to any particular centre in the face of what the situation ethically demands.

Here it might be asked: is it possible to be completely acentric or de-centred? There is a psychotic version in the fetishization of a totally objective 'view from nowhere' or 'view from everywhere'.[18] At the other end of a scale of sanity, perhaps, there is also a Buddhist version, namely enlightenment. That entails *not* a lack of centres (or egos or selves), however, but a lack of attachment *to* them, such as they are. I daresay there will always be centres as long as there is anything, and no position – even ones advocating the radical uncertainty of full acentrism such as Middle Way Buddhism, apophatic Christian theology, Derridean poststructuralism, etc. – can actually enforce non-attachment, even to those positions themselves.

My own view is therefore that the closest to what is both desirable and practically possible (certainly collectively and perhaps individually) is a poly- or multicentric world. As Plumwood points out, 'Depending on how it is developed, a sufficiently inclusive and flexible polycentrism might also be described as a (relatively) de-centred world' (2002: 256).[19] And insofar as there must, or at least almost certainly will, be the horizon of an effectively ultimate 'centre', let us have one that is genuinely pro-life (if I may put it that way), and whose starting-point is as roomy, inclusive, democratic and pluralist as possible: ecocentrism.

12

Green Citizenship and Education

Making it Real

This book is not intended to offer a detailed analysis of the practical implementation of an ecocentric ethic. However, it would be irresponsible to say nothing about it whatsoever. So what would be required to make it one of the ethics, at least, that determines what actually happens?

As that question implies, an ecocentric ethic (I suggest) must be consequentialist; it must be able to make a real positive difference in the world. But it also must be deontological, inasmuch as it involves rules which are, through both rewards and punishments, actively enforced (rewarding a culture of encouraging ecocentric behaviour and shaming its opposite being at least as important as legal sanctions, although those too are needed). Finally and most crucially, however – as that last point implies – an ecocentric ethic requires a green virtue ethic (GVE), in which ecological virtue becomes a central value in our societies and cultures. Another way to put it is that an ecological virtue ethic, if it is to be more than a way for a few people to feel good about themselves, depends on practically realizing the idea of *green citizenship*: being good citizens of the Earth community.[1]

Being primarily a citizen is already an extremely significant departure from being primarily a consumer or customer; it is the inherently social relationality of the former that leads, rather than the possessive individualism of the latter. Community takes in all the generations – of whom the eldest, being potentially the wisest, are by no means least – and, as I have argued throughout, its sociality is biotic. Both ethically and ecologically, we can no longer afford to restrict the social to humans alone, as if we had nothing to learn from or give to all the others, or could even exist without them. (In indigenous traditions, of course, this is no news.)

Most broadly put, the goal is to 'create and maintain structures and procedures that give as much scope as possible to the laborious working out, individually and in concert, of courses of action that are the "best" (all things considered . . .) for each, and each set, of us' (Smith 1988: 179). In this process, there are educational, political, economic, social and cultural dimensions to green citizenship, all of which are important.

For example, deep ecological ethics must be brought to the attention of both the relevant authorities and the public (although not in the same way, of course). Authorities must be helped to reconceptualize their perceived political and economic remits in relation to the ecological dimension; the public, to imagine plausible cultural and social life-narratives which include that dimension. Somewhere in between, sharing both these challenges, are the community decision-makers.

For many people and organizations directly involved with ecological ethics, the primary task is to get ecocentric ideas and values into the 'collective mindstream' of the NGOs, think-tanks, quasi-academic institutes and the media, which tend to determine what become 'issues' and how they are treated, and which are themselves trying to influence state/government policy regarding these issues. This can be more productive and important than lobbying the government ('up one level') directly, although of course that too is often necessary. Doing so will often involve articulating and construing the concerns and fears of so-called ordinary people ('down one level'), though again, not just doing that. Getting an idea 'onto the table' is often a prerequisite for getting it to influence action – whether action by the state or in some grassroots way.[2]

Of course, pressure must be put on governments at all levels finally to begin putting practices of green citizenship at the top of their civic and political agenda. (Some enlightened leadership once in a while would help too.) As with any political programme, both carrots and sticks will be needed. But it won't succeed without a popular groundswell in its favour: that is, a *culture* of green citizenship. And that will depend vitally on people 'doing it for themselves': collectively organizing themselves and acting as citizens. Indeed, ultimately, all that governments can do (although it is a lot) is help or hinder that process. (In the next chapter, we shall be looking at what could be done, and what is already under way.)

Noteworthy in this context is the finding by the Program on International Policy Attitudes (PIPA) that public opinion is frequently more progressive than that of its so-called representatives. Its polls consistently show, for example, that 'world publics strongly favour requiring more wind and solar energy and more efficiency even if it increases costs [and] that oil needs to be replaced as an energy source', that 'international polls find robust global support for increased efforts to address climate change' and that 'most would pay higher energy bills to address climate change'.[3]

The work that needs doing also includes patient and dogged efforts to influence the institutions – e.g., all the media, schools and universities – that in turn tend to control how people perceive natural goods.[4] Textbooks, monographs and research reports certainly have their place in this process, but they are almost entirely overwhelmed by the immense, and immensely damaging, popular power of celebrity money-worship, which effectively sends out the message that the most important thing to do in life is to make as much money for yourself as fast as you can, or else marry someone who has. Conversely, a few 'green' popular TV soap operas would probably do more to propagate ecocentric values, and faster, than any number of specialist books.[5] But who owns the media? A green bandwagon might tempt them to do it, because it would attract viewers, but that would encourage advertisers to sell more products and reinforce a culture of consumerism – even if they are 'green' products.

In any case, a culture of green citizenship urgently needs popular life-narratives which allow and encourage people to imagine and begin to inhabit fulfilling ecocentric lives as Earth citizens, rather than as the anthropocentric consumers that companies want to create. Such narratives are central to the proper work of culture. And central to specifically ecocentric counter-narratives must be the theme of *limits*, showing that you can live a good life despite them

– indeed, that it is only possible to do so through recognizing and working *with* them. Besides, the intrinsic goods of partner, family, friends, colleagues, animals and nature can afford deep pleasure (untainted by the suspicion that they are only providing it because you have paid for it). But note: 'one can get love only for love', not for usefulness (Peterson 2009: 156).

There are not only practical constraints but limits *in principle* to the amount of energy each of us can fairly consume, the number of children we can responsibly have, the amount of rubbish we can throw away, and so on. And not only are 'resources' not infinite (a fact no amount of technology can finally overcome), thus requiring them to be carefully shared with all kinds of others; personal security too is necessarily limited. The ultimate limit of all embodied life, which is therefore profoundly ecological, is, of course, death. The bedrock assumption of consumerism – what makes it a culture of denial – is that you can ultimately somehow buy and/or believe your way out of anything, maybe even that. (As Lewis Lapham observed, 'Dying is un–American'.) In contrast, ecocentrism asserts that only 'When we belong to the world' – not, note, the reverse! – do 'we become what we are'. Thus there is an important psychological dimension, both individual and collective, to this project.[6]

For the great majority of people, it must be said, the idea of the survival of biodiversity, or even of the human species as such, is so abstract as to be virtually meaningless. But this too is the sort of thing that requires cultural as well as political work, creative as much as intellectual or political, enabling it to become real in our collective imagination.

On this theme, I highly recommend Anna Peterson's recent *Everyday Ethics and Social Change: The Education of Desire* (2009). As Peterson writes, we need to 'construct an ethic based on the values that we [already] enact in our most meaningful encounters with other people and with nonhuman nature'. That arises from *experiencing* ourselves 'as social creatures enmeshed in and joyfully dependent upon a web of relationships and practices over which we do not have ultimate control'. It also connects our particulars to the bigger picture of more–than–human structures and processes. (It is to open our eyes to the possibility of doing so, and give us some ideas and encouragement to that end, that corresponding narratives are so important.) As Peterson points out:

Our particular bonds provide not only entryways but also concrete examples for the gradual construction of a practice-based ethic. . . . The education of desire that we need must be first and foremost a practical education, which takes place in and through practices of community, of play, of un-self-interested giving and receiving. (2009: 150–1, 160)

This is precisely the lifelong ecosocial project of developing a green virtue ethic that we discussed in Chapter 4, as well as its Buddhist version in Chapter 10, and now here.

Eckersley too has some helpful things to say under the rubric of **ecocommunitarianism**. Notwithstanding the global effects of ecocrisis, and programmes to deal with it globally (such as reducing everything to issues of carbon), the fact remains that

human loyalties are typically more intense at the embodied, face-to-face level . . . because this is how humans learn to become social beings . . . wherever the circle of human compassion *ends*, it always *begins* with the local . . . [and] it is these formative, local, social and ecological attachments that provide the basis for sympathetic solidarity with others.

Therefore 'the *primary* ecocommunitarian response to transboundary ecological problems would still be to work creatively with the moral resources within particularistic communities towards sustainability' (2006: 103, 104; emphases in original). Seen in this light, the attempt currently gathering pace in the global North to stave off ecological disaster and save our selfish and unsustainable lifestyles by reducing everything to issues of carbon and creating a corresponding financial market is only the latest abstract monism, and a particularly iniquitous one in that it sacrifices the natural world in the *name* of ecology.

A Long Revolution?

One of the practical-political problems here is that, to the extent an ethic remains fundamentally conventional (anthropocentric), it will tend to be persuasive but effect little change; whereas, to the extent it is radical (ecocentric), it will tend, for that very reason, to be easily marginalized. As Andrew McLaughlin observes: 'A radical critique that questions society's basic belief system and also wishes to gain assent from the members of that society must confront the fact that any appeal to "common sense" or intuitions will not go deeply enough because our common sense is part of the problem' (1993b: 170).

A related point is that an appeal *purely* to ecocentric altruism seems in general almost certainly bound to fail. Yet an appeal to 'enlightened' self-interest is highly vulnerable to people's selfishness, short sense of time-scale and narrow interpretations of 'self', e.g., myself and my family, now and maybe for the next few years – all of which invites more ecological destruction. There is no escaping these general dilemmas, and every actual situation will require a different mix and balance, a compromise with reference to its particular problem and context.

Of course, if an ecocentrically radical politics is sufficiently pragmatic, and an anthropocentrically reformist politics is sufficiently extensive, they meet, rendering the distinction irrelevant in practice. It is also true that 'we do not in all cases need to await agreement on principles (much less on social solutions in which they are applied) before particular problems can be recognized as such' (Attfield 1983: 7).[7] However – and this is the key point – the ecocrisis requires an ecocentric ethic as a *regulative horizon*, an ethical context and ideal which may never be fully attained but which nonetheless indicate the right direction and help move things that way. As F. M. Alexander remarked: 'There is no such thing as a right position, but there is a right direction' (2000: 73).

Sylvan and Bennett have pointed out that real change can come about in two basic ways – and there are serious problems with both. One is slowly, through *reform*. But 'the overwhelming evidence is that not nearly enough will happen in time for anything but a grossly impoverished natural environment to emerge. . . . For much of the world's remaining wildernesses, for most of its remaining species, it is going to be all over in the next 20 years or so' (1994: 218–19): given some latitude with the 'or so', a prediction that, in 2010, still looks like coming true. Reform virtually never happens with that sort of speed, especially when the initial odds are so heavily against it.

The alternative is *revolution*, at least in a few key states. But 'were the styles of historic revolutions emulated, it would be a problematic and likely nasty medicine' (1994: 218–19). Such a revolution – for which it seems there would be little public support anyway – is very hard to achieve satisfactorily, and there is always the possibility that a state could 'fall the wrong way, for instance to a totalitarian far right' (1994: 218–19). The historical record of revolutions by the left is not encouraging either; paradigmatically, Bolshevism, Maoism and the Khmer Rouge, like the French Revolution they were modelled on, resulted in yet more Terrors and millions upon millions of violent deaths. It is also significant that both revolutionaries and reactionaries agree on not just the desirability of power (as long as they have it) but the need to control if not eliminate civil society, voluntary associations and middle-class professionals – in other words, any possible sources of independent thinking and action.

The moral, I think, is that strengthening and renewing *civil society, citizens' initiatives and locally-led movements* – with a real measure of autonomy from both the state (although they need some protection by, as well as from, the state) and corporations (for which private profit remains paramount) – is the most promising route to radical but relatively peaceful change. No real hope lies in trying to *start* at the top, with either state or business reforms; they are too compromised (especially the former by the latter). Nor can those at the very bottom, the hardest-hit victims of industrial capitalism, offer much; they have their hands full simply trying to survive. Given limited time and energy, therefore, the most promising place to start is with those intermediary associations and related citizens' initatives, and thence to put pressure on both governments and businesses to change accordingly. (And no, this is not a perfect prescription either; but absent a perfect world, there is no such thing.)

Of course, public opinion and political conditions could change if something goes badly wrong. Herman Daly rightly says that it may well take 'a Great Ecological Spasm to convince people that something is wrong with an economic theory that denies the very possibility of an economy exceeding its optimal scale. But even in that unhappy event, it is still necessary to have an alternative vision ready to present when crisis conditions provide a receptive public' (quoted in McLaughlin 1993: 218). Would there be ready and available, in that case, sufficiently well-thought-out and detailed ecocentric alternatives? Sylvan and Bennett wisely conclude that

'Requisite organization, well-thought-through directions, plans for action, and restructuring: such features are critical. Deep environmental groups should begin to prepare, carefully and thoroughly' (1994: 120). Also important is the attitude suggested by Ken Jones, to be a practical idealist: 'one who is accepting of her fear (and there is plenty to be afraid of) without being possessed by it. Living beyond optimism and pessimism, she is a patient and clear-sighted *possibilist*' (1993: 190).

Indeed, the question of attitude should not be neglected in a rush to green activism. It is to the credit of the green movement – including what might be said to be its 'spiritual' wing, neo-paganism – that, compared to the New Age movement and new religious movements, there is less self-indulgent spirituality in which the 'external' or 'outer' world, including nature, is regarded as secondary or inferior. (To see nature in such away simply accepts the premise of modern science of a nature without significant agency, subjectivity or soul.) But that does not mean that questions of one's own personal and subjective involvement with ecocentrism are entirely optional. Their complete neglect can result not only in losing touch with what one is trying to defend, but in 'burn-out' and despair that puts an end to activism too.[8]

Of course, the need for change is urgent; biotechnology, global warming, overpopulation, deforestation, extinctions and too many other crises are already well under way. But a longer view too is necessary, and much of it has to do with encouraging practices embodying the ethical virtue of green citizenship. It could be said, without much exaggeration, that it is only in the light of an ecocentric ethic that humans causing these things can be perceived as acting wrongly, even criminally; and it is only by the public expression of such an ethic through active green citizenship that anything will be done about them. Transnational companies are unlikely to forgo huge profits unbidden, any more than governments are to vote themselves out of office for a poor environmental record. 'A steady-state economy', as Jones points out, 'cannot exist without a whole steady-state culture to support it' (1993: 115). Further to that point, there is, for example, an urgent need for 'ecoliteracy' (Capra 1997: 289–95).

Ecological Education

Ecological education is central to developing green citizenship and a green virtue ethic.[9] Positively, as Jones's point implies, there is no long-term hope without *a culture of nature*, and negatively, its current decline (at least in the global North) is alarming. The trend could not be more clear: a large majority of British children now play more indoors than out, spending more than five hours a day in front of a screen, and the average American 8–18-year-old apparently now spends more than 53 hours a week (more than 7 hours a day!) using 'entertainment media'.[10]

An early pioneer of eco-education was Edith Cobb. In a paper entitled 'The Ecology of Imagination in Childhood' (1959) about 'the childhood experience of Nature', she emphasized how human potential is rooted in 'the child's perceptual relations with the natural world'. Such experience involves the child as a 'whole organism', not just his or her 'mind', and it is a qualitative and sensuous one.[11] As Livingston adds, developing Cobb's approach, '[t]he pre-adolescent seeks heterogenous experience with non-human phenomena of all kinds as essential nutrition for its further development into whole maturity' (1994: 129-30). The same experience supplies the basis of that child's relations as an adult with nonhuman nature. And whereas 'Wild Nature is of all things heterogenous', increasingly everything a young person now 'sees, hears, smells, touches, and tastes is a human artifact' (1994: 135). This should be recognized for what it is: an impoverishment and a deprivation, with correspondingly dangerous developmental effects.

Even in terms of straightforward information, it should and easily could be a fundamental part of every child's education to learn where his or her food (in all its kinds), water and energy come from, and how they get there, and where wastes (of all kinds) go to, and with what other effects for whom. But this kind of 'objective' knowledge should, as Bender says, be complemented by '[f]inding out, subjectively, where the most beautiful spots are, where we feel most empowered, afraid or happy, and what we share spiritually with the animals and other people (past and present) . . . Activities of both kinds are necessary to establish a healthy balance and a sense of kinship with our place' (2003: 375).

I would add that burdening children prematurely with eco-doom (turn out the lights or polar bears will die, etc.) without allowing and helping them to have direct experience of wild nature, and a personal relationship with its sensuous, plural qualities, is stupid, if not cruel. It will do nothing to help the natural world. And not wasting energy, etc. can be taught as a good thing in itself, without giving children an inflated sense of what they are personally responsible for and against which they might very well rebel, thus going to the opposite and equally unhelpful extreme of taking no responsibility whatever.

Up to a point, eco-education can be supported through media, both formally and informally educational, not only those showing nature in its richness and complexity, but telling stories in which nature is more than simply a background for the usual human drama. As Abram (e.g. 2007) has insisted, however, electronic media have serious inherent limitations. Most notably, the child is a passive recipient, not an active participant. Even 'interactive' media take place within the narrow cognitive parameters of visual simulation, and the most sophisticated kinds are still inescapably a kind of cartoon that objectifies the world and removes the viewer from it. Such (in effect) cartoons are undeniably entertaining, but it is dangerous to mistake them for an accurate representation of how the world works, either 'inner' or 'outer'; and their power and frequency today, combined with increasing nature deprivation, makes that all too easy.

Relatedly, computer simulation encourages the fantasy of ultimate human control. And a flat screen, no matter what is shown *on* it, can never replace a three-dimensional and multisensory encounter in real time and place. (I would add that what is selected to be shown can easily be influenced by ideological biases, e.g. a social Darwinian nature, 'red in tooth and claw', to the exclusion of cooperation and harmony.) The essential problem boils down to this: we can see the animals, but they can't see us. What this one-way gaze signifies, and *teaches*, is not relationship, or any kind of equality; rather, it is human mastery and nature as spectacle, ultimately entertainment. But real ecology is not something 'out there'. It is what we are *in*, and that is in *us*.[12]

C. A. Bowers (1993, 2000) also provides a critique of the ecological failure of modern educational theory and practice, including the fallacy of thinking that a computer on every school desk (or in every home) will help. The point is 'not so much what children *know* about nature that's important, as what happens to them when they are *in* nature (and not just in it, but in it by themselves, without grown-ups)'. To quote Kristen Lambert, an educator working with eco-education, children engaged in unstructured outdoor play 'set their own challenges, assess their own risks, take their own responsibility, have their own adventures, and learn from them. And what they learn can't be taught.'[13] Strikingly, this is just what Ivan Illich pointed out nearly four decades ago: 'paradoxically, what people most need to learn, they cannot be *taught* or *educated* to do' (1975: 81; emphases in original). The resistance to this truth from mainstream educators hasn't changed since then. (We'll put everything into telling children what they need to know rather than letting them discover it, or helping them to do so, because we can control teaching, and thereby the children. And above all, we must be in control.)

Illich also presciently remarked, in 1981, that 'machines which ape people are tending to encroach on every aspect of people's lives, and that such machines force people to behave like machines . . . to "communicate" with them *and* with each other *on the terms of the machine*' (1992: 47; my emphases). In the global North, the amount of time children spend 'communicating' with and through electronic media, on its terms, continues to spiral upwards. Those terms are a human artefact's terms – ones which take certain cognitive aspects of human being, create a model of them in the form of a computer and universalize the result. This cart then pulls the human horse. The whole apparatus is deeply anthropocentric: recall the long history of 'reason' (operationalized by psychology as cognition and now integrated with evolutionary theory) as a supposedly distinctive human (and particularly male) attribute which licenses 'our' unique privileges. And it would be absurd to think that that attitude is not communicated through the technology it informs.

David Orr and Richard Louv are two of the most influential eco-educators today.[14] Both recognize the acute challenge of urbanization but rightly insist that there is really no substitute for enabling children to have at least a minimum of unmediated access to, and unstructured play in, relatively wild nature, preferably local.

Negatively, the relentless educational emphasis on an endless instrumental succession – achieving high grades in order to land a top job in order to be financially and socially secure in order to . . . – is deadening, and sometimes deadly. The entire 'knowledge economy', with its 'impact agenda', 'targets' and 'learning outcomes' (and the ugly impersonal language is entirely appropriate) is homage to the anthropocentric rule of capital. So too is the privileging of its chief servants, maths and science, over the humanities.[15] This process is now starting earlier than ever, given a parental culture of fear (one wonders how many parents have ever compared actual 'stranger danger' with traffic fatalities, say) and hypercontrol, together with many parents' vicarious hyperambition that drives the same sort of educational culture. And the rule of Health and Safety, striving for impossibly total security, does not help either.

Orr, Louv and other authors present much evidence that the effects of media-driven 'nature deficit' can include alienation, depression, both cognitive and affective disorders, and a seriously stunted sense of, and relationship with, the natural world. Conversely, direct contact with nature tends to result in healthier physical, emotional, psychological and social development, starting with a stronger sense of wonder and of being *alive*, and extending to greater creativity, learning ability, self-esteem, flexibility, curiosity, social cooperation and appreciation of boundaries.

They also include many excellent practical proposals that cannot detain us here. But one I'm not sure receives sufficient emphasis is the importance of group rituals (whether of family or peers) to celebrate the seasons through appreciating what each season comes up with in that natural place. Thus we can learn to know the nature of our place – which is to say, in important part, *who* we are – and to love the cyclical round of life with which our places and lives are so intertwined.

As usual, Peterson makes some excellent points. The important thing, she says, is to create conditions

> in which reciprocity, emotional intimacy, and aesthetic pleasure can take precedence over use-value, profit, time management, and efficiency. These alternative values come to the fore when humans encounter nonhuman nature – when we spend time in places that are not structured primarily by human priorities and in interactions with nonhuman animals, who experience the world in distinctive ways, without the same goals, priorities, or assumptions as humans. (2009: 82)

Key to this is *play*: not 'educational', 'guided' or 'structured' play, but the real thing: unplanned, spontaneous and open-ended play, non-instrumental and open to all kinds of intrinsic value. There is a reason why other animals and most children (unless their desires have already colonized by capital, especially through advertisers) are good at play: they have 'little interest in the abstract and values of exchange and use'. Peterson even argues that play 'helps make possible utopian moments that can serve as critical grounds for evaluating and perhaps transforming the aspects of our lives that are dominated by utility and calculation' (2009: 156–7). This plausibly suggests in turn that commercial efforts to control and direct play through their 'games' is not just about selling specific products for a profit, but about capturing their desires and creating generations, a whole culture, of loyal consumers without the desire or ability to critically evaluate what is going on.

When play is out in nature (small-scale intimate places will serve perfectly well, as long as they are *relatively* wild), there is another important dimension involved: an experience of the intrinsic value of nature, and nature as non-instrumental. Or, in a word, its *wonder.* What could be more important for an ecological ethic? But note the paradox that surfaces with the point that 'time spent in nature is an end in itself, not a means to any other goal' (2009: 89). We encountered this before when considering an ecocentric ethic: the deepest positive effects of green education only work, are only good for us, if we value nature for its *own* sake. Intrinsic value will not be tricked: 'one can only get love for love'. Without that love, it has failed, and we are back to the anthropocentric and modernist agenda, no matter how subtle, of reason, knowledge and control.

The ideal situation, of course – actually, the most realistic one, properly speaking – would be for education for all and at all levels to cultivate and honour ecological intelligence. At the moment, only a few green shoots have appeared. There are some autonomous initiatives showing the way, however. In addition to the greening of the mainstream Scouts and Girl Guides, one is *Forest School Camps*, a British educational charity inspired by the Woodcraft movement, Native Americans, Quakers and others, which enables children to play and work together in nature in ways that encourage awareness of their interdependence and thus ethical responsibilities, both natural and social. Another more recent initiative is *Earth Scouts*, a national program in the USA based on the Earth Charter (discussed in Chapter 8) which engages children in personally developing

Earth-citizen virtues.[16] In this sort of context there are good things to be taught as well as learned: survival skills or 'bushcraft', traditional crafts, and uses of nature that are not exploitative.[17] But perhaps most important of all is for parents to let and help their own children to do these things, whether playing in the park or camping or helping with the gardening.

What about at the other end of the formal educational system: universities? Here, too, there are serious systemic problems. Going straight to the point, the Belgian philosopher of science Isabelle Stengers warns us:

> [T]he multifaceted machine called technoscience is in the process of redefining our own worlds in terms that makes them available for its comparative operations. The relative passivity of the academic world, lending itself to ranking systems of evaluation and productivity comparison which reshape it in a radical manner, is sufficient to demonstrate how easy it is to have people, [even those] who are not naive or impressed or overpowered, to submit to questions that are not only irrelevant but, as such, sound the death-knell of what matters for them.

She adds: 'Daring to speculate will not save us, probably, but it may at least give us words that both disentangle us from what is in the process of destroying us, and affirm a proximity with those who were already destroyed in the name of rationality, objectivity and the great divide between nature and culture.'[18] There is a weight of wisdom in these words that speaks directly to our subject as a whole.

Universities which are ever-increasingly led by the corporate agenda, especially direct funding and funding of research, and (even in the absence of this) a corporate, managerial and administrative model of education, raise uncomfortable questions. How is it possible to teach genuinely ecological values and concepts in an intellectual environment dominated by anthropocentrism, economism and scientism? Where it is not only a question of defending wisdom against knowledge, but knowledge against information? Where the trajectory is from questions of substance, pre-eminently ethical, to questions of method, culminating in what Midgley has aptly called 'methodolatry'? Especially given, in addition, the subtle and not-so-subtle pressures to toe the appropriate line in order to retain a decent career (a worthy goal in itself, when not so distorted). The answers will be as various as there are teachers, and I have faith in the latter; but they won't be easy to find, and sometimes one wonders.[19]

More generally, there is a damaging split in the culture of higher education between two opposing camps: scientific materialists on the one hand and cultural constructionists on the other, where each is trying to capture nature as a whole with, and for, their unsustainably one-sided versions. We have already mentioned this problem, which I have discussed in detail elsewhere (Curry 2003, 2008a), so I will just point out that both sides regard the natural world as essentially a passive resource, whether as one to be physically mastered or as one to be culturally appropriated and, with equally anthropocentric arrogance, given meaning and used for some human purpose or other.[20] Against this, a heartening tender green shoot is the appearance of the ecological humanities or **ecohumanities**.[21]

Traditional Ecological Knowledge

As I have mentioned, the nature that figures so importantly in eco-education is local. As Eckersley (2006: 104) asks, 'without some knowledge and attachment to our own riverbank – to this riverbank, not any old riverbank', or indeed riverbanks in general, why would we be motivated to defend other ones? Or to revert to Plumwood's point, whence solidarity? I want to suggest that, to a significant extent, the cultural dimension of our relationships with local nature will either consciously derive from surviving local indigenous traditions or it will involve *re*discovering what they knew. That should not be surprising. After all, who has lived in place the longest and in the least 'mediated' way? As a Crow elder ventured (quoted by Snyder 1990: 42) – generously, all things considered – 'You know, I think if people stay somewhere long enough – even white people – the spirits will begin to speak to them. It's the power of the spirits coming up from the land. The spirits and the old powers aren't lost, they just need people to be around long enough and the spirits will begin to influence them.'

I have already suggested that ecological ethics, even (or especially) a 'global' one, must have strong roots in particular places. 'Deep roots are not reached by the frost.' Local ethics can connect up to become effectively global, but the latter cannot exist without the former. An ecological ethics cannot be successfully imposed by diktat or purely as a matter of policy. Indeed, strictly speaking, it cannot be 'created' at all; it must be encouraged and articulated (joined up as well as voiced) on the basis of what is ecological and ethical in what people already value, know and do where they are.

Historically speaking, modernity is a very recent experiment, which, it is now very clear, has already had disastrous ecological results. It consists of about 1 per cent of the time that has lapsed since humans (anatomically identical with their present form) are thought to have first appeared. The main engine of modernity is commodity capitalism, the corresponding culture of which is consumerism (The other two engines, tightly intermeshed with the first, are techno-science and the modern nation-state.) We shall look at this in more detail in Chapter 13, but for now let me just point out that the entire modern economic system, or what Lewis Mumford (1964) called 'the megamachine', is based on, and requires, endless growth – in a single planet with finite resources.

The inability of capitalism (and orthodox socialism, its modern twin) to recognize real, natural and ultimately non-negotiable limits is what makes it inherently unsustainable, as well as anti-ecological. And the cultural dimension of this process is principally to replace local distinctiveness, variety and qualities (plural) with flattened, homogenized and standardized units, tending towards identical and interchangeable, of quantity (single: more or less of the same stuff). The prophet of this process was Max Weber, speaking in 1918: 'The fate of our times is characterised by rationalisation and intellectualisa-tion and, above all, by the "disenchantment of the world"' (Weber 1991: 155). That is not the whole story, by any means, but it is true as far as it goes – which is pretty far.[22]

The contrast that concerns us here is with the *local* and the *sustainable*: not the nonsense of 'sustainable development' or 'sustainable growth' which currently adorns the economic Emperor, lavishly praised by his courtiers, but real sustainability (to be explored in Chapter 13). It is internally entwined with local distinctiveness and, although I won't develop the point here, enchantment. Together, they are a central feature of what preceded modernity and has survived it, if only just, in the great array of different indigenous and traditional cultures whose peoples managed to live on the Earth, more-or-less sustainably, for tens of thousands of years before the ecocrisis. As Irvine says: 'There is no need to romanticise the past to appreciate that often people did find comparatively sustainable and convivial ways of organising their livelihoods.'[23] And as Manes points out, this is not just a thing of the past:

> [T]he path of environmental modesty is not utopian; it is being lived this minute by millions of tribal peoples around the world. And up until a few centuries ago it was the predominant way humans related to the natural world. On the contrary, our way of life is utopian, in the sense that it is unrealistic and naïve and cannot realize its fantasy of unlimited affluence and power free from all ecological restraints. (1990: 238)

Here we have rejoined our main topic in this section, because at the heart of non-modern sustainability is a fluid but tightly-knit mixture of local or bioregional scientifically ecological wisdom, spiritual values and corresponding ritual practices – ones which directly connect with our discussion in Chapter 10 of animism – and socio-political ethics which, altogether, is known as *traditional ecological knowledge* (TEK). TEK encodes values, facilitates perceptions, prescribes some practices and proscribes others, growing out of experience acquired over hundreds, often thousands, of years of direct contact with the natural world. Thus where such knowledge survives, it is extremely important to protect and encourage it; and where it does not, it must essentially be rediscovered and re-embodied in 'invented traditions', ones which reconnect in new ways with a very old sensibility.

A joint report by the Worldwide Fund for Nature and Terralingua cross-mapped the world's ecoregions of the highest biological diversity with the areas of greatest cultural and linguistic diversity (more than 80 per cent of the diversity of which is supplied by indigenous peoples, despite them constituting only 5 per cent of the global population). The result – a highly significant coincidence of the two – strongly implies that biodiversity and cultural diversity are interdependent and stand or fall together: where TEK survives and thrives, so does biodiversity, and where it suffers or disappears, so do ecosystems.[24] To quote from Toledo's report on the exhaustive research on this issue, the 'world's biodiversity only will be effectively preserved by preserving diversity of cultures and vice-versa' (2001: 9). (The research also shows that a degree of *non-industrial* human intervention in nature can actually enhance biodiversity.)

As I said, it is not surprising that peoples who have lived longest on their lands and love them will tend to be those who know its ecology best, including how to live sustainably on its terms, and to pass on that knowledge down the generations in culturally transmitted forms. But modern hypermobility – encouraged in order to have a rootless and disenchanted set of workers, both labourers and managers – cuts this process off at the roots.

In fact, a key part of the dynamics of globalized corporate capitalism and industrialization is precisely to replace local and vernacular knowledge, values and lifestyles with a global consumerism, and central to that in turn is the abstract, technical calculability of quantitative units and their administration and management – both of nonhuman nature (as 'resources') and humans (as 'consumers' of 'products').[25] As Livingston says,

> The most important export of the northern industrial-growth ideology has always been itself, meaning both its means and its ends. . . . In the process of neutralizing any vestiges of a cultural immune system from within, they import more experts, more consultants, more technicians, more resource administrators, more 'environmental' planners, more micro-computer salesmen, more priests of the exotic ethos of 'sustainable development.' Like goats and rabbits, such transplants 'take'. (1994: 70–1)

The popularity in recent years of debunking a straw man called 'the ecological Indian' is therefore somewhat suspicious. In addition to being economical with the truth, it is too convenient for those who want to persuade us that *homo economicus* was, is and ever will be the sole master here.[26] Anderson (1996), Berkes (1999) and Brody (2002), among others, have shown that there are ecologies of the heart as well as mind, and they do make a practical difference.[27] Furthermore, most of the attacks on aboriginal ecological 'balance' are unfair insofar as such systems are always *relatively*, not absolutely, stable. To quote Michael Novack:

Most traditional societies were operationally stable in the environmental sense but usually lacked mechanisms to resist disturbance if faced with factors they did not co-evolve with. Thus a traditional American Indian hunting society might have had mechanisms in place that would prevent human unbalancing of the food animal species but no corresponding mechanism for animals just being killed for their skins; after all, how many skins could a semi-nomad carry around, how many were useful, and what sane person would waste time killing more fur-bearers than the fur of which they had use for? Bring outside fur-traders into the equation and the system collapses.

'The reality', he adds, 'is that this is not a fault which can be prevented. No matter what mechanisms are proposed to maintain stability and balance, it will always be possible to find some perturbation large enough or alien enough to upset the apple-cart. . . . We can only hope our solution will not encounter what it is not designed to withstand.'[28] So to hold this against aboriginal 'solutions' is manifestly unfair, and indeed hypocritical.

In short, recognizing, protecting and encouraging traditional ecological knowledge is one of the indispensable keys to addressing the ecocrisis. Given that indigenous or traditional people now constitute only about 5 per cent of the world population, however, it is clearly not enough. Successfully contesting consumerism through green citizenship, as already discussed, will need to include the *re-creation* of TEK through renewed contact with the local land, plus renewed cultural forms for its protection and transmission: community values, including nonhuman others, that result from what Gary Snyder (with characteristic elegance and precision) calls 'deliberately, knowledgeably, and affectionately "living in place"'. Of course, this agenda connects directly with the matter of eco-education discussed earlier in the chapter, together with the importance of place and of narratives.[29]

Given the modern obsession with hypermobility (which also happens to be ideal for providing a compliant labour force that will follow the work without undue resistance), this will not be easy. But there are some powerful voices of encouragement: especially, in addition to Snyder, Wendell Berry, Wes Jackson and those of the **bioregional** movement.[30] The last is directly concerned with placing social and cultural as well as economic concerns within, and in relation to, ecological ones. The result would be political and administrative boundaries that follow natural ones, instead of ignoring or trying to overrule them, and economies sustainably adapted to rather than dominating and exploiting locale. Whatever the problems of trying to do so – and not surprisingly, they are considerable – the intention to put the horse (nature) back before the cart (human society) is wholly exemplary.

Ecological Republicanism

I now want to consider citizenship from another perspective. The political tradition in which both citizenship and virtue are most important is not modern liberal democracy; it is *civic republicanism*. Let me introduce it by flagging up a few more problems facing the project of green citizenship.

One: we can dispense with the notion, which some greens have inherited from anarchism, that left to themselves (whatever that may mean), human beings will just naturally 'do the right thing'; or that human life, beyond a very small population indeed, is possible without social and political structures. The evidence in support of either idea is in extremely short supply. Nor can such structures ever be purely emancipatory: that about them which enables is also, in different ways and/or for different people, what unavoidably constrains. (Contrariwise, as Foucault recognized, nor are they ever purely repressive; at the very least, they create new patterns of resistance.)

Two: while there are many unsung heroes – courageous, giving and uncomplaining – among ordinary people, there are also many selfish, callous and unscrupulous people, both ordinary and powerful. Opportunists abound, and many people know (technically, so to speak) what is ethical but simply do not *care*. Serious advocates of a better world had better have some idea of how to prevent the good work of the first kind of people from being destroyed by the second – but without becoming like them.

As Adrian Oldfield remarks, 'The moral character which is appropriate for genuine citizenship does not generate itself; it has to be authoritatively inculcated' (1990: 164).[31] Certainly, 'authoritative' should not mean 'authoritarian', and need not. But to expect it to work without duties as well as rights, penalties as well as rewards, losers as well as winners, is indefensibly naive; these will unavoidably figure strongly in any green citizenship worth the name. (They do so *already*, of course, in its absence; but for very different ends, virtually all of them anthropocentric.) In some cases, what is required may well take the form, in Hardin's words, of 'mutual coercion, mutually agreed upon by the majority of people affected' (in Benson 2000: 194), although, if so agreed, does it remain 'coercion'? Again, in any case, it is absurd to pretend that we are presently not subjected to coercion, both directly and indirectly.

There is much to learn here from the tradition of civic republican-ism, perhaps even more than from its younger, more cautious sibling, communitarianism.[32] Virtue ethics is closely related to it, and argu-ably inseparable. The fundamental concern in civic republicanism is with cultivating *virtù* through *a self-governing citizenry actively participat-ing in its own governance*. And the corresponding fear is of *corruption*, almost always by a small unaccountable clique with too much power – often but not necessarily financial or commercial – which is used for selfish private ends. Does that sound familiar? It should.

> The assumption that corporations are legal persons and thereby beyond effective public scrutiny, control, or law is foolishness and worse. The latest corporate scandals are only that: the latest in a recurring pattern of illegality, self-dealing, and political corrup-tion surpassing even that of the robber baron era. The solution is to enforce corporate charters as public license to do business on behalf of the public that are revocable if and when the terms of the charter are violated. . . . By the same logic, we must remove the corrupting influence of money from politics beginning with corporate campaign contributions and the hundreds of billions of dollars of public subsidies for cars, highways, fossil fuels, and nuclear power that corrupt the democratic process and public policy. (Orr 2003)

David Orr's fears here are completely in line with those of civic republicanism. It is not an outdated political philosophy of merely antiquarian interest, but a vibrant tradition that speaks to the heart of an ecological virtue ethic. For civic republicans, in cases of conflict, *public* values always take precedence over private, and the *common* good is the ultimate value. From this point of view, present liberal democracies, dominated by massive concentrations of democratically unaccountable economic power and with political participation largely reduced to voting for parties (frequently indistinguishable) every few years, are a hollow shell.

The immediate relevance of such a philosophy to our concerns here is obvious. Each issue can be recast in ecological terms: a green virtue ethic cultivated through participation in a more-than-human community based on an ecological common good, and vigilant in resisting the corresponding kind of corruption. The appropriate political project then becomes one of setting a renewed framework for humanity *within* nature, especially for determining what counts as ethically acceptable behaviour.

In an interesting essay, Dobson points to three significant overlaps between civic republicanism and political ecology:

- A 'key idea' of the former is 'that the citizen has a duty to promote the common good. Where the citizen's own interests clash with the common good, the latter should take precedence.' This is also an inalienable ecological truth and value.
- A second shared value is 'the importance of the exercise of virtue', although there are arguably different emphases: for the former, 'courage, sacrifice, manliness', while for the latter he suggests 'care, concern and compassion'.
- For both, ideally, 'the citizen as an active political animal'. Politics is fundamentally about local citizen participation. (Dobson and Eckersley 2006: 222–3)

This confluence suggests fertile ground for an ***ecological citizenship***. Dobson is right to remark on the different emphases in the kind or style or virtue exercised – drawing the ecological kind largely from ecofeminism, I think – but are they mutually exclusive? Could they not just as well be seen as complementary? For their part, ecofeminists are right to emphasize practices of caring and nurturing, which have a vital contribution to make – not least, in this case, by helping to prevent an ecological republicanism from degenerating into yet another masculinist programme (only this time in the name of the

Earth), and, more positively, by reminding us that a great deal of the kind of attitude that is needed already exists as the unrecognized and undervalued work of (overwhelmingly) women. But the problems remain with which I opened this section, and for which the remedies must surely include the option of a 'masculine' firmness in insisting on appropriate responsibilities, duties and limits.

It is a tall order: to combine republican toughness and ecofeminist tenderness, so to speak, in a green virtue ethics for the twenty-first century. (Although both also contain the contrary virtues in their own way: the tender dream of a self-governing citizenry, for example, and the toughness of feminine realism.) Nonetheless, the situation we are in demands no less. And it is significant, and hopeful, that they share a fundamental concept, and value, that has been lost in the modernist worship of Progress: the common good. Only now, it must be an ***ecological common good***, that of all the communities that make up the republic of life on Earth.[33]

There should be no illusions about establishing a green utopia, however. In addition to the obvious political dangers, as Callicott says: 'An ethic is never [fully] realized on a collective social scale and only very rarely on an individual scale. . . . An ethic constitutes, rather, an ideal of human behaviour . . . [but] it nonetheless exerts a very real force on practice' (1994: 2–3). A powerfully ecocentric version of such an ethic, where there is now effectively very little, would help get us closer, at least, to heaven on Earth – which is where we most need it.

A Note on Wisdom

It hardly needs stressing that the project of green virtue, or ecocentric citizenship, faces many serious difficulties. It will require both political and emotional intelligence, will and (not least) luck. It has many enemies, in both high and low places, and, as Machiavelli pointed out, '[t]he fact is that a man who wants to act virtuously *in every way* necessarily comes to grief among so many who are not virtuous' (1981: 91; my italics). Furthermore, as I have said, living in a plural world means that values sometimes conflict, with no ideal or painless resolution. Taking these points together, it follows that although it is both ethically and strategically important for ecocentric activists to accommodate as many different virtuous ideals as possible, it will rarely be possible to accommodate them all.

There is no single blueprint for how to act, no set of infallible rules or guidelines; but act we must. (Doing nothing is, of course, just another kind of action.) Yet although the extent of our present eco-crisis is unprecedented, such uncertainty is not, and negotiating it is inherent in being alive. For that reason, major cultural traditions such as religions have some pertinent advice to offer here. For example, Christ advised us to be not only harmless as doves but also wise as serpents (Matthew 10:16). Buddhism emphasizes the inseparability of compassion for suffering on the one hand and *upaya*, or 'skilful means', on the other.

The Greek philosophical tradition we in the West have inherited (and spread) identified only *logos* – reason, theoretical and mascu-line, and the word – as truth, ultimately scorning the emotions, the body, the feminine and nature, and their truths. (I am speaking of the tradition to which Plato gave rise.) This had extremely damag-ing consequences, ecologically and otherwise, especially when it was absorbed into Christianity through Paul and Augustine. Aristotle redressed the balance slightly by stressing the value of *phronesis*, the practical wisdom of non-transferable skills. But there is a still more ancient Greek term, *metis*, with a strikingly cross-cultural equivalent in the Chinese concept of *zhi*. Both denote 'cunning wisdom': the ability, completely unamenable to being formalized and turned into a method, to intuitively 'do the right thing' in a precise situation where there is no clear right thing to do, nor time to study it and reflect.[34] Machiavelli spontaneously rediscovered the same phenomenon: the need to be *able* to act wrongly, in relation to one principle, in order to act virtuously in relation to what one judges to be more important in the present situation. (It is a misunderstanding that he asserted that the end 'justifies' the means, however; in such situations, such an action remains morally wrong, and there is a price to be paid for it.)

Another unlikely cross-cultural agreement is also significant: both the Chinese neo-Confucians and Montaigne, their approximate contemporary and perhaps the most influential European human-ist, concurred that one cannot be fully human if one's concern is only for humans; in other words, without being *humane*.[35] Chu Hsi (1130–1200) influentially defined *jen*, or humanity, as 'the feeling of love, respect, being right, and discrimination between right and wrong – and the feeling of commiseration pervades them all' (Chan 1963: 594). There was, quite deliberately, no attempt to stipulate a restricted class of appropriate *objects* of commiseration. The source of *jen* was life itself, and so too, in all its manifestations, was its appropriate object. Similarly, Montaigne (1533–92) reflected:

> There is a kind of respect and a duty in man as a genus which link us not merely to the beasts, which have life and feelings, but even to trees and plants. We owe justice to men; and to the other creatures who are able to receive them we owe gentleness and kindness. Between them and us there is some sort of intercourse and a degree of mutual obligation. (1991: 488)[36]

It is no coincidence that one of these writers was non-Western and the other pre-modern: Montaigne in a time when our ancient kinship with all life had not been entirely overruled, officially at least, in favour of our own kind alone (although the foundations were already well-laid), and Chu Hsi in a place where that policy had not yet been cemented into place by imperialism and latterly globalisation. (The greatest Western conquest of China was not by gunboats but by Marxism-Leninism, including its industrial freight.)

This point should remind us of the importance, vital in every sense, of green virtue ethics: just the kind which, being essentially non-modern, offers the most hopeful way forward. Without compassion – for fellow human beings, certainly, but for the rest of life no less – we would not care about the ecological holocaust, and there would be nothing more to discuss. But without intelligence, wisdom and sometimes even cunning, we shall not get very far in stopping it, nor in bringing about something better. And without lifelong lives of learning and teaching (by example) ecocentric practices, supporting and supported by corresponding values, we shall hardly get started.

13

Grounding Ecological Ethics

In this chapter, we consider some aspects of modern life in relation to ecological ethics. I shall not be able to do such large subjects justice as a whole, but do hope to bring out that dimension in each. The reason for doing so is simple: presenting an ecological ethics without any consideration of how it could become more of a reality in daily material life is a job half-done.

The Food System

Food cannot be ignored. It connects us to some of the most fundamental aspects of our lives, ones which sheer physical need does not begin to exhaust. Perhaps the most basic of those, with eco-ethics at its heart, is our relationship with nonhuman nature: our dependence, our impact and, not least, our pleasure and appreciation. Pollan observes that 'the way we eat represents our most profound engagement with the natural world' (2006: 10), and Peterson concurs: 'The most common way most people in [the] industrialized world encounter nonhuman nature is as food.' Inseparable here is the immense cultural role of food in our lives, and the role of culture in what food means to us. Peterson adds: 'In eating, and in consumption generally, we enact our values, consciously or unconsciously' (2009: 104). Those values are seamlessly personal and shared, instinctive and learned, and so are the corresponding ethical virtues and vices.

In this context, then, let us briefly review the present industrial food system, also known as ***agribusiness***, before turning to more ecologically ethical alternatives. In addition to mass plant production, agribusiness includes industrial agriculture, meat production and commercial fishing. We have already seen, when discussing animals in Chapter 7, the resulting systematic cruelty to animals. With record levels now of diet-related diseases – from obesity (from overprocessed 'edible foodlike substances')[1] to CJD (from bovine BSE) and avian flu (H_5N_1, from poultry 'farms') – the effects are almost equally dire for human health, although that is not our concern here. But the ecological consequences, both local and global, are. A few pointers, then:

1 Almost half the world's people are undernourished and 20 per cent (2.5 billion) live in absolute poverty without basic necessities.[2]

2 As the number of hungry human mouths continues to increase, calls to increase global food production yet again are unaccompanied by any serious attempts to address the former. Perhaps the callers (who in 2008 included the head of the World Bank) think this can go on indefinitely, but living on a single planet of limited resources suggests it cannot.

3 The 'Green Revolution' in agriculture continues to be trumpeted as a success despite its dependence on oil, the destructive effects of large amounts of artificial fertilizers, and the fact that an estimated one billion people remain undernourished. (Its chief agronomic architect, William Paddock, warned at the outset 'that the increased agricultural productivity would simply produce more malnourished people if curbs were not applied to the increase in human numbers that would result from increased food availability'. His warning was, typically, ignored by those for whom it was inconvenient.)[3] As McKibben says, 'the Green Revolution lured us into a kind of ecological debt that we're only starting to comprehend' (2010: 157).

4 Soil erosion continues to increase, significantly lowering the potential of global food productivity.[4]

5 Food production is now forced to compete with biofuels in order to feed our energy addiction. These are also often grown at the expense of precious rainforest.

6 The extent of water-use by agribusiness is completely unsustainable; for example, a kilogram of grain for animal food requires about a ton of water; each kilogram of beef requires about seven kilograms of grain. Yet at the same time, the industry systematically reduces usable fresh water through run-off from chemical fertilizers and untreated slurry.

7 Livestock raised for meat and milk constitutes the largest of all anthropogenic land uses: 70 per cent of all agricultural land and 30 per cent of the ice-free terrestrial surface of the planet. It is also the most wasteful in terms of the space and water it takes (compared to raising plant proteins) and the most destructive kind of monoculture ever and anywhere, on virtually any measure. In addition to the unimaginable scale of animal suffering, livestock is profoundly implicated in generating greenhouse gases, destroying biodiversity, stressing ecosystems, deforestation, polluting fresh water (and, when animal fat and red meat are a major part of the diet, damaging human health).[5]

8 Concentrated Animal Feeding Operations (CAFOs) result in massive amounts of shit which, being exempt from the most elementary environmental regulations, is simply dumped. This poisons not only land and water – the EPA estimates that some 35,000 miles of American waterways have been contaminated – but also the air: the livestock industry produces 18 per cent of total global CO_2 emissions.[6]

9 The 'input' is equally disturbing: 90–95 per cent of the world production of soya – much of it grown in razed Amazonian rainforest – and about 50 per cent of wheat are fed to livestock, in the course of which up to 90 per cent of its food value, which could have fed perhaps ten times as many humans as the meat feeds, is lost. (And those responsible for this are often the people claiming to be 'efficient' and 'realistic'.)

10 As well as further compromising the long-term ecosystemic health of the land, and thus its ability to supply food in the

future, the cheap price-tag of fast food disguises its true costs to animals, to the environment, and to public health.[7] (Obesity is now the third highest risk factor in the overdeveloped world, after tobacco and alcohol.)

11 Distribution requires hundreds, sometimes thousands, of miles of transport, with its own fossil-fuel impacts in addition to those of extremely energy-intensive conventional agricultural production.

12 Fast-food giants intensively (and successfully) lobby governments to exclude nutrition from official consideration and keep regulation of advertising and marketing minimal. They also systematically target children with multi-million-dollar advertising to sell products whose health-value ranges from indifferent to pathogenic. (As an exercise, how would you characterize the ethics at work there?) But this is only the most blatant instance of the system deliberately encouraging unsustainable and unhealthy overconsumption.[8]

13 The basis of industrial agriculture – oil, not only for artificial fertilizers but for processing, storing and transporting food – has started to decline and/or to become prohibitively expensive, and its continuing extraction to damage the Earth's ecosystemic integrity upon which food (along with everything else) depends.

Two things arise from this list which need more discussion. The last item highlights the extraordinary insecurity of the modern food system stemming from the terrible simplifications that high-tech industrial agriculture and husbandry require, and the magnified dependencies that result.[9] Its vulnerability is systemic: as a monoculture, it is (and therefore we are) dependent on a few key items for which the system has left no alternatives – especially oil, for fertilizer, processing and transport – and which are at the mercy of large-scale availability, market volatility, climate change and a host of other largely unpredictable factors. The contrast to be drawn here is with the relative security of food supply that comes from resilient and diverse nature-cultures, with far shorter supply-chains and locally adapted crops that need less artificial assistance and protection.

The other matter follows on from the items indicting industrial meat-eating. In a recent book, Simon Fairlie (2010a) analyses the ratio of plant food to meat – in other words, the amount of plant food (which could directly feed humans) it takes to produce an equivalent amount of meat – in an attempt to drastically reduce it from currently accepted estimates of 10:1. His methodology has been severely criticized by Wardle (2010). Even if Fairlie was right, however, in terms of the full eco-ethical spectrum, his position stops somewhere between light and mid-green. Indeed, his title, *Meat: A Benign Extravagence*, shows up the problem at once: 'benign' for whom? I argued in Chapter 7 that our treatment of individual domestic animals (and even wild ones, subject to nonhuman ecological exigencies) – including the question, do they really need to die for us? – is a genuinely ecocentric ethical issue. If so, it certainly cannot be reduced to questions about 'the efficiency of meat production'; and even assuming those are resolved, it does not necessarily mean we can then eat meat 'with a clean conscience'.[10]

Two excellent analyses of the food system as a whole are Pollan's *The Omnivore's Dilemma* (2006) and Raj Patel's *Stuffed and Starved* (2008). Neither strays far from solely human concerns, but given how those are so intertwined with nonhuman nature, the ecocentric can learn much there nonetheless. As Pollan says:

> [T]here exists a fundamental tension between the logic of nature and the logic of human industry, at least as it is presently organized. Our ingenuity in feeding ourselves is prodigious, but at various points our technologies come into conflict with nature's way of doing things, as when we seek to maximize efficiency by planting crops or raising animals in vast monocultures. This is something nature never does, always and for good reasons practising diversity instead. . . . By replacing solar energy with fossil fuel, by raising millions of food animals in close confinement, by feeding those animals foods they never evolved to eat, and by feeding ourselves food far more novel than we even realize, we are taking risks with our health and the health of the planet that are unprecedented. (2006: 9, 10)

Patel's book shows how global hunger and obesity (often within the same country) are equally a product of the modern food system, with its systemic but hidden constraints on our choices. The control of food by a few wealthy and powerful companies results in a set of relationships with food that suit them but are seriously and systematically damaging for everyone else: the lives of producers (farmers and rural communities) through low wages and few rights, the health of consumers and the integrity of the environment.

Food giants are helped by their own affiliates in the World Trade Organization, the World Bank and national governments anxious for their fiscal share of the profits. (Recall the triple engine of modernity mentioned above in Chapter 12; add technoscientific innovation, as per GMOs, and the match is complete.) Their most powerful single weapon is the trade agreement. As Patel says, whenever there is a conflict between producers' or consumers' rights and corporate rights, especially in the form of 'free trade' – that is, 'trade free of ethical, health and environmental considerations' (2008: 297) – governments, even the most democratic, invariably side with the latter, underwriting agribusiness with enormous subsidies, taxing them in ways that fail to reflect true costs, and turning a blind eye to effective monopolies.

Peterson points out that the very long chains of transport not only have a large fossil-fuel impact: 'Worst of all, perhaps, they sever the ties between producers and consumers.' As a result, 'end-point consumers are far removed from the origins and processing of what they buy and use. . . . [This] breaks the direct links of accountability between producers and consumers and also eliminates the feedback necessary to restrain resource use' (2009: 104, 105).

Much of the unsustainability of the food system and its damaging effects results from the grip of supermarkets, tending to monopoly, on how we can buy our food. Large supermarkets undermine local food cultures by standardization, and destroy local and regional economies and communities by driving out local smaller firms. (There is evidence that Wal-Mart puts an estimated 100 small firms out of business for each of their outlets that opens.) Supermarkets also damage the environment by encouraging large-scale industrial farming of crops for cash, which damages the soil and wildlife along with local resilience, and debilitates social capital. It is significant that when supermarkets appear in communities, civic participation of all kinds declines: fewer people vote, support local charities, participate in voluntary associations or attend churches. Local distinctiveness starts to die, and where cultural diversity goes, ecological is not far behind.

Yet in the UK, entire 'Tesco Towns' are planned, controlling not only food but housing, schooling and 'public' places.[11]

The ideology at work here goes under the more general banner of Progress, in which increasingly few people believe any more, but then their belief is no longer needed: dependency will do. Its byword is efficiency: 'a word that is becoming more important every year, as global lenders and global markets demand ever higher profit, ever lower costs, ever greater efficiency. Machines are often more efficient than people. Big stores are more efficient than small stores. Mass production is more efficient than craftsmanship' (Longworth 1998: 210). Here too is a direct tie-in with the ideology of utility dominating education, with the 'function' of schools and universities viewed as being a resource of new generations of producers, managers and consumers (but preferably not citizens, let alone independently minded ones).

Genetically modified (GM) food is another instance of the toxic effects of capital, working with technoscience and protected by national governments to appropriate food. The pretence is that there is a single powerful technical fix to the problem (and the masculinism here is pretty obvious), when food security is actually an intricate and messy amalgam of biology, culture and political power. The goal, and increasingly the reality, is an unprecedented concentration of corporate power in commercial seed companies selling bioengineered seeds, agrochemical companies selling pesticides, and corporations selling commodities, all protected by national governments, whose own scientists and sometimes ministers come from the same stable. (Six companies control three-quarters of the global agrochemical market.).

Basically, the market is prised open by introducing GM food, especially soya, into the food chain in such a way that it becomes practically impossible to keep non-GM food uncontaminated. This thin end of the wedge is then used to take over the entire market, on the logic that it is already effectively GM, and they can supply that more cheaply (because of economies of scale) than anyone else. Meanwhile, research results from trials are neglected, pre-empted or manipulated. (A *Scientific American* editorial concluded that 'Only studies the seed companies have approved see the light of day.')[12] Significantly, in such trials as there are, the only alternative tested is conventional crops grown with the usual pesticides. Organic farming simply isn't allowed into the discussion, although – or rather, just because – it doesn't use any pesticides at all, benefits wildlife and results in high-quality food.

As we have already noted, one-size-fits-all monocultures increase the risk of disastrous failure, including malnutrition and even starvation. Traditional crops adapted to local climatic variations and grown organically are the only long-term way to 'feed the world', and such an agroecological approach goes hand-in-hand with maintaining ecological as well as cultural diversity.[13]

Brennan's sharp summary rings true:

> Biotech companies claim that genetic-engineering technology will help feed the world. The old canard about feeding the Third World is trotted out each time a risky [but potentially profitable] technique needs ethical justification for its implementation. (There are variations on the theme, such as the drug companies' tune about preventing illness in the Third World.) There are food shortages, but they derive from overpopulation in relation to the earth's resources, as well as the degradation of those resources resulting from disturbed ecosystems. Interfering further with those ecosystems will only exacerbate the problem it is meant to solve. (2003: 58–9)

My only reservation is her apparent naivety in assuming that hunger really is what the biotech companies see as 'the problem'; actually, of course, their biggest problem is how to show a higher rate of return for investment, while protecting their humanitarian image to that end.

In recent years, food has entered the high-risk financial commodities market. Speculation by hedge funds and investment banks has artificially driven up food prices, causing new hardship and hunger. It seems that Goldman Sachs invented a mathematical formula to convert food into a commodity (the 'food index') for investors. Even though there was no less food being produced than before, the resulting speculative frenzy artificially drove food prices up, increasing the number of seriously hungry people by 250 million in a single year (2008). The 'success' of this scheme (!) has inspired other multinational players to devise their own commodity index funds, and now, 'Imaginary wheat bought anywhere affects real wheat bought everywhere' (Kaufman 2010: 33). Another part of this ecologically deeply unhelpful development is 'the growing trend for investors and sovereign wealth funds to snap up overseas land and marginalise local producers'.[14] Could they be anticipating profits from a coming scarcity? And wouldn't that make scarcity a good thing, from their point of view?

This phenomenon perfectly captures the magical mechanics of industrial capitalism and its dislocating effect: take something that everyone once knew was real without having to think about it (food); then, using a mathematical formula that turns that reality's sensuous qualities into abstract quantities, transform it into a completely hypothetical abstraction (a food commodity); then sell the latter for a great deal of money. I say 'transform it', but the food still exists; so should we say, rather, '*apparently* transform it'? But for the powerful manipulators, the new entity is more real than the original (except, perhaps, when they need to eat); and what is more, they are able to bring the new abstract reality to bear directly on the lives of those who merely produce food that was formerly real! So what is now really real?

Trying to understand this surreal situation, it may seem hyperbole to describe it as an act of magic, but hear the definition of someone well placed to know, by scholarship as well as insight: 'Magic produces, or pretends to produce, an alteration in the Primary World. . . . [I]t is not an art but a technique; its desire is *power* in this world, domination of things and wills' (Tolkien 1988: 49–50). The food system is but part of the anthropocentric empire of modernity which proceeds by turning unique places into measurable units of space, unique moments into interchangeable units of time, and plural qualities into a quantity of ultimately indistinguishable stuff, all of which can then be manipulated. (For these people, it is 'matter'; for their idealist collaborators, it is 'spirit'.) And the means are frighteningly efficient, but the end, as so often with magicians, is quite irrational. Is the goal ethical, or even sensible? That is a question the operators, servants and immediate beneficiaries of the system are strongly discouraged from asking.

Although they were following the lead of Max Weber (and to some extent, Karl Marx), Max Horkheimer and Theodor Adorno, writing in 1944, remain among the clearest and most prescient analysts of this overall process. Their chilling critique resonates with a great deal of what we have already discussed in this book, from anthropocentrism, economism and scientism to animism, quality and place: 'What human beings seek to learn from nature is how to use it to dominate wholly both it and human beings. Nothing else counts.' Thus: 'There shall be neither mystery nor any desire to reveal mystery.' In fact, '[t]he disenchantment of the world means the extirpation of animism', because 'its ideal is the system from everything and anything follows'. And what does that system do? It 'makes dissimilar things comparable by reducing them to abstract quantities' (2002: 2, 4, 5).

What, then, is food sanity? By way of contrast to the above, a list would include:

- the importance of resilience in food security;
- local adaptedness and self-sufficiency (as far as possible), including growing your own, in gardens or allotments, and short supply-chains: e.g., buying as much as possible from farmers' markets and community-supported sources and outlets;
- respecting local, traditional and vernacular agricultural knowledge;
- protecting diversity, both ecological and cultural;
- light or no use of artificial fertilizers and chemical pesticides;
- eating seasonally as well as locally (as much as possible);
- celebrating that unique and wonderful meld of nature and culture that is cooking, not least by eating slowly and socially rather than fast and privately; and
- eating far less (or no) meat and dairy products.

It is our good fortune and hope, then, that these are not only *desiderata*; despite the oppressive dominance of the global food system, to greater or lesser extents they already exist. If a single name for them is needed, the best candidate is *agroecology*, or ecological farming. (There is a reason why it is no longer 'organic food', as we shall see.) We cannot go into detail here, so shall mention only a few salient issues and promising developments. For those who want to delve deeper, the work of Wendell Berry, Wes Jackson and Bill Mollison is vital.[15]

Feasibility

Agroecological farming moves towards ecological sustainability by respecting the land and working with instead of against it; socially, it draws upon and encourages local knowledge and local solutions, and therefore respects the human growers and their indispensable contributions. Encouragingly, there is also evidence that, encouraged globally, it could 'feed the world'. Of course, that task would be vastly easier if the global human population significantly decreased, and it verges on becoming insoluble as that continues to increase. In addition – *both* points need addressing – the politics and economics of food ownership and access urgently need to shift from private gain to public good. However, it seems it is still possible to feed very large human populations, and to do so without sacrificing 'non-essential' parts of the natural world. A recent report by Compassion in World Farming and Friends of the Earth, 'Eating the Planet? How We Can Feed the World Without Trashing It' (2009),[16] concludes that overall food security can be realized while retaining humane livestock farming (albeit with much-reduced meat consumption: a near-universal requirement) and meeting basic environmental objectives in crop production. That conclusion is supported by the work of the Pimentals (2008) and Halweil (2006), among others, and the empirical/historical experience of Cuba, with its enforced low-energy agroecology, suggests the same.

Food sovereignty

This is a key issue in any move away from agribusiness towards an ethical and ecological agriculture. It offers a viable alternative to the rules of financial markets fixing food prices, sidelining issues of environmental impacts, the health of consumers and the rights of producers (except insofar as these measurably impact on profits). As Carlo Petrini (2009) shows, a growing number of local alliances between food producers and food consumers offers the basis for redressing the balance by forming regional but globally linked food communities with a real say in what and how they grow and eat. These alliances consist mainly of farmers' and peasants' groups in India, Mexico, the USA, Brazil and elsewhere, many of them under the umbrella of *La Via Campesina* (The Peasant Way), which numbers an estimated 150 million people worldwide. This makes it easier to campaign for the rights of farmers and peasants – especially women, who play a major role in the whole cycle from seed to table, and especially in the global South – as well as consumers.[17] Significantly, those rights are communal as well as individual, thus opening the door to that concern for the common good which is fundamental to ecological ethics.

Food sovereignty has an important local and small-scale dimension in the form of growing food in gardens or allotments and/or buying it from cooperative community-supported agriculture farms (CSAs), local and farmers' markets and locally owned businesses. These are all valuable steps beyond mere green consumerism. As Patel says, even with corporate social responsibility, 'good works are constrained by profitability'. He adds: 'The honey trap of ethical consumerism is to think that the only means of communication we have with producers is through the market, and that the only way we can take collective action is to persuade everyone else to shop like us' (2008: 310, 312).

In short, shopping *is* political, but political action is far from limited to shopping – or even voting. The most radical and positive political actions, I suggest, are those that transcend our habitual anthropocentrism. It could be something as simple as walking in woods, growing food in a garden, or eating locally: all things, as Peterson says, that 'can help us reeducate our desires for more sustainable, humane, mutual relations with nature'. Then when that extends into more overtly political actions (campaigning, etc.), as it well might, they are well rooted. 'The responsible, sacramental sense that we must care for this natural drama, see that it is maintained and not destroyed or compromised, will be a natural outgrowth of our sustained engagement and work with it' (2009: 108).

Celebrations, festivals and rituals showcasing local cuisine, food and drink also have an important role to play, especially if done in a way that connects, implicitly or explicitly, with the ethical issues. To pick only a couple of examples: in May 2009, the Belgian town of Ghent instituted a vegetarian day once a week, to reduce its citizens' carbon footprint and improve their health, turning it into a public celebration. And every October now in England, thanks largely to the impetus of the charity Common Ground, there is an Apple Day – or rather, a lot of Apple Days, in almost every county, celebrating local varieties of apple and the drinks, foods and customs they have inspired and the orchards where they grow. (There are 2,300 different varieties in the British Isles alone, although you would never guess it from the few, mostly spotless and tasteless, on offer in supermarkets.) This sort of thing, where nature and culture meet in enacted story, is fertile ground for ecological ethics. At least initially, there is no need for the latter to be explicit, as it is in the Institute for Critical Animal Studies' campaign for cruelty-free campuses, although that is also an excellent project.

Slow Food Movement

Petrini was a central figure in founding the Slow Food Movement (SFM) in Italy in the late 1980s. The initial spark, appropriately, was resistance to a new McDonald's near the Spanish Steps in Rome. There are now groups in more than 130 countries comprising more than 100,000 members.

The SFM is much more than a middle-class *divertissement*. Its manifesto states that 'A firm defence of material pleasure is the only way to oppose the universal folly of Fast Life', but it also notes that 'food is grown, and eaten, in a particular *place*'. In other words, the pleasures of growing, cooking and eating locally and slowly are indissolubly linked with defending agroecology and resisting industrialized food-production, commodification and eating habits. Of course, that involves choosing and celebrating local and regional cuisines, surely one of Europe's chief cultural-natural glories. But it also entails maintaining close relations with and support for farmers, seeing that they are paid a fair wage and insisting that the food is grown in a way that respects the long-term integrity of local ecosystems as well as animal welfare. In these ways, the SFM, together with food sovereignty, embodies a defence of local distinctiveness, pluralism and qualities, extending to the independent identity and integrity of the land: all indispensable to developing a green virtue ethic and citizenry.[18]

There is another aspect of the 'slow' sensibility that deserves mention. McKibben writes that, when eating locally, he realized that 'everything came with a story attached to it. Every night when we sat down to dinner, we knew how and why our food had come to us . . . the good taste eating locally leaves in your mouth is not just the food, but the strong sense of community; the food really means something.'[19] In other words, it also invites to the table the *places* and *narratives* which, as we have already seen, are such important parts of an ecocentric way of life.

The SFM has already inspired many related movements, including Slow Cities (resisting the urban homogenization resulting from commercial globalization) as well as Acoustic Cities (no forced 'music' in public places), Slow Money (facilitating donor investments in local, small and/or ecological enterprises), Slow Parenting (parents: lighten up, pull back and trust them a bit), Slow Travel (remember journeys that were exciting, interesting and fun?), Slow Architecture (designing and building slowly, and with reduced machismo) and even Slow Sex (orgasmic but *mindful* . . . based in San Francisco).

Organic food movement

This is not the place for even a potted history of the organic food movement; suffice it to say that it has an important and honourable place in the struggle to grow food in ways that treat nonhuman nature as a partner, not a slave. In recent years, however, organic food has been colonized by agribusiness; it is increasingly grown in ever-larger monocultures and sold in supermarkets and fast-food outlets. It even has its own supermarkets.[20] Good, you might think; and it is something of an advance. But, as McKibben says, when you buy organic food at a supermarket, 'instead of building stronger local communities [and ecologies], the money you spend buying it just builds the bank accounts of a few huge firms' (2010: 187).[21]

The net effect of allowing corporations to take over organic farming, as Patel points out, 'is to legitimate their rule, to concede that no kind of food system is possible without their participation'. But they 'can only comprehend the potentially radical call for sustainable agriculture as customer demand for processed food grown with fewer pesticides. This sets at zero the importance of social relations through which food is produced, and the politics that permits these relations.' (We should take 'social relations' here to include those with nonhumans.) In the absence of any personal connections with the persons and places who grow our food, or at least awareness of them as such, 'we're tricked by the simulacrum, mistaking the dead green "Certified Organic" packaging for a living connection' (2008: 246–7).

Thus, 'industrial organic' is a contradiction in terms, just as is 'green consumerism'. Industrially produced organic food remains narrowly environmental: not ecological (where humans are part of, and dependent upon, a much larger set of 'social' relationships) and certainly not ecocentric (where those are given first priority). Furthermore, large whole-food stores, replicating the supermarket experience but 'ethically', encourage the delusion that, as Bahro said, you can have a megamachine that doesn't hurt anyone. Encouraged to believe that buying organic blueberries grown on big farms 1,000 miles away is an ethical act, you pay for this small truth (the organic bit) by signing up to a big lie: that sustainable consumer capitalism is actually possible, and that you can support it while being an ecologically virtuous person whose actions don't harm the 'environment' or 'nature'. I'm afraid it isn't, and you can't. No wonder that supermarkets, even organic, fail to delight and engage the way a genuinely local small market can, and leave a bad ethical taste in the mouth. The answer to agribusiness (or part of it, at least) is not a global chain of big organic and fairtrade supermarkets. It is supporting many *small*, *local* and *independent* organic and fairtrade outlets, and buying locally as well as organically: in short, agroecologically.

On Malthus

The work of Robert Malthus (1766–1834) occupies an awkward but unavoidable place (not unlike that of Garrett Hardin) at the juncture of food and population. Malthus was a political economist and demographer. In *An Essay on the Principle of Population*, he argued that '[t]he power of population is indefinitely greater than the power in the earth to produce subsistence for man'; in other words, that sooner or later, population would necessarily exceed food resources, resulting in a collapse. He therefore opposed trying to meet the needs of people who would not stop reproducing, insofar as doing so would not only merely postpone disaster but make it worse when it happened.

For these ideas, Malthus has been vilified with a bitterness that suggests his critics' attachment to some deeply (and not necessarily consciously) held belief that they feel is threatened. Interestingly, these critics have come from both the political left (Marx and Engels prominent among them) and the right (e.g. techno-cornucopians such as Julian Simon). We will ask what unites them in a moment, but the latter have pointed to the fact that there has been no overall Malthusian crash, and cite the success of the Green Revolution as evidence that (overlooking the couple of billion people who still go hungry) industrial agriculture can keep pace with population indefinitely. We have already reviewed reasons why that claim should be treated sceptically.

Despite being killed off many times, Malthus's idea continues to resonate. Hardin (1977: 112) defined *carrying capacity* – a key concept in all such discussions – as 'the maximum number of a species that can be supported indefinitely by a particular habitat, allowing for seasonal and random changes, without degradation of the environment and without diminishing carrying capacity in the future'. In his important update, *Overshoot*, William Catton adds that 'The cumulative biotic potential of *any* species exceeds the carrying capacity of its habitat' (1980: 127; emphasis in original).

Rees points out that '*without constraints*, whether "internal" or "external", all animal populations will grow to the point of exhausting critical resources and consequently collapsing'.[22] And Bender usefully reminds us that Malthusian *analysis* should not be confused with *policy* prescriptions.[23] In other words, it is quite possible to agree with Malthus's central point without necessarily accepting any of his suggested remedies.[24]

Was – is – that point correct? In principle, yes. Unless you believe that the Earth and its 'resources' are infinite, which seems extremely implausible at best and delusional at worst, then it is clear that carrying capacity can be exceeded, but not permanently, and its defining limits deferred, but not forever; mitigated, but not completely. So the complex dance between P (population), L (lifestyle), O (organization) and T (technology) takes place entirely within Malthus's proposition and its implications.

Does this view seem confirmed historically and/or empirically? Malthus predicted that, ultimately, agricultural production would not be able to keep pace with population growth. True, that has not yet happened on a massive scale. Is that a cause for complacency? From the perspective of the present, with massive overpopulation (see

Chapter 14) combined with diminishing returns in food production, not really. The one-off bonanza of non-renewable energy sources (now dwindling) that fuelled the Industrial Revolution, plus the colonization of huge new lands (relatively unpopulated after massive indigenous die-off from European diseases) and the exploitation of their resources, permitted and then required increased industrial food production that led to increased population, which then required more food, 'development' and intensive management; and so on.

As we have already seen, the most recent instalment of the programme, the 'Green Revolution' in agriculture, bought more time but merely postponed the problem by failing to address its root causes. The net result is now an even bigger problem, with many more lives at risk. This was in fact precisely predicted by the prime mover behind the Green Revolution, Norman Borlaug, when accepting the Nobel Peace Prize in 1970:

> The Green Revolution has won a temporary success in man's war against hunger and deprivation; it has given man a breathing space. If fully implemented, the revolution can provide sufficient food for sustenance during the next three decades. But the frightening power of human reproduction must also be curbed; otherwise the success of the Green Revolution will be ephemeral only.[25]

And so it has proved – as will the next high-tech instalment, unless Borlaug's and Malthus's points are acknowledged and acted on.

The most plausible view, then, is all our cleverness has only postponed a Malthusian reckoning which is drawing closer, as the practical limits of technological innovation and of a capitalist economy dependent upon growth, but whose very growth is destroying its own base, start to bite. As Livingston insists: ' "Malthusian" is not a dirty word. It is shorthand for "the natural and inevitable effects of population pressure" ' (1994: 193–4).

Rees's formulation introduces the possibility, at least, of *self-restraint* pre-empting forcible external restraint. The evidence of collective human self-restraint is extremely thin, of course, but unlike fantasies of an infinitely expanding resource base thanks to miraculous technological advances, at least this possibility is a real one. As Michel Serres optimistically remarked: 'Reason puts aside some reason to restrain itself', and 'Science will become wise when it restrains itself from doing all it can do' (1991: 186). It might be possible – it may *only* be possible – as part of a green virtue ethic.

What, then, is the reason for the extremity of hostility to Malthus? There is no mystery here. His critics, left and right, are united in their anthropocentrism, and the ideology of human Progress says it must be indefinite or not at all. The idea that there are any real, natural and ultimately non-negotiable *limits* to which humanity is subject is completely unacceptable. That may be the case for other animals, but not this one, because this one is special. (So too are all the others? Ah, but we are special in a *special* way.) All of which helps maintain the central plank of the toxic anti-ecological fantasy that humans, uniquely, are outside and above nature, masters not equals, doing to but never done to . . . Could we finally grow up now, please?

Climate Change

This is another very large subject, so once again I shall try to follow the ecocentric thread without us getting too lost. The basic situation is as follows. To begin with, *climate change is happening*. On the basis of the scientific evidence – and, for that matter, personal 'anecdotal' evidence – there is vanishingly little doubt of that. (We shall say here 'climate change' not 'global warming' because although the global temperature trend overall is sharply up, that trend is not uniform everywhere, and accompanying extreme weather conditions are also important which temperature alone doesn't cover.) The effects, which we are already experiencing in both extreme temperatures (with consequent effects on rainfall) and storms, will become more severe. The best evidence points to at least a four degree overall rise over the rest of this century – that's six degrees, on average, on land – with significant effects within the next two decades. The consequences for other species are at least equally dire; those who are temperature-sensitive are facing extinction, while the habitats of others (of whom polar bears are only one well-publicized example) will drastically shrink or disappear.[26] In short, 'if it's bad, it's really bad, and if it's good, it's still pretty bad'.[27]

A significant amount of climate change is almost certainly anthro-genic (human-caused): hence, ACC. 'Significant' means a major part of it, at least, and 'almost certainly' means: with as much certainty as the extreme complexity of the phenomenon permits, which is necessarily short of total certainty. It is true that the almost perfect coincidence of a rising global temperature with the rate of CO_2 emissions from the burning of fossil fuels beginning with the Industrial Revolution is not 'proof' of a causal connection, but the same argument was used against the link between cigarette-smoking and lung cancer – and, as we shall see, by some of the same people, with the same backers – until it wore too thin to be credible even with those who wanted to believe it. Hopefully, at some point before too long, although we are not there yet, the same sort of awakening will happen again.

The key point is this: *even if* the anthropogenic contribution to climate change is less than the current consensus holds to be, continuing with business as usual is not a viable option.[28] One reason is that we need to reduce our contribution, whatever it is. Still more importantly, measures to reduce our energy consumption and economic production, as well as to reduce our population, are needed as part of *a number of interlinked measures* reducing our impact *across a wide range of contexts in crisis* (perhaps most notably, biodiversity crash). It doesn't make any sense to be trying to 'develop' less, slaughter less, pollute less, breed less and (for some of us) eat less, especially less meat, while generating more oil spills, pumping more CO_2 into the atmosphere and creating more undisposable nuclear waste!

In what the media dubbed (unoriginally enough) 'Climategate', the Climate Research Unit of the University of East Anglia became the target of a concerted attempt in late 2009 to undermine its scientific authority, as thousands of hacked emails to and from its members were made public. Several subsequent investigations cleared them of all serious charges of scientific misconduct, although the affair did reveal a culture among climate scientists of secrecy and fear – one which the attack on them, ironically, showed was not without foundation. But moving to discourage or even suppress dissent played into the hands of the so-called **climate sceptics**, who sought to 'reposition global warming as a theory (not a fact)'.[29]

Philosophically speaking, it is misleading to call this group 'sceptics'. In the original sense of the word, sceptics are even-handedly sceptical about *all* propositions or truths without exception. For this reason, it seems more accurate to call them *climate (change)* **deniers**. Evidently their grasp of the philosophy of science is also shaky, because no hard-and-fast distinction between a 'theory' and a 'fact' is possible, and science always admits of uncertainty to some degree or other. One hundred per cent certainty is simply not an option, nor is 'proof'. To quote two working climate researchers: 'Scientists are not in the business of handing down incontrovertible truth. We deal in observations and theories, couched in uncertainty, to produce our best models of how the world works; it is a messy and difficult business.'[30] In this process, scientists are unavoidably influenced by many different factors, including personal, ideological and practical ones. As Larry Lohmann says, 'Acknowledging and examining these lines of influence – rather than claiming that "good science" is somehow immune from them – would give all sides incentives to be more aware of what kind of politics is involved in any particular research scheme, and what the consequences are' (2006: 39).

As it happens, the degree of scientific consensus garnered by the Intergovernmental Panel on Climate Change (IPCC) – to whose latest Assessment Report more than 2,500 scientific expert reviewers, 800 contributing authors and 450 lead authors contributed – is unusually strong. So the climate deniers, who mostly take their stand not on denying climate change as such but any human contribution to it, are obliged to split science into two: 'good science' (the obedient servant of capital) and 'bad science' (making things more difficult). The process of separating the two is now under way.

A closer look at the climate deniers, who also fight attempts to institute clean energy measures, is instructive. It turns out they are a relatively small number of extremely well-organized and well-funded people, mainly in organizations dedicated to lobbying, publicity and campaigning that are backed by ExxonMobil ($8.9 million between 2005 and 2008), the American Petroleum Institute and other industry donors, but even more, Koch Industries: the second-largest private company in the USA, largely based on oil and owned by two billionaire brothers, David and Charles Koch, whose combined wealth is exceeded only by that of Bill Gates and Warren Buffett. The $24.9 million that Koch industries donated in the same period to 35 climate denial groups (and 20 congressmen and senators) is only part of more than $100 million so far given to various libertarian and right-wing causes.[31]

As part of this pattern, several of the same figures who were active in denying the smoking–cancer link, and subsequently those between coal emissions and acid rain and CFCs and the ozone hole, have resurfaced to sow systematic doubt on ACC. To quote one tobacco company executive: 'Doubt is our product.'[32] The Advancement of Sound Science Coalition, a major corporate-funded agitator for climate change denial, was an offshoot of a PR firm hired by the tobacco company Philip Morris to fight legislation based on the connection between cancer and passive smoking: nice lineage.[33] *Plus ça change, plus c'est la même chose*, as they probably don't say at head office.

Climate deniers play very skilfully (they are not wise, but they certainly are clever) upon some deep-seated human tendencies: to prefer the devil ones knows; to ignore what one doesn't want to admit because doing so would make one feel uncomfortable, even bad; and to indulge in wishful thinking. A MORI poll of British public opinion in 2007 concluded:

> The public want to avert climate change and play their part but at the same time they also want to go on holiday, drive to work, own a second (or third or fourth) home and buy the latest electrical products. . . . They hope for technical innovations or efficiency improvements – such as airplanes and cars that don't emit CO_2 – rather than contemplate radical changes in lifestyle. (Quoted in McIntosh 2008: 88)

There's that desire for a kinder, fluffier megamachine again – and plenty of fodder for reactionary manipulation. But this attitude doesn't just exist among the general public. Bjørn Lomborg, as the acceptable face of climate denial, has based an entire and, in its own terms, very successful career on catering to the demand among policy-makers and CEOs to hear what they want to hear.[34]

For their part, climate change scientists and lobbyists, and environmentalists generally, have naively and grossly overestimated the importance of individual cognition and information as opposed to affect (emotion) and group dynamics. David Orr's bitter assessment in 2003 still rings true, unfortunately ('we do science, write books, publish articles, develop professional societies, attend conferences, and converse learnedly. But they do politics, take over the courts, control the media, and manipulate the fears and resentments endemic to a rapidly changing society').

One moral is clear: big issues that bring into play fundamental values – ecocentrism versus anthropocentrism comes to mind – are not won or lost on the basis of reasoned arguments alone; making a good case based on fact will never suffice. (As one lightning rod for denial, journalist George Monbiot, remarked wonderingly: 'The more I stick to the facts, the more virulent the abuse becomes.')[35] Any long or broad hope must include telling *a better story*, with all the elements that involves: a powerfully affective narrative, more mythic than analytical and skilfully told, which opens doors for those it reaches and shows them how things, and they themselves, could be better.

The climate deniers are not just 'conservative', but often openly reactionary libertarians. In 2007, however, Britain spawned a small group of deniers with a very different provenance: ex-members of the Revolutionary Communist Party whose subsequent forums (*Living Marxism*, later *LM*, and *Spiked*) were a toxic brew of libertarianism, ultra-modernism and scientism. One of their members is repeatedly given an influential public platform by a seemingly unscrupulous TV station, Channel 4.[36] But this crew wouldn't be worth mentioning except for their apparently unlikely common cause with American right-wing Republicans. What unites them all is profound anthropo-centrism and hostility to the possibility of natural limits, especially as these might affect private profit.

Hear Frank Furedi, one of the British contingent: 'Instead of bowing to the divine authority of the planet, we ought to uphold the age-long project of humanizing the planet.' And Lowell Wood, Edward 'Father of the H Bomb' Teller's heir at the Lawrence Livermore National Laboratory, now of the George C. Marshall and Hoover Institutes, defending geo-engineering: 'It is the manifest destiny of the human race . . . we are the builders of new worlds. In this country we took a raw wilderness and turned it into the shining city on the hill of our world' (both quoted in Hamilton 2010: 114, 186).

To Furedi one could simply ask, are those the only alternatives? But Wood's rhetoric repays closer analysis. 'Manifest destiny' was the phrase used, with an overtly racist dimension, to justify the nineteenth-century American war to take over the Western part of the continent from Mexicans and Native Americans; 'raw wilderness' implies that no one was already living in America when 'we' arrived (or no one who matters); and 'shining city on the hill', from Matthew 5:14, was influentially used by the Puritan divine John Winthrop to express unique divine approval of America. As usual, Livingston was right: 'The goal, simply put, is the humanization of the entire planet, its remaking in our image – domesticated, predictable, and control-lable' (1994: 177). The contrast with anything ecological, let alone ecocentric, could hardly be clearer.

At the other end of an ethical scale is surely the Bolivian gov-ernment's initiative, led by Evo Morales, to fight ACC based on the values of indigenous people: the World People's Conference on Climate Change and the Rights of Mother Earth, held in Cochabamba, Boliva in April 2010, demanded:

- a 'universal Declaration of Mother Earth Rights', protecting ecosystems from destruction, and enforced;
- a 'climate justice tribunal', to bring offenders to justice;
- 'climate debt', not aid, recognizing that most poor countries are the victims of something for which they are not responsible;
- a 'world people's referendum on climate change', encouraging wider participation in a more democratic debate.

Morales added what almost no one wants to hear: 'We have a stark choice between capitalism and survival.' Hence the conference's call for less consumption and more conservation, less development and global trade and more local self-reliance.[37]

Agarwal and Narain (1991) distinguish between luxury emis-sions and survival emissions, the former as hard to defend ethically as the latter are to criticize. Rising Tide, an international grassroots network combatting climate change, calls for 'climate justice through solutions that address structural inequalities and recognise the his-torical responsibility of the rich nations for the problem', and a rapid transition away from a fossil fuel economy that compensates those who will be hardest hit. Other encouraging movements are 350.org and 10:10 (the first originally American and the second British, but both now global). We could add that even among the poor, women are disproportionately affected, while, at the same time, 'climate change is sex-gendered'; that is, the lifestyles of affluent white men are its primary drivers (Salleh 2010: 186, 187; see also her 2008–9). In all, such approaches are not in themselves ecocentric, but they are important, even necessary, and have considerable positive ecological potential.

Another good point has been made by Paul G. Harris, who advocates a shift from international to global climate justice. He argues that 'people, rather than states alone', are the agents 'of climate change and the bearers of related rights, responsibilities and obligations', and points out that there are now hundreds of millions of affluent and high-polluting people living outside the so-called developed countries. 'Cosmopolitan justice', then, as well as practicality, 'points us to a fundamental conclusion: that affluent people *everywhere* should limit, and more often than not cut, their atmospheric pollution, regardless of where they live' (2010: vii, 7). Putting all the emphasis on nation-states downgrades what is needed most: an active and responsible green citizenry.

The fact is that, after decades of IPCC assessments, the Kyoto Protocol, various G8 conferences, *emissions are still rising*. And as Hamilton (2010: 201) points out: '[T]he relentless logic of the models proves over and over again that the poor and vulnerable will be hardest hit by climate change, even though they are not responsible for causing it and are in the weakest position to defend themselves against it.' How much more so, then, and in all respects, the world's other animals?

For these reasons, Mike Hulme suggests: 'Perhaps this particular way of framing climate change (as a mega-problem awaiting, demanding, a mega-solution) has led us down the wrong road.' Quite, and the still more spectacular failures of a single, universal and enlightened carbon-market, or binding international treaty, or geo-engineering intervention, or mass spiritual conversion wait in the wings. Hulme adds: 'Science has universalised and materialised climate change; we must now *particularise and spiritualise it*' (2009: 333, 330; my emphasis).

The attitude I am criticizing occurs among the 'good guys', too. As Ruth Thomas-Pellicer points out, the international climate change regime 'features all the traits proper to the ecocidal mode of being: anthropocentrism, priority accorded to the mode of production, binary logic, abstract – as opposed to embodied, embedded, situated – conceptualism, restricted economy, and teleology of progress'.[38] Rees (2009), who developed the concept of 'ecological footprint', despairs that 'intelligence and reason are not the primary determinants of human behavior'. Rather, 'brutish passion and instinct often overwhelm the godly gift of reason'. (Note, as ever, the language, which here asserts a radical and value-laden dualism between humans and 'brutes', and invokes divine sanction, yet again, for human exceptionalism.) Rees realizes that it is the 'economic growth paradigm' (or 'industrial capitalism') which is 'wrecking the ecosphere', but he attributes it to the 'biological drivers' of our 'lower brain centres'. It seems more plausible to see that economic system as a perverse *realization* of human 'reason'.

In any case, Rees's rationalist exhortations are the authentic voice of anthropocentrism, the very structure of values and ideas of human exceptionalism and privilege that is so implicated in ecocide. As such, they not only fail in ecological terms, but collude with it. What will 'save' us, if anything, is not what apparently separates us from other animals but a conscious recognition and revaluing of what we all share: the common good of our embodied and embedded life as Earthlings, and our common vulnerability to its abuse.

The reality is that even if the radical cuts in emissions needed (but for which there is little popular or political will) were instituted, the time-lag in their effects, plus the irreversibility of changes we have already wrought, mean that barring unforeseen developments such as a major volcanic eruption, the planet is *already* facing the 4°+ rise overall mentioned at the outset. (The last time when action might well have worked was the early 1980s, when Reaganism and Thatcherism wrecked its chances.)

Considering this lack of progress, and the lack of realistic prospects of progress, several sober commentators have recently called for a new realism. Adam D. Sacks has anatomized 'the failure of climate activism', arguing that two errors need addressing:

> The first error is our failure to understand that greenhouse gases are not a cause but a symptom, and addressing the symptom will do little but leave us with a devil's sack full of many other symptoms, possibly somewhat less rapidly lethal but lethal nonetheless. The root cause, the source of the symptoms, is 300 years of our relentlessly exploitative, extractive, and exponentially growing technoculture, against the background of ten millennia

of hierarchical and colonial civilizations. . . . The second error is our stubborn unwillingness to understand that the battle against greenhouse-gas emissions, as we have currently framed it, is over. *It is absolutely over and we have lost.* . . . Our version of life on earth has come to an end. Moreover, there are no 'free market' or 'economic' solutions. And since corporations must have physically impossible endless growth in order to survive, corporate social responsibility is a myth. The only socially responsible act that corporations can take is to dissolve. . . . We can either try to plan the transition, even at this late hour, or the physical forces of the world will do it for us – indeed, they already are.[39]

Bill McKibben's most recent book (2010), which is about (to quote the subtitle) 'making a life on a tough new planet', confirms that global warming is no longer a threat but a reality, so it's time to begin deciding 'what parts of our lives and our ideologies we must abandon so that we can protect the core' (2010: xiii, xiv). Clive Hamilton, in his excellent (if slightly melodramatically titled) *Requiem for a Species: Why We Resist the Truth about Climate Change*, opens on a similar note: 'No one is willing to say publicly what the climate science is telling us: that we can no longer prevent global warming that will this century bring about a radically transformed world that is much more hostile to the survival and flourishing of life' (2010: x–xi). I recommend both books.

I believe that Sacks, McKibben and Hamilton are correct, particularly if one adds to the picture something that is subject to an even more deafening official silence: peak oil. That is, the process in which remaining oil reserves become scarce and/or increasingly expensive, difficult and damaging to extract to the point of overall economic unviability in terms of *net* energy. As Richard Heinberg (2009) says, with admirable concision: '[T]here is no clear practical scenario by which we can replace the energy from today's conventional sources with sufficient energy from *alternative* sources to sustain industrial society at its present scale of operations.'[40]

What then follows, however? Certainly, we should stop believing in the 'solutions' on offer, particularly those which are being literally sold to us and stand to make a lot of money for someone else. (We will come back to those in a moment.) Nor, however, is despair a viable response. For one thing, it grants to the modernists their self-important delusion that without the accoutrements of capitalist modernity, life isn't worth living. For another, retreating to a cabin in the woods stockpiled with baked beans and guns contributes nothing to the one thing that we will need most, and that stands the best chance to save the best of what we are and have: in a word, *community*.

That is the clear lesson emerging from the wreck of the high-level conferences in Copenhagen (2009) and Cancún (2010). Writing after the latter, in words which independently resonate with my own conclusions, Gustavo Esteva declared: '[W]e must stop asking governments and international organisations for solutions they don't want to – and can't – implement. And we must stop pretending to be God, thinking we can "fix" the planet.' The only hope, he argues, is for people to bypass both the state and the market, together with their institutional allies, and take charge of their own lives by rejecting waste rather than recycling more of it, reclaiming mobility through bikes and shared public transport rather than more 'green' cars, and so on.[41] That is now the greater part of the work that can be and needs to be done.

Strengthening sustainable local communities will do the most both to slow or mitigate the effects of unavoidable climate change and to help us and our fellow species survive what cannot be stopped. As Guy R. McPherson wisely remarked: '[C]ommunity is the least regarded, yet most important, characteristic for the post-carbon era.'[42] This is an insight that John Michael Greer develops at length in his 'user's guide to the end of the industrial age', entitled *The Long Descent* (2008): neither continuance as usual nor a sudden all-encompassing crash, but a series of descents and temporary plateaus until a new stability is found.

> There's a wide middle ground between contemporary society and a Road Warrior struggle of all against all . . . and aiming for a constructive response to the futures of the middle ground is in all probability the best strategy we have. The longer we try to cling to the peak, the harder and faster the fall is going to be, and the fewer are the people and cultural resources that are likely to survive it. If we accept that the Long Descent is inevitable and try to make it in a controlled manner, on the other hand, the way is open not only for bare survival, but for surviving in a humane and

creative fashion while preserving as much of value as possible for the future. (2008: 128, 130–1)

Before considering in more detail the possibilities offered by this approach, however, we need to look at other schemes that are currently carrying a heavy load of human hopes.

Wind Power and Energy

Many people's hopes are currently invested in wind power. Perhaps it can 'save' us? The answer depends on what that means. In a nutshell, if it means 'Can wind power, intelligently and sensitively undertaken, contribute significantly to a *sustainable* energy programme overall?' then the answer is yes, almost certainly. But if it means 'Can wind power enable us to continue with our *present* rate of energy consumption but without damaging the environment to the extent coal and oil have?' then the answer is unequivocally no. Not even – indeed, especially – if the wind farms are on a massive scale.

Let us note right away that, as they have become bigger and more intensive, it is increasingly misleading to speak, as the industry prefers, of 'wind farms', as if they were some mom–and–pop operation. We should really call them 'wind factories', but I shall settle for putting 'farms' in quotation marks. Here are some of the companies most heavily invested in wind power in North America: General Electric, Halliburton, Goldman Sachs, J. P. Morgan Chase and the FLP Group. Have these huge corporations converted to the green cause? Hardly. They see another chance for private profit, this time in the name of 'environmentally responsible energy'. As a result, in remaining wildernesses throughout North America and increasingly Europe, local and national governments are collaborating with business to install large turbine assemblies, complete with new clear-cut roads, the felling of trees or draining of wetland, more power lines, a new electrical sub-station, lights on some of the turbine blades for aircraft, increased human traffic and noise. Potential health issues, let alone ecological impacts on wildlife and biotic integrity, are not allowed a look-in.

Perhaps their proponents will ignore personal evidence of noise pollution and consequent physical stress for those living near them, and an absence of the usual wildlife, presumably for the same reason. ('Merely anecdotal' is the first weapon of choice when technoscience doesn't want its well-paid services to capital to be inconvenienced.) Perhaps they will also dismiss, despite mounting evidence, the losses of birds and bats as, say, 'a necessary price to pay' (but by whom?).[43] In that case, the objection that, when they are sited in areas of exceptional natural beauty and/or wildness, wind 'farms' are ugly and intrusive will pose no problem at all; the charge of being the subjective concern of a middle-class NIMBY (Not in My Back Yard) will fly.

Those for whom ecological ethics matters should not be fooled. First, Aldo Leopold's dictum was, if you remember, that 'A thing is right when it tends to preserve the integrity, stability *and beauty* of the biotic community. It is wrong when it tends otherwise' (1970: 262). Aesthetics have a complex but real connection with ecology, and the ugliness of an industrially violated landscape is also, more often than not, a reliable sign of its biotic degradation and desecration.

Second, wild nature should be understood 'not as that which is free of all trace of our interventions', to repeat Wiggins (2000: 10; see above, Chapter 2), 'but as that which has not been entirely instrumentalized by human artifice, and as something to be cherished . . . in ways that outrun all considerations of profit'. Quite, and that is just what a wind 'farm' in such a place destroys.

Third, as already mentioned, the charge of NIMBYism is often used to undermine just the sort of popular resistance to industrial instrumentalization that politically progressive people should be supporting. (And not only popular. The principal reason why the English city of Oxford is not an ugly and polluted sacrificial victim to the motorcar and large-scale commercial property development, like virtually every other major British city, is the powerful elite resistance of the University.) Seen through the new 'green' looking-glass, defenders of local distinctiveness – places which have not already been engineered to fit in with human needs and desires, and whose value lies rather in what they mean to those who live there or nearby, both human and nonhuman – are selfish hypocrites, while landowners, developers and energy companies whose motives are private profit are the new environmental heroes!

Finally, not the least important element of ecocide is the ideology of allowing measurable utility (such as energy output) to ride roughshod over everything else (especially non-economic, in fact non-quantifiable, aesthetic or spiritual qualities). Interestingly, the logic of wind 'farm' advocates is identical with that of the recent so-called war on terror: 'Surrender your civil liberties, or terrorists will take them.' In this case, it's 'Surrender your last places of wild nature, or climate change will destroy them.' Elevated natural areas such as mountain ridges, especially, are now being added to the list of 'resources' for anthropocentric exploitation. Terence Black, rueing the forced conversion of a local patch, writes:

> To those who do not enjoy or understand the countryside – like most politicians, one suspects – the idea that a few fields and birds, a bit of woodland, can be set against a great global concern will seem bizarre. Yet, as they become increasingly rare, these unspoilt, ordinary places matter, each in its own particular way. . . . The great abstract ideals of environmentalism mean nothing when they are achieved against the grain of local environments.[44]

David Orton and Helga Hoffmann-Orton point out that 'We are not talking here about a small group of wind turbines ecologically situated, community owned and controlled, and helping to supply energy to the local bioregion, with the revenues community-generated, not privately accumulated, within an overall societal strategy of seriously reducing citizen energy lifestyles and hence greenhouse gas emissions.'[45] And the so-called environmental assessment process, in the case of a new wind development in their part of rural Nova Scotia, was highly instructive. The project was registered on 5 August 2008 and approved by the Minister of the Environment on 2 September 2008, with public comments being accepted for *two weeks* (which was just long enough for the leader of the Green Party of Canada enthusiastically to endorse it).

If the situation was as Orton and Hoffmann-Orton say, by way of contrast, it would be a very different matter. But placing giant banks of wind turbines (or for that matter, giant solar panels) in areas relatively little impacted by humans (so they are good candidates for 'development') or little populated by humans (so no one who matters will be disturbed, i.e. nonhumans) connected through lengthy transmission lines to where the energy is actually needed – all this is simply industrial capitalism's 'green' attempt to keep its show on the road. Even in technical terms, wind turbines are physically unable to generate the amounts of energy that would allow us to carry on as we have been without covering a staggering amount of the habitable surfaces of the planet.[46] No matter how you look at it, then, industrial wind 'farms' are an extension of what is destroying the Earth and which will end, if unchecked, by eating itself and its dependents.[47]

Let me summarize. Industrial wind 'farms', without a serious programme to (a) radically reduce energy consumption and (b) conserve energy, as well as (c) bring down human numbers as quickly and humanely possible, are an ecological travesty and an ecocentric betrayal. Conversely, however, *if* those parts of the programme are in place, together with considerably reduced consumption, microhydro, tidal, solar and energy conservation through much better design, insulation and use of buildings, then wind power could help provide the basis of an energy economy that doesn't destroy nonhuman nature and nearby human communities alike.[48]

Nuclear Energy

I don't intend to spend so long on this topic, partly because the gist of what has just been said applies with equal force to nuclear power, and partly because we have already discussed it briefly in Chapter 8, where I criticized Lovelock's contrarian advocacy. But the issues mentioned there do not exhaust the problems. David Lowry, the former director of the European Proliferation Information Centre, points out that recycling plutonium to generate energy 'will normalise the use of prime nuclear explosive material in international commerce, and ensure the movement . . . of huge quantities of weapons–usable nuclear material . . . inviting terrorist interventions'. Leonard Weiss, of the Center for Arms Control and Non-Proliferation, reminds us that: 'Expanded nuclear power in industrial countries will inevitably mean expanded nuclear exports to less developed countries as manufacturers try to recoup their investments in a limited domestic market by selling abroad. It can be shown statistically that countries that receive nuclear assistance are more likely to build nuclear weapons.'[49]

In terms of specifically ecological ethics, what is also deeply problematic is how nuclear power stations exemplify and reinforce the 'large is beautiful' attitude of industrial hypertechnology. In addition, there is its potential environmental impact, on all forms of life; the problem of how safely to store radioactive nuclear waste is still unsolved. (A recent study concluded that, in all, nearly one million people around the world have died from exposure to radiation released by the 1986 nuclear disaster at the Chernobyl reactor.)[50] Finally but not least, it is unforgivably naive to assume or hope that nuclear power would be used to enable a transition to genuine eco-sustainability, rather than to prop up the current hugely destructive levels and kinds of energy production and consumption for as long as possible.

Unfortunately, Lovelock is not alone in that assumption. The Bay Area of California is home to one of the most progressive concentrations of people in the world. In what is probably a package, however – being a rich place, in every way – it also occasionally throws up some unfortunate instances of vision (or visionariness, perhaps) in the service of techno-cornucopian libertarianism. Stewart Brand's most recent book, subtitled *An Ecopragmatist Manifesto* (2009), is one. Actually, Brand's defence of nuclear power and genetic engineering is not surprising; his love of technology has long been evident, starting with his early adoption of Buckminster Fuller's metaphor of 'Spaceship Earth'. It's a pity that Gregory Bateson, another of Brand's mentors, isn't still here to skewer his enthusiasm for nuclear and gene hypertechnology. A truth voiced by Sunita Narain will have to do: 'All technofixes – biofuels, GM crops or nuclear power – will create the next generation of crisis, because they ignore the fundamental problems of capitalism as a system that ignores injustices and promotes inequity' (quoted in Hulme 2009: 268).

In fairness, I should add that for every Global Business Network (co-founded by Brand) in San Francisco, helping businesses, NGOs and governments survive in a changing 'global environment', there is a Planet Drum Foundation or an International Forum on Globalization, helping people to survive businesses and governments, and connect with local ecology. (And whatever else the planet may be, it is closer to a drum than to a spaceship: a shiny metal phallic artefact, operated by and for men in order to 'escape' from the Earth.)

Geo-Engineering

What has been said concerning wind 'farms' and nuclear power stations applies with equal force, if not more so, to proposals for huge hypertechnological interventions intended to 'geo-engineer' the Earth's climate. In a sane world it wouldn't be necessary, but let's review the problems.

One is their sheer scale: dangerously insensitive not only to what's happening on the ground but to small effects that can then become the causes of big effects (as per chaos and complexity theory). For the dire track record of brutalist 'engineering' of this size and scope, see James C. Scott, *Seeing Like a State: How Certain Schemes to Improve the Human Condition Have Failed* (1998). And remember DDT and CFCs (chlorofluorocarbons): both hailed as breakthroughs and boons, both deadly.[51]

Then there is the arrogant assumption that our (relevant) knowledge of something as complex and delicate as the Earth's climate exceeds our ignorance; and relatedly, that it can be modelled on, or as, a machine – something *we* have *made* – and hence, engineered. To quote the dazed comment of one survivor of the Deepwater oil rig in the Gulf that blew up in 2010: 'Everything they said couldn't go wrong went wrong.' And when it does, it's always a surprise, especially to the 'experts'. That might be because, in the words of one rightly angry woman at a town hall meeting in Louisiana, addressed to the officials of BP, the government and the state: '[You] act like you know when you don't know.'[52] We certainly don't know how to refreeze the Arctic, how to regrow a rainforest, or how to restore a complex ecosystem and the human culture it once supported.

'Countering the damage caused by one technological dinosaur with another gargantuan engineering venture reflects the characteristic technological hubris of modern industrial capitalism' (Hamilton 2010: 163). Tennekes (1990) is less restrained: '[T]he hubris, the conceit, the arrogance implied by words like "managing the planet" and "stabilising the climate" . . . We cannot even manage ourselves!' Geo-engineering moves in precisely the opposite direction to recognizing our vulnerability and our dependence on the Earth, an insight which is at the heart of ecocentric ethics. As Wendell Berry says, 'the work now most needing to be done – that of neighbourliness and caretaking – cannot be done by remote control with the greatest power on the largest scale' (2008: 2).

Hubris is 'arrogance, such as invites disaster', as the ancient Greeks well knew but some people today have clearly forgotten. Such arrogance has dimensions that are our direct concern in this book; one is certainly anthropocentrism. Hear Rowe again, ever a touchstone of sanity and sanctity: 'It is time to eschew human self-interest and recognize the inherent worth and surpassing values of Earth's miraculous ecosystems whose workings we do not understand. Anthropocentrism says we know how to control and manage them; ecocentrism says "not yet; maybe never"' (1994: 107).

Another dimension is secularism. 'Calling the Earth "sacred" is another way of expressing humility in the face of forces we do not fully comprehend. When something is sacred, it demands that we proceed with caution. Even awe.'[53] Conversely, as we have already seen, desacralizing the Earth is a necessary prerequisite to its ruthless exploitation: in short, to desecrating it.

Finally, the arrogance involved is androcentric in its facile assumption of a single, technical, silver bullet/killer app solution to a messy, complex problem that requires personally engaging with its emotional, cultural, social and political aspects, all of which have highly material effects. The words 'boys' and 'toys' come irresistibly to mind. The ethical attitude seems to be: don't bother me with details, this is basically simple and it might work, so let's do it and see what happens. After all, we *can*, so we *should*, right? Anyway, we (the ones doing it) will be disproportionately shielded from any adverse consequences.

Carbon Trading and Ecosystem Services: The New Gods of the Market

Attempts to stave off ecocrisis through industrial-scale renewable energy, nuclear power and/or geo-engineering are deeply implausible if you admit the simple truth that 'you can't grow your way out of a crisis if growth is what's causing the crisis in the first place' (Greer 2008: 5–6), or, as Kingsnorth says, that '[a]n economy predicated on constant growth cannot be the engine of a change that

urgently demands less of it'. But that is just what seems to be difficult
to see and admit. As Kingsnorth continues, 'Democracies predicated
on giving their consumer citizens what they want are unable to tell
them what they cannot have.'[54] Such corruption of citizenship and
the common good makes use of the human tendency to rely heavily
on habit, narrowly perceived self-interest, wishful thinking and
denial, and the whole ensemble is then easy meat for manipulation
at the skilled and unscrupulous hands of those with a private gain at
stake. So it doesn't help to overestimate the importance of reason
or plausibility; like it or not, as I argued in Chapter 11, there are no
self-evident truths.

That analysis is no conspiracy theory, although I am sure there are
such conspiracies. (Indeed, according to George Bernard Shaw, 'All
professions are conspiracies against the laity.') My point is that there
is an anthropocentric *culture* of capitalism, as well as capitalist societies, that supports and is supported by such enterprises. And just as
the best, most convincing liar is one who believes his own lies, so the
belief of capitalists in capitalism is passionate and complete: in short,
religious. (Or, more precisely, since it's not supposed to be a religion
and therefore cannot admit to being one: crypto-religious.)

Hamilton notes that the reason for the outrage that met both
Carson's *Silent Spring* and Meadows et al.'s *The Limits to Growth* (discussed later in this chapter) 'is that they challenge the most deeply
held assumptions of Western civilisation – that the Earth's resources
are infinite and that humans have the right to exploit them without
restraint for their own benefit. . . . At its core, the preoccupation
with growth is a religious urge, but one displaced from the genuinely
sacred to the nominally profane' (2010: 37–8, 65). (Although note
that to cast the Earth in terms of its 'resources' is already to concede
the terms of the argument to the anthropocentrics.) George Monbiot
throws another insightful light on it: '[T]he central immortality
project of western society [is] perpetual economic growth, supported
by an ideology of entitlement and exceptionalism.'[55] And in a superb
essay, Wendell Berry calls our present ruling religion 'a sort of autistic
industrialism' (2008: 1).

The alternative is not *no* religion. There is virtually nil prospect of
that, despite the fantasies of the 'New Atheists'. In any case, it's not
at all clear that the 'atheist anthropolatry of Richard Dawkins and
his peers', being another form of anthropocentrism, would be an

improvement (Greer 2008: 216). The only real alternative, as I have tried to show, is a better kind of religion, one with the Earth and all its life, rather than money, at its heart, which I describe as animism.

Of course a great deal could be accomplished through political and economic measures such as large-scale public works, radically shifting subsidies, conventional regulation, green taxes and other non-trading market mechanisms, and legal action. But just as a steady-state economy requires a steady-state culture to support it, such measures will never be legislated and enforced (not successfully, at least) without a great deal of public pressure from citizens. Governments will not act against their fiscal interests unless they have to, and capital too 'will not act against its own interests by respecting environmental measures' (Brennan 2003: 160). That kind of pressure is not only political; it can only come from, and be sustained by, deep roots in *shared emotional and spiritual values* that can then be articulated and mobilized. As Sarkar remarks, 'Economic contraction, a steady-state economy, equality or even reduction in inequality are . . . things that must be put through against the laws of market economy and against the bitter resistance of capitalists' (1999: 174). Athanasiou too recommends 'admitting that there is no easy path to a green transition, and perhaps no path at all – for powerful minorities everywhere do not want change' (1997: 304). It is not a good idea to be so 'realistic' you are paralysed, however; after all, as a wise man once remarked: '[D]espair is only for those who see the end beyond all doubt. We do not.'

I would like to move on to hopeful strategies around the issue of community that I mentioned above. First, however, we are obliged to consider the latest and most daring attempt by capital to turn the ecocrisis which threatens its existence along with ours to its own twisted account, by reinventing itself and selling us more of what caused the ecocrisis (along with overpopulation) as its solution. And if that sounds laughably unlikely, it would be a bad mistake to underestimate corporate cunning. If one was a gambler, one might even admire this last daring throw of the dice. The project has two main connected faces: *carbon trading* and *ecosystem services*, culminating in *Earth Inc.*

These enterprises have powerful backers among the true believers. Maurice Strong, Secretary-General of both the 1972 UN Conference on the Human Environment in Stockholm and the 1992

Earth Summit in Rio, and the First Executive Director of the United Nations Environment Programme (UNEP), asserted in 1996: 'In addressing the challenge of achieving global sustainability, we must apply the basic principles of business. This means running "Earth Incorporated" with a depreciation, amortization and maintenance account.' Similarly, the Stern Review (2005) was a major report by (Lord) Nicholas Stern, commissioned by the British government, on the economic impact of climate change. It positioned climate change as 'the greatest market failure the world has ever seen'. Tony Blair, hailing it in 2006, said: '[W]hat the Stern Review shows is how the economic benefits of strong early action easily outweigh any costs. It proves tackling climate change is the pro-growth strategy.' In other words, ultimately, no matter how serious, climate change is only a *technical* problem, requiring a technical – that is, *market* – solution. Any ethical or political dimension is negligible.[56]

Also in 2005, the multi-authored, multi-volume UN Millennium Ecosystem Assessment (MEA) was published. This gave an enormous boost to the idea of turning the Earth into a corporation providing priceable and tradable goods and services, and ecosystems into an abstraction to that end. Four years later, the Deputy Head of the International Union for Conservation of Nature (IUCN) – one of the oldest and largest environmental NGOs – asserted that 'it's time to recognize that nature is the largest company on Earth working for the benefit of 100 per cent of humankind' (quoted in Sullivan 2010b). As with all such statements, this is not a description so much as an intervention: one that contributes to *turning* nature into a business company, one whose only function is to *work*, and for whom? For *humankind*. That is what anthropocentrism offers the rest of nature: more or less enlightened, and more or less efficient, slavery.

Ecocrisis is thus becoming (from an article in the *Harvard Business Review*) 'one of the biggest opportunities in the history of commerce', with companies 'selling solutions to the world's environmental problems' (quoted in Sullivan 2010a: 2–3). I quoted earlier the motto of the giant management company McKinsey: 'Everything can be measured, and what gets measured gets managed.' *The McKinsey Quarterly* reports that 'executives are now beginning to recognise the importance of biodiversity for their future strategies. Many are also discovering business opportunities, not just threats.' In fact, a majority of the executives interviewed 'identify a variety of potential opportunities, such as bolstering corporate reputations with environmentally conscious stakeholders by acting to preserve biodiversity and developing new products or ideas from renewable natural resources.'[57] In short, the firm that brought you enclosures, colonialism, privatization and ecocrisis itself is still in business, only now it's green . . .

What are 'ecosystem services', then? The basic idea is that the 'environment' provides a number of 'services' to humans which enable them to do, well, anything, but which have so far been ignored as economic 'externalities'. That was bad enough, it's true, but what of the 'solution'? What is on offer is not to recognize and respect the intrinsic value of nature, both for its own sake and (so to speak) for ours, as a bulwark against yet more dangerous exploitation and destruction. It is just the opposite: to instrumentalize ecosystems even more thoroughly, bringing them into the financial and economic system by quantifying, commodifying, pricing, selling and trading them.

In what follows, I shall rely heavily on the excellent work of Sian Sullivan (2010a) in order to summarize the steps by which the natural world is turned into a financial instrument:

1 Propagate the concept of nature as a 'provider' of 'services' to humans. (I shall henceforth refrain from putting scare-quotes on all these terms, but please try to keep in mind how questionable, even downright weird, they are when applied to the natural world.) This begins the work of turning the Earth into a corporation.
2 Conceptually break those services down into categories that lend themselves to being quantified and given financial values.
3 Bring in the quantification wizards from ecological science, economics and finance to assign prices to each service, thus turning them into fictional commodities. (At this point, a river you could swim in, a forest you could walk through or food you could eat starts to melt into a set of digits; or, rather, the latter starts to become more real, so to speak, than the former.)
4 Get more financial investment experts to help create new markets where these commodities can be traded. (And, as Sullivan points out, the value of a commodity increases with its scarcity: helpful with carbon pollution, as long as the

scarcity isn't purely notional, but not so good for rainforests or species.)

5   Introduce the resulting commodities into the financial markets and develop complex derived products such as options and futures that can acquire more value (or 'value') through speculative trading. Thus already there is a species credit trading industry, an ecosystem marketplace, environmental asset management and investment companies, biobanks, biodiversity derivatives, natural capital – in short, a few people making a lot of money without any evidence that any of this has had any positive environmental impact whatsoever.

By now it should be no surprise to find that 'The global mega-NGOs of Conservation International (CI), The Nature Conservancy (TNC), and the World Wide Fund for Nature (WWF), in collaboration with CEOs on their boards and wealthy, largely US-based, philanthropic foundations, are all endorsing and developing market-approaches to conservation based on newly created environmental products that can be exchanged remotely' (Sullivan 2010a: 120). Even a recent Worldwatch Report on a 'Green New Deal' rests on productivist assumptions of endless growth, treating nature as 'natural capital' and managing 'nature-based assets' for profit. It shows no recognition of 'the basic incompatibility between capitalist accumulation and ecosystem integrity . . . deepening the humanity versus nature contradiction and people's alienation from their embodiment' (Salleh 2010).

Already in 1993, the Natural Resources Defense Council, the National Wildlife Federation and the Environmental Defense Fund sided with the US government against old-school environmentalists to support the neoliberal NAFTA measure. Afterwards, a member of the first organization bragged: 'We broke the back of the environmental opposition to NAFTA' (quoted in Hertsgaard's useful 1999: 308). Note the language of the boast, worthy of any hyped-up CEO or politician; and the Orwellian names, in context, of the organizations. Another NGO, the National Wetlands Coalition, lobbies on behalf of business interest to oppose legislation protecting wetlands.

The ugliness of the discourse of capital eating nature is aesthetic and spiritual, too. Terms like 'sustainable resource management' fall into the same category as the obfuscation lashed by Orwell in his essential essay, 'Politics and the English Language': they are 'designed to make lies sound truthful and murder respectable, and to give an appearance of solidity to pure wind'. A good counter-example would be Abram's *Becoming Animal: An Earthly Cosmology* (2010), a beautifully written work, opening our eyes to animist enchantment. In contrast to 'ecosystem services' and the like, that sounds fluffy and subjective; yet what Abram calls 'the practice of wonder', being fully embodied and embedded, is actually as solid as it gets. It is also (therefore?) highly resistant to being instrumentalized, and carries ecocentrically egalitarian implications that would horrify the market.

At its present rate of growth, by 2030 carbon will be the largest commodity market in the world (around $2 trillion, about the same as oil now). There have already been more than $300 billion worth of carbon transactions since 2005: a staggering amount. These are a form of 'pollution trading', and, very briefly, they work like this: an official cap is set to the total permissible amount of emissions, and firms hold a limited number of permits to emit a specified amount, the total number of which limit the overall amount. Firms that want to emit more may buy more permits from those who have more than they need. (Hence, 'cap and trade'.) There is then a financial incentive to reduce your emissions.

There is a small problem, however: it doesn't work. (As a way to reduce overall carbon emissions, that is, not as a nice little earner.) A recent investigation by Mark Schapiro concluded that the carbon market 'is, in essence, an elaborate shell game' – as in three shells, a pea under one of them, and a sharp wager – 'a disappearing act that nicely serves the immediate interests of the world's governments but fails to meet the challenges of our looming environmental crisis' (2010: 39). In the words of a subsequent commentator, 'There is a real chance that billions of dollars will change hands via the exchange of phantom offsets and that the climate will benefit not one iota from the effort.'[58]

Should we be surprised? The Tropical Rainforest Action Plan (TRAP) has overseen billions of dollars spent since 1985 promoting 'responsible' industrial logging. Result: deforestation has rapidly increased. As Athanasiou points out in his excellent book, 'corporate environmentalism . . . offers a misleading win–win fantasy of environmental protection in which tough choices will not be necessary' (1997: 241). Yet such approaches continue to displace and obscure measures not depending on commodification which could actually reduce emissions. Gar Lipow, a systems analyst and activist, put it this way: 'Mommy, where do carbon offsets come from?' 'Well, you see, honey, when a polluter and a consultant love money very, very much, they come together in a very special way to produce an extremely long piece of paper' (quoted in Lohmann 2006: 61).

There is actually a perfectly good precedent for recognizing the intrinsic value of nature without betraying it by instrumentalizing it. It only appears radical in the light of the reactionary politics and economics that has subsequently become so dominant. As Don Brown says:

> The best alternative to an instrumental value of nature is not to put an economic value which represents its 'intrinsic' value, but simply to create a rule that prohibits destruction of natural resources because of their intrinsic value. Many environmental laws do this, particularly those passed [in the USA] before the mid-1980s when economic efficiency arguments became the dominant policy discourse. Such acts required protection of fish, other species, and human health without regard to their economic value, nor did they limit regulatory action on the basis of the results of a cost-benefit analysis which required valuing everything as a commodity.[59]

One might object: but who decides what has intrinsic value? But that was always a political decision anyway. All that turning the answer over to the market does is disguise its unavoidably political and thus contested nature with a spuriously naturalized 'objectivity'.

In short, the answer to destructive economic assessments of environmental impacts, sinks and costs is not to assign nature an economic value; that simply feeds the megamachine. It is, rather, to resist and contest the underlying assumption that nature's chief value is economic, and that its value can be entirely captured in economic terms.

Larry Lohmann is one of the most acute and industrious analysts of carbon markets and his work, with that of other authors on the subject published by the Corner House, is required reading on this subject. Among other points, he reminds us of the extent to which 'carbon colonialism' is at work; the decisions are almost all taken by powerful men in the global North, but their direct effects are overwhelmingly felt by men and women in the global South. An influential IPCC report in 2000, for example, was written by a panel which

> included no representatives of indigenous peoples who live in or depend on forests, or of communities directly affected by plantation projects. It included no representatives of communities damaged by fossil-fuel pollution that would be licensed by 'forestry off-set' projects, who also would have had incentives to insist on better science. To the middle-class natural scientists and economists who dominated the panel, it was likely to be simply a given that there were vast 'degraded lands' in the South (but not the North) that could be taken over for carbon projects without land or forests being degraded elsewhere as a result; that project development agencies could do what they promised; and that it would be easy to determine from a distant office whether projects actually 'saved' carbon. (Lohman 2006: 38)

Feyerabend's observation from two decades earlier still stands: '[A]n abstract discussion of the lives of people I do not know and with whose situation I am not familiar is not only a waste of time, it is also inhumane and impertinent' (1987: 305). Nigel Cooper makes another good point: rather than relying on an economic model, especially when the intrinsic value of places and considerations of human livelihood, for example, conflict, 'the process of decision-making also needs to be spiritual in the broad sense of the term, earthed in real life rather than financial abstractions and alert to the wonders of the human condition'.[60]

A related programme is Reducing Emissions from Deforestation and Forest Degradation (REDD), in which you can emit greenhouse gases to an equivalent amount stored in a protected forest. Note three crucial assumptions: (i) the validity of the magical abstraction by which a carbon emission and some trees are interchangeable (or, rather, that the latter are, in effect, *only* carbon); (ii) that forests will stay protected in perpetuity; and especially (iii) that it works. But again, it doesn't. A Greenpeace investigation found that in the model example in Bolivia, set up by the Bolivian government, the Nature Conservancy, BP, Pacificorp and American Electric Power, logging companies were simply taking the money not to chop down one part of the forest and moving operations to the next part, sometimes even using the same money to do so. The estimate that only one-tenth of the original amount of carbon claimed would actually be saved is almost certainly too high. Another major assessment by Friends of the Earth International reveals a mass privatization of forests in train, with indigenous and local communities shut out and no overall reduction in losses.[61] And as Hari (2010) points out:

> When you claim an offset and it doesn't work, the climate is screwed twice over – first because the same amount of forest has been cut down after all, and second because a huge amount of additional warming gases has been pumped into the atmosphere on the assumption that the gases will be locked away by the now-dead trees. So the offset hasn't prevented emissions – it's doubled them.

Sullivan argues:

> Markets do not care if rainforests fall, if glaciers shrink, or if the values of indigenous cultures are displaced or captured in the service of capitalism: and it seems to be mad to think that it is only their correct construction, e.g. through pricing mechanisms, that will prevent the manifestation of these losses. When nature health becomes converted into a dollar sign, *it is the dollar not the nature that is valued*. (2010a: 127; my emphasis)

Something that all financial and economic instrumentalization does is to establish an apparent equivalence between one 'bit' of nature here and another somewhere else, so that someone wishing to 'develop' one 'bit' can justify doing so by 'protecting' another. In this way, the plural, sensuous qualities of the living world are progressively replaced with a dead materialist monism (a perfect parody of the One God) consisting entirely of identical quantifiable stuff, entirely bound and ruled by money, itself an abstraction. Here the virtuality of the speculative financial markets really comes into its own: full of abstract entities with vanishingly tenuous connections to anything you could eat, wear, live in or even watch or read, but dangerously 'normal' in the mental world of investors, speculators, traders and bankers. (And that, I would add, is just the world currently being protected by its arm in government – for the entire financial services industry depends on state patronage – as everywhere in the global North, the financial failures of *those* people, plus their overseers in office, are rebranded as the fault of *the* people.)

Remember Horkheimer and Adorno: modernity 'makes dissimilar things comparable by reducing them to abstract quantities. . . . All gods and qualities must be destroyed' (2002: 4–5). As they understood, despite its hardnosed technoscientific and bureaucratic appearance, the act of converting the unfathomably rich and complex world of nature, at once material and qualitative, into an abstraction of quantifiable and equivalent indices – but with powerful material effects – is fundamentally one of dark magic.[62] In that process, all intrinsic value other than that of money, now not for what it can do for anyone or anything but for its own sake, is instrumentalized. As Sullivan says: 'These processes, and the institutions and structures with which they are linked, seem to be further conceiving and producing the Earth as a smooth, abstract, space for "nomadic" capture and exchange by the realm of the disembedded and disembodied: namely a transcendent corporate capital and finance' (2010a: 119).

In particular, the new 'green' capitalism tries to destroy the intrinsic value of nature, which cannot be captured by use- or exchange-values, and of the nonhuman lives, agencies or agendas that an animistic mode would respect. Ominously, any sense of natural limits that must be respected also vanishes. The only alternative on offer, tolerated by capital because it is both unavoidable and conveniently amenable, by and large, to sharing power, is worship of an equally abstract and anti-ecological God.[63] Green capitalism is thus the sharp end, and hypermodern expansion, of Max Weber's definition, more than a century ago, of modernist disenchantment: 'the unity of the primitive image of the world, in which everything was concrete magic . . . split[s] into rational cognition and mastery of nature, on the one hand, and into "mystic" experiences, on the other' (1991: 282). (Our masters are quite happy for us to have mystical experiences as long as they don't result in criticizing or inconveniencing the smooth running of the megamachine. Popular New Age nonsense like *The Secret*, purveying fantasies of private spiritual power, will do nicely.)

As Sullivan reminds us, the market 'does not in and of itself embody or produce virtuous behaviour. The market does not care. . . . [W]hat is being promoted under these proposals is a valuing of nature *as money*, not of nature's immanence or sentience, or as a community of which we humans are one of many companions' (2010b: 18). It is, of course, the entire argument of this book that what we and the Earth need most is for humans collectively to *re*-embody and *re*-embed their lives – something which requires re-evaluating the intrinsic value of life and other lives.[64]

Sustainability

Tim Murray, in the course of a useful discussion, says: 'There really is only one kind of sustainability.'[65] That's wrong, because there are two: the genuine article and the other kind. And the fraudulence of the latter doesn't mean it doesn't exist or matter. The signs to look out for are the terms '*sustainable growth*' or '*sustainable development*'. Growth in a finite physical world necessarily reaches a point where it is no longer sustainable, i.e. it *must* stop, although it can stop for two different reasons: either because it reached the point of unsustainability (also known as *overshoot*) and has therefore tipped over into crash, or because it is stopped voluntarily before reaching that point. But advocates of so-called sustainable growth are not interested in entertaining either possibility.

More often than not, those advocating sustainable development mean the same thing as those who are pro-growth, but they may be more sensitive to the second option: hence, 'let's develop to that point and if we're lucky we may never get there, but if not we will consider stopping development voluntarily'. If that sounds like a less than entirely rigorous policy, you're right. It is based on ignoring the fact that *indefinite* 'sustainable development' is an oxymoron. A good example provided by Hardin B. C. Tibbs: 'Our challenge now is to engineer industrial infrastructures that are good ecological citizens [*sic*], so that the scale of industrial activity can continue to increase – to meet international demand without running into environmental constraints' (cited in Sarkar 1999: 119). (And for my next trick . . .)

The more mendacious proponents are indeed using sustainability as, in Thomas-Pellicer's apt metaphor, 'neo-liberalism's Trojan

Horse in ecocidal times': ideological camouflage for 'its classical agenda, viz. private property and free trade'. Thus the only version of sustainability on offer at the Copenhagen Accord meetings in 2010 was, to quote her summary, 'agrifuels + GM monocultures = carbon offsets'.[66] Anything approaching genuine sustainability, such as agro-ecology, local self-reliance or power for producers and consumers, was kept firmly off the table (where the presence of the global South was only grudgingly tolerated in any case).

Even progressive types, however, still apparently consider ecology and ecological ethics as only one consideration out of several. As Murray says:

> economic considerations have achieved a delusional parity in a 'holistic' paradigm that sees 'environmental' sustainability balanced off against 'economic' and 'cultural' sustainability. In this three-legged stool model of viability, environmental issues must compete with other 'sustainability' concerns on a level playing field with other equally valid objectives so as to achieve the optimal 'trade-offs'. This misconception may be termed 'The Fallacy of Equivalent Concerns'. We make our living in an economy, but we live in a biosphere. . . . Without clean air, productive soils, replenished aquifers – without [so-called] biodiversity services – any economy will collapse.[67]

He gives two classic examples of ecologically delusional reasoning. One is from a former Premier of British Columbia: 'To have a healthy environment we need a healthy economy.' (Now try that the other way round.) As Murray points out, the environment was actually doing quite well before humans arrived to 'manage' it! The other is from the Planning Department of a typical Canadian city: 'Several growth allocation/land use scenarios will . . . be developed and tested for impacts on *various* sustainability criteria (financial, environmental, social and cultural).'[68]

It is always awkward to have to state the obvious, so this time I'll let Sandy Irvine do it: 'Unless humans suddenly become capable of personal photosynthesis, digesting their own wastes and many more such capabilities, their well-being is conditional upon that of the life-sustaining Ecosphere *whose well-being must be the litmus test of all other policies.*' As I have argued above (especially in Chapter 8), ecocentrism is the ultimate horizon, practically as much as ethically, and when strictly human interests (as they do sometimes appear to be) conflict with ecological, *the former must give way* – either voluntarily, with as much grace and skill and compassion as we can manage, or else willy-nilly, without them. And even in the former case, for people formed by life in the relatively wealthy middle-classes (let alone the truly rich), the hard fact remains that, in Irvine's words, 'what one can sustainably get will be a great deal less than one expects'.[69]

What of genuine sustainability? The Brundtland Commission of 1987 influentially defined sustainable development as 'development which meets the needs of the current generation without impairing the ability of future generations to meet their own needs'. There are at least three problems here. One is that it fails to recognize the reality of ultimate natural limits. Another is that it doesn't explicitly include the effects of population growth. The third is that it is entirely anthropocentric; what about the needs, present and future, of other beings? A better definition is one by Dave Greenfield:

> A sustainable society (or economy) is one which makes use of renewable earth material at a rate that is well within the natural cycles of renewal, makes use of non-renewable material extremely sparingly if at all, focuses on inward, non-material human growth and chooses not to make use of earth material if it is not necessary for a reasonably liveable life.[70]

This too is not explicitly ecocentric, but it is much more eco-friendly. (Implicit is the additional point that, as Sarkar [2010] says, 'a sustainable society would cease to be sustainable if its population continues to grow'.)

The best detailed discussion of (genuine) sustainability I have found is by Richard Heinberg.[71] However, the present book is principally one of ecological ethics, not economics, so I shall only point out two things. One is that, substantively, as Sarkar among others makes plain, '[t]here is a fundamental contradiction between the logic of capitalism and that of a sustainable economy', because 'in a capitalist economy there is a built-in growth dynamic'. For both 'internal' (psycho-social) and 'external' (structural economic) reasons, '[c]apitalists cannot say "enough"' (1999: 150–1).

Second, empirically, the best recent estimate indicates that the resources currently being used by the human race to feed itself, deal with its waste, house itself, amuse itself and so on *already* exceeds the capacity of the Earth's land and water to provide those resources, sustainably – that is, such that they can be replenished – by 30 per cent.[72]

The Limits to Growth

For a grasp of ecological ethics, it is good to know something about this important idea. It stems from a book of the same name by Donella Meadows, Dennis L. Meadows and Jørgen Randers (known collectively as the Club of Rome), published in 1974 and, with a 30-year update, in 2004. Its central idea is that there are natural limits to economic growth stemming from the fact of living in a physically finite world with ultimately limited resources; and that technological innovation, being subject to the same exigency, can only go so far in postponing or mitigating those limits. Not surprisingly, since this contradicts the central belief of modernity in human 'progress' without limits, it met with a mixture of fury, derision and passive resistance (the same response as to ecological Malthusians from the political left and Carson's *Silent Spring* from the right, in fact). The growth ideology of capitalism (and most socialism) felt under threat.

Larry Summers, President Obama's chief economics adviser until late 2010, former president of Harvard University and part-time hedge fund consultant, said: 'The idea that we should put limits on growth because of some natural limit is a profound error.' Summers's view is consistent: we 'cannot and will not accept any "speed limit" on American economic growth. It is the task of economic policy to grow the economy as rapidly, sustainably, and inclusively as possible' (quoted in McKibben 2010: 47; note the token 'sustainably'). And 30 years after the original report, growth having failed to hit the buffers yet, ExxonMobil exalted that 'The Club of Rome was wrong.' But as McKibben, from whose lucid discussion I have borrowed here, comments, 'Not wrong, as it turned out. Just ahead of the curve' (2010: 95).

The basic position of *Limits* was, in fact, that (i) 'If the present growth trends in world population, industrialization, pollution, food production, and resource depletion continue unchanged, the limits to growth on this planet will be reached sometime within the next 100 years'; (ii) however, there is still a chance 'to alter these growth trends and to establish a condition of ecological and economic stability that is sustainable far into the future'; and (iii) the sooner people start on that the better, because the window won't stay open forever (Meadows et al. 1992: xv). But that didn't happen; instead, we got the 1980s. As a result, the collapse predicted by the Club of Rome now appears 'almost inevitable, since we didn't take our foot off the gas when we had the chance' (McKibben 2010: 98).

Dobson (2007) identifies a commitment to recognizing the limits to growth as one of the two distinguishing features of what he calls 'ecologism', the other being ecocentrism and its critique of anthropocentrism. That is true as far as it goes, but it needs to be added that the limits thesis, as it usually stands, is anthropocentric; the only interest its proponents seem to have in nonhuman nature is instrumental, as that which sustains human life. I have argued here that that approach will eventually fail even on its own terms.

The distinction between the idea of natural limits and ecocentrism is not quite so clean, however. A superb essay by Wendell Berry that I have already mentioned makes that clear. As he says:

> To recover from our disease of limitlessness, we will have to give up the idea that we have a right to be godlike animals, that we are potentially omniscient and omnipotent, ready to discover 'the secret of the universe.' We will have to start over, with a different and much older premise: the naturalness and, for creatures of limited intelligence, the necessity, of limits. (2008: 1, 6)[73]

Returning to being the animals we are, as I have already suggested, puts us on a fundamentally equal footing with all the other beings under the ecocentric horizon.

A Left Ecocentric Guide to Capitalism

Rushing in where I should (and do) fear to tread, some comments on the ethical dimension of capitalism, as the currently undisputedly dominant way of doing business, are unavoidable. Here are a few points to consider.

Industrial capitalism is the most widespread, powerful and probably virulent form of anthropocentrism.[74] Its entire point is to generate a private profit for its particular few human shareholders alone. Everyone and everything else, from stakeholders or society to the natural environment, global well-being or the common good, is *secondary*. In this sense, to complain about it not behaving any other way is really to have missed the point. It is quite permissible, however – indeed, vitally important – to ask: are these good people? Is this virtuous behaviour? What are its effects? The capitalist's answer might invoke Adam Smith's faith in the beneficent unintended effects of the so-called 'invisible hand' of the market. It seems to me that a remark sometimes attributed to John Maynard Keynes was closer to the mark: 'Capitalism is the extraordinary belief that the nastiest of men, for the nastiest of reasons, will somehow work for the benefit of us all.'[75]

Proponents of capital often praise choice, but usually in terms of the number of brands selling the same kind of products; the choice on offer is never reflexive in relation to itself as a paradigm. When it comes to that, apparently there is, in Margaret Thatcher's famous phrase, 'no alternative'. This monopoly (in which monism appears again) has long been justified ideologically by presenting capitalism as 'natural', and thus inevitable: something that evolutionary psychology, with its reductive emphasis on competition (but not cooperation) and instrumentality (nothing for its own sake but only for the sake of 'success'), both feeds off and feeds into. The appropriate response is, again, to insist on asking hard questions: *Who says?* And *who benefits thereby?*

What about the benefits of capitalism to the many? Has it in fact been a big success? I recommend a sobering review of the evidence (in case you aren't already pretty sober) by William Rees (2009), the Canadian ecologist who developed the concept of the ecological footprint. As he notes in his summary:

- Development is driving ecocide, 'and the problem is not just climate change. Humans are acidifying the oceans; deserts are spreading; tropical forests are disappearing; biodiversity is declining; fisheries are collapsing; soils are eroding; aquifers are falling; surface waters are polluted beyond life and use, etc.'

- 'We know that the world's most serious ecological problems (e.g., climate change) can be traced mainly to high-income consumers. . . . The wealthy have per capita ecological footprints twenty times or more larger than the very poor.'
- '[T]he absolute number of poor has never been higher.'
- '[T]he greatest share of national and global income growth flows to upper income groups who need it least.'[76]
- 'Beyond a certain point, a point long past in the development of high-income countries, there is no significant positive relationship between various . . . indicators of . . . health [or well-being] and incomes.'[77]
- '[T]he income gap both between and within countries is widening.'[78]
- '[O]ne of the most significant contributors to declining population health and increasing civil unrest in poor and rich countries alike is income disparity',[79] which nonetheless continues to increase.

Rees concludes:

It seems that over the past few decades virtually the entire world has bought into an economic growth paradigm that, contrary to its implict assumptions and stated goals, is wrecking the ecosphere, undermining essential life-support systems, failing the chronically poor, making the already rich richer without improving well-being, and increasing inequality virtually everywhere with negative implications for population health and social stability. Not exactly a stellar record.

In addition to the central importance of profit, and its private nature, the imperative of the bottom line means there will always be pressure on companies to operate in ways that are anti-ecological, such as 'externalizing' costs and scaling up as much as possible. (The latter imperative moves inexorably towards globalization.) For the same reason, and with the same sort of effects, the capitalist ideal is a shared *monopoly* of production/supply (shared only because it looks more like fair competition) and on the consumption/demand side, *dependency*, the ultimate form of which is managed addiction (managed because the dead buy nothing). And it is predicated on perpetual *growth*, since companies are always in competition with others also seeking to grow; so to stop growing is to lose out and vanish or be taken over.

Hence the key role played by the billion-dollar advertising industry in manipulating old desires and creating new ones: wants that have nothing to do with genuine needs. Freya Stark described advertising as 'untruthfulness combined with repetition'. Orwell was blunter; he called it 'the rattling of a stick in a swill bucket'. The advertising industry creates dissatisfaction, waste, debt and social misery. Almost unregulated, its domination of public places with private interests is inescapable, as is its malignant presence on TV, both fuelling the consumerism that helps drive ecocide.[80] Close kin is corporate public relations and spin, used to bully and seduce both the public and politicians. When adopted by companies to improve their public image without addressing anything of ecological substance, trying to persuade us that nuclear power stations or cars or supermarkets are actually ecologically virtuous, PR is known as **greenwashing**.[81] The kind of ethics involved in all this should be obvious: not just anthropocentric but contemptible.

Now I am perfectly aware that there are many small firms, shops and companies which it will be hard to recognize in this description. I myself buy most of my food from small local markets and shops, some of them wholefood, my music CDs from an excellent independent trader, my toiletries from a quirky 'all-natural' outlet that is part of a small chain, and my electricity from an energy company that actively supports renewables. With the owners/employees of all of them (except the last, whom I haven't met yet) I enjoy some sort of personal relationship, and all mix business with some measure of idealism and appreciation for the intrinsic value of what they're doing.

I also realize that local businesses have a very important role to play in any transition to a eco-sustainable economy and society, and (in some appropriate form) in maintaining them. Furthermore, one should be careful criticizing companies that are genuinely trying to become 'green' or sustainable within the limits set by capitalism, for it can play into the hands of those attacking such efforts as hypocrisy, etc. from the political right, which wants to stop them from even trying.

Nonetheless, two big problems remain. One is that such businesses are outweighed many times over, in both the amount of business they do and the effects they have, by the giant supermarkets (whose impacts we have already reviewed), energy companies, media conglomerates, cosmetics firms, power companies and shopping malls. The size, wealth and power – not only financial and economic, but political, social and cultural – of multinational corporations, as concentrations of democratically unaccountable power, the civic republican nightmare, is extraordinary.

Second, all firms must compete against others, so there is always both pressure and the temptation (especially if they're doing well!) to upsize and become one of the big boys, or else sell out to one. The classic example is the sale of The Body Shop in 2006 by its founders Anita and Gordon Roddick to L'Oréal, itself more than a quarter owned by Nestlé, for £652 million (plus £130 million for the Roddicks). Included in the sale was The Body Shop's commitment to no animal testing and fairtrade. Another (there are so many to choose from) was the acquisition in 2000 of Ben and Jerry's ice-cream by the multinational food giant Unilever. In both cases, transnational companies were enabled literally to profit from unwary 'enlightened' consumers without changing their own basic structures and impacts.[82]

Another way we often get fooled is exemplified by *recycling*. Manes isn't:

> To have recycling technologies . . . requires people to design and produce the machinery, roads to transport raw materials and finished products, institutions of learning to train people for this end, currency, governments to print currency, police to protect government interests – in short, the entire structure of technological culture we now have. (1990: 237)

But someone will profit, so capital will tolerate it, using recycling as 'public relations cover for the garbage society' (Athanasiou 1997: 244). What it will never accept, unless it is forced to, is what would actually begin to get to the root problem of overconsumption and waste: *reduced use* in the first place. I would add that the same point applies to 'green' (electric, hybrid, etc.) cars, whose manufacturing impacts are considerable and which contribute to the whole socially and ecologically destructive infrastructure of driving. What is needed are *fewer* cars.

These phenomena are part of the culture as well as the logic of capitalism – which is to say, a culture of anti-ecology and any ecological ethic but the thinnest environmentalism – that we have already discussed in relation to corruption and the loss of the common good. That culture now dominates almost every walk of modern life: not only economics, shutting out more socially and ecologically sustainable ways of life, but democratic politics (successful corporate funding and lobbying by extremely wealthy and unregulated special interest groups), culture (celebrity worship – fame for being famous – and art of all kinds as profitable commodity) and sports (as true fans know). Of course, in all these activities good things are still happening – but overwhelmingly despite business, not because of it. (As Van Morrison once bitingly observed: 'Music is spiritual, but the music business is *not*.')[83]

As a single symbol of how capitalism kills sustainable civic and ecological community and replaces it with a simulacrum that it can control, nothing is better than the shopping mall.[84] A new one recently appeared where I live, like a huge spaceship from Planet Shopping that has crash-landed on Shepherds Bush. As far as any connections with existing communities there, it might as well be, and local shops are already suffering grievously. The message seems to be: the more you spend, the happier you will be. Another lie is proclaimed over the entrance gate, in ominously large, iron letters: 'The Village'.

A related perspective is afforded by Misha Glenny's *McMafia: A Journey Through the Global Criminal Underworld* (2008). Crime now is a billion-dollar enterprise, as much as a fifth of the global economy as a whole, with its proceeds increasingly indistinguishable from the rest. Not a little of it directly sponsors the murder of animals for their body parts, the destruction of habitat by 'logging mafia' as a profitable business, etc. In fact, the parallels with business, both of activities and attitudes, are striking. There is certainly a significant difference between business as legal criminality and crime as illegal business; but it is not fundamental. As Sarkar (1999: 147, 150) observes: 'In capitalism, ethics can only play an insignificant role, the upper limit of which is observance of the rules of the game and the laws of the state. . . . Its basic principles – self-interest, greed, and competition

– promote criminality.' And as ever, in both cases, the helpless and least to blame suffer the most: the natural world and other animals, then women, children and the poor. (From which it follows that the last kinds of humans have a disproportionately large stake in enacting ecocentrism: hence the potential importance of ecofeminism and ecosocialism.)

Of course, there are good individual businessmen and women. To pick only one example, they include those taking part in recent campaigns led by Peter Singer (in the USA) and Toby Ord (in the UK) enjoining those who can afford it to give regularly and generously to charity. But the dynamics and culture of capital make it far too easy to act unethically, even viciously, and even in purely anthropocentric terms, never mind ecocentric ones; and the system itself, as a whole, tends that way. The price for 'enterprise culture' is too high when the effect of the enterprise is ecocide.

More generally, due allowance must be made for the fact that significant instances of ecological destruction either predated capitalism (e.g. some Stone Age megafauna extinctions) or proceeded independently of a market economy (e.g. the Soviet destruction of the Aral Sea). Nonetheless, its centrality in modern ecocide is unmistakeable. Its overall significance of capitalism for us here was thus well summarized by Steven Best:

> Of course, capitalism did not pioneer the reduction of living beings to things and exploitable resources. The domination of humans, animals, and the Earth has ancient institutional and ideological sources in Western culture and, ultimately, agricultural society (spawned some ten thousand years ago) that transcend class and economic dynamics. But while the domination of nature and nonhuman animals hardly began with capitalism, the capitalist system raises human alienation from, and contempt for, the natural world to its highest expression in a global system of individualistic property rights and an advanced technological empire governed by transnational corporations. And when ancient pathologies are conjoined to modern technologies; to an industrial paradigm that subjects work, production, and living processes to mechanized procedures (such as the transformation of agriculture into agribusiness and farming into factory farming); to a bureaucratic state driven by efficiency imperatives; and to an economic system

organized solely around accumulation and profit, the result is an unprecedented crisis stemming from a culture of carcinogenic growth and murderous extermination imperatives. (2009: 43)[85]

At this point, another complexity, if not paradox, presents itself. For the reasons just given, *an ecocentric virtue ethic must be non- (or anti-) capitalist,* but *anti-capitalism is not in itself ecocentric.* That is, because industrial capitalism contributes so grievously to ecocide, it must be radically reformed or replaced; but that alone (so to speak) will not suffice, because it could leave a dominant anthropocentrism in place. It is, as philosophers like to say, a necessary but insufficient condition. Unless anti-capitalism has an ecocentric context or horizon, it won't touch anthropocentrism, the deepest root of our destructiveness and self-destructiveness, which dictates that success or failure lie solely in meeting human needs. So an anthropocentric ecosocialism could 'succeed' in those terms while still condemning other life-forms to death and even as – given our utter interdependency – it is merely postponing the sentence on humanity too. (It is quite possible to imagine a completely egalitarian socialist society that still exploits nonhuman nature and other animals for as long as it can.)

Can capitalism be reformed? That depends. Not internally, either by 'voluntary self-restraint' or 'self-regulation', nor by subjective and voluntaristic idealism on the part of a few entrepreneurs. None of these stands the slightest chance of altering the logic of the market.[86] Somewhat better placed to have a positive impact is *corporate social responsibility* (CSR), also known as *sustainable responsible business* (SRB) and *socially responsible investing* (SRI). This is an attempt to use self-regulation to broaden corporate responsibility beyond shareholders to stakeholders (i.e. all those affected by the company) and communities. Ideally, firms which have embraced CSR would even positively promote community development and voluntarily refrain from socially harmful practices, motivated by a bottom line of people and planet as well as profit.

Before we get too hopeful, however, it would be wise to remember that even if it is not just a cynical ploy (which in some cases it may be), this effort is still framed by the profit imperative. In hard times, if it became a question of company survival, what are the odds that either planet and/or the people, probably in that order, wouldn't be sacrificed first? And I would point out that CSR is still a long way from realizing or recognizing that those three items do not exist on the same plane of importance; in fact, profit depends on people who depend on the planet, which last must therefore take pride of place.

So capitalism can only be 'reformed', or at least its destructiveness effectively controlled, by political and legal regulation that is imposed and monitored externally. That in turn requires broader social and cultural support to succeed – which is why the corporations have a profound interest, beyond simply increasing their sales, in getting inside our heads, and indeed souls. In ecological perspective, the contemporary struggle for the human soul is not between God and the devil, or unbelief; it is between *industrial capitalism*, with its consumer culture, and *green citizenship*. The former is anthropocentric; and if the latter is anything less than ecocentric, the former will have won.

At the time of writing, the former is 'winning'. Here are a few recent headlines. 'Warnings of "Shale Rush" after Canada's Tar Sands Success' (17.5.10). So, despite decades of ecological economics, a method of producing more oil that will further contribute to irreversible climate change, and which is itself up to five times more carbon-intensive than drilling and trashes the environment, is a 'success'. Another one reads, 'Anger as Obama Freeze on Deepwater Drilling puts 46,000 Oil Jobs at Risk' (10.6.10). I don't want to underplay the problems of those whose livelihoods depend on industries that are destroying the world, especially when so very many others (including myself) are also implicated, even if in less direct ways. (Whether deliberately or not, positioning all criticism as hypocrisy seems to be one of the ways the system protects itself.) But immediately after the worst single environmental disaster ever to befall North America, as a direct result of deep-sea drilling – indeed, while the oil is still flowing out – anger at not simply resuming, or maybe even stepping it up?

A third says, 'Greenland's Prime Minister Lambasts Greenpeace for Raiding Arctic Oil Rig' (31.8.10). (That's 'Greenland's socialist prime minister', supported by most of his electorate, and just after the Deep Water disaster.) Positively wicked: trying to stop increased oil and gas extraction in an extremely fragile environment, development of which has been made possible by climate change caused in large part by the same industry. In fact, in January 2011, BP, the principal party behind Deep Water, chirpily announced a massive new deal with the Russian energy firm Rosneft to 'develop' oil and gas reserves in the Arctic. Four degrees plus here we come, I guess. But watching governments and companies trying to buy their way out of the results will not be adequate compensation.

In the meantime, the hard lesson is that there are no solutions to ecological problems in which corporations or the so-called free market play a dominant role. Nor can they coexist for long with an ecocentric ethic.

Perhaps capitalism can be replaced by something else that would be ecologically ethical? While recognizing the force of the Marxist critique of capitalism, I have already argued that its prescription is too compromised by what the two share: principally, a Promethean anthropocentrism and an emphasis on production that leads to industrialism. ('Eco-Marxism' is not very different from 'sustainable growth'.) So let's turn to some other possibilities.

Alternatives

One fascinating analysis, full of Marxist insights but leading through and out of Marx*ism*, is that of Teresa Brennan. She develops the idea 'that environmental degradation is the inevitable consequence of the pursuit of profit. One can either side with Mammon, or with the living against the dead.' Siding with the living means fulfilling what she calls the 'prime directive: we shall not use up nature and humankind at a rate faster than they can replenish themselves and be replenished' (2003: x, 164).

Capital has to speed up production and, with it, consumption; the dynamic of globalization, its latest phase,

> is born of speeding up time while extending further through space, increasing the degrees of separation in relation to control (few have more) and in relation to geography (more people and things have further to go) . . . This same dynamic is responsible for con-suming more of nature than we allow to be replenished, for stress and related illness, and for the destruction of air, water, food and climate. It is this situation which can be countered, without loss of the lives of humans and other species, only by reversing course. (2003: 156)

In other words, 'reversing the accelerated pace of production with its overconsumption of energies means moving back toward a local and nonspecialized economy'. And this, Brennan adds, 'was precisely what Gandhi advocated. . . . When production and consumption both become localized, the temptation to speed up production, indefinitely and at any price, disappears' (2003: 152, 153).

Such a conscious and deliberate return to viability is not borne of 'nostalgia but out of the desire to keep living'. Furthermore, to 're-create the form and scale of an earlier market is not to advocate that its technology be reinstituted. Whatever genuine technological advances we have made (from solar and wind power to anaesthetized and sterile surgery) we retain and build on. But we cannot capitalize upon them, for to do this is to use up more of nature than we return, in one form or another'. Politically, it is both revolutionary and pragmatic, uniting two traditional opponents, both with important truths: progressive advocates of distributive justice, on the one hand, and conservative advocates of local or regional autonomy, on the other. (The positive potential of this point is something no one trying to bring about an ecological ethics should neglect.) As Brennan says: 'To say that we need to "go back, slow down" will be portrayed as antiprogress. But progress lies in straining the human imagination to its limits in cleaning up the mess – while retaining the information that mess has yielded' (2003: 156, 157, 165).

I too am not in a hurry to live in a world without anaesthetics, antibiotics or sophisticated dentistry. But are these a package, so to speak, with nuclear energy, advanced military technology and mass production? Perhaps, and that is a sobering thought. But it should encourage, not paralyse, an impulse to enquire further and ask: *to what extent* are these a package? Maybe, after all, it is not so tightly bound as to rule out some significant picking and choosing, encouraging this and discouraging, even eliminating, that.

What Brennan is suggesting could also be framed as a steady-state economy, as opposed to growth economy – something that was advocated as long ago as 1848 by John Stuart Mill, and a century later by John Maynard Keynes. Its principal and most tireless contemporary theorist is Herman Daly. However, the literature is vast and this is not a book about ecological economics as such.[87] The basic idea should already be clear: a steady-state economy – and the society of which it is part – is a sustainable one because it genuinely respects ecological limits. In Daly's words, it is '[a]n economy with constant stocks of people and artifacts, maintained at some desired, sufficient levels by low rates of maintenance throughput, that is, by the lowest feasible flows of matter and energy from the first stage of production to the last stage of consumption' (1991: 17). I also want to bring to the reader's attention some other work that is more robustly eco-logical, however, and which includes, from that perspective, some potent criticism of both Kovel's eco-Marxism and Daly's ecological economics.

Along with Brennan's work, Saral Sarkar's *Eco-Socialism or Eco-Capitalism?* is an in-depth treatment that is indispensable.[88] (Still another is the work of Ted Trainer, which we shall touch on below.) As Sarkar says, 'a serious ecology movement is today the biggest enemy of capitalism'. But he points out that it poses big problems for socialism, too. Marxist socialism remains 'deeply embedded in a growth paradigm', and not only must the cake to be fairly shared not grow, 'it must shrink. . . . For the first time in history, a social movement "promises" a lower standard of living.' Crucially, the fundamental 'contradiction' is not between capitalism and ecology but between *any* kind of industrial society and ecology. So 'Eco-socialists must not tell voters that they can have their cake and eat it too' (1999: 227, 226, 199, 228).

Sarkar is equally tough on 'eco-capitalism', however – not only unreconstructed capitalism but the kind apparently espoused by Daly and many others. Given the fundamental tension between the growth dynamic of capitalism and what is required for a sustainable steady-state economy, how can one claim, he asks, that the latter is simply a better, greener version of the former? 'Capitalism plus co-operation plus ethics' will not, as he shows in detail, suffice (1999: 176).

Of course, we should not allow terms to unduly dominate ques-tions of substance; if changes under the name of 'capitalism' become sufficiently deep, comprehensive and radical, then that would be fine. Part of Sarkar's point, which certainly seems valid, is that unless such changes alter the socioeconomic *framework* within which such things function, then ecological sustainability will be unable to take root and flourish as we need it to. Thus, cooperatives, joint stock compa-nies, mutual and worker-owned companies, etc. are all good things, but they cannot fully succeed unless their *context* is ecosocialist. (And that means *eco*socialist: the context of anthropocentrically oriented state ownership will not do, either.)

Movements in the Right Direction

It is important to remember that the most important decisions and actions respecting the host of pressing matters that besets us cannot be made solely on economic, scientific or any other 'objective' or 'systematic' grounds. They can only be made on *primarily ethical grounds*. The decision to leave the answer to economics or science alone isn't itself economic or scientific; it simply reflects the fact that for its proponents, economics or science have ultimate value. (And as Brennan says, refining this point, 'deregulation does not mean the absence of all forms of regulation; it means passing regulation to the machine' [2003: 220].)

Perhaps for that reason, some of the most helpful guides to achieving ecological ethics on the ground have turned out to be those who are not afraid of its emotional, personal, cultural and spiritual dimensions: writers like John Michael Greer, Alistair McIntosh, Starhawk, Bill McKibben, Clive Hamilton and Anna Peterson.[89] The subtitle of one of McIntosh's books, 'Climate Change, Hope and the Human Condition' (2008), and the title of another, *Soil and Soul* (2004), strike the right sort of note. Nor do those dimensions, including embodied and 'material' spirituality, exclude political considerations, or intellectual rigour, or mental toughness. Far from it, as I hope to have shown (and the ecofeminists have already).

I want now to mention some grassroots movements and networks that are doing good work and have even more positive potential. As we often find, they are not necessarily ecocentric in themselves, but, in true ecological fashion, they support ecocentrism in action – and would undoubtedly benefit from it, too. There are almost certainly very many more local and particular activities in which you can participate, of course, where you live. But here, in brief, are a few of the more established and better-known ones in addition to Slow Food and the other 'slow' movements discussed earlier in this chapter.

Local Exchange and Trading Systems (LETS) link people locally to enable them to share their time and skills. Through such networks, goods and services can be traded on a non-profit basis. Everyone's time is treated equally: one hour of your time earns you one 'time credit' to spend on what you need from someone else. Time banking in the UK has witnessed a spectacular increase since it first started in 1998. And although this happens without the need for any printed currency, it is close neighbour to the development of local currencies.

The Commons Movement reflects the importance of the common good that I have already emphasized, and the urgent need to protect and reclaim public spaces, with varying green elements, from private interests, developers and commercial invasion. That value extends to open-source and accessible cultural and intellectual initiatives. There is an active organization, On the Commons (formerly the Tomales Bay Institute), as well as more specific groups putting the idea into action in their area.[90] On the west coast of America, the Pacific Forest Trust, founded in 1993, is a non-profit trust that acquires working forest conservation easements by which owners can harvest trees sustainably but not clear-cut or subdivide their land, or sell it off – rules which are binding on new owners too – in the knowledge that the forest will be managed sustainably indefinitely.

An important idea in this context is that of *usufruct*: the right to derive benefit from a portion of land that belongs to an other(s) which also entails some responsibility to take care of it. In this case, the ultimate owner of the land – all land – is the Earth itself. That awareness, especially given legal standing, could help undermine the destructive effects of private property as a lynchpin of corporate capitalism, which concept is also (as so often) a strange fantasy: that human beings can 'own' the Earth, when, if anything, the reverse is the case! In practice, usufruct makes a sort of pair with satisization, the ecosocial idea and practice of 'enough', as opposed to maximization.

Silke Helfrich has helpfully articulated the commons as a paradigm for social movements.[91] Not the least of its virtues is that it cannot be slotted into the antediluvian binaries of capitalist market versus state 'alternative', nor public (when it is state-owned) versus private. Commons encourage self-determination, in line with a participatory civic republican model, together with diversity, cooperation ('out-cooperate instead of out-compete'), long-termism and respect for traditional knowledges. The model also recognizes the ultimate indivisibility of social and ecological dimensions. In words that resonate elsewhere in this book, Helfrich says: 'Remember: the commons are not for sale.'

The Global Ecovillage Movement (GEN) is an impressive network of sustainable communities and initiatives across different cultures, countries and continents that serves as an umbrella organization for ecovillages, transition town initiatives, intentional communities and ecologically minded individuals. It connects and advises thousands of communities, both directly and through other networks, such as Sarvodaya (which supports 2,000 sustainable villages in Sri Lanka), Damanhur in Italy, Nimbin in Australia, small rural ecovillages in Argentina and Mexico, urban rejuvenation projects like Los Angeles EcoVillage and Christiania in Copenhagen, permaculture design sites in Australia, Bolivia and Brazil, and educational centres such as the Findhorn in Scotland, Centre for Alternative Technology in Wales, and Earthlands in Massachusetts.[92]

The Voluntary Simplicity Movement is also based on the idea and value – radical and scary for capitalists, but actually both ancient and sensible – of 'enough', as already mentioned.[93] Its appeal comes from recognizing the positive virtues of living a life rich in intrinsic values and personal, social and ecological goods, and the unhealthy stresses and impacts, contrariwise, of a life veering between driven acquisitiveness and overconsumption or 'affluenza', to use the term popularized by Oliver James (2007). Thus, in circumstances of affluence, provided one went about it intelligently, lowering one's material 'standard of living' (as measured by income/consumption) could actually increase 'quality of life' (subjective well-being). There are now a number of books and websites exploring this subject.[94] Closely related is the growing body of work clearly showing that beyond a certain minimum level of income, happiness levels do not rise with further increases. Robert Skidelsky makes the interesting point that one reason why the 'accumulation of wealth, which should be a means to the "good life", becomes an end in itself [is] because it destroyed many of the things that make life worth living. Beyond a certain point the accumulation of wealth offers only substitute pleasures for the real losses that it extracts.'[95]

Another movement with closely overlapping ideas and values

(which I therefore won't repeat) is that of *degrowth*. Inspired largely by the work of Serge Latouche (most recently, 2007; but see also Gorz 2010), it also emphasizes sufficiency and non-material sources of happiness, and opposes both the overconsumption and overproduction of an economy addicted to growth.

The Transition Town Movement (TTM) is one of the largest and most influential of these networks. It started in Ireland in 2003 and soon spread across the globe. The initial stimulus was the prospect of peak oil and its impact on communities that have grown dependent on fossil fuels for its energy needs, especially as it coincides with the increasingly serious effects of climate change. Attempting to address that issue, however, has naturally led the TTM to all the unavoidably connected ones – just as any resolution to it will have positive effects in other ways. A Transition Initiative is a group working together to address this question: '[F]or all those aspects of life that this community needs in order to sustain itself and thrive, how do we significantly increase resilience (to mitigate the effects of peak oil) and drastically reduce carbon emissions (to mitigate the effects of climate change)?'

Local movements undertake education, awareness-raising and other projects, form groups to take on different key areas, connect with already-existing groups and local governments, and work towards launching a 'community-defined, community-implemented "Energy Descent Action Plan" over a 15 to 20 year timescale', moving towards a low-energy and locally resilient economy. But such collective planning and action will encourage ways of living that are more socially, culturally and ecologically sustainable in other ways too. The movement's manual speaks of the importance of head (why peak oil and climate change are inevitable), heart (why a positive vision is crucial) and hands (the transition model for inspiring local resilience-building) – homely but accessible, as it should be.[96]

Ted Trainer, the author of some important books on the need for a 'conserver society', has written a critically sympathetic piece on the TTM. He points out that in the context of the ongoing and worsening ecocrisis, present global rates of resource use and ecological impact are already grossly unsustainable. So the professed ambition of liberal capitalists to raise them for billions more people is farcical; in which case, the very rich are actually condemning everyone else to poverty. This situation follows from the present paradigm. 'The global economy is a market system and in a market scarce things always go mostly to the rich, that is, to those who can pay most for them.' It also results in seriously inappropriate development (what Shiva calls 'maldevelopment'), which especially in the global South will benefit not local people or environments, but rich corporations and consumers elsewhere, e.g. through cash crops and products for export, 'a form of legitimised plunder'.[97]

All these problems have worsened since the 1970s, with globalization attacking every form of resistance to so-called free trade and market forces. As Brennan (2003) points out too, the social and psychological consequences even in the global North are reflected in burgeoning physical as well as mental health problems, social breakdown, etc. In a society where maximizing your monetary wealth is the supreme value driving ethics, 'market forces drive out good social values and behaviour, because they are only about individuals competing to maximise self-interest' (Trainer 2010).

Trainer concludes that inasmuch as these problems cannot be solved *within* a consumer-capitalist society, 'a good society cannot be an affluent society'. He is therefore critical of Daly, Latouche, Jackson and other writers who think we should retain market capitalism, albeit radically reformed. Instead, we must move towards a zero-growth economy, with a far lower GDP than at present, consisting of 'small, highly self-sufficient, localised economies under local cooperative control' based on meeting needs rather than making a profit, and a corresponding culture of communal cooperation and non-material satisfactions: what he calls 'The Simpler Way'.[98]

Trainer admits that this is asking a lot, voluntarily at least, and may not be possible within the short time that is probably left. In any case, Trainer says – and here it is hard to disagree – we cannot wait for governments or businesses to act. Although 'there will be no significant change while the supermarket shelves remain well-stocked', i.e. while people's faith in the system remains unshaken, which is unlikely to happen until serious fuel shortages start, we can start building a new economy (able to produce the basic goods and services needed to survive) and society (with cooperative and communal values, structures and events) now, under and alongside the old one. That is where the TTM and similar efforts can contribute. Trainer warns trenchantly:

It's not oil that sets your greatest insecurity; it is the global economy. It doesn't need your town. . . . In the coming time of scarcity it will not look after you. You will only escape that fate if you build a radically new economy in your region, and run it to provide for the people who live there.

And he worries that 'the things that green/transition people are doing now, such as setting up community gardens, food co-ops, recycling centres, Permaculture groups, skill banks, home-craft courses, commons, volunteering, downshifting, etc.' will fail if they are contained and subverted by the dominant market system.

Trainer has a point – they need to be articulated as part of a common vision – but I think he overlooks the fact that the new economy can only come from just such efforts, even if it will ultimately take more. Besides, 'big picture thinking' can be paralysing without stuff to do on the ground. (And it takes a lot of work to get a communal garden or local food co-op, say, up and running!) So 'resilience is not enough', but neither is revolutionary theory; they need each other.[99]

In a parallel way, we cannot rely on either big collectivities like government or business *or* individuals acting alone, no matter how green their lifestyle. The only hope, such as it is, lies with citizens, networks and movements acting together. If they can do so with sufficient diligence and persistence, they may bring sufficient pressure to bear on the collectivities to induce structural change (and may also inspire more individuals to join in).

Trainer (2010) concludes that the most important single thing to do to help get this process in motion is to set up a *Community Development Cooperative* (CDC), starting with a community garden, workshop and meeting-place, for your town, suburb or region. 'If you want to help us save the planet, this is by far the most important kind of work you could take on.' His advice chimes with the position that has emerged from the analysis in this book, and others working towards the same end.

We may seem to have wandered from our main subject, but an ecological ethics that exists only in the mind, or as a theory, or even only as an ideal, has failed. Any adequate treatment of the subject must therefore include ways for it to become fully real.

14

Human Overpopulation

The Problem

We have already touched on human population as a factor in the I=PLOT equation (that is, population, lifestyle or consumption, organization and technology). Now at 6.9 billion, it has more than doubled since the 1960s and is expected to reach about 9.3 billion by the middle of this century. But out of all the possible ecological problems, why choose population as an example? Because it is a kind of test case for ecocentrism. Population is significantly different from factors of the dynamic of ecocide because unlike, say, consumption or technology, it directly involves – indeed, in a sense, *is* – human beings as such, and therefore an ecocentric challenge.

More precisely, in order to recognize it *as* a genuine problem, you have to be able to challenge a fundamentally anthropocentric assumption which, although rarely articulated, amounts to a gut feeling that 'Of course, human beings are good – indeed, the highest good – so the more human beings, the better!' And conversely, 'Anyone who wants to see fewer human beings here must hate them!' (We find it difficult to think of ourselves *as* the problem, rather than *having* problems caused by, you know, other things. Or other people, at a pinch.)

Now a moment's thought will show that these two statements are deeply flawed, and that the conclusions don't necessarily follow at all from their premises even if those are granted. Consider the following points:

1 We should ask ourselves: are humans necessarily, always and everywhere, a good (let alone the highest good)?

2 We should remember that a good very rarely increases arithmetically (or geometrically) without any limits past which it starts to become a problem instead (think of the consumption of food, for example). Why should collective human good be any different?

3 If the measure of civilization is quality of achievement (rather than the sheer number of people), then two of the towering cultural peaks of all human history, by most reckonings, occurred in Athens of the fourth–fifth century BCE and Florence of the fifteenth–sixteenth century CE, where the population was no higher than the tens and hundreds of thousands respectively: a tiny percentage of their current populations. The same general point could be made of Sung dynasty China and Tokugawa era Japan.

4 It is perfectly possible to want fewer new people because you fear for those who already exist. To quote the present Dalai Lama, 'There are six billion precious lives on Earth. All of them are under direct threat from other precious lives that are being added by the million.'[1]

5 Is there no ethical problem with all the individuals of other species (indeed, sometimes whole species) and places who are killed or destroyed as a direct result of humans taking over and remaking new territory? What about the individuals, places and species that are the victims of mass extinction as a direct result of human beings continually taking and making over new territory?

But when it comes to thinking about and discussing human population, we are not usually dealing with logic, concepts or evidence so much as a *mentality*, and one which embodies a deeply defended anthropocentrism. (This was clearly evident in the often outraged response to Bill McKibben's cautious and measured book in 1998, *Maybe One: A Personal and Environmental Argument for Much Smaller*

Families.) Thus, even many otherwise enlightened and progressive individuals, who have no trouble in arguing for lower levels of consumption and green technologies, bitterly resist looking human population – and all the more so, the present *over*population – in the face. The result is what Irvine (2002) calls the 'overpopulation denial syndrome' (ODS):[2] a disgraceful silence on this subject, enforced by the justifiable fear of being accused of misanthropy, authoritarianism, racism or sexism, since anyone who does raise it is frequently accused of one or more of those unpleasant things simply for doing so.

This silence often involves an unholy alliance of political left and right. For the *right*, when religious, 'overpopulation' represents an intolerable threat to dogma of the sanctity of individual human life, no matter in what conditions; when non-religious, the threat is to the secular cult of what now passes for humanism.[3] For the *left*, which shares a good deal of ground with the previous position, just to raise the issue of overpopulation is evidence of hatred of humanity, or people of colour, or women. It seems to make no difference when the point is also made that since a child born in Britain, say, will put 30–40 times more strain on global resources than one born in Bangladesh, population control is therefore probably most urgent in the overdeveloped world.

Even NGOs tiptoe around the P-word, addressing it, if at all, as a mere side effect of another supposedly more basic and politically acceptable problem, such as poverty, women's lack of education and access to reproductive health facilities and healthcare, etc. We shall review these points later; they are certainly all valid and urgent concerns, but they do not remove the need to recognize population as a fundamental and pressing dynamic *in itself*. Note too that these are all anthropocentric concerns; but even within that ambit, as McLaughlin notes, 'Combining social justice with an increasing population is like running down the up escalator. Increasing effort is required just to stay in place' (1993b: 216).

It is true that no single one of the PLOT factors offers a complete solution to ecological crisis. In all major human-caused ecological problems, more than one is implicated and needs addressing: 'both-and', not 'either-or'. Nor are all ecological problems the direct result of overpopulation; in particular, if the overdevelopment and overconsumption powered by global corporate capitalism continues unabated, their effects will need no help from other quarters.

Nonetheless, it does not require genius to realize that if human population continues to grow at a sufficient rate for long enough, then no amount of technological tweaking (assuming it is politically feasible) or reduction of consumption (which, at the moment, is certainly *not* politically feasible) will suffice to control and then reduce our ecological impact.

In addition, overpopulation has the peculiarly vicious result that simply by force of numbers, the most natural human activities, relating most directly to survival and the continuation of the species – finding fuel, shelter, growing food, procreation, excretion and so on – themselves become pathological: direct threats to personal survival and to that of the species, plus other lives and species.

Analysing Overpopulation

This is the context in which world population has now reached very nearly seven billion and still rising. Despite recent publicity about a trend 'reversed', what has started to decline (with no guarantees that it will continue) is the rate of increase; but the number of people is still growing, *and it is already far too high*. To quote Ward Churchill, the American Indian Movement leader:

> Any serious discussion of global problem resolution must begin with the observation that a 5.25 billion human population [as it then was] is in itself outrageously unrealistic. The question then becomes not how we sustain such a ludicrous overburden of one species, but how we begin to inculcate a broad consciousness leading to the steady scaling back of human numbers to some point well below 50% of the present level, and keep it there. (Quoted in McCormick 1994: 6–7)

Why is it too high? There are powerful reasons, both anthropocentric, concerning purely human well-being, and ecocentric, directly affecting the survival of most other animal species too, along with any remaining wilderness. In the earlier section on ecocrisis, we touched on the dimensions of that crisis in terms of biodiversity, habitat loss, species extinction, climate change and pollution.[4] Overpopulation has a direct hand in all of these. Other perspectives point to the same conclusion.

First, it directly contributes to human over-use of biological resources, which has exceeded the rate at which they can renew themselves since around 1985.[5] Furthermore, using up this natural 'capital' (a metaphor to be used carefully) contributes to a reduction in the rate of replenishment itself, which means that any overshoot is especially dangerous even though it is not immediately obvious what is going on.[6] Yet the overshoot by 2005 was 29 per cent,[7] and in 2009 the Global Footprint Network published data which shows that in 2006 the overshoot had already increased to an alarming 40 per cent.[8] (And if you aren't alarmed, you aren't paying attention.)

Second, in 1999, there were only about 2.2 hectares of eco-logically productive land per person on Earth. When the population grows to 9 billion, that figure will come down to 1.5 – barely enough to provide everyone with a good diet, never mind sustainably supply energy requirements, etc. In addition, some ecologists have suggested that in order to attain long-term viability and sustainability, as much as 50 per cent of the Earth's major ecosystems need to be either retained or restored; others, to the same end, have envisaged one-third natural, one-third small settlements and low-impact agriculture and one-third urban. In either case, a major reduction in population would be required.[9]

Third, as we see, population has a major impact on anthropogenic climate change. Martin Desvaux (2009) recently concluded, after a rigorous quantitative analysis, that 'without fossil fuels, the planet cannot support the current population of 6.8 billion, except at sig-nificantly lower average levels of consumption'. Furthermore, the population is still growing (projected to 9.4 billion by 2050) while available energy and global biocapacity is set to decline due to the effects of global warming, so there is 'an urgent case' for limiting family size.[10]

At this point, I need to introduce two concepts which are impor-tant to understanding population and its ecological impact. **Carrying capacity** is 'The estimated human impact which a defined zone of the Earth can sustain over a given timescale without long-term deg-radation.'[11] It is determined by the amount of renewable resources available and the amount of waste that can be assimilated by natural processes without resulting in long-term deterioration of the ecosystem. The most important single criterion for establishing human carrying capacity is the amount of ecologically productive land. And that amount, to state the obvious, is limited. Technophiles believe that limitation can be overcome through increased agricultural efficiency. Certain questions, however, remain conspicuously unanswered, starting from the fact that when (again, not 'if') the decline of global oil production starts to impact on fertilizer and pesticide production, the productivity of the industrial agriculture that supports otherwise unsustainable population growth will start to fall dramatically.[12] But even if this were *not* the case, do they believe present levels could continue indefinitely? With no effects that undermine the ecological base? And with no other significant costs, such as impact on human and/or environmental health, other species and ecosystems?

Ecological footprint is 'the total area of productive land and water required on a continuous basis to produce all the resources consumed, and to assimilate all the wastes produced, by that population, wherever on Earth that land is located' (Wackernagel and Rees 1996).[13] The concept originated with William Rees (1992). When demand in a particular area, such as a country, exceeds supply – as it now frequently does – the ecological deficit is made up by appropriating the produce of land elsewhere. So the ecological footprint of a small, crowded 'developed' country such as the Netherlands or the UK, for example, vastly exceeds its geographical size. That deficit could be reduced either by reducing per capita consumption and/or reducing the number of consumers.

These concepts are interrelated, of course. As already mentioned, humanity's current ecological footprint already exceeds the entire Earth's long-term carrying capacity by as much as 40 per cent. This situation invites some pertinent if uncomfortable questions:

1 Is it ethically defensible for the ecological footprint of a country or region to exceed its own borders, and, if so, under what circumstances? Does this happen voluntarily, and if so is the recompense for those elsewhere who are supporting it (since we can assume they are not doing so as an act of charity) fair and just?

2 Relatedly, is it ethically defensible to encourage ideas, values and/or activities that collectively entail exceeding the carrying capacity of the Earth as a whole? That, of course, is just what

the current world economic system does, with its unsustainably polluting and high-energy technologies; but the same question applies to encouraging large families.

3 Advocates of a growth economy as well as uncontrolled population-growth also seem quite unconcerned about our duty to future generations of humans; we are reeling in the resources of the future, and damaging – perhaps irreparably – the ability of the Earth to replenish them.

4 Here's a thought-experiment to try: after your next bowel movement, pause and consider it before flushing it away. Now multiply what you're looking at another time or two a day for the duration of an average life in years; then multiply that 6.9 billion times (and rising) . . . Rich or poor, professor or peasant, high carbon-emitter or low – that stuff has all got to go somewhere. (And, of course, it is not all.)

5 Now add everything else every individual needs and has a 'right' to: clean water, nourishing food, housing, medical care, a healthy (non-polluted) environment, education, employment, community and social life . . . Here is the ethically intolerable situation that overpopulation places us in: if you condone still more preventable births now, and the new arrivals *get* all this, then you are supporting yet more ecological destruction and degradation, including continuing mass extinctions of other species; but if they *don't* get it, then you are supporting intolerable human misery and deprivation. (The solution is simple, even if insufficient in itself: support humane population reduction!)

6 Is it not true, in however rough-and-ready a way, that the more people *have* to share their bit of the planet with others, the more the value of human life cheapens and declines? I don't mean the 'actual' value, whatever that might be and however we might agree what it is; I mean its perceived and experienced value: its actual value in practice. As Isaac Asimov once remarked, neither democracy, decency nor human dignity can survive overpopulation. This point applies with as much force to the global North as to the global South. (Here's another exercise: while fighting your way through the rush hour of any major city, try deeply appreciating the priceless intrinsic value of every individual you encounter.)

7 How many people do we arguably *need*, or are *desirable*, as opposed to how many can we squeeze onto the planet? Sheer numbers are certainly no guarantee of creativity or happiness, as I have suggested. The prerequisite for all other human interests is ecological health. John Ruskin, that prophet without honour, was right: 'THERE IS NO WEALTH BUT LIFE' – all kinds of life, and without requiring the destruction of what life depends on (1998: 270).[14]

It turns out that the most closely reasoned estimates for a human population for the Earth that is within its total carrying capacity – allowing for an average 'European' standard of living for all (although with reduced or more efficient energy consumption), sustainable use of natural resources, and some remaining wild places – agree that it is a maximum of *around 2 billion people*.[15] Indeed, Mosquin and Rowe of the Manifesto for Earth arrive at the figure of the global population when it was last sustainably within the planet's overall carrying capacity, roughly at the beginning of the Industrial Revolution: one-sixth of its present number, or *1 billion*.

Of course, this point has more local versions. For example, the UK's population – already high, still rising, and with ongoing immigration – is about 61 million and rising. Its ecological footprint thus greatly exceeds its own area. Furthermore, as Optimum Population Trust (OPT) researcher Andrew Ferguson points out, it is only by 'extravagant use of fossil fuel' that even the present number can be supported, and that is starting to run out; he estimates a sustainable figure to be, at most, 30 million. Yet Britain's runaway number of unplanned teenage pregnancies (about 40,000 a year, far ahead of the nearest European country) attracts little policy attention, and calls to rethink immigration are associated firmly with the far right. 'Genuine asylum seekers and others reasonably admitted can be black, khaki, purple or green', argues OPT patron John Guillebaud, 'as long as we bring immigration and emigration into balance and control teenage pregnancies over five to six generations . . . . That could bring the UK to 30 million by 2130.'[16] Yet this is a generous time-frame, and there is very little evidence of either joined-up governmental thinking or informed public concern. And this national example could be multiplied many times over.

Taking on the Arguments

At this point, let us review the most common objections to taking overpopulation seriously, as opposed to viewing it as not very important and/or as a mere function of something else.

'*The population explosion is over.*' This ignores the fact of *population momentum*, which means that total numbers will keep on rising long after a fall in the rate of increase. (It is easy to miss the implications of simple maths applied to planetary limits: a 1 per cent or 0.5 per cent increase sounds small, but starting from a base of 8 billion, the latter per annum increase yields another billion in 24 years, i.e., within a generation; a 1 per cent increase does it in 12 years.) As John Caldwell says, 'With regard to the long-term stability of the world's ecosystems and our ability to feed everyone adequately and to give them a reasonably good life, that margin of 3 or 4 billion extra people could be critical' (quoted in Kates 2004: 52–3).

'*Affluence is the answer*', also known as the 'Demographic Transition Theory', according to which a country's birth rate will fall when it achieves sufficient wealth. The USA, whose burgeoning population (from births as well as immigration) does not exactly manifest sub-replacement fertility, exposes this fallacy. So does Saudi Arabia.

'*Poverty is the problem*', or 'Only rich countries are the problem.' But huge numbers of the not-so-affluent also have an impact. Even with very low levels of consumption, sheer numbers can turn a once-sustainable practice, such as slash-and-burn cultivation, into a devastating one. 'Granted the rich are more destructive than the poor, but the poor too require shelter, clothing and food that has to come from somewhere on Earth. They've got an ecological footprint too. The numbers matter.'[17]

Furthermore, raising the poor out of poverty (currently about 1.3 billion people, with millions more arriving every month) will unavoidably increase per capita pollution and consumption. Yet this is something a progressive agenda cannot *not* support. In addition, citizens of the rich 'North' have a much higher impact through consumption and technology, but immigrants soon adopt the same patterns. The consequence of immigration is therefore significantly to increase ecological impact, while the resulting population reduction in their country of origin is negligible. (Remember, the Earth is completely non-discriminatory. If two persons' impact is identical, their class, race and gender is, in this context, irrelevant.) Finally, almost no one seems to have considered the possibility that 'population stabilisation and then reduction (by whatever humane and just means are appropriate to each situation) could actually be *precursor* to the take-off out of poverty' (Stevens 2003).

'*Reproductive and sexual healthcare and family planning are the answer.*' It *is* scandalous that more than one-third of all couples worldwide do not have access to proper contraception, and equally so that about 600,000 women every year die preventable deaths in pregnancy and childbirth (roughly the equivalent of four fully loaded jumbo jets crashing every day).[18] These are ethical issues in their own right, and contraception is certainly a vital part of reducing population. The implications for overpopulation, however, are not necessarily straightforward (see the following point).

'*Female empowerment, especially education, is the answer.*' Again, this is highly desirable in itself, and in most situations probably helps to reduce the number of births. But the work of Virginia Abernethy has shown that there is no simple connection, and certainly no necessary one, between increasing prosperity, healthcare and the education of women and fewer children. These do have positive effects but they can be overruled by the fact that, ultimately, 'people have as many children as they think can be raised well, according to their own standards'. So a sense of expanding opportunities can easily lead to larger families, and of shrinking ones to smaller.[19]

'*There are enough resources to go around if properly distributed*', or (even more wishfully mantra-like), 'Always enough for need, never enough for greed.' But in addition to the points above concerning affluence/poverty, sooner or later, if unchecked, ongoing expansion of population and/or consumption will catch up with *any* redistribution of a finite cake.

'*Increasing food production alone can cure world hunger.*' This assumes that present levels of production will continue or even increase, despite worsening soil impoverishment and depletion, aquifer exhaustion, chemical contamination, etc., not to mention (human-induced) climate change (see the questions raised earlier about agricultural innovation), and countenances turning over virtually all remaining wilderness with any agricultural potential to cultivation. Even more implausibly, it assumes that overpopulation will somehow take care of itself (kindly, of course). Without any steps to control population, it thus locks humanity further into the zero-sum dynamic of more food, leading to more births, requiring more food, requiring more industrialization of food production, resulting in more births. Pointing to the achievements of the Green Revolution (and ignoring their costs), advocates now promise new miracles from biotechnology. But there is no exit strategy from the tightening spiral (or at least, no humane one), for which *collective addiction* would seem to provide the best model. This position is the height of ethical irresponsibility, especially when it comes from those who are offering, for a handsome profit, to supply not the solution but a fix.[20]

'*We don't need to reduce population because environmental problems can be solved by technological means.*' But all technologies have an environmental impact, and despite endless promises, there are limits on how clean *and* affordable they can become. More people with the same overall per capita consumption will therefore inevitably cancel out gains from more efficient and less polluting technologies.

'*We need more young people to look after old people.*' But, 'If we all have more children in order to look after more old people, you only have to wait for 70 years and you will have even more old people to look after.'[21] To maintain the support ratio of workers to dependents characteristic of the twentieth century in the UK, for example, a permanent pyramidal population structure would be necessary, with those of child-producing years always more than reproducing their own numbers. Does it need to be said that this is obviously unsustainable?[22]

Nor is it any less so if the 'shortfall' is supplied through immigration. And in that case, is it ethical, or even simply intelligent, for nations with lower birth rates to be asked to absorb large excess populations from those with high rates? Surely the latter should be encouraged (and helped) to act responsibly and control their own birth rates, rather than exporting the problem in a finite world. Equally, 'developed' countries should try to assist them (always assuming local governments are trying too) to improve the conditions that make people want to emigrate. And in any case, local people cannot fairly be asked to bear fewer children if at the same time you ask them to accept the immigration of others not making the same sacrifice, which will defeat the effect of theirs. The overall level of consumption increases, of course, with the introduction of every additional person. But the overdeveloped world engages in disproportionately high consumption. Unless the countries of origin can succeed in lowering their birth rates, therefore, immigration to countries where consumption levels are already too high simply further increases the net strain upon the Earth without significantly relieving the countries of origin, where those leaving are quickly replaced.[23]

'*Reproductive rights are a non-negotiable freedom.*' But are they unaccompanied by any corresponding duty or responsibility? Is *any* right absolute in that sense? The civic republican and communitarian traditions, at least, suggest not. We should also consider the right of those already here not to have their share of what is needed for a good life taken away by those who reproduce irresponsibly (i.e. beyond a certain [very low] number, and without being prepared or even able to support their children). In any case, the ethically unacceptable impacts of human overpopulation point firmly to the conclusion that now, 'All of the world's peoples must come fully to terms with the fact that a person's (biological) right to have children must be mediated by his or her (social) responsibility not to have too many' (Smail 1997: 189). I might add that anyone who nonetheless insists on reproduction as their absolute right or freedom, thus denying that they have any limits or duties in regard to that right, might reflect that they are inviting a corresponding denial from others that *they* have any duty to feed or support those children.[24]

Of course, just as a steady-state economy requires a steady-state culture to support it, that responsibility will require a global small-family culture. But it will not happen without political leadership too, and regulatory measures encouraging population control *as such*. In addition to encouraging female education, family planning and widespread access to birth control, these should include such measures as removing government subsidies for children after the second, and perhaps recovering the social and ecological costs of any further children through taxation. As Norman Myers (1998) says:

> Of course two children are every couple's right. It is their right too to have a third child without asking anybody's approval. But everybody else has a right to ask the couple to pay the additional costs entrained for everybody else by that third child. These are costs the child will impose upon everybody's environment and hence on everybody's economy.

But success would ultimately depend on a wider and deeper realization that it no longer makes sense to allow parents the 'right to
procreate as much as they please, while in doing so they restrict
everybody else's right to live as they please' (Myers 1998).

The 'right' to have any number of children (and now at almost any
age, with expensive medical assistance) is widely upheld. Similarly, as
noted earlier, advocates of measures to control population – humane
and sensible measures involving cheap and simple technology, not
forced sterilizations or eugenics – are often accused of misanthropy,
while those who make the charge implicitly lay claim to compassion
(within a strictly human context). Couples who have decided not to
bear children are still widely regarded as odd, at best.[25] But what if
some restraint now for some people means a better quality of life for
more people in the not-so-distant future? And what if indulgence
today means drastically greater hardship and suffering tomorrow?
The ecological evidence strongly suggests that population planning,
as Jack Parsons writes, 'is not an invasion of liberty but a safeguard
of liberty. . . . The key question is not "Would population control
reduce individual liberty?" but "Would population control reduce
individual liberty more than unrestricted population growth?"'
(1971: xxii).[26]

Climate Change Again

It might be thought that since the global North contributes massively more per capita to the emissions that drive climate change,
population is not an issue in that context. There are a number of
reasons why that would be wrong. Parts of the global South are now
industrializing, and even within largely non-industrial countries,
energy-hungry middle classes are starting to emerge, with predictable
ecological consequences, including increased emissions. The same
consideration applies to efforts to move people out of poverty; not
only is overpopulation one of the things undermining those efforts,
but the all-important question remains of how to escape poverty
without simply reproducing and adding to the unsustainable consequences of 'Western' growth and development. The more people
involved, the more critical that question becomes. So yes, population

reduction is especially important among the richer countries, but neither is it of negligible importance among the poorer. Population growth is now a problem wherever it occurs.

A couple of studies make the case in detail. Murtaugh and Schlax show that the positive environmental consequences of *not* having a child are vast, and 'ignoring the consequences of reproduction can lead to serious underestimation of an individual's long-term impact on the global environment' (2009: 18). This does not mean that no one should have children. It *does* mean that the decision to have even one child is one with serious consequences for everyone else, so it should be taken seriously. That in turn makes it the responsibility of governments, at whatever level, to encourage individuals and couples to take that decision seriously, and to discourage them from taking it lightly.

Philip Cafaro, in the course of a detailed study, concludes that population growth is one of the two main drivers of global climate change, so reducing it could make a huge contribution (which is reasonably quantifiable) to mitigating it. As he notes, 'Talk of limiting or reducing human numbers makes many people uncomfortable, despite the fact that we are not talking about killing people, but preventing births that would otherwise occur.' Nevertheless:

> Resources are limited. People living in many developing nations well understand the human costs of crowding, urban populations that outgrow basic services, and large numbers of unemployed young people; meanwhile, even confirmed anthropocentrists might well hesitate before accepting the total displacement of wild nature in order to maximize human numbers. People are wonderful, but it is possible to have too many people: in a family, an apartment, or a nation. GCC [global climate change] may be telling us that it is possible to have too many people on the earth itself. Part of its message may be that with freedom to reproduce comes responsibility to limit reproduction, so as not to overwhelm global ecological services or create a world that is solely a reflection of ourselves. (2010: 16)[27]

Overpopulation and Ecocentrism

The upshot of the discussion in this chapter so far is the need for a decent, but urgent, reduction of human population as soon as possible.[28] But unlike the rest of this book, it argues that case mostly on anthropocentric grounds. We have had to do so because Overpopulation Denial Syndrome has so obscured the whole subject, even from the viewpoint of human self-interest, together with the disastrous consequences of overpopulation for nonhuman nature. Some have been mentioned, but it is now time to clarify them.

The basics should be fairly obvious. Humanity has already taken over at least a quarter of the planet's natural energy, two-thirds of its habitable land surface and 50 per cent of its fresh run-off water. The result is energy, room and water that is ever-increasingly *not* available to all other species which are not directly or indirectly subservient to our needs and wants. So much for the wild! And this is a process which the demands resulting from sheer numbers – at least as much as consumption and technology – are causing to accelerate all the time. As Manes says, even if the present number of humans is sustainable, that discussion 'leave[s] out the whole question of the effect *present* population levels have on the nonhuman world' (1990: 234; my emphasis).

In addition to the shallow or light green reasons, there is also a powerful intermediate or mid-green case for population control, in two respects:

1 Colonizing ever more land for ever more human beings, for shelter, food and fuel, involves killing off its aboriginal nonhuman inhabitants, so to speak, and taking away their land. The present rate of extinctions is already ample evidence, although what they fail to communicate is the brutality of the slaughter, the shame on us, and the tragedy of the loss. In the words of Alice Walker:

> Part of what justice means for non-human animals is that there will just have to be fewer people, because I think the insistence of people on covering the Earth itself is a grievous insult to the non-human animals whose space is squeezed into nonexistence. Just because people can have three, four

and five children does not mean that that's best for all creation. It definitely is not. (Quoted in McCormick 1994: 6–7)

2 Ever more human beings, demanding ever more cheap food,
are causing immense suffering for billions of intelligent social
animals in 'efficient' factory farms, along with millions in
laboratories so they can have 'safe' medicines, cosmetics, etc.
Although that suffering is, strictly speaking, unnecessary (except
on the part of subsistence hunters where there are few or no
alternatives), increased numbers will mean increasing demand,
leading to more suffering.

Finally, there is the deep or dark green case. This is at once the
most urgent one and the hardest to argue. Urgent because (as the
Earth Manifesto, in particular, makes clear) what is ultimately at
stake – nature itself – is the source of all value, human and nonhuman
alike. Hard, because, overwhelmingly, people seem unaware of their
utter eco-dependence.

Gaia Theory[29] implies that the Earth as such will survive our dep-
redations nicely, thank you. But in addition to this providing rather
cold comfort, consider the post-human New World. The odds are
high, especially if (human-caused) climate change is the primary
factor, that we would take most of the planet's remaining complex
life-forms with us, or those still left, and render it uninhabitable for
the foreseeable future by any possible heirs. Will anyone argue that
this is ethically admirable or even defensible behaviour, even as a
risk?

Here too, the statistics cannot do justice to the ethical obscenity
of (say) an old-growth forest – literally irreplacable, biotically rich
beyond our comprehension, and home to countless nonhuman lives
– devastated and converted into more plywood shuttering, mail-
order sales catalogues and toilet-paper, not to mention cattle-feed in
order to supply hamburgers. Other examples are possible, of course,
but as a matter of fact, most of the new land continually being appropriated to meet the demands of ever more humans and to make up
for cropland lost to urbanization and degradation (yet another function of overpopulation) comes from forests.[30]

This is also where the limitations of the anthropocentric case are
most apparent. The argument above for taxing large families, for

example, assumes that all significant effects on the environment of overpopulation are costable economically. But it is a fallacy to assume that all value can be converted into a single financial calculus; indeed, I have argued that it is one of the most ecologically destructive beliefs today.[31] As Paul Erhlich remarked, 'The economy is a wholly-owned subsidiary of the Earth's ecology', and it is so in ways that far outrun any possible full financial or fiscal accountancy.[32] Similarly, my criticisms of an unrestricted right to bear children were all limited to its effects on other people. But the effects on the natural world are at least as dire. Meanwhile, the entire debate about rights is about purely *human* rights. But what about all the others?

Carrying capacity *can* be entirely defined in human terms: how many people, living in what ways, can the Earth support? But as we have seen, to speak of 'biological resources' or 'capital' in this way is deeply anthropocentric. As I hope this book has made clear, to assume that the planet's entire biomass is at our sole disposal is ethically reprehensible. Willey is quite right that fewer people would mean an overall better quality of life for all: fewer houses (less urbanization), fewer cars (less road-building and congestion), fuller employment, higher incomes and 'a harder life for pathogens'.[33] He also includes less intensive agriculture and factory farming, and more countryside. This is all quite true and important, but ethically speaking it rather stops short. It would mean a much better life for the rest of the natural world, too.

15

Postscript

In the course of this book, we have considered the problems with much the greater part of existing ethics when it comes to recognizing and rising to the challenge of global ecocrisis. Those problems centre on anthropocentrism as a perspective which locates virtually all value in humanity, as opposed to nonhuman nature. They include related dynamics such as an objectifying attitude to nonhuman nature and the accompanying instrumentalist ethos which sanctions its undue exploitation, i.e. 'resourcism'; a rigid distinction between human and nonhuman life and the systematic privileging of the former, i.e. 'speciesism'; and the narrow and short-term character of so-called enlightened self-interest.

The only truly sustainable human culture is one based on ecological sustainability. That in turn requires ecocentrism, for a way of life that recognizes only human needs and values will never be sustainable. Only a nonhuman nature whose flourishing in its own way is permitted, indeed encouraged, will suffice. It won't flourish if it is only allowed to do so within the narrow range of ways that suit us alone. So that in turn requires us to respect and love nature, and recognize its intrinsic value as a whole. However paradoxical it may seem, the conclusion is clear: any philosophy concerned only with humans fails both humanity and the rest of life.

I admit that it is very hard to love the Earthian matrix of life when it manifests as lethal tsunamis, horrible diseases and the like. But these are parts of life as a whole, and therefore of what enables us all to live at all. (Nor are they personally directed at humans; life is risky for everyone.) Ecocentrism doesn't try to forbid sensitive attempts at cure or mitigation, nor does it condemn understandable failures to love nature. Yet in the end, that is what is most fitting as well as what is most needed.

We have therefore explored a much more promising kind of ethics than 'environmental', namely ecocentric. That was defined, in its fullest or deepest sense, as one which locates value in the more-than-human world: the Earth, or nature as such, including but vastly exceeding humanity, is holistic, extending to both species and places. So it strives to be impartial in relation to conflicts between human and nonhuman nature. Various such ethics were examined, especially of the dark or deep green kind. However, it has also turned out that ecocentrism is not limited to dark green ethics. The latter, being cumulative, is the most ecocentric kind. (In this it parallels the idea of a more-than-human nature that includes humanity.) However, a light green concern for the well-being of humans in ecological terms (which therefore takes it out of pure anthropocentrism), and a mid-green concern for the well-being of other animals ('animal welfare'), are also ecocentric to a significant degree.

It was further suggested that an ecocentric ethics at its best is pluralist and pragmatic, post-secular in an animist way, and part of a programme of green citizenship that also draws on ecofeminism, civic republicanism and traditional ecological knowledge. And what brings these strands together is deep green virtue ethics, which develops through the exercise of green citizenship and lifelong ecocentric education. I then tried to show how, to really take root, that requires strong, sustainable economies and communities which can support, and be supported by, such an ethics. Conversely, a green virtue ethics withers and dies in economies, societies and cultures dominated by the ethos, equally inhuman and unnatural, of industrial capitalism. So we reviewed some hopeful alternatives.

Both civic republican and feminist perspectives strongly emphasize sociality and relationality (which, given their other differences, is already significant), and their ecological versions all the more so, insofar as the relevant relationships and societies are more-than-human. Accordingly, it is fitting that one of the conclusions to be drawn from this book is that strengthening local communities, together with emphasizing their ecocentric dimension, is probably the most important single thing we can do in response to the gathering storm. Even if doing so does not stop ecocrisis and its consequences, which is too much to ask at this late stage, it will help ensure that in the long decline of industrial society, the smallest number of persons possible (human and nonhuman) get hurt, and the most things of real value possible (natural and cultural) are saved from the wreck.

In arguing that an ecological ethics is not only desirable but urgently needed, I am aware that it could also be asked: but is it feasible? A number of answers come to mind. One, the simplest but not the least important, is: who knows? But it has got to be worth a try, because if we don't then the answer will certainly turn out to be 'no'. Even if we do try, there are no guarantees; but then there is a chance. The work in, with, and for communities needs other things to succeed, and that is one: hope without guarantees.[1]

The authors of a book on Easter Island remark that their now extinct inhabitants

> carried out for us the experiment of permitting unrestricted population growth, profligate use of resources, destruction of the environment and boundless confidence in their religion to take care of the future. The result was an ecological disaster leading to a population crash. . . . Do we have to repeat the experiment on [a] grand scale?[2]

Can we hope not – not least since, as I have been at pains to point out, the effects of an ecological disaster, even if it is human-caused, are by no means restricted to humans? And can we begin, individually and collectively, to imagine an alternative future, a different storyline, a promising narrative? I have suggested that for humans to partake of sanity and sanctity, they must feel themselves to be part of a greater, more ancient and important story, and one that will survive us too. Nature offers the ultimate liveable and sustainable narrative.

Here too, there is vitally important work to be done, not a whit less so for being 'cultural'. It could be defined as *the resacralization* (or re-enchantment) *of living nature*, including human nature, *in the local cultural idiom*. At stake is nothing less than a new ethical emphasis on

conviviality, respect for life and ultimate humility.[3] And, as Adrian
Parr says, '[s]ustainability considerations that are not cultural are not
sustainable'. But as he also immediately adds (and this is something
some greens forget), 'Yet a theory and practice of sustainability that
is only cultural ultimately compromises the complexity and dynamics
of life' (2009: 166).

The Dark Mountain Project is one recent example of such cultural work.[4] Another example is the journal *Archipelago*. Connecting
with the rich tradition of 'nature writing', whether poetry, fiction
or essays, is another activity with much to contribute to sustaining an engagement with nonhuman nature in the teeth of despair.[5]
I am also struck by the way that many of the writers whom we
have found with much to offer in the course of this book are
ones who not only respect the importance of culture, imagination and narrative but are not afraid of their spiritual dimension
(which, let me remind you, is not supernatural, transcendentalist or
idealist).[6]

That is not surprising. Maybe more than anything else, an
awareness of the immediate as well as ultimate mystery of more-
than-human nature guards against anthropocentric and especially
technoscientific hubris.[7] To such an understanding, the idea of
willed one-way manipulation of nature without inviting terrible
unintended consequences (and the more so the grander its scale) is
laughable, when it is not tragic.

Finally, still another doubting question suggests itself. We could
be asked, should we adopt ecocentrism because it is true or because
it would be good for the Earth? But the very way this question is
posed, in the distinction between 'true' and 'good' which it assumes
as fundamental, carries within it a non-ecological sensibility so it
cannot be answered in its own terms without betraying the ecocentrism it questions. As Abram reminds us:

> Ecologically speaking, it is not primarily our verbal statements
> that are 'true' or 'false,' but rather the kind of relations that we
> sustain with the rest of nature. A human community that lives
> in a mutually beneficial relation with the surrounding earth is a
> community, we might say, that lives in truth. . . . [Whereas a]
> civilization that relentlessly destroys the living land it inhabits is
> not well acquainted with *truth*, regardless of how many supposed

facts it has amassed regarding the calculable properties of its world. (1996a: 264)[8]

What such a question and its implicit attitude forgets is that we cannot stand outside the Earth and judge its value or truth from elsewhere, or from nowhere. Ultimately, nature is what enables us to do anything, including assess truth; so barring a collective death-wish, we can only consider it not only a good, but for us and all other Earthlings the ultimate good, and, as such, sacred. For the same reason – which is to say, an inclusive ecology – to 'know' or 'assess' or 'consider' is not possible without participating in a relationship with what is being known, assessed or considered. So an ethical dimension is already present from the start.

Aldo Leopold once observed that: 'One of the penalties of an ecological education is one lives alone in a world of wounds' (1993: 165). It is indeed often painful, but to recognize that world and those wounds is the first step to healing. And we are far from alone.

Notes

Chapter 1   Introduction

1   E.g., Kohák 2000; Des Jardins 2001; Wenz 2001; Benson 2000. Anthologies include Light and Rolston 2003; Zimmerman et al. 2005; and Keller 2010.
2   The term 'ethical extensionism' was first used, I believe, by Singer 1981.
3   As Bateson (1972; 1979), for example, influentially argued. The same point follows from Latour's Actor Network Theory (1993). See also The Alliance for Wild Ethics initiated by Abram: http://www.wildethics.org/.
4   This question was first raised in print by Richard Routley (later Sylvan) in "Is There a Need for a New, an Environmental Ethic?" (1973: 205–10).
5   See my 2007.
6   See Scott 1998.
7   See Bender 2003; Manes 1990; Gare 1993; and Diamond 2004.
8   There is a precedent for my choice: Kohák 2000.
9   See Cooper 1992.
10 See Smith 1988: 160.

Chapter 2   The Earth in Crisis

1   For an excellent overview, see Ponting 2000, 2007. Also see McNeill 2001, although his neglect of modern capitalism as the principal engine of environmental change is extraordinary; see the review by Donald Worster, 'On the Planet of the Apes', *Times Literary Supplement* (13.7.01), p. 12.

2   E.g., North 1995; Easterbrook 1995; Lomborg 2001. For scientific critiques of the latter, see reports by the Danish Committee on Scientific Dishonesty (7.1.03) and the Danish Ecological Council (28.6.03), and in the pages of those bastions of fringe radical environmentalism, *Nature* (8.11.01) and *Scientific American* (January 2002).

3   Data for what follows in this chapter comes from publications by the United Nations Environment Programme (UNEP) (2007); the Worldwide Fund for Nature (WWF) *Living Planet Report* (2008); and the Millennium Ecosystem Assessment (MEA) (2005). These are all based on the best current peer-reviewed scientific studies; the first alone was produced by almost 400 scientists, all experts in their fields, whose findings were subjected to review by another 1,000 of their peers. See also the annual *State of the World* reports by the Worldwatch Institute.

4   Intergovernmental Panel on Climate Change (IPCC) 2001, confirmed in subsequent assessments.

5   See Speth 2004; Gelbspan 2004.

6   'Put us all on rations', the *Guardian* (26.8.04). For a good layperson's discussion, see Verlyn Klinkenborg, 'Be Afraid. Be Very Afraid', *The New York Times Book Review* (30.5.04).

7   UNEP, 'GEO-3: Past, Present and Future Perspectives' (2002).

8   Lord (Robert) May (President of the Royal Society) and Janet Larsen (Earth Policy Institute), quoted in the *Guardian* (2.10.03 and 10.3.04 respectively). See also Leakey and Lewin 1996.

9   Figures from the International Union for the Conservation of Nature, and the *Guardian* (22.7.04).

10 Gardner-Outlaw and Engelman 1999: 26.

11 Richard Aronson, Dauphin Island Sea Lab (the *Guardian* 19.2.04).

12 The MEA (2005).

13 Smil 1993: 181.

14 E.g., Solomon et al. 2003; IUCN/UNEP 2003.

15 *Environmental Health Perspectives* 112: 5 (April 2004).

16 Thomas 2004.

17 Speaking at the February 2004 meeting of the AAAS (the *Guardian*, 14.2.04).

18 Jones 1993; Nicholsen 2003.

19 The original idea is usually attributed to Paul and Anne Erhlich, but I have been unable to find the exact first reference. But for a good discussion see Sylvan and Bennett 1994: 36–53. I am grateful to Harry Cripps for his suggestions in this section.

20 From p. 11 of a paper written by David Willey for the Optimum Population Trust entitled 'Some Hopes and Thoughts for the Future' (September 2000).

21 UN Population Division 2002.

22 Saral Sarkar and Bruno Kern, 'Ecosocialism or Barbarism: An Appeal' (27.2.10): http://dandeliontimes.net/2010/02/eco-socialism-or-barbarism-an-appeal/.

23 Forman 1997.

24 See Ekins 1992 and Foreman 1997.

25 This led Paul Feyerabend (1978: 106–7) to argue that 'Science is one ideology among many and should be separated from the state just as religion is now separated from the state.' See also Kitcher 2001; Brown 2002.

26 See, e.g., Feyerabend 1978, 1987; Midgley 1992, 2001; Dupré 2001.

27 In addition to Feyerabend, see Bauer 1994.

28 See Bulger et al. 1995; Jasanoff 1990; Horton 2004.

29 See Stenmark 2001.

30 See Bulger et al. 1995; Jasanoff 1990; Horton 2004.

31 The $9 billion supporting the construction of the Large Hadron Collider is a good example, along with the clouds of quasi-theological rhetorical camouflage about answering fundamental questions about where we came from, etc.

32 This is what Paul Feyerabend (1987) called 'democratic relativism'. See also Midgley's excellent work (1992, 2001). The same point was made much earlier, of course, by (e.g.) William James and Max Weber.

33 Latour continues: 'Reality is not defined by matters of fact. Matters of fact are only very partial and very polemical, very political renderings of matters of concern. It is this second empiricism, this return to a realist attitude, that I'd like to offer as the next task for the critically minded' (2004: 18).

Chapter 3 Ethics

1 For an introduction, see Blackburn 2001.

2 See Smith 1998; Curry 2000; and Dobson 2006.

3 I am running together the metaphysical and epistemological aspects of both realism and relativism, but in an introductory context the distinction seems to me unnecessarily confusing. For the same reason, I will

stick with the commonly posited opposition between realism and relativism (rather than calling the latter, say, 'anti-realism').

4   See my discussion in Curry 2008a.

5   See the excellent discussion in Smith 1997: ch. 5.

6   The best discussion of these issues is in Smith 1988, 1997; but see also
    Latour 1993: ch. 4; Feyerabend 1987: ch. 1; and *Common Knowledge* 13,
    2–3 (2007), 'A "Dictatorship of Relativism"?'. In relation to ecological
    philosophy, see also Curry 2003 and 2008a.

7   From Hume 1740; Moore 1903.

8   Philosophers of science call the first point the 'theory-laden' nature of
    facts, and the second the 'underdetermination of theory by facts'.

9   With thanks to Nigel Cooper for this point.

10 Kohák 2000: 137.

11 With thanks to Michael Novack for pointing this out.

12 By those who have wanted to understand it that way. Cf. Kohák 2000:
    62–3.

13 See also Psalms 96: 11–13, 148: 9–10, 13.

14 See Sorrell 1988 and, more generally, Hessel and Ruether 2000;
    McDonagh 1990; and Dunlap 2004. It is not entirely mischievous to
    add that one might feel surer of Francis's ecocentrism if he were known
    to have *listened* to the birds as well as preaching *to* them.

15 For the UK, see www.ely.anglican.org/environment (accessed 10.8.09).

16 See Haught 1996. For more recent general reflections by Christians on
    ecology, out of a large literature, see Northcott (2010) and Bauckham
    (2010).

17 See Shklar 1984. (Christ specified that blasphemy against the Holy
    Ghost was unforgivable: Matthew 12: 31.)

18 See Henry 2002.

19 Among its exemplars are Richard Dawkins, Daniel Dennett, Peter
    Atkins, Lewis Wolpert and Nicholas Humphrey. By way of contrast,
    see the work of (among others) Mary Midgley, Barbara Herrnstein
    Smith and Paul Feyerabend.

20 See Toulmin 1990 and 2010 for an excellent discussion of the differ-
    ence between the genuine scepticism of Pyrro, Sextus and Montaigne
    as against the modern pseudo-scepticism initiated by Descartes.

21 See Ehrenfeld 1981.

22 For a careful analysis which takes this point seriously, see Hern
    1997.

23 Boyle 1996: 15. For a good discussion of Bacon and Descartes in this
    context, see Merchant 1980; Henry 2002.

24 Although the contract was among subjects about the state, not directly
    with the state (a point which I owe to an anonymous reviewer).

25 I have borrowed this basic analysis from Ekins 1992; see also Bauman 1992, Scott 1998, and Toulmin's excellent 1990.

Chapter 4 Three Schools of Ethics

1 I take some comfort from the extent of disagreement about Kant among professional philosophers themselves.
2 I have been helped here by Scruton's discussion in his 2001.
3 *On the Basis of Morality*, p. 83; quoted in Janaway 2002: 90.
4 See Janaway 2002: 92.
5 See the criticisms in Gray 1993, and more recently Sen 2009.
6 See Skinner 1998.
7 That is, preferences can be criticized, but not, without circularity, on preference-utilitarian grounds.
8 With thanks to Michael Novack for help with this point.
9 See Scott 1998.
10 Wittgenstein put paid to this notion in his *Philosophical Investigations* of 1953.
11 On the recently renewed interest in virtue ethics, see McIntyre 1981; Hursthouse 1999; Foot 2001. By 'disillusionment', I mean fear, uncertainty, lack of hope.
12 In addition to those I am about to discuss, see Fox 1984; Frasz 1993; Wensveen 2000; Swanton 2004.

Chapter 5 Value

1 See Callicott 1985, 1989.
2 Cf. Smith 1988, 1997; in relation to ecocentrism and intrinsic value, see Curry 2003.
3 E.g., respectively, Rolston 1997 and Callicott 1985; again, see Curry 2003.
4 Jordanova is actually taking Keith Thomas, in his *Man and the Natural World* (1983), to task for being insufficiently anthropocentric! (Emphasis in the original.)
5 See also Fox 1995: 20–2 for a good discussion.
6 Hayward 1995, 1998.
7 Respectively: as first suggested by Routley and Routley 1979; Ryder 1973; Eckersley 1998; see also Hayward 1998.
8 Although for the story of its modern corruption, see the excellent analysis in Ehrenfeld 1981.
9 John Muir (1875), *Wild Wool*: http://www.sierraclub.org/john_muir_exhibit/writings/favorite_quotations.aspx.

10 See, e.g., Bahro 1994.

11 A term I have borrowed from David Orton. See the important critique by David Livingston in his books of 1981 and 1994.

12 I also find questionable, indeed implausible, his flat statement, 'Nor do nonhumans love' (2010: 12).

13 There may be a case for (or at least a parallel with) 'ecologism'. The problem is the latter has at least three current and highly conflicting meanings: ecological philosophy, extremist ecological ideology and eco-scientism (see, respectively, Dobson 2007; Bramwell 1989; Naess 1989).

14 Ecofeminist critics in particular (e.g. Ariel Salleh, Val Plumwood and Mary Mellor).

15 See Taylor 2010 for a careful consideration of the evidence. Much of the charge rests on a single instance in 1987 where Christopher Manes, writing as 'Miss Ann Thropy' in an Earth First! journal, suggested that AIDS could help reduce human overpopulation. Frankly, however shocking a suggestion, it is a very slender reed to bear all the rhetorical weight placed on it by Deep Ecology's enemies; and if it makes them feel any better, Manes has paid for his youthful sensationalism many times over. (I would add that his 1990 book has also been charged with macho environmentalism, but it makes some very good points, and nowhere does he say that his perspective is the only valid or relevant one.)

16 This is consistent theme in the work of Murray Bookchin, among other social ecologists.

17 See Hargrove 1989.

18 'Our Natural Selves', *Times Literary Supplement* (8.9.95): 10–11.

Chapter 6   Light Green or Shallow (Anthropocentric) Ethics

1 'Light green' comes from Sylvan and Bennett 1994, 'shallow' from Naess's influential 1973. Dave Greenfield has helpfully identified nine distinct shades of green: light, business, state, citizen, centre-left, far left, radical action, deep and deep left (see 'Nine Shades of Green' (14.4.09): http://greenpolitics.ca/2009/04/nine-shades-of-green/).

2 With thanks to Michael Novack for the points in this paragraph.

3 The term 'megamachine' is Lewis Mumford's.

4 With thanks to Nigel Cooper for a helpful discussion of this point.

5 Such as Botkin 1992; Budiansky 1995; Easterbrook 1995.

6 E.g., influentially, Pearce et al. 1989. On 'ecosystem services', see the excellent analysis of Sullivan 2010a and Chapter 13 of this book.

7 The reference is, of course, to Rudyard Kipling's notorious justification of imperialism as 'the white man's burden'.

8 For an excellent analysis of the scale of scientistic fantasy, see Midgley 1992.

9 Cf. the excellent critique by Eckersley 1989.

10 Since writing this, I have learned to exempt the excellent work of social ecologist John Clark.

11 These are the two prerequisites Dobson (2007) specifies for what he calls 'ecologism'.

12 Terry Hamblin, quoted in the *Guardian* (8.8.98), G2, p. 20.

13 See also the earlier arguments to this effect by Livingstone 1981 and Ehrenfeld 1981.

14 Quoted in *The Higher Education Supplement* (5.8.10), p. 51.

15 See McKay 1996.

16 http://www.countercurrents.org/dobson200810.htm (accessed 20.8.10).

17 Quotations by Hardin here and the following quotation about 'a managed commons' are from the useful website www.garretthardin-society.org (accessed 29.8.10). I also thank Sandy Irvine for a helpful discussion (including the apt point that in attacking Hardin wholesale, the left are shooting themselves in the foot).

18 The seminal text here is Polanyi 1957.

19 Cf. Ostrom 1990.

20 Most recently, Fairlie 2010b.

Chapter 7   Mid-Green or Intermediate Ethics

1 'Who' is appropriate for any subject or agent, just as 'that' or 'what' are appropriate for any object. It is therefore incorrect to limit the former term to human beings; we are human because we are a (kind of) subject, not subjects because we are human beings.

2 The term was first coined by Ryder 1973.

3 A hopeful sign at the time of writing was the Compassionate Conservation Symposium in September 2010 in Oxford, hosted by the University of Oxford's Wildlife Conservation Research Unit (WildCRU) and the Born Free Foundation. (I learned about this from *Wolf Print* 42 [Spring 2011].)

4 Although I wasn't able to read it before writing, to judge by what I have seen of his work, Best 2010 is to be recommended. See also Phelps 2007 and Cockburn 1996.

5 Jonathan Franzen, 'Emptying the Skies', *The New Yorker* (26.7.10).

6 Note the excellent work of Global Tiger Patrol, led by Peter Lawton.

7 The *Guardian* (17.11.10).

8 Jeffrey Goldberg published an attack on the Owens in *The New Yorker* on 5.4.10; see their response in 'Letters' on 26.4.10.

9   I do not believe this position outlined here supports the acts of some animal liberation activists who send letter bombs to experimenters through the mail, which is ethically indefensible. As well as being excessively random and therefore potentially highly unfair, as well as cowardly, it is hard to believe that the potential of campaigning, including agitating peacefully for stronger legislation, embarrassing companies through adverse publicity, public demonstrations and NVDA, had been exhausted first. In addition, such actions are massively offensive to the moral instincts of the public at large, and therefore damage the cause they seek to further.

10   Guha 2006: 25–8, which I reviewed in the *Times Literary Supplement* (22.6.07), p. 23. See also Guha's paper of 1989. On his absurd portrayal of Deep Ecology, see Witoszek and Brennan 1999: 314.

11   See the excellent chapter by Barbara Smuts in Coetzee 1999; also see Haraway 2008.

12   Quoted in the epigraph to Patterson 2002.

13   The fifth-century writer Plautus remarked that 'Man is a wolf to man', which became a popular Latin saying. It would have been truer to say, 'Man is a man to man, and to wolf'. (On lupine–human relations, Farley Mowat's *Never Cry Wolf* remains the classic account.)

14   The views expressed by Coetzee's character Elizabeth Costello are almost certainly his own, although using her voice subtly changes the dynamic in ways beyond what can be explored here.

15   Quoted in *Harper's Magazine* (April 2010), p. 78.

16   Sources: *Journal for Critical Animal Studies* (2007), V/2; Balcombe 2010. See also Gellatley 1996.

17   Not himself a vegetarian, by the way.

18   See also Plumwood's important work in her 2000a and 2008. Gary Snyder's excellent essay, 'Survival and Sacrament' (1990: 187–97), is another must-read.

Chapter 8   Dark Green or Deep (Ecocentric) Ethics

1   Sylvan and Bennett 1994: 90.

2   Cf. Pimentel et al. 2000.

3   One exception, which rather confirms the point, is Bender 2004: an important new analysis of ecocentrism.

4   Such as is being developed, in different ways, by people like Susan Bratton, Jane Lubchenko and Carl Safina (with thanks to Jack Stillwell for this point). On an ocean ethic, see the excellent Shaw and Francis 2008.

5   Sylvan and Bennett assign the Land Ethic to Intermediate Environmental

Ethics, a decision with which I do not agree. (Leopold's moral extensionism is not, in itself, sufficient grounds.)

6 For an excellent discussion of 'ecofascism', see Orton 2000.

7 He was preceded by Bateson 1972, 1979.

8 See Curry 2000.

9 Those are the three Buddhist 'sins', which seem to me to be ecologically more relevant than the Christian ones.

10 See Smith 1988, 1997; Latour 1993.

11 As for developing a genetically modified cow resistant to BSE – something which was reported in 2004 – that is simply and in every sense sad.

12 See Curry 2003; Viveiros de Castro 2004.

13 Lovelock 1979, 1988.

14 See the bibliography in Bunyard 1996.

15 E.g., Lynn Margulis, in Bunyard 1996: 54.

16 See Abram 1996b. The objection also ignores the considerable subsequent work modelling Gaia (e.g., 'Daisyworld').

17 See Rawles 1996.

18 With thanks to Clay Ramsay for points I have incorporated here.

19 See Quammen 1998, 1999.

20 As Machiavelli argued.

21 Margulis, in Bunyard 1996: 64; Lovelock 1991.

22 See also David Rothenberg, in Naess 1989.

23 Taken from Naess 1989: 29. These differ slightly (but not substantively) from the way they are stated in Devall and Sessions 1985.

24 Naess 1989: 28; Naess and Sessions 1984.

25 For a very different (and preferable) definition of depth ecology, see Abram 2005.

26 See Chase 1991 for a good summary.

27 See List 1993. See also Chapter 7, note 6.

28 See Sylvan and Bennett 1994: 99–102.

29 See also Fox 1995: 223–4.

30 See Sylvan and Bennett 1994: 102–4, 107–10; Katz 2000; and for a good discussion, James 2004: 76–82.

31 See Curry 2010a for a critique.

32 In Mahayana Buddhism, a Bodhisattva is one who is ready to transcend the world of suffering (*samsara*) for *nirvana* but chooses instead to stay, or return, in order to help others do the same.

33 See Bateson 1972, 1979; Abram 1996a. (Not idealism in the sense of having ideals, but in the philosophical sense of according the 'spiritual' world primacy over the 'material'.)

34 See Barry 1999; Curry 2000.

35 See Plumwood 1995 and Curry 2010a.

36 See Abram 1996: 66–7.

37 Li 1998: 300.

38 Salleh adds that 'There is surely a large portion of illusion and self-indulgence in the North's comfortable middle-class pursuit of the cosmic "transpersonal Self"' (1993: 229).

39 Cf. Abram 1996.

40 To be fair, this point has a Madhyamaka provenance which may not carry the same weight in other Buddhist schools.

41 Perhaps apocryphal, but to the point nonetheless. I have also seen this remark attributed to T. S. Eliot.

42 With respect to David Bennett, whose role as Sylvan's co-author I am sure was crucial, I shall treat DGT as primarily the work of Sylvan. It is certainly of a piece with his earlier writing.

43 Cf. McLaughlin 1993a: 214.

44 Such as those of Guhu 1989.

45 I'm afraid I cannot now locate the reference for this wonderful remark.

46 http://home.ca.inter.net/~greenweb/index.htm. Extant at the time of writing.

47 Cf. Kohák 2000: 64.

48 For one well-informed answer in the negative, see Rees 2002.

49 McLaughlin 1993a.

50 I am grateful to Penny Novack for the points in this paragraph.

51 Michael Novack, private communication.

52 David Orton, 'A Deep Ecology Talk' (4 July 2003).

53 See, e.g., McLaughlin 1993a and Eckersley 1992.

54 E.g. the depressingly orthodox and sectarian Foster 2009.

55 See Orton's indispensable analyses in his 'Ecological Marxism, Intrinsic Value, and Human-Centeredness' (December 2005), http://home.ca.inter.net/~greenweb/Ecological_Marxism.html; 'Mixed Thoughts on Ecosocialism', MS (17.3.10); and 'A Short Talk on Left Biocentrism' (2008) http://home.ca.inter.net/~greenweb/A_short_talk_on_Left_Biocentrism.pdf.

56 'The creatures outside looked from pig to man, and from man to pig, and from pig to man again; but already it was impossible to say which was which' (the concluding sentence of Orwell's *Animal Farm*). And this is leaving aside the dispiriting tendency to already knowing all the answers (it's been foretold, it's all in the Book . . . as with so much revolutionary Marxism, the template is not far to seek) and sectarianism (of which The People's Front of Judea – *not* to be confused with that splitter, the Judean People's Front – remains a deadly accurate parody).

57 David Orton, 'Ecological Marxism, Intrinsic Value, and Human-Centeredness' (Dec. 2005): http://home.ca.inter.net/~greenweb/Ecological_Marxism.html (accessed 4.5.10).

58 Imhoff et al. 2004; Vitousek et al. 1986; Daily 1995; Haberl et al. 2008.

59 Galadriel's words from J. R. R. Tolkien's *The Lord of the Rings*. (For a qualified ecocentric reading of the latter, see Curry 2004.)

60 As Rudolf Bahro always insisted, to the disquiet of the socialist left.

61 Orton, 'Ecological Marxism, Intrinsic Value, and Human-Centeredness'.

62 See http://www.ecospherics.net.

63 Earth Charter USA (2000). See the special issue of *Worldviews* 8: 1 (2004), especially Lynn 2004.

64 As with most other such statements discussed here, please see the original document, which is freely available – in this case, at www.earthcharter.org – for the full text.

Chapter 9   Ecofeminism

1 I would like to thank Ariel Salleh for her patient and invaluable help with this chapter. (Its shortcomings remain mine.) I have also drawn, for the revised edition, on Mellor's excellent 1997.

2 I also like Mellor's suggestion that the problem now is *filiarchy*: rule by the sons. We need our powerful and heedless sons 'to acknowledge their embodiment and embeddedness and what that means for their claims to autonomy and transcendence' (1997: 194).

3 Cf. Plumwood 1993: 60.

4 See Merchant 1980; Keller 1985; Rose 1994; Harding 1986 and 2008.

5 King is quoted in Mellor 1997: 6; Irvine and Ponton in Dobson 2007: 142.

6 See e.g. Mellor 1997: 178–9.

7 See Salleh 1997; Warren 1994; Plumwood 1993 and 2002. It is worth noting the convergence here with the work of David Abram.

8 Gilligan 1982; Noddings 1984; Ruddick 1989.

9 For one supportive philosophical argument (excepting his occasional lapses into scientism), see Williams 1993. On the wrecks, see Scott's excellent 1998. (It is not irrelevant either that virtually all such schemes have been led by ambitious, egomaniacal and decidedly masculinist men.)

Chapter 10   Deep Green Ethics as Post-Secular

1 Note the typically light touch in his subtitle: 'Against Antihumanism, Misanthropy, Mysticism and Primitivism'.

2 See Weber 1991: 143, 153; Midgley 1992, 2001; Feyerabend 1987.

3 Or what Max Weber (1991: 282) called 'concrete magic'. Cf. Bateson 1972, 1979; Abram 1996a.

4 See the *Religions of the World and Ecology* series edited by Mary Evelyn Tucker and John Grim (Harvard University Center for the Study of World Religions); Tucker and Grim 1994; McDonagh 1990; Gottlieb 1996; and Dunlap 2004; also see Curry 2007. I am grateful, here as elsewhere, to Michael Winship and Nigel Cooper for obliging me to be more fair-minded (and accurate) on the subject of Christianity than I sometimes tend to be!

5 Cf. the distinction between religion and enchantment made by Max Weber 1991: 129–56.

6 The Dalai Lama and Vaclav Havel, among others, have advocated a post-secular spirituality. See also Curry 2007.

7 Despite our disagreement over the issue, I am grateful to David Keller for pressing me to clarify this point; and to Greg Garrard, to the same end, regarding animism.

8 See, e.g., Anderson 1996.

9 See, e.g., Salleh 1997; Plumwood 2002. See also Curry 2000; Clifford and King 1993.

10 See Bird-David 1999; Viveiros de Castro 1998; Harvey 2005. For an excellent account of how animism coheres with critical pluralism, see Mathews 1999. Regrettably, Taylor's recent discussion (2010) is misleading. He writes: 'Animism has to do with the *perception* that spiritual intelligences or lifeforces *animate* natural objects or living things', and terms it '*super*natural' (2010: 15; my emphases). But that way of putting it simply assumes what is at stake, namely that 'natural objects' are as defined by Cartesian science – fundamentally, once reduced to physics, *in*animate particles of 'purely physical' stuff – so any spiritual dimension must be *added* in order to 'animate' them. Furthermore, Taylor presents animism not as a way of living or being (ontology) but as a matter of *perception* (epistemology); this not only misunderstands animism but offers it up, trussed and gagged, to the modernist science which now owns 'knowledge'.

11 See especially the brilliant work of Hutton 1991, 1999 and 2003; as well as Harvey 1997; and Jones and Pennick 1995.

12 This continues. See Jay Griffiths's (2006) disturbing contemporary account of the complicity of evangelical missionaries with mercenary corporate exploitation in and of the developing world (specifically West Papua, Peru and Nunavut).

13 See Kaza and Kraft 2000; Badiner 1990; Batchelor and Brown 1992; Ryan 1998; Tucker and Williams 1997. For a promising recent meeting

of Buddhism and Deep Ecology, see the Dharmagaia website: http://www.dharmagaians.org.

14 Inspired to a large extent by the excellent writings of David Loy and Ken Jones, as well as Thich Nhat Hanh and Sulak Sivaraksa.

15 See also James's lucid 2004, in some ways a companion volume, and the excellent discussion in Clark 2008.

16 Hence the famous 'emptiness' (śūnyatā).

17 To oversimplify Cooper and James's argument: 'Buddhism is virtue ethical in character because it regards virtue as *constitutive* of its goal of nirvanic felicity. . . . If virtue is constitutive of wisdom, and wisdom of nirvanic felicity, then virtue itself is constitutive of the Buddhist goal' (2005: 79).

Chapter 11 Moral Pluralism and Pragmatism

1 See James 1977; Weber's seminal essay 'On Science as a Vocation' in his 1991; Berlin 1969 and his superb essay 'The Originality of Machiavelli' in his 1998.

2 See also Kontos 1994.

3 Abram 1996; Weston 1994.

4 Barbara Herrnstein Smith's analyses of this point in her 1988 and 1997 remain peerless.

5 On epistemological pluralism, see Feyerabend 1987 and Smith 1997; on axiological (value) pluralism see Smith's exemplary 1988; on moral pluralism, see Berlin 1969; on pluralism in a political context, and in relation to ecocentrism, see Stone 1987, 1995; Brennan 1995a, 1995b; Midgley 1997; Curry 2003.

6 Cf. Brennan 1995b

7 See Stone 1995; Brennan 1995a; also Laclau and Mouffe 1985.

8 She adds: 'The idea that reductive simplicity here is particularly rational or "scientific" is mere confusion' (1997: 100).

9 This is also something that Machiavelli and Weber recognized.

10 See Swanton 2004.

11 I am thinking of the work of William James and John Dewey (more than Peirce), as well as Michael Polanyi and Michael Oakeshott. See Light and Katz 1996; and Cormier 2001 (on James).

12 See Plumwood 2002: 124–6 for an excellent critique of Norton's position.

13 In addition to Rowe, Livingstone and Orton, some of the names that come to mind are Val Plumwood, Gary Snyder, Ursula Le Guin, Wendell Berry, Loren Eisley, Mary Midgley, Barry Lopez, David Abram, Gregory Bateson and Hugh Brody. 'Sanity and sanctity' was

how one reader described the work of J. R. R. Tolkien (see Curry 2004). It was and is appreciated as such by some members of the same class, such as Eisley, Le Guin and David Ehrenfeld.

14 I would like to record a significant debt to Francesco Barravechia for conversations around the subject of this following discussion, although he would probably still disagree with my conclusion.

15 *Chambers Dictionary*, and basic Pierre Bourdieu, respectively.

16 Weber 2005: 215. On animist perspectivism, see Viveiros de Castro 2004. On Buddhism, see my remarks in this volume. (There is of course a large literature on the last.)

17 A wonderful word and concept, which I have borrowed from the nature-culture writer Tim Robinson.

18 Thomas Nagel's and Donna Haraway's phrases, respectively. (They amount to the same thing, of course.)

19 Concerning Buddhist spiritual development, consider the truth of a remark by Jack Engler: 'You have to be somebody before you can be nobody.'

Chapter 12   Green Citizenship and Education

1 See Berry 2000 and Heyd 2007.

2 Clay Ramsay, personal communication.

3 See www.worldpublicopinion.org (accessed 2.3.11).

4 See Smith 1988: 132.

5 Mention might be made at this point of the popular film *Avatar* (2009). One possible response might be: it's all a cynical con to make people feel better about their ecocidal lives. Another might be: it's more evidence of a global change of consciousness that will save us in the nick of time. Both, alone, would be wrong (and not just because 'consciousness' apparently means whatever anyone wants it to). The fact that *Avatar*'s ecological and indigenous storyline was financed by, and made profits for, the multinational company News International, and that its anti-technological message was made possible by the most advanced and expensive media machines, does not altogether cancel out its reach and emotional power, or determine what viewers will take away from it. Nor, however, does that message obviate the pointed ironies involved. Only this sort of 'both-and' thinking can even begin to get to grips with the relevant complexities (ecological in the fullest sense). I would add that the film was interesting for the way it laid bare the actual relationship, when push comes to shove, between capital and technoscience: the latter is the servant of the former.

6 Lewis H. Lapham's editorial, *Harper's Magazine*, June 2009. Anne Stevenson, from 'Poem for a Daughter', in Neil Astley, *Staying Alive: Real Poems for Unreal Times* (Tarset: Bloodaxe Books, 2002), p. 185. See Nicholsen 2003, Jones 1993 and Loy 2005.

7 Cf. Norton 1991. A good antidote, to mention only one example, might be the mindfulness meditation of Jon Kabat-Zinn.

8 See Jones 1993 for an excellent discussion.

9 I am grateful to Suzanna Saumarez for helpful suggestions for this section.

10 *Guardian*, 17.8.10 and 16.1.08.

11 I have taken these quotations from Livingston's discussion in his 1994: 129.

12 See also the seminal essay 'Why Look at Animals?' by Berger (2009), as well as the poem 'They Are the Last', in the same collection.

13 John Henley, 'Nature's Lost Generation', *Guardian* (17.8.10); also the source for Lambert.

14 Orr 1991 and 2004; Louv 2008. But in addition to Bowers, see Heyd 2007; Joyce 2009.

15 See Mark Slouka, 'Dehumanized. When Math and Science Rule the School', *Harper's Magazine*, Sept. 2009, pp. 32–40. (Let alone the eco-humanities!)

16 See http://www.earthcharterus.org (accessed 2.3.11).

17 On the distinction between use and exploitation, see Zwicky 1992 and my recent discussion in 2010b.

18 From a talk given in Copenhagen on 3.9.09, 'Comparison as a Matter of Concern', the final version of which appeared as Stengers 2011. See also Curry 2010b and Rowe, 'Role of the University' in his 2002: 122–31.

19 The entire section on Deep Ecology was excised from the most recent edition (2005) of the influential undergraduate reader, *Environmental Philosophy: From Animal Rights to Radical Ecology*. One reason given by J. Baird Callicott, one of the editors, was that Deep Ecology now seemed 'vaguely anti-intellectual', but the real reason, it turns out, was that since 11 September 2001, 'responsible environmental philosophers wish to distance themselves from militant ideologies'. It is indefensible to associate Deep Ecologists, however extreme a very few might be, with the violent Islamists of 9/11; evidence for doing so is nil, and semi-hysteria is not a reliable moral or intellectual guide. One effect is to deny political ecology its most radical voice at exactly the time when the environmental crisis is deepening and widening. If this is the price of respectability, it is too high. On the other hand, the third edition (2001) of the same reader contained a positive reference by the social

ecology activist and philosopher John Clark to left biocentrism, which is repeated in the current fourth edition.

20 Sometimes, bizarrely, the two meet, as in Donna Haraway's (1991: 181) preference for being a cyborg over a goddess. Even critical feminist and environmental philosophers, it seems, are not altogether immune to the allure of hegemonic masculinist fantasies of mastery (shiny, clever, secular biomachines: good/messy, dark, earthy, feminine sacrality: bad). Another recent ecowriter in the academy, Timothy Morton, denies the reality, or at least importance, or at any rate helpfulness (it's not clear which) of what he calls Nature in favour of 'the ecological thought': 'Ecology equals living plus Nature, plus consciousness' (2010: 19). But the entire theoretical edifice seems to be built on the assumption, which I have contested here, that nature excludes both humanity and consciousness; and the emphasis on the latter should immediately alert us, as Sylvan noted of some Deep Ecologists' emphasis on Self-realization, to the presence of Enlightenment anthropocentrism. (Not for the first time do I miss Plumwood: in this case, for what she would have had to say about Morton's work! But see the pertinent comments by Salleh 2010.)

21 For an initiative out of all proportion to its apparent size, see an Australian network, partly inspired by Plumwood, under the name of ecohumanities: http://www.ecologicalhumanities.org/index.html; and Rose and Robin's article of 2004, accessible at http://www.australianhumanitiesreview.org/archive/Issue-April-2004/rose.html. Some equally exciting work is also taking place in Canada, more on the edge of the academy than in it; see the discussion in my 2010b. For an excellent general introduction and reader, see Coupe 2000 and (with some reservations) Garrard 2004.

22 Out of a vast literature: for a bracingly gloomy follow-up to Weber, see Horkheimer and Adorno 2002; for contemporary sociological exemplification, see Ritzer 1996 and 2004; for a brilliant analysis bringing Weber up to date, see Scaff 1989; for an important supplementary corrective, see Latour 1993.

23 Irvine's remark is in an unpublished MS. I would add that assumptions of Neolithic anthropogenic megafauna extinctions are arguably simplistic; a few large killing sites do not constitute a species extinction.

24 See Oviedo and Maffi 2000. With thanks to Elizabeth Reichel for drawing my attention to this report and supplying related material.

25 See Geertz 2000; Scott 1998.

26 See Deloria 2000 for an incisive review of Krech 1999; and Isenberg 2000 for a critical alternative view.

27 See also Harrop 2010.

28 Personal communication (28.11.03).
29 Quoted in *The Utne Reader* (5.6.95) p. 69. I would also like to mention the books of Caduto and Bruchac (1991, 1994a, 1994b), which combine activities for children, Native American stories, and local natural worlds in an exemplary way.
30 See (in all cases, among many other publications by the same authors) Snyder 1990; Clifford and King 1993; Jackson 1994; Berry 1987, 2010. On bioregionalism, see Sale 1985; McGinnis 1999; Thayer 2003; and the excellent work of the Planet Drum Foundation (www.planetdrum. org). See also Martin 1992.
31 Cf. Barry 1999: 233.
32 See Sandel 1996; Pettit 1997; Oldfield 1990. On communitarianism, see Tam 1998 for a promising (although non-ecocentric) version.
33 See Curry 2000. 'Life' here is intended to include the abiotic whose matrix it shares, as discussed above.
34 See Detienne and Vernant 1991; Raphals 1992.
35 Tucker and Berthrong 1998; Chan 1963; Montaigne 1991.
36 With thanks to Michael Novack for reminding me of this wonderful passage.

Chapter 13   Grounding Ecological Ethics

1 Michael Pollan's excellent term.
2 Ponting 2007.
3 Salonius 2008.
4 See Montgomery 2008.
5 See Steinfeld et al. 2006; and Cockburn's excellent paper of 1996.
6 For water statistics, see Elizabeth Kolbert, 'Flesh of Your Flesh', *The New Yorker* (9.11.09); for air statistics, see Patel 2008: 299. The recent lower estimate of Fairlie 2010a has been thrown into serious doubt by Wardle (2010).
7 See Schlosser 2001.
8 See Princen et al. 2002; also the work of Juliet Schor and the Center for a New American Dream (CNAD); and not least, Reverend Billy and the Church of Stop Shopping.
9 See Pimental and Pimental 2008; Roberts 2008.
10 Quoting from George Monbiot's encomium in the *Guardian* (7.9.10). (It is dismaying to find a prominent green spokesperson practising just such a reduction to efficiency.)
11 On Wal-Mart, see Quinn 2000. On Tesco, see Simms 2007. For the effect on social capital, see Goetz and Rupasingha 2006. See also a report in the *Guardian* (5.5.10).

12 Felicity Lawrence, 'It is too late to shut the door on GM foods', the *Guardian* (17.10.09).

13 See the excellent work of Shiva, especially (in this connection) her 1993.

14 *Guardian* (16.6.10). For the immediately following discussion, see Kaufman 2010.

15 Berry has written so many excellent books that it would be unwise to try to pick out only one or two. Jackson 1994 stands out, as does Mollison 1988. See also Holmgren 2003; Netting 1993; Wirzba 2003; Smith 2003.

16 www.ciwf.org/eatingtheplanet.

17 See Windfur and Jonsén 2005.

18 In addition to the SFM websites, see Patel 2008: 281–6.

19 Quoted in Peterson 2009: 107.

20 See Nick Paumgarten, 'Food Fighter', *The New Yorker* (4.1.10) for a revealing interview with Whole Foods', er, colourful entrepreneurial founder and CEO, John Mackey.

21 Also see Pollan 2007 and Patel 2008 for good discussions.

22 Quoted in Salonius 2008; my emphasis.

23 See Bender 2003: 321–8 for a good discussion of 'Updating Malthus Ecologically'. Sarkar, discussing Malthus, agrees: 'We must differentiate between problem and policy' (1999: 130–1).

24 See also Ferguson 1998; also Al Bartlett, 'The Massive Movement to Marginalize the Modern Malthusian Message' (1998): http://www.albartlett.org/articles/art1998spring.html (accessed 15.2.11).

25 http://nobelprize.org/nobel_prizes/peace/laureates/1970/borlaug-lecture.html.

26 See Locke and Mackey 2009.

27 Bart Verheggen on Keith Kloor's website: http://www.collide-a-scape.com/2010/06/11/bridging-the-climate-divide/. On the issue of four/six degrees, in addition to the latest IPCC report, see Lynas 2007 and, for a recent review, Hamilton 2010.

28 For a view (which I am not competent to judge) that 'at least 60% of the global warming observed since 1970 has been induced by the combined effect of . . . natural climate oscillations' derived from solar-system cycles, see Nicola Scafetta, 'Empirical Evidence of a Celestial Origin of the Climate Oscillations and its Implications', *Journal of Atmospheric and Solar-Terrestrial Physics* (2010), doi:10.1016/jastp.2020.04.015 (with thanks to Graham Douglas for this reference). But note that even in this scenario, the suggested current astrophysical cooling downswing will not last, and when it starts to rise in the 2030s, if it does so together with unabated anthropogenic emissions, the effect will be truly fierce.

29 Alex Bojanowski, 'The Climategate Chronicle: How the Science of Global Warming Was Compromised', *Spiegel* Online (14.5.10): http://www.spiegel.de/international/ (accessed 15.2.11).

30 Stephen Curry and Bill Hanage, 'We're not on a Pedestal', *Guardian* (11.2.10).

31 See the Greenpeace report 'Koch Industries: Secretly Funding the Denial Machine': http://www.greenpeace.org/usa/en/media-center/reports/koch-industries-secretly-fund/ (accessed 15.2.11); Jane Meyer, 'Covert Operations', *The New Yorker* (30.8.10). Recently the Coalition for Responsible Regulation, connected to the chemical firm Solvay, has been funding directly efforts to stop the EPA from addressing ACC; see the *Guardian* (22.4.10).

32 See Oreskes and Conway 2010. For an overview of the crucial role of advertising in this context, see McIntosh 2008.

33 Hamilton 2010: 105–6.

34 See Friel 2010.

35 *Guardian* (9.3.10).

36 Martin Durkin, whose earlier documentary linked environmentalists and Nazis, repeated the trick on Channel 4 (in November 2010) with a call to solve the economic crisis by simply privatizing and deregulating everything. See Hamilton 2010: 113–16.

37 See http://pwccc.wordpress.com/ and the excellent article by Jerry Mander, 'Climate Change v. Capitalism: The Feast Is Almost Over', *Guardian* (15.10.10).

38 'The ICCR & The Re-Embodiment of the Global Polity: An Ecofeminist Approach' (25.2.10): http://www.ecopaxmundi.org/docs/kernels/theicc.pdf (accessed 15.2.11).

39 http://www.grist.org/article/2009-08-23-the-fallacy-of-climate-activism (accessed 15.2.11). Emphases in the original.

40 See also Greer 2010.

41 Gustavo Esteva, 'The arrogance of Cancún', *Guardian* (16.12.10).

42 http://www.countercurrents.org/mcpherson300609.htm (accessed 15.2.11).

43 Siting wind 'farms' offshore – sensitively – would probably have significantly less ecological impact, although it is too early to say for sure.

44 Terence Blacker, 'An Ordinary Beauty', *Countryside Voice* (Spring 2010), the magazine of the Campaign for the Protection of Rural England, which does good work of this kind. So does the excellent charity Common Ground, on behalf of local natural/cultural distinctiveness.

45 http://home.ca.inter.net/~greenweb/Wind_turbine_questions.pdf; see also http://home.ca.inter.net/~greenweb/Wind_Farms_and_Deep_Ecology.pdf (both sites accessed 15.2.11).

46 Ignoring the salutary recent lessons of wind-power in Denmark, the British government recently blithely issued a target that would requite a 'turbine footprint' of half the area of Wales or a strip 10km-deep around the entire British coastline ('Denmark's Wind Turbines', *THE* [29.7.10]: 39).

47 For a detailed analysis, see Trainer (2007).

48 See http://www.aweo.org/Lake.html.

49 Lowry: letter to the *Guardian* (16.4.10); Weiss: letter to *The New Yorker* (5.4.10).

50 Yablokov et al. 2001. Like other investigations to date, however, it remains controversial.

51 With thanks to Ian Whyte for this point.

52 From Naomi Klein's excellent report 'Gulf Oil Spill: A Hole in the World', *Guardian* (19.5.10). On the crucial difference between ecological wisdom and scientific brilliance – and in the case of Freeman Dyson, a climate change denier and geoengineering enthusiast, complete disconnect – see Brower's important 2010 article.

53 Klein, 'Gulf Oil Spill: A Hole in the World'.

54 Paul Kingsnorth, 'A Climate Deal is Like Trying to Halt the Rains in Cumbria', *Guardian* (25.11.09).

55 *Guardian* (3.11.09). For an excellent and detailed analysis, see Loy 2002, as well as Harvey Cox, 'The Market as God: Living in the New Dispensation', *The Atlantic Online* (1999): http://www.theatlantic. com/past/docs/issues/99mar/marketgod.htm (accessed 15.2.11).

56 For Strong, see Sullivan 2010a: 116; For Stern and Blair, see Hulme 2008: 125.

57 See http://www.mckinseyquarterly.com/Strategy/Strategy_in_Practice/ The_next_environmental_issue_for_business_McKinsey_Global_Sur vey_results_2651 (accessed 24.9.10); with thanks to Stephen Fitzpatrick for bringing this to my attention.

58 Terry Dressler, an air pollution control officer in Santa Barbara; letter in *Harper's Magazine* (April 2010).

59 On the International Society for Environmental Ethics (ISEE) list-serv (25.5.10).

60 Nigel Cooper, 'The Spiritual Value of Ecosystem Services: an Initial Christian Exploration' (2009): http://www.cambridgeconservationforum. org.uk/wp-content/uploads/Ecosystem-service-discussion-papers. zip.

61 For more on the Greenpeace investigation, see Hari 2010. The FOE report is 'REDD: The realities in black and white' (Nov. 2010), accessible on www.foei.org under 'Resources' – Publications – Forests.

62 Recall Tolkien's definition of magic quoted above, including the way

it 'produces, or *pretends* to produce, an alteration in the Primary World' in order to dominate 'things and wills'.

63 Which is why some missionaries and transnational companies work hand-in-hand in remaining indigenous areas; see Griffiths 2006.

64 See also Sullivan 2009/10; Robertson 2006; and also Cooper, 'The Spiritual Value of Ecosystem Services'. Also see Ruth Thomas-Pellicer, 'The ICCR & The Re-Embodiment of the Global Polity: An Ecofeminist Approach' (25.2.10): http://www.ecopaxmundi.org/docs/kernels/theicc.pdf, and 'Sustainability as (Neo)liberalism's Trojan Horse in Ecocidal Times': http://www.ecopaxmundi.org/docs/kernels/SustainabilityAsTheTrojanHorseOfNeoliberalismInEcocidalTimes15022010.pdf, both on: http://www.ecopaxmundi.org/.

65 Tim Murray, 'There Really Is Only One Kind Of Sustainability' (2.4.10) – http://www.countercurrents.org/murray020410.htm (accessed 15.2.11).

66 Thomas-Pellicer, 'The ICCR & The Re-Embodiment of the Global Polity'.

67 Murray, 'There Really Is Only One Kind Of Sustainability'.

68 For a dire recent example of elite economic wishful thinking, see Paul Collier 2010, who recommends rescuing a 'plundered planet' by a better class of plundering, and 'reconciling prosperity with nature' by turning more of the latter into still more cash.

69 I quote from Irvine's 'Cornucopia Scam: Contradictions of Sustainable Development', published over three issues of *Wild Earth*: Fall 1994: 73–84; Winter 1994/95: 72–82; Spring 1995: 76–80. Irvine and Ponton's 1988 is still a classic of genuinely ecocentric political ecology. See also the passage quoted earlier, on pages 208–9, from Adam Sacks.

70 From a post on the Left Bio list. Cf. Sarkar 2010 to the same end.

71 Richard Heinberg, 'Five Axioms of Sustainability', *MuseLetter* 178 (1.2.07): http://heinberg.wordpress.com/2007/02/01/178-five-axioms-of-sustainability/ (accessed 20.12.10). But see also Jackson 2009.

72 See Jackson 2009: xvii.

73 Cf. the novelist Robertson Davies: 'I'm fascinated by those who assume that man with his five senses and his remarkable ability to think and investigate will somehow put salt on the tail of all the secrets of the universe.'

74 The dominant form of which is *neoliberal economics*, the toxic spawn of neoclassical economics (utilitarian, materialist and positivist) and neoliberal politics (elitist, managerial and ruthless). For a good recent discussion, see Söderbaum 2008.

75 Perhaps this is where Tertullian's theological justification for belief in

God, almost extinct in the Church, lives on in modern culture: *credo quia absurdam* (I believe it because it is absurd).

76 The neoliberal 1980s and 1990s saw 'the largest transfer of wealth from the poor to the rich in human history', with the result that 'In 1999 nearly half of American families had a lower real income than in 1973' (Eherenberg 1999: 245–59).

77 See Lane 2000.

78 In London, where I live, the richest 10th of the population has 273 times the wealth of the poorest 10th: a gap not seen since slave-owning society.

79 Wilkinson 1996, Wilkinson and Pickett 2010. It is significant that the latter has recently been subjected to the same sort of attacks as those on climate science (see the *Guardian* [14.8.10]).

80 See Gannon and Lawson 2010.

81 See Clegg 2009; Tokar 1997.

82 On a point of social psychology, the pathetic self-justifications of the original owners also revealed how easy long-term immersion in business culture can make it to lose the ethical plot.

83 You have to say or hear this in a Belfast accent to get its full force. (I would add, however, that anyone fighting for better treatment of animals would be a fool to refuse the help of a Pamela Anderson; or for renewable energy, an Arnold Schwarzenegger.)

84 Actually, two other items could give it a run for its money: the huge, military-style SUV, and the leaf-blower. (And no, converting either of them to solar or hydrogen would not make any real difference!)

85 Cf. Bender (2003: 342): 'Though capitalism is inherently anti-ecological, it cannot be overshoot's ultimate cause, since the culture of capitalism began long before capitalism arose. It began with the transition from seasonally nomadic horticulture to agriculture. . . . We can say only that capitalism has hugely exacerbated anthrogenic [*sic*] impact.'

86 Idealistic entrepreneurs: see The Body Shop and Ben & Jerry's (and Innocent Smoothies, and Seeds of Change, and . . .). Self-regulation: in addition to the 'restraint' shown recently by City of London banks in awarding themselves huge publicly funded bonuses, banks continue to back environmentally destructive mega-projects, despite the seven years of voluntary 'self-policing' under the Equator Principles they agreed in 2003. See also Rich 1994.

87 See, e.g., Daly and Cobb 1997 (perhaps the most important in relation to eco-ethics); Daly and Townsend 1993; Daly and Farley 2004; Daly 2008; Douthwaite 1999 (among several others); Nickerson 2009; McKibben 2007; Brian Czech, 'Steady State Economy', *The*

Encyclopedia of Earth (2006): http://www.eoearth.org/article/Steady_
state_economy (accessed 15.2.11); and the website http://steadystate.
org/ (accessed 20.12.10). Some of the others besides Daly and his
colleagues whose work contributes to bringing about positive changes
include Hazel Henderson as well as Jerry Mander and Edward
Goldsmith (contesting globalization and promoting local self-reliance),
and Richard Douthwaite (contesting economic growth and promoting community economies and energy), together with Colin Hines
(both on localizing economies), Serge Latouche (voice of the promising 'degrowth' movement), and Bill McKibben (2007). (Some of their
books are included in my bibliography.)

88 It is not perfect; he is patronizing, almost racist, towards indigenous
cultures and vernacular knowledge, an attitude which also results from
his unfortunate scientism. But that can be put to one side for the sake
of his socioeconomic analysis. See also the important work by David
Orton on this subject.

89 Mike Hulme (2009) probably belongs here too, although his book is
somewhat weakened by its occasional pedagogical blandness, e.g.: 'One
of the reasons we disagree about climate change is that we receive mul-
tiple and conflicting messages about climate change and we interpret
them in different ways' (p. 215).

90 http://onthecommons.org (accessed 15.2.11). See also 'Commons
Rising: A Report to Owners from the Tomales Bay Institute' (2006).

91 http://commonsblog.wordpress.com/2010/01/28/the-commons-
as-a-common-paradigm-for-social-movements-and-beyond/ (accessed
15.2.11).

92 http://gen.ecovillage.org/ (accessed 15.2.11).

93 See Sylvan and Bennett 1994: 169–72.

94 James 2007; de Graaf et al. 2005; Segal 1999; Siegal 2008; Alexander
2009. See also www.simplicitycollective.com (accessed 15.2.11).

95 Robert Skidelsky, 'Enough is not enough', *Guardian* (23.11.09).

96 From the TTM website: http://transitiontowns.org. See also Hopkins
2008.

97 Ted Trainer, 'The Transition Towns Movement: Its Huge Significance
and a Friendly Criticism' (16.2.10): http://www.culturechange.org/cms/
content/view/605/65/. See responses such as that by Brian Davey: http://
www.energybulletin.net/node/50894. (Both sites accessed 15.2.11.)

98 Trainer is rightly critical of techno-fixes such as suggested by Weizacher
and Lovins 1998. (He calculates that to succeed would require a Factor
100+ *reduction*.) Trainer's website is http://ssis.arts.unsw.edu.au/tsw/
(accessed 15.2.11).

99 For another very good discussion, see Roseland 1998.

Chapter 14   Human Overpopulation

1 Quoted in the Optimum Population Trust (OPT) Newsletter (January 1998): 6.

2 In Irvine's unpublished MS 'Missing Numbers'. Cf. the British Medical Journal 319 (9.10.99): 931–4, 977–97; also the work of Al Barlett: http://www.albartlett.org/articles/articles_by_al_bartlett.html (accessed 15.2.11).

3 See Ehrenfeld 1981.

4 See too the point about human appropriation of global photosynthetic energy, made in the section in Chapter 8 on Left Biocentrism.

5 WWF 2008.

6 With thanks to Harry Cripps for clarifying this point.

7 WWF 2008.

8 http://footprintnetwork.org/images/uploads/EcologicalFootprintAtlas 2009.pdf (accessed 28.4.10).

9 Ted Mosquin, personal communication.

10 In addition to the authors directly cited or quoted here, much good thinking is carried out by members of the UK-based Optimum Population Trust (OPT), some of it appearing in its journal *The Jackdaw*.

11 *Pherology* is a term coined by Alec Ponton to mean 'the science of the human carrying-capacity of the Earth or specific parts of the Earth' (2001: 2). Regrettably, it seems to have fallen into disuse.

12 See Youngquist 1999.

13 Also see Rees 1996.

14 Including, as Gaia Theory and the Earth Manifesto do, the inorganic elements that are essential to life.

15 Willey 2000; Smail 1997; Ferguson 1999 (and writings in general for the OPT). See the entire issue that includes Smail's paper, that is, pp. 181–354, for an excellent discussion.

16 Cf. Stanton 2004.

17 Stan Rowe, personal communication.

18 Willey 2004: 6.

19 Virginia Abernethy, *The Pherologist* 2: 3 (1999): 7 (with references).

20 Another analogy might be: responding to a growing debt by repeatedly increasing the overdraft limit – as if this could be kept up indefinitely.

21 John Guillebaud, quoted in a letter by Doeke Oostra of EPOC (6.2.01). Cf. the demographer Tomáš Sobotka, 'Europe is not heading for a population collapse', *Guardian* (5.2.10): 'a slow decline in European pop should be welcomed by all who care about climate change and global pressure on resources.'

22 With thanks to Edmund Davey for this point.

23 Cf. Paul Watson (statement issued in November 2003): 'I don't believe it is anti-immigrant to be in favor of lower immigration levels for the same reason I don't think it is anti-baby to be in favor of less babies being born.'

24 On this subject, see the excellent paper by Kates 2004. With thanks to Michael Novack for discussions concerning this point.

25 Some non-academic books on this subject are: Casey 1998; Carroll 2000; Cain 2001.

26 Again, see also Kates 2004.

27 See also Meyerson 1998, O'Neill et al. 2005.

28 As called for, e.g., by Smail 1997.

29 James Lovelock is an OPT patron.

30 See Jensen and Draffan 2003.

31 For this reason, I strongly disagree with a recent campaign by the OPT for a financial incentive not to have children based on a calculated amount of carbon thereby not released (by those children); see my analysis above of the iniquitous effects of the market instrumentalization of nature, which apply equally to human nature.

32 Quoted in an interview in 'Green' (28.5.08): http://current.com/green/89058022_paul-ehrlich-talks-about-earths-dominant-animal.htm.

33 Quoted in EPOC press release (14.2.99).

Chapter 15   Postscript

1 A phrase of Tolkien's, describing our existential situation. (Note that he didn't see his deep Catholic faith as a guarantee, on this side of the grave, of salvation; nor the lack of a guarantee as impugning his faith.)

2 Bahn and Flenley (1992), quoted by Ronald Wright in the *TLS*, 19.11.04. See also Diamond 2005.

3 Quoting, in this and the preceding sentence, from my 2004: 19, 140. Abram (2010) argues just this case.

4 http://www.dark-mountain.net/ and Kingsnorth and Hine 2010. See too Lear 2006 and, for a discussion explicitly related to ecocrisis, Peter Case and Jonathan Gosling, 'Leading through the veil: seeing to the other side of catastrophe', forthcoming paper.

5 See the excellent collections of Coupe 2000 and, for poetry, Astley 2007; also Barry Lopez's essay 'Landscape and Narrative' in his 1988. The Dark Mountain project takes its name, and to some extent lead, from Robinson Jeffers, and while there are many fine 'nature' poets – most of them in Astley's collection – I cannot leave the subject without a bow to Jeffers, D. H. Lawrence, Mary Oliver and W. S. Merwin.

6 John Michael Greer, Alistair McIntosh, and Starhawk, for example. See also the 'food sanity' list offered in chapter 13 (with apologies for the inevitable omissions).

7 'It was the spiritual dimension of the world, its enchanted, magical quality that rendered it infinite, not amenable to complete calculability; spirit could not be quantified; it permitted and invited mythologization' (Kontos 1994: 225).

8 Perhaps we need a new term for ecological truth. I suggest VERIDITY, from Latin *viridis* (green) → viridian + Latin *veritas* (truth) → verity.

References

Abernethy, Virginia (1993) *Population Politics: The Choices that Shape Our Future* (New York: Plenum).

Abram, David (1996a) *The Spell of the Sensuous: Perception and Language in a More-Than-Human World* (New York: Random House).

Abram, David (1996b) 'The Mechanical and the Organic: Epistemological Consequences of the Gaia Hypothesis', in Bunyard (ed.).

Abram, David (2005) 'Depth Ecology', in Taylor (ed.).

Abram, David (2007) 'Earth in Eclipse: An Essay on the Philosophy of Science and Ethics', in Suzanne L. Cataldi and William S. Hamrick (eds), *Merleau-Ponty and Environmental Philosophy* (Albany: State University of New York Press).

Abram, David (2010) *Becoming Animal: An Earthly Cosmology* (New York: Pantheon).

Agarwal, Anil and Sunita Narain (1991) *Global Warming in an Unequal World* (Delhi: Centre for Science and the Environment).

Alexander, F. M. (2000) *Aphorisms*, ed. Jean M. O. Fischer (London: Mouritz).

Alexander, Samuel (ed.) (2009) *Voluntary Simplicity: The Poetic Alternative to Consumer Culture* (Aotearoa, NZ: Stead & Daughters Ltd.).

Anderson, E. N. (1996) *Ecologies of the Heart: Emotion, Belief, and the Environment* (Oxford: Oxford University Press).

Astley, Neil (ed.) (2007) *Earthshattering: Ecopoems* (Tarset, Northumberland: Bloodaxe).

Athanasiou, Tom (1997) *Slow Reckoning: The Ecology of a Divided Planet* (London: Secker & Warburg).

Attfield, Robin (1983) *The Ethics of Environmental Concern* (Oxford: Blackwell).

Badiner, Allan Hunt (ed.) (1990) *Dharma Gaia: A Harvest of Essays in Buddhism and Ecology* (Berkeley: Parallax Press).

Bahn, Paul and John Flenley (1992) *Easter Island, Earth Island* (London: Thames & Hudson).

Bahro, Rudolf (1986) *Building the Green Movement* (London: GMP).

Bahro, Rudolf (1994) *Avoiding Social and Ecological Disaster: The Politics of World Transformation*, rev. edn (Bath: Gateway Books).

Balcombe, Jonathan (2010) *Second Nature: The Inner Lives of Animals* (London: Palgrave Macmillan).

Barry, John (1999) *Rethinking Green Politics* (London: Sage).

Batchelor, Martine and Kerry Brown (eds) (1992) *Buddhism and Ecology* (London: Cassell).

Bateson, Gregory (1972) *Steps to an Ecology of Mind* (New York: Ballantine).

Bateson, Gregory (1979) *Mind and Nature: A Necessary Unity* (New York: Dutton).

Bauckham, Richard (2010) *Bible and Ecology: Rediscovering the Community of Creation* (London: Darton, Longman & Todd).

Bauer, Henry (1994) *Scientific Literacy and the Myth of the Scientific Method* (Urbana: University of Illinois Press).

Bauman, Zygmunt (1992) *Intimations of Postmodernity* (London: Routledge).

Bender, Frederic L. (2003) *The Culture of Extinction: Toward a Philosophy of Deep Ecology* (Amherst, NY: Humanity Books).

Benson, John (2000) *Environmental Ethics: An Introduction with Readings* (London: Routledge).

Bentham, Jeremy (1907) *The Principles of Morals and Legislation* (Oxford: Oxford University Press).

Berger, John (2009) *Why Look at Animals?* (London: Penguin).

Berkes, Fikret (1999) *Sacred Ecology: Traditional Ecological Knowledge and Resource Management* (Philadelphia: Taylor and Francis).

Berlin, Isaiah (1969) *Four Essays on Liberty* (Oxford: Oxford University Press).

Berlin, Isaiah (1998) *The Proper Study of Mankind: An Anthology of Essays*, ed. Henry Hardy and Roger Hausheer (London: Pimlico).

Berry, Thomas (2000) *The Great Work: Our Way into the Future* (New York: Three Rivers Press).

Berry, Wendell (1987) *Home Economics* (New York: North Point Press).

Berry, Wendell (2008) 'Faustian Economics: Hell Hath No Limits', *Harper's Magazine* (May): 1–7.

Berry, Wendell (2010) *Imagination in Place* (Berkeley: Counterpoint).

Best, Steven (2009) 'The Rise of Critical Animal Studies: Putting Theory into Action and Animal Liberation into Higher Education', *Journal for Critical Animal Studies* 7(1): 9–52.

Best, Steven (2010) *Moral Progress and Animal Liberation: The Struggle for Human Evolution* (Lanham, MD: Rowman and Littlefield).

Bird-David, Nurit (1999) '"Animism" Revisited: Personhood, Environment, and Relational Epistemology', *Current Anthropology* 40: S67–S91; repr. in Graham Harvey (ed.), *Readings in Indigenous Religions* (London: Continuum, 2002).

Blackburn, Simon (2001) *Being Good: A Short Introduction to Ethics* (Oxford: Oxford University Press).

Blackburn, Simon (ed.) (1994) *The Oxford Dictionary of Philosophy* (Oxford: Oxford University Press).

Bookchin, Murray (1990) *The Philosophy of Social Ecology* (Montreal: Black Rose Books).

Bookchin, Murray (1995) *Re-Enchanting Humanity: A Defense of the Human Spirit Against Antihumanism, Misanthropy, Mysticism and Primitivism* (London: Cassell).

Botkin, Daniel B. (1992) *Discordant Harmonies: New Ecology for the Twenty-First Century* (Oxford: Oxford University Press).

Bowers, C. A. (1993) *Critical Essays on Education and the Recovery of the Ecological Imperative* (New York: Teachers College Press).

Bowers, C. A. (2000) *Let Them Eat Data: How Computers Affect Education, Cultural Diversity and the Prospects of an Ecologically Sustainable Future* (Athens: University of Georgia Press).

Boyle, Robert (1997 [1686]) *A Free Enquiry into the Vulgarly Received Notion of Nature*, ed. Edward B. Davis and Michael Hunter (Cambridge: Cambridge University Press).

Braithwaite Victoria (2010) *Do Fish Feel Pain?* (Oxford: Oxford University Press).

Bramwell, Anna (1989) *Ecology in the 20th Century* (New Haven: Yale University Press).

Brand, Stewart (2009) *Whole Earth Discipline: An Ecopragmatist Manifesto* (New York: Viking).

Brennan, Andrew (1995a) 'Ecological Theory and Value in Nature', in Elliott (ed.).

Brennan, Andrew (ed.) (1995b) *The Ethics of the Environment* (Aldershot: Dartmouth).

Brennan, Andrew (ed.) (1998) *Thinking About Nature: An Investigation of Nature, Value and Ecology* (London: Routledge).

Brennan, Teresa (2000) *Exhausting Modernity: Grounds for a New Economy* (London: Routledge).

Brennan, Teresa (2003) *Globalization and its Terrors. Daily Life in the West* (London: Routledge).

Briggs, Robert (2001) 'Wild Thoughts: A Deconstructive Environmental Ethics?', *Environmental Ethics* 23(2): 115–34.

Brody, Hugh (2002) *The Other Side of Eden: Hunter-gatherers, Farmers and the Shaping of the World*, 2nd edn (London: Faber & Faber).

Brower, Kenneth (2010) 'The Danger of Cosmic Genius', *The Atlantic* (December): 48–62.

Brown, James Robert (2002) *Who Rules in Science?* (Cambridge, MA: Harvard University Press).

Brown, Lester (2000) 'Challenges of the New Century', *State of the World 2000* (New York: Norton).

Budiansky, Stephen (1995) *Nature's Keepers: The New Science of Nature Management* (London: Weidenfeld and Nicolson).

Bulger, Ruth Ellen, Elizabeth Meyer Bobby and Harvey Fineberg (eds) (1995) *Society's Choices* (Washington, DC: National Academy of Sciences).

Bunyard, Peter (ed.) (1996) *Gaia in Action: Science of the Living Earth* (Edinburgh: Floris Books).

Butchart, Stuart H. M. et al. (2010) 'Global Biodiversity: Indicators of Recent Declines', *Science* 328 (29 April): 1164–8.

Caduto, Michael J. and Joseph Bruchac (1991) *Keepers of the Animals: Native American Stories and Wildlife Activities for Children* (Golden: Fulcrum Publishing).

Caduto, Michael J. and Joseph Bruchac (1994a) *Keepers of Life: Discovering Plants Through Native American Stories and Earth Activities for Children* (Golden, CO: Fulcrum Publishing).

Caduto, Michael J. and Joseph Bruchac (1994b) *Native American Stories and Nocturnal Activities for Children* (Golden, CO: Fulcrum Publishing).

Cafaro, Philip (2010) 'Economic Growth or the Flourishing of Life: The Ethical Choice Climate Change Puts to Humanity', *Essays in Philosophy* 11(1): 44–75; http://commons.pacificu.edu/cgi/viewcontent.cgi?article=1354&context=eip.

Cain, Madelyn (2001) *The Childless Revolution: What it Means to be Childless Today* (New York: Perseus Publications).

Callicott, J. Baird (1985) 'Intrinsic Value, Quantum Theory, and Environmental Ethics', *Environmental Ethics* 7: 357–75.

Callicott, J. Baird (1989) *In Defence of the Land Ethic* (Albany: State University of New York Press).

Callicott, J. Baird (1994) *Earth's Insights* (Berkeley: University of California Press).

Callicott, J. Baird (1999) *Beyond the Land Ethic: More Essays in Envrionmental Philosophy* (Albany: State University of New York Press).

Callicott, J. Baird (ed.) (1987) *A Companion to the Sand County Almanac* (Madison: University of Wisconsin Press).

Capra, Fritjof (1997) *The Web of Life: A New Synthesis of Mind and Matter* (London: Flamingo).

Carroll, Laura (2000) *Families of Two: Interviews with Happily Married Couples without Children by Choice* (Philadelphia: Xlibris).

Carson, Rachel (1962) *Silent Spring* (Boston: Houghton Mifflin).

Casey, Terri (1998) *Pride and Joy: The Lives and Passions of Women without Children* (Hillsboro, OR: Beyond Words Publications).

Catton, William R. Jr. (2009) *Bottleneck: Humanity's Impending Impasse* (Bloomington: Xlibris).

Catton, William R. Jr. (1980) *Overshoot: The Ecological Basis of Revolutionary Change* (Urbana: University of Illinois Press).

Chan, Wing-Tsit (1963) A *Source Book in Chinese Philosophy* (Princeton: Princeton University Press).

Chappell, T. D. J. (ed.) (1997) *The Philosophy of the Environment* (Edinburgh: Edinburgh University Press).

Chase, Steve (ed.) (1991) *Defending the Earth: A Dialogue Between Murray Bookchin and Dave Foreman* (Boston: South End Press).

Cheetham, Tom (1993) 'The Forms of Life: Complexity, History, and Actuality', *Environmental Ethics* 15 (4): 293–311.

Clark, John (2008) 'On Being None with Nature: Nagarjuna and the Ecology of Emptiness', *Capitalism, Nature, Socialism* 19(4): 6–29.

Clegg, Brian (2009) *Eco-logic: Cutting Through the Greenwash: Truth, Lies and Saving the Planet* (London: Eden Project).

Clifford, Sue and Angela King (1993) *Local Distinctiveness: Place, Particularity and Identity* (London: Common Ground).

Cobb, Edith (1959) 'The Ecology of Imagination in Childhood', *Daedelus* 88(3): 537–48.

Cockburn, Alexander (1996) 'A Short, Meat-Oriented History of the World. From Eden to the Mattole', *New Left Review* 215: 16–42.

Coetzee, J. M. (1999) *The Lives of Animals*, ed. Amy Gutman (Princeton: Princeton University Press).

Coleman, Jon (2004) *Vicious: Wolves and Men in America* (New Haven: Yale University Press).

Collier, Paul (2010) *The Plundered Planet: How to Reconcile Prosperity with Nature* (London: Allen Lane).

Cooper, David E. (1992) 'The Idea of Environment', in Cooper and Palmer (eds).

Cooper, David E. and Joy A. Palmer (eds) (1992) *The Environment in Question* (London: Routledge).

Cooper, David E. and Simon P. James (2005) *Buddhism, Virtue and Environment* (Aldershot: Ashgate).

Cormier, Harvey (2001) *The Truth is What Works: William James, Pragmatism, and the Seed of Death* (Lanham, MD: Rowman and Littlefield).

Coupe, Laurence (ed.) (2000) *The Green Studies Reader: From Romanticism to Ecocriticism* (London: Routledge).

Curry, Patrick (1999) 'Magic vs. Enchantment', *Journal of Contemporary Religion* 14(3): 401–12.

Curry, Patrick (2000) 'Redefining Community: Towards an Ecological Republicanism', *Biodiversity and Conservation* 9(8): 1059–71.

Curry, Patrick (2003) 'Rethinking Nature: Towards an Ecopluralism', *Environmental Values* 12(3): 337–60.

Curry, Patrick (2004) *Defending Middle-Earth:Tolkien, Myth and Modernity*, 2nd edn (Boston: Houghton Mifflin).

Curry, Patrick (2007) 'Post-Secular Nature: Principles and Politics', *Worldviews: Environment, Culture, Religion* 11(3): 284–304.

Curry, Patrick (2008a) 'Nature Post-Nature', *New Formations* 26: 51–64.

Curry, Patrick (2008b) 'Comment', *Environmental Ethics* 30(2): 223–4.

Curry, Patrick (2010a) 'Grizzly Man and the Spiritual Life', *Journal for the Study of Religion, Culture and Nature* 4(3): 195–209.

Curry, Patrick (2010b) 'From Ecocriticism to Ecohumanities: An Essay-Review', *Green Letters* 13: 95–109.

Curtin, Deane (2000) 'A State of Mind Like Water: Ecosophy T and the Buddhist Traditions', in Katz et al. (eds).

Daily, G. (1995) *People and the Planet* 4(4): 18–19.

Daly, Herman (1991) *Steady-State Economics*, 2nd edn (Washington, DC: Island Press).

Daly, Herman (2008) *Ecological Economics and Sustainable Development: Selected Essays* (Cheltenham: Edward Elgar Publishing).

Daly, Herman E. and John B. Cobb Jr. (1997) *For the Common Good: Redirecting the Economy towards Community, the Environment and a Sustainable Future*, rev. edn (Boston: Beacon Press).

Daly, Herman E. and Joshua Farley (2004) *Ecological Economics: Principles and Applications* (Washington, DC: Island Press).

Daly, Herman E. and Kenneth N. Townsend (eds) (1993) *Valuing the Earth: Economics, Ecology, Ethics* (Cambridge, MA: MIT Press); first published as *Toward a Steady-State Economy* (1973).

de Graaf, John, David Wann and Thomas H. Naylor (2005) *Affluenza: The All-Consuming Epidemic*, 2nd edn (San Francisco: Berrett-Koehler).

Deloria, Vine, Jr. (2000) 'The Speculations of Krech', *Worldviews* 4(3): 283–93.

Des Jardins, Joseph R. (2001) *Environmental Ethics: An Introduction to Environmental Philosophy*, 3rd edn (Belmont, CA: Wadsworth).

Desvaux, Martin (2009) 'Footprints to the Future', *Medicine, Conflict and Survival* 25(3): 221–45.

Detienne, Marcel and Jean-Pierre Vernant (1991) *Cunning Intelligence in Greek Culture and Society*, trans. Janet Lloyd (Chicago: University of Chicago Press).

Devall, Bill and George Sessions (1985) *Deep Ecology: Living as if Nature Mattered* (Salt Lake City, UT: Peregrine Smith Books).

Diamond, Jared (2004) *Ecocide* (London: Allen Lane).

Diamond, Jared (2005) *Collapse: How Societies Choose to Fail or Succeed* (London: Allen Lane).

Dobson, Andrew (2006) 'Citizenship', in Dobson and Eckersley (eds).

Dobson, Andrew (2007) *Green Political Thought*, rev. edn (London: Routledge).

Dobson, Andrew and Robyn Eckersley (eds) (2006) *Political Theory and the Ecological Challenge* (Cambridge: Cambridge University Press).

Douthwaite, Richard (1996) *Short Circuit: Practical New Approaches to Building More Self-Reliant Communities* (Dartington, Devon: Green Books)

Douthwaite, Richard (1999) *The Growth Illusion: How Economic Growth Enriched the Few, Impoverished the Many, and Endangered the Planet*, rev. edn. (Dublin: Lilliput Press).

Drengson, Alan and Inoue, Yuichi (eds) (1995) *The Deep Ecology Movement: An Introductory Anthology* (Berkeley: North Atlantic Books).

Dunlap, Thomas (2004) *Faith in Nature: Environmentalism as a Religious Quest* (Seattle: University of Washington Press).

Dupré, John (2001) *Human Nature and the Limits of Science* (Oxford: Oxford University Press).

Earth Charter USA (2000) *Exploring the Earth Charter: Resources for Community Study* (Washington, DC: Earth Charter USA); www.earth-charterusa.org/resources.

Easterbrook, Gregg (1995) *A Moment on the Earth* (New York: Penguin Books).

Eckersley, Robyn (1989) 'Divining Evolution: The Ecological Ethics of Murray Bookchin', *Environmental Ethics* 11: 99–116.

Eckersley, Robyn (1992) *Environmentalism and Political Theory: Toward an Ecocentric Approach* (Albany: State University of New York Press).

Eckersley, Robyn (1998) 'Beyond Human Racism', *Environmental Values* 7: 165–82.

Eckersley, Robyn (2006) 'Communitarianism', in Dobson and Eckersley (eds).

Eherenberg, John (1999) *Civil Society: The Critical History of an Idea* (New York: New York University Press).

Ehrenfeld, David (1981) *The Arrogance of Humanism*, 2nd edn (Oxford: Oxford University Press).

Ekins, Paul (1992) *A New World Order: Grassroots Movements for Global Change* (London: Routledge).

Elgin, Duane (1998) *Voluntary Simplicity*, rev. edn (New York: Quill).

Elliott, Robert (ed.) (1995) *Environmental Ethics* (Oxford: Oxford University Press).

Erlich, Anne and Paul Erlich (1990) *The Population Explosion* (New York: Simon & Schuster).

Evernden, Neil (1985) *The Natural Alien: Humankind and Environment* (Toronto: University of Toronto Press).

Evernden, Neil (1992) *The Social Construction of Nature* (Baltimore: Johns Hopkins University Press).

Fairlie, Simon (2010a) *Meat: A Benign Extravagence* (East Meon, Hampshire: Permanent Publications).

Fairlie, Simon (2010b) 'The Tragedy of the Tragedy of the Commons', in Kingsnorth and Hine (eds).

Ferguson, A. R. B. (1998) 'For Debate: The Bicentenary of Thomas Malthus', *Medicine, Conflict and Survival* 14: 321–5.

Ferguson, A. R. B. (1999) 'The Logical Foundations of Ecological Footprints', *Environment, Development and Sustainability* 2: 149–56.

Ferry, Luc (1995) *The New Ecological Order*, trans. Carol Volk (Chicago: Chicago University Press).

Feyerabend, Paul (1978) *Science in a Free Society* (London: NLB).

Feyerabend, Paul (1987) *Farewell to Reason* (London: Verso).

Foer, Jonathan Safran (2009) *Eating Animals* (London: Little, Brown).

Foot, Philippa (2001) *Natural Goodness* (Oxford: Clarendon Press).

Forman, Paul (1997) 'Recent Science: Late-Modern and Post-Modern', in Thomas Söderqvist (ed.), *The Historiography of Contemporary Science and Technology* (Amsterdam: Harwood Academic).

Foster, John Bellamy (2009) *The Ecological Revolution: Making Peace with the Planet* (New York: Monthly Review Press).

Fowles, John (1979) *The Tree* (St Albans, UK: The Sumach Press).

Fox, Warwick (1984) 'Deep Ecology: A New Philosophy of Our Time?', *The Ecologist* 14(7): 194–200.

Fox, Warwick (1986) 'Approaching Deep Ecology: A Response to Richard Sylvan's Critique of Deep Ecology', Hobart: University of Tasmania, Environmental Studies. Occasional paper 20.

Fox, Warwick (1989) 'The Deep Ecology-Ecofeminism Debate and its Parallels', *Environmental Ethics* 11: 5–25.

Fox, Warwick (1995) *Toward a Transpersonal Ecology: Developing New Foundations for Environmentalism* (Totnes, Devon: Green Books).

Frasz, Geoffrey B. (1993) 'Environmental Virtue Ethics: A New Direction for Environmental Ethics', *Environmental Ethics* 15: 259–74.

Friel, Howard (2010) *The Lomborg Deception: Setting the Record Straight About Global Warming* (New Haven: Yale University Press).

Gandhi Mahatma (1969), *Collected Works* (New Delhi: Government of India, 1969), vol. 31.

Gannon, Zoe and Neal Lawson (2010) *The Advertising Effect: How Do We Get the Balance of Advertising Right* (London: Compass).

Gardner-Outlaw, Tom and Robert Engelman (1999) *Forest Futures: Population, Consumption and Wood Resources* (Washington, DC: Population Action International).

Gare, Arran (1993) *Nihilism Incorporated: European Civilzation and Environmental Destruction* (Bungendore, NSW: Ecological Press).

Garrard, Greg (2004) *Ecocriticism* (London: Routledge).

Geertz, Clifford (2000) *Local Knowledge: Further Essays in Interpretive Anthropology*, 3rd edn (New York: Basic Books).

Gelbspan, Ross (2004) *Boiling Point: How Politicians, Big Oil and Coal, Journalists, and Activists are Fueling the Climate Crisis – and What We Can Do to Avert Disaster* (New York: Basic Books).

Gellatley, Juliet, with Tony Wardle (1996) *The Silent Ark* (London: HarperCollins).

Gilligan, Carol (1982) *In a Different Voice: Psychological Theory and Women's Development* (Cambridge, MA: Harvard University Press).

Gilligan, Carol (1994) 'Reply to my Critics', in Mary Jeanne Larabee (ed.), *An Ethic of Care: Feminist and Interdisciplinary Perspectives* (London: Routledge).

Glenny, Misha (2008) *McMafia: A Journey Through the Global Criminal Underworld* (New York: Random House).

Goetz, Stephan J. and Anil Rupasingha (2006) 'Wal-Mart and Social Capital', *American Journal of Agricultural Economics* 88(5): 1304–10.

Gorz, André (2010) *Ecologica*, trans. Chris Turner (Chicago: University of Chicago Press).

Gottlieb, Roger (ed.) (1996) *This Sacred Earth* (New York: Routledge).

Gould, Stephen Jay (1993) *Eight Little Piggies* (New York: W. W. Norton).

Gray, John (1993) *Post-Liberalism: Studies in Political Thought* (London: Routledge).

Greer, John Michael (2008) *The Long Descent: A User's Guide to the End of the Industrial Age* (Gabriola Island, BC: New Society).

Greer, John Michael (2010) 'The Falling Years: An Inhumanist Vision', in Kingsnorth and Hine (eds).

Grey, William (2000) 'A Critique of Deep Green Theory', in Katz et al. (eds).

Griffiths, Jay (2006) *Wild: An Elemental Journey* (London: Hamish Hamilton).

Guhu, Ramachandra (1989) 'Radical American Environmentalism and Wilderness Preservation: A Third World Critique', *Environmental Ethics* 11: 71–83.

Guhu, Ramachandra (2006) *How Much Should a Person Consume? Environmentalism in India and the United States* (Berkeley: University of California Press).

Haberl, Helmut et al (2008) 'Quantifying and Mapping the Human Appropriation of Net Primary Production in Earth's Terrestrial Ecosystems'; http://www.eoearth.org/article/Global_human_appropriation_of_net_primary_production_(HANPP).

Halweil, Brian (2006) 'Can Organic Farming Feed Us All?', *WorldWatch Magazine* 19(3): 18–24.

Hamilton, Clive (2010) *Requiem for a Species. Why We Resist the Truth about Climate Change* (London: Earthscan).

Haraway, Donna J. (1991) *Simians, Cyborgs and Women: The Reinvention of Nature* (New York: Routledge).

Haraway, Donna J. (2008) *When Species Meet* (Minneapolis: University of Minnesota Press).

Hardin, Garrett (1968) 'The Tragedy of the Commons', *Science* 162: 1243–8; repr. in Benson 2000.

Hardin, Garrett (1977) 'Ethical Implications of Carrying Capacity', in Garrett Hardin and John Baden (eds), *Managing the Commons* (New York: W.H. Freeman & Co).

Hardin, Garrett (1992) *Living within Limits: Ecology, Economics and Population Taboos* (New York: Oxford University Press).

Harding, Sandra (1996) *The Science Question in Feminism* (Ithaca, NY: Cornell University Press).

Harding, Sandra (2008) *Sciences from Below: Feminisms, Postcolonialities, and Modernities* (Durham, NC: Duke University Press).

Hargrove, Eugene C. (1989) *Foundations of Environmental Ethics* (Denton, TX: Environmental Ethics Books).

Hari, Johann (2010) 'The Wrong Kind of Green', *The Nation* (22.3.10); http://www.thenation.com/doc/20100322/hari.

Harris, Paul G. (2010) *World Ethics and Climate Change: From International to Global Justice* (Edinburgh: Edinburgh University Press).

Harrop, Stuart (2010) 'The Carbon Footprint of Oracles: How Green is Divination?', in Patrick Curry (ed.), *Divination: Perspectives for a New Millennium* (Aldershot: Ashgate).

Harvey, Graham (1997) *Listening People, Speaking Earth: Contemporary*

Paganism (London: Hurst); also published as *Contemporary Paganism: Listening People, Speaking Earth* (New York: New York University Press).

Harvey, Graham (2005) *Animism: Respecting the Living World* (London: Hurst & Co. and New York: Columbia University Press).

Haught, John F. (1996) 'Christianity and Ecology', in Roger S. Gottlieb (ed.), *This Sacred Earth: Religion, Nature, Environment* (New York: Routledge).

Hayward, Tim (1995) *Ecological Thought: An Introduction* (Cambridge: Polity).

Hayward, Tim (1998) *Political Theory and Ecological Values* (Cambridge: Polity).

Heinberg, Richard (2009) *Searching for A Miracle: Net Energy Limits and the Fate of Industrial Society* (The Post Carbon Institute and International Forum on Globalization); http://www.postcarbon.org/report/44377-searching-for-a-miracle.

Henderson, Hazel (1999) *Beyond Globalisation: Shaping a Sustainable Economy* (London: Kumarian Press).

Henderson, Hazel (2007) *Ethical Markets: Growing the Green Economy* (White River Junction, VT: Chelsea Green).

Henry, John (2002) *The Scientific Revolution and the Origins of Modern Science*, 2nd edn (Basingstoke: Palgrave).

Hern W. M. (1997) 'Is Human Culture Oncogenic for Uncontrolled Population Growth and Ecological Destruction?' *Human Evolution* 12(1–2): 97–105.

Hertsgaard, Mark (1999) *Earth Odyssey: Around the World in Search of Our Environmental Future* (London: Abacus).

Hessel, Dieter T. and Rosemary Radford Ruether (eds) (2000) *Christianity and Ecology: Seeking the Well-Being of Earth and Humans* (Cambridge, MA: Harvard University Press).

Heyd, Thomas (2007) *Encountering Nature: Toward an Environmental Culture* (Aldershot: Ashgate).

Hines, Colin (2000) *Localization: A Global Manifesto* (London: Earthscan).

Holmgren, David (2003) *Permaculture: Principles and Pathways Beyond Sustainability* (Hepburn, Victoria: Holmgren Design Services).

Hopkins, Rob (2008) *The Transition Handbook: From Oil Dependency to Local Resilience* (Dartington, Devon: Green Books).

Horkheimer, Max and Theodor W. Adorno (2002) [1944] *The Dialectic of Enlightenment*, trans. Edmund Jephcott, ed. Gunzelin Schmid Noerr (Stanford: Stanford University Press).

Horton, Richard (2004) 'The Dawn of McScience'. Review of Sheldon Krimsky's *Science in the Private Interest*, *New York Review of Books* 51(4) (14 March).

Hulme, Mike (2008) *Why We Disagree About Climate Change. Understanding*

Controversy, Inaction and Opportunity (Cambridge: Cambridge University Press).

Hume, David (1740) *A Treatise on Human Nature* (Oxford).

Hursthouse, Rosalind (1999) *On Virtue Ethics* (Oxford: Oxford University Press).

Hutton, Ronald (1991) *The Pagan Religions of the British Isles* (Oxford: Blackwell).

Hutton, Ronald (1999) *The Triumph of the Moon: A History of Modern Pagan Witchcraft* (Oxford: Oxford University Press).

Hutton, Ronald (2003) *Witches, Druids and King Arthur* (London: Hambledon and London).

Illich, Ivan (1975) *Tools for Conviviality* (London: Fontana).

Illich, Ivan (1992) *In the Mirror of the Past: Lectures and Addresses 1978–1990* (London: Marion Boyars).

Imhoff, Marc L., Lahouari Bounoua, Taylor Ricketts, Colby Loucks, Robert Harriss and William T. Lawrence, (2004) 'Global Patterns in Human Consumption of Net Primary Production', *Nature* 429 (6994): 870–3.

IPCC (2001) *Climate Change 2001: Synthesis Report* (Intergovernmental Panel on Climate Change).

Irvine, Sandy (2001) *The Deeply Green Book Guide* (Newcastle upon Tyne: Real World Publishing).

Irvine, Sandy 'Missing Numbers: The Overpopulation Denial Syndrome'; unpublished MS.

Irvine, Sandy and Alec Ponton (1988) *A Green Manifesto: Policies for a Green Future* (London: Macdonald Optima).

Isenberg, Andrew C. (2000) *The Destruction of the Bison* (Cambridge: Cambridge University Press).

IUCN/UNEP (2003) '2003 World Database on Protected Areas': CD-ROM.

Jackson, Tim (2009) *Prosperity without Growth: Economics for a Finite Planet* (London: Earthscan).

Jackson, Wes (1994) *Becoming Native to This Place* (Lexington: University of Kentucky Press).

Jackson, Wes (2008) 'Toward an Ignorance-Based Worldview', in Wes Jackson and Bill Vitek (eds), *The Virtues of Ignorance: Complexity, Sustainability, and the Limits of Knowledge* (Lexington: University Press of Kentucky).

Jackson, Wes (2010) *What Matters? Economics for a Renewed Commonwealth* (Berkeley: Counterpoint).

James, Oliver (2007) *Affluenza* (London: Vermilion).

James, Simon P. (2004) *Zen Buddhism and Environmental Ethics* (Farnham, Surrey: Ashgate).

James, William (1977) [1909] *A Pluralistic Universe* (Cambridge, MA: Harvard University Press).

Janaway, Christopher (2002) *Schopenhauer: A Very Short Introduction* (Oxford: Oxford University Press).

Jasanoff, Sheila (1990) *The Fifth Branch: Science Advisers as Policymakers* (Cambridge, MA: Harvard University Press).

Jensen, Derrick and George Draffan (2003) *Strangely Like a War: The Global Assault on Forests* (White River Junction, VT: Chelsea Green Publishing Co).

Jones, Ken (1993) *Beyond Optimism: A Buddhist Political Ecology* (Oxford: Jon Carpenter Publishing).

Jones, Prudence and Nigel Pennick (1995) *A History of Pagan Europe* (London: Routledge).

Jordanova, Ludmilla (1987) 'The Interpretation of Nature: A Review Article', *Comparative Studies in Society and History* 27(1): 195–200.

Joyce, Rosaleen (2009) 'Outdoor Learning: An Enquiry into its Relation to Social and Historical Constructions of Children and Childhood', MA dissertation, University of Sheffield.

Kaebnick, Gregory E. (2000) 'On the Sanctity of Nature', Hastings Center Report 30(5): 16–23.

Kane, Sean (1998) *Wisdom of the Mythtellers*, 2nd edn (Peterborough, ONT: Broadview Press).

Kates, Carol A. (2004) 'Reproductive Liberty and Overpopulation', *Environmental Values* 13 (1): 51–79.

Katz, Eric (2000) 'Against the Inevitability of Anthropocentrism', in Katz et al. (eds).

Katz, Eric, Andrew Light and David Rothenberg (eds) (2000) *Beneath the Surface: Critical Essays in the Philosophy of Deep Ecology* (Cambridge, MA: MIT Press).

Kaufman, Frederick (2010) 'The Food Bubble: How Wall Street Starved Millions and Got Away With It', *Harper's Magazine* (July).

Kaza, Stephanie and Kenneth Kraft (eds) (2000) *Dharma Rain: Sources of Buddhist Environmentalism* (Boston: Shambhala).

Keller, David R. (ed.) (2010) *Environmental Ethics: The Big Questions* (Malden, MA: Wiley-Blackwell).

Keller, Evelyn Fox (1985) *Reflections on Gender and Science* (New Haven: Yale University Press).

Kingsnorth, Paul (2010) 'Confessions of a Recovering Environmentalist', in Kingsnorth and Hine (eds).

Kingsnorth, Paul and Douglas Hine (eds) (2010) *Dark Mountain 1* (n.p.: The Dark Mountain Project).

Kitcher, Philip (2001) *Science, Truth, and Democracy* (New York: Oxford University Press).

Kohák, Erazim (2000) *The Green Halo:A Bird's-EyeView of Ecological Ethics* (Chicago and La Salle: Open Court).

Kontos, Alkis (1994) 'The World Disenchanted, and the Return of Gods and Demons', in Asher Horowitz and Terry Maley (eds), *The Barbarism of Reason: Max Weber and the Twilight of Reason* (Toronto: University of Toronto Press).

Kovel, Joel (2007) *The Enemy of Nature: The End of Capitalism or the End of the World?*, 2nd edn (London: Zed Books).

Krech, Shepherd (1999) *The Ecological Indian* (New York: W. W. Norton and Company).

Kundera, Milan (1984) *The Unbearable Lightness of Being* (London: Faber & Faber).

Laclau, Ernesto (1991) *New Reflections on the Revolution of Our Time* (London: Verso).

Laclau, Ernesto and Chantal Mouffe (1985) *Hegemony and Socialist Strategy: Towards a Radical Democratic Politics* (London: Verso).

Lane, Robert (2000) *The Loss of Happiness in Market Societies* (New Haven: Yale University Press).

Latouche, Serge (2007) *Petit Traité de la décroissance sereine* (Paris: Mille et Une Nuits).

Latour, Bruno (1993) *We Have Never Been Modern*, trans. Catherine Porter (Hemel Hempstead: Harvester Wheatsheaf).

Latour, Bruno (2004) 'Why Has Critique Run Out of Steam?', *Harper's Magazine* (April): 15–22; repr. from *Critical Inquiry* (Winter 2004).

Leakey, Richard and Roger Lewin (1996) *The Sixth Extinction: Biodiversity and its Survival* (London: Weidenfeld & Nicolson).

Lear, Jonathan (2006) *Radical Hope: Ethics in the Face of Cultural Devastation* (Cambridge, MA: Harvard University Press).

Le Guin, Ursula K. (1992) *Dancing at the Edge of the World. Thoughts on Words, Women, Places* (London: Paladin).

Leopold, Aldo (1949) *A Sand County Almanac with Essays on Conservation from Round River* (New York: Oxford University Press; repr. 1989).

Leopold, Aldo (1991) *The River of the Mother of God and Other Essays*, ed. Susan Flader and J. Baird Callicott (Madison: University of Wisconsin Press).

Leopold, Aldo (1993) *Round River* (New York: Oxford University Press).

Li, Huey-li (1998) 'Some Thoughts on Confucianism and Ecofeminism', in Mary Evelyn Tucker and John Berthrong (eds), *Confucianism and Ecology* (Cambridge, MA: Harvard University Press).

Lifton, Robert Jay (1987) *The Future of Immortality and Other Essays for a Nuclear Age* (New York: Basic Books).

Light, Andrew and Eric Katz (eds) (1996) *Environmental Pragmatism* (London: Routledge).

Light, Andrew and Holmes Rolston III (eds) (2003) *Environmental Ethics: An Anthology* (Oxford: Blackwell).

Linzey, Andrew (2009) *Why Animal Suffering Matters: Philosophy, Theology, and Practical Ethics* (Oxford: Oxford University Press).

List, Peter C. (ed.) (1993) *Radical Environmentalism: Philosophy and Tactics* (Belmont, CA: Wadsworth).

Livingston, John A. (1981) *The Fallacy of Wildlife Conservation* (Toronto: McClelland and Stewart).

Livingston, John A. (1994) *Rogue Primate: An Exploration of Human Domestification* (Toronto: Key Porter Books).

Locke, Harvey and Brendan Mackey (2009) 'The Nature of Climate Change: Reunite International Climate Change Mitigation Efforts with Biodiversity Conservation and Wilderness Protection', *International Journal of Wilderness* 15(2): 7–40.

Lohmann, Larry (2006) *Carbon Trading: A Critical Conversation on Climate Change, Privatisation and Power* (Upsalla: The Dag Hammarskjöld Centre).

Lomborg, Bjørn (2001) *The Skeptical Environmentalist: Measuring the Real State of the World* (Cambridge: Cambridge University Press).

Longworth, Richard C. (1998) *Global Squeeze: The Coming Crisis for First World Nations* (Chicago: Contemporary Books).

Lopez, Barry (1988) *Crossing Open Ground* (New York: Charles Scribner's Sons).

Louv, Richard (2008) *Last Child in the Woods: Saving Our Children from Nature-Deficit Disorder*, 2nd edn (Chapel Hill, NC: Algonquin Books).

Lovelock, James (1979) *Gaia: A New Look at Life on Earth* (Oxford: Oxford University Press).

Lovelock, James (1988) *The Ages of Gaia: A Biography of our Living Earth* (New York: Norton).

Lovelock, James (1991) *Healing Gaia: Practical Medicine for the Planet* (New York: Harmony).

Lovelock, James (1995) *Gaia: A New Look at Life on Earth*, rev. edn. (Oxford: Oxford University Press).

Loy, David R. (2002) *A Buddhist History of the West: Studies in Lack* (Albany: State University of New York Press).

Loy, David R. (2005) *The Great Awakening: A Buddhist Social Theory* (Boston: Wisdom Publications).

Lynas, Mark (2007) *Six Degrees: Our Future on a Hotter Planet* (London: Fourth Estate).

Lynn, William S. (2004) 'Situating the Earth Charter: An Introduction', *Worldviews* 8(1): 1–14.

Maathai, Wangari (2009) *The Challenge for Africa: A New Vision* (London: William Heinemann).

MacDonald, Christine (2008) *Green Inc.: An Environmental Insider Reveals How A Good Cause Has Gone Bad* (Guilford, CT: The Lyons Press)

Machiavelli, Niccolò (1981) *The Prince*, trans. George Bull (London: Penguin).

Mackey, Brendan G. (2004) 'The Earth Charter and Ecological Integrity – Some Policy Implications', *Worldviews* 8(1): 76–92.

Mander, Jerry and Edward Goldsmith (eds) (1996) *The Case Against the Global Economy, and for a Turn Toward the Local* (San Francisco: Sierra Club.)

Manes, Christopher (1990) *Green Rage: Radical Environmentalism and the Unmaking of Civilization* (Boston: Little, Brown & Co.).

Martin, Calvin Luther (1992) *In the Spirit of the Earth. Rethinking History and Time* (Baltimore: Johns Hopkins University Press).

Mathews, Freya (1999) 'Becoming Native: An Ethos of Countermodernity II', *Worldviews: Environment, Culture, Religion* 3(3): 243–72.

McCormick, Bill (1994) 'Identity Crisis', *Real World* 9 (Autumn), 6–7.

McDonagh, Sean (1990) *The Greening of the Church* (Maryknoll, NY: Orbis).

McGinnis, Michael Vincent (1999) *Bioregionalism* (London: Routledge).

McIntosh, Alastair (2004) *Soil and Soul: People vs. Corporate Power* (London: Aurum).

McIntosh, Alastair (2008) *Hell and High Water: Climate Change, Hope and the Human Condition* (Edinburgh: Birlinn).

McIntyre, Alastair (1981) *After Virtue* (London: Duckworth).

McKay, George (1996) *Senseless Acts of Beauty* (London: Verso, 1996).

McKibben, Bill (1990) *The End of Nature* (London: Penguin; 2nd edn New York: Random House, 1992).

McKibben, Bill (1998) *Maybe One: A Personal and Environmental Argument for Much Smaller Families* (New York: Simon and Schuster, 1998).

McKibben, Bill (2007) *Deep Economy: The Wealth of Communities and the Durable Future* (New York: Henry Holt).

McKibben, Bill (2010) *Eaarth: Making a Life on a Tough New Planet* (New York: Times Books).

McLaughlin, Andrew (1993a) 'Marxism and the Mastery of Nature: An Ecological Critique', in Roger S. Gottlieb and Richard Schmitt (eds), *Radical Philosophy: Tradition, Counter-Tradition, Politics* (Philadelphia: Temple University Press).

McLaughlin, Andrew (1993b) *Regarding Nature: Industrialism and Deep Ecology* (Albany: State University of New York Press).

McNeill, J. R. (2001) *Something New Under the Sun: An Environmental History of the Twentieth-Century World* (London: Allen Lane).

Meadows, Donella, Dennis L. Meadows, Jørgen Randers and William W. Behrens III (1974) *The Limits to Growth* (London: Pan).

Meadows, Donella, Dennis L. Meadows and Jørgen Randers (1992) *Beyond the Limits* (White River Junction, VT: Chelsea Green).

Meadows, Donella, Jørgen Randers and Dennis L. Meadows (2004) *Limits to Growth: The Thirty-Year Update* (London: Earthscan).

Mellor, Mary (1997) *Feminism and Ecology* (Cambridge: Polity).

Merchant, Carolyn (1980) *The Death of Nature: Women, Ecology and the Scientific Revolution* (San Francisco: Harper & Row).

Merchant, Carolyn (1995) *Earthcare:Women and the Environment* (New York: Routledge).

Meyerson, Frederick (1998) 'Population, Carbon Emissions, and Global Warming: The Forgotten Relationship at Kyoto', *Population and Development Review* 24: 115–30.

Midgley, Mary (1983) *Animals and Why They Matter* (Athens: University of Georgia Press).

Midgley, Mary (1992) *Science as Salvation: A Modern Myth and Its Meaning* (London: Routledge).

Midgley, Mary (1997) 'Sustainability and Moral Pluralism', in Chappell (ed.).

Midgley, Mary (2001) *Science and Poetry* (London: Routledge).

Midgley, Mary (2000) 'Biotechnology and Monstrosity: Why We Should Pay Attention to the "Yuk Factor"', *Hastings Center Report* 30(5): 7-15.

Millennium Ecosystem Assessment (2005) *Ecosystems and Human Well-Being*, 4 vols (Washington, DC: Island Press).

Mollison, Bill (1988) *Permaculture, a Designers' Manual* (Tyalgum, NSW: Tagari Publishers).

Montaigne, Michel de (1991) *The Complete Essays*, trans. M. A. Screech (London: Penguin Books).

Montgomery, David R. (2008) *Dirt: The Erosion of Civilizations* (Berkeley: University of California Press).

Moore, G. E. (1903) *Principia Ethica* (Cambridge: Cambridge University Press).

Morton, Timothy (2010) *The Ecological Thought* (Cambridge, MA: Harvard University Press).

Mosquin, Ted and Stan Rowe (2004) 'A Manifesto for Earth', *Biodiversity* 5 (1): 3-9; www.ecospherics.net.

Mowat, Farley (1963) *Never Cry Wolf* (Boston: Little, Brown & Co).

Mumford, Lewis (1964) *The Myth of the Machine*, vol. 1 (New York: Harcourt, Brace).

Murtaugh, Paul A. and Michael G. Schlax (2009) 'Reproduction and the Carbon Legacies of Individuals', *Global Environmental Change* 19: 14–20.

Myers, Norman (1998) 'Population: Some Overlooked Issues', *The Environmentalist* 18: 135–8.

Naess, Arne (1973) 'The Shallow and the Deep, Long-Range Ecology Movements', *Inquiry* 16: 95–100.

Naess, Arne (1989) *Ecology, Community and Lifestyle*, ed. David Rothenberg (Cambridge: Cambridge University Press).

Naess, Arne and George Sessions (1984) 'Basic Principles of Deep Ecology', *Ecophilosophy* 6: 3–7.

Naess, Arne and George Sessions (1985) 'Platform Principles of the Deep Ecology Movement', in Bill Devall and George Sessions (eds), *Deep Ecology: Living as if Nature Mattered* (Salt Lake City, UT: Peregrine Smith Books).

Naess, Arne and George Sessions (1989) *Ecology, Community and Lifestyle*, ed. David Rothenberg (Cambridge: Cambridge University Press).

Nagel, Thomas (1986) *The View from Nowhere* (Oxford: Oxford University Press).

Netting, Robert (1993) *Smallholders, Householders: Farm Families and the Ecology of Intensive, Sustainable Agriculture* (Stanford: Stanford University Press).

Nicholsen, Shierry Weber (2003) *The Love of Nature and the End of the World. The Unspoken Dimensions of Environmental Concern* (Cambridge, MA: MIT Press).

Nickerson, Mike (2009) *Life, Money and Illusion: Living on Earth As If We Want to Stay*, 2nd edn (Gabriola Island, BC: New Society Publishers).

Noddings, Nel (1984) *Caring: A Feminine Approach to Ethics and Moral Education* (Berkeley: University of California Press).

North, Richard D. (1995) *Life on a Modern Planet: A Manifesto for Progress* (Manchester: University of Manchester Press).

Northcote, Michael S. (2010) *Cuttlefish, Clones and Cluster Bombs: Preaching, Politics and Ecology* (London: Darton, Longman & Todd).

Norton, Bryan (1991) *Toward Unity Among Environmentalists* (New York: Oxford University Press).

Oldfield, Adrian (1990) *Citizenship and Community: Civic Republicanism and the Modern World* (London: Routledge).

O'Neill, Brian C., F. Landis Mackellar and Wolfgang Lutz (2005) *Population and Climate Change* (Cambridge: Cambridge University Press).

Oreskes, Naomi and Erik M. Conway (2010) *Merchants of Doubt: How a Handful of Scientists Obscured the Truth on Issues from Tobacco Smoke to Global Warming* (London: Bloomsbury Press).

Orr, David W. (1991) *Ecological Literacy: Education and the Transition to a Postmodern World* (Albany: State University of New York Press).

Orr, David W. (2003) 'Walking North on a Southbound Train, pt. 1', *Rachel's Environment & Health News* (25.6.03): 766; http://www.david-worr.com/files/Walking_North.pdf.

Orr, David W. (2004) Earth in Mind (Washington, DC: Island Press).

Orton, David. Green Web Publications: Bulletins (Part I), Bulletins (Part II), and Book Reviews and Other Articles; http://home.ca.inter.net/~greenweb/index.htm.

Orton, David (2000) 'Ecofascism: What is It? A Left Biocentric Analysis'; http://home.ca.inter.net/~greenweb/Ecofascism.html.

Orwell, George (1970) 'Some Thoughts on the Common Toad', in *The Collected Essays*, vol. 4 (Harmondsworth: Penguin).

Ostrom, Elinor (1990) *Governing the Commons: The Evolution of Institutions for Collective Action* (Cambridge: Cambridge University Press).

Oviedo, Gonzalo and Luisa Maffi, with Peter Bille Larsen (2000) *Indigenous and Traditional Peoples of the World and Ecoregion Conservation: An Integrated Approach to Conserving the World's Biological and Cultural Diversity*, Report by the WWF and Terralingua (Gland, Switzerland: WWF).

Parr, Adrian (2009) *Hijacking Sustainability* (Cambridge, MA: MIT Press).

Parsons, Jack (1971) *Population versus Liberty* (London: Population Policy Press).

Parsons, Jack (1977) *Population Fallacies* (Llantrisant: Population Policy Press).

Passmore, John (1974) *Man's Responsibility for Nature*, 2nd edn (London: Duckworth).

Patel, Raj (2008) *Stuffed and Starved: The Hidden Battle for the World Food System* (New York: Melville House).

Patterson, Charles (2002) *Eternal Treblinka: Our Treatment of Animals and the Holocaust* (New York: Lantern Books).

Pearce, David, Anil Markandya and Edward B. Barber (1989) *Blueprint for a Green Economy* (London: Earthscan).

Peterson, Anna L. (2009) *Everyday Ethics and Social Change: The Education of Desire* (New York: Columbia University Press).

Petrini, Carlo (2009) *Terra Madre: Forging a New Global Network of Sustainable Food Communities* (White River Junction, VT: Chelsea Green Publishing).

Pettit, Philip (1997) *Republicanism: A Theory of Freedom and Government* (Oxford: Clarendon Press).

Phelps, Norman (2007) *The Longest Struggle: Animal Rights from Pythagoras to Peta* (New York: Lantern Books).

Pimental, David and Marcia Pimental (2008) *Food, Energy, and Society*, 3rd edn (Bocas Raton, FL: CRC Press).

Pimentel, David et al. (1999) 'Will Limits of the Earth's Resources Control Human Numbers?', *Environment, Development, and Sustainability* 1: 19–38.

Pimentel, David, Laura Westra and Reed F. Noss (eds) (2000) *Ecological Integrity: Integrating Environment, Conservation, and Health* (Washington, DC: Island Press).

Plumwood, Val (1993) *Feminism and the Mastery of Nature* (London: Routledge).

Plumwood, Val (1995) 'Nature, Self and Gender: Feminism, Environmental Philosophy and the Critique of Rationalism', in Elliott (ed.); first published in *Hypatia* 6 (1991): 10–16, 23–6.

Plumwood Val (1999) 'Being Prey', in David Rothenberg and Marat Ulvaeus (eds), *The New Earth Reader: The Best of Terra Nova* (Cambridge, MA: MIT Press, 1999).

Plumwood Val (2000a) 'Integrating Ethical Frameworks for Animals, Humans, and Nature: A Critical Feminist Eco-Socialist Analysis', *Ethics and the Environment* 5(2): 285–322.

Plumwood Val (2000b) 'Deep Ecology, Deep Pockets, and Deep Problems: A Feminist Ecosocialist Analysis', in Katz et al. (eds).

Plumwood, Val (2002) *Environmental Culture: The Ecological Crisis of Reason* (London and New York: Routledge).

Plumwood, Val (2006a) 'The Concept of a Cultural Landscape', *Ethics and the Environment*, 11(2): 115–50.

Plumwood, Val (2006b) 'Feminism', in Dobson and Eckersley (eds).

Plumwood Val (2008) 'Tasteless: Towards a Food-Based Approach to Death', *Environmental Values* 17(3): 317–22.

Polanyi, Karl (1957) *The Great Transformation: The Political and Economic Origins of Our Time* (Boston: Beacon Press).

Pollan, Michael (2006) *The Omnivore's Dilemma. A Natural History of Four Meals* (London: Penguin Books).

Ponting, Clive (2000) *World History: A New Perspective* (London: Chatto & Windus).

Ponting, Clive (2007) *A New Green History of the World: The Environment and the Collapse of Great Civilizations*, 2nd edn (London: Vintage).

Ponton, Alec (2001) Editorial, *The Pherologist* 4(3) (August): 2.

Princen, Thomas, Michael Maniates and Ken Conca (eds) (2002) *Confronting Consumption* (Cambridge, MA: MIT Press).

Quammen, David (1998) 'Planet of Weeds', *Harper's Magazine* (October): 57–69.

Quammen, David (1999) 'An Interview with David Quammen', *Wild Duck Review* 5(1) (Winter): 15–21.

Quammen, David (2003) *Monster of God: The Man-Eating Predator in the Jungles of History and the Mind* (New York: W. W. Norton & Co).

Quinn, Bill (2000) *How Wal-Mart is Destroying America and the World and What You Can Do About It* (Berkeley, CA: Ten Speed Press).

Raphals, Lisa (1992) *Knowing Words: Wisdom and Cunning in the Classical Traditions of China and Greece* (Ithaca, NY: Cornell University Press).

Rawles, Kate (1996) 'Ethical Implications of the Gaia Hypothesis', in Bunyard (ed.).

Rawls, John (1993) *Political Liberalism* (Oxford: Oxford University Press).

Rees, William E. (1992) 'Ecological Footprints and Appropriated Carrying Capacity: What Urban Economics Leaves Out', *Environment and Urbanisation* 4: 121–30.

Rees, William E. (1996) 'Revisiting Carrying Capacity', *Population and Environment* 17: 195–215.

Rees, William E. (2000) 'Patch Disturbance, Eco-footprints, and Biological Integrity: Revisitng the Limits to Growth (or Why Industrial Society is Inherently Unsustainable)', in David Pimentel et al. (eds).

Rees, William E. (2009) 'Are Humans Unsustainable by Nature?' Trudeau Lecture (28.1.09); http://www.plancanada.com/Unsustainable%20 by%20Nature.rees.pdf.

Regan, Tom (1983) *The Case for Animal Rights* (Berkeley: University of California Press).

Rich, Bruce (1994) *Mortgaging the Earth: The World Bank, Environmental Impoverishment and the Crisis of Development* (London: Earthscan, and Boston: Beacon Press).

Ritzer, George (1996) *The McDonaldization of Society* (Thousand Oaks, CA: Pine Forge Press).

Ritzer, George (2004) *The Globalization of Nothing* (Thousand Oaks, CA: Pine Forge Press).

Roberts, Paul (2008) *The End of Food* (Boston: Houghton Mifflin).

Robertson, Morgan M. (2006) 'The Nature that Capital Can See: Science, State, and Market in the Commodification of Ecosystem Services', *Environment and Planning D: Society and Space* 24(3): 367–87.

Rodman, John (1977) 'The Liberation of Nature?', *Inquiry* 20: 83–131.

Rolston III, Holmes (1988) *Environmental Ethics* (Philadelphia: Temple University Press).

Rolston III, Holmes (1992) 'Challenges in Environmental Ethics', in Cooper and Palmer (eds).

Rolston III, Holmes (1997) 'Nature for Real: Is Nature a Social Construct?' in Chappell (ed.).

Rose, Hilary (1994) *Love, Power and Knowledge: Towards a Feminist Transformation of the Sciences* (Cambridge: Polity).

Roseland, Mark (1998) *Toward Sustainable Communities: Resources for Citizens and their Governments*, 2nd edn (Gabriola Island, BC: New Society Publishers).

Routley, Richard (1973) 'Is There a Need for a New, an Environmental Ethic?' (Varna: Proceedings of the 15th World Congress of Philosophy): 205–10.

Routley, Richard and Val Routley (1979) 'Against the Inevitability of Human Chauvinism', in K. E. Goodpaster and K. M. Sayre (eds), *Ethics and Problems of the 21st Century* (Notre Dame, IN: University of Notre Dame Press).

Rowe, Stan (1994) 'Ecocentrism: The Chord that Harmonizes Humans and the Earth', *The Trumpeter* 11(2): 106-7; http://www.ecospherics.net.

Rowe, Stan (1995) 'Managing Profligacy Effciently', *Real World* 12 (Summer): 7–9.

Rowe, Stan (1997) 'From Reductionism to Holism in Ecology and Deep Ecology', *The Ecologist* 27 (4) (July/August): 147–51.

Rowe, Stan (2002) *Home Place: Essays on Ecology*, 2nd edn (Edmonton, Canada: NeWest Press).

Rowe, Stan (2006) *Earth Alive. Essays on Ecology* (Edmonton, Canada: NeWest Press).

Rowell, Andrew (1996) *Green Backlash: Global Subversion of the Environmental Movement* (London: Routledge).

Ruddick, Sara (1989) *Maternal Thinking: Towards a Politics of Peace* (New York: Ballantine).

Ruskin, John (1998) *The Genius of John Ruskin: Selections from his Writings*, ed. John D. Rosenberg (Charlottesville: University of Virginia Press).

Ryan, P. D. (1998) *Buddhism and the Natural World: Towards a Meaningful Myth* (Birmingham: Windhorse Publications).

Ryder, Richard (1973) 'Victims of Science', in Stanley Godlovitch, Rosalind Godlovich and John Harris (eds), *Animals, Men and Morals* (New York: Grove Press).

Sale, Kirkpatrick (1985) *Dwellers in the Land: The Bioregional Vision* (New York: Random House).

Salleh, Ariel (1984) 'Deeper Than Deep Ecology: The Ecofeminist Connection', *Environmental Ethics* 6: 335–41.

Salleh, Ariel (1992) 'The Ecofeminism / Deep Ecology Debate: A Reply to Patriarchal Reason', *Environmental Ethics* 14: 195–216.

Salleh, Ariel (1993) 'Class, Race, and Gender Discourse in the Ecofeminism Deep Ecology Debate', *Environmental Ethics* 15: 225–44.

Salleh, Ariel (1997) *Ecofeminism as Politics: Nature, Marx and the Postmodern* (London: Zed Books).

Salleh, Ariel (2000) 'In Defence of Deep Ecology: An Ecofeminist Response to a Liberal Critique', in Katz et al. (eds).

Salleh, Ariel (2008–9) 'Climate Change – and the Other Footprint', *The Commoner* 13: 15–19.

Salleh, Ariel (2010) 'Green New Deal – or Globalisation Lite?', *Arena* 2:105; a review of the World Watch Institute report, *Toward a Transatlantic Green New Deal: Tackling the Climate and Economic Crises* (Brussels: Heinrich-Boell-Stiftung, 2009).

Salonius, Peter (2008) 'Agriculture: Unsustainable Resource Depletion Began 10,000 Years Ago', *The Oildrum* (21.10.08); http://www.theoildrum.com/node/4628.

Sandel, Michael J. (1996) *Democracy's Discontent* (Cambridge, MA: The Belknap Press).

Sandler, Ronald (2005) 'Introduction: Environmental Virtue Ethics', in Sandler and Cafaro (eds).

Sandler, Ronald (2007) *Character and Environment: A Virtue-Oriented Approach to Environmental Ethics* (New York: Columbia University Press).

Sandler, Ronald and Philip Cafaro (eds) (2005) *Environmental Virtue Ethics* (Lanham, MD: Rowman & Littlefield).

Sarkar, Saral (1999) *Eco-Socialism or Eco-Capitalism? A Critical Analysis of Humanity's Fundamental Choices* (London: Zed Books).

Sarkar, Saral (2010) 'Ecosocialism or Barbarism', *Dandelion Times* (February); http://dandeliontimes.net/category/socialism/.

Scaff, Lawrence A. (1989) *Fleeing the Modern Cage: Culture, Politics, and Modernity in the Thought of Max Weber* (Berkeley: University of California Press).

Schapiro, Mark (2010) 'Conning the Climate', *Harper's Magazine* (Feb.): 31–9.

Schlosser, Eric (2001) *Fast Food Nation: The Dark Side of the All-American Meal* (Boston: Houghton Mifflin).

Scott, James C. (1998) *Seeing Like a State: How Certain Schemes to Improve the Human Condition Have Failed* (New Haven: Yale University Press).

Scruton, Roger (2001) *Kant: A Very Short Introduction* (Oxford: Oxford University Press).

Segal, Jerome (1999) *Graceful Simplicity: Toward a Philosophy and Politics of the Alternative American Dream* (New York: Henry Holt).

Sen, Amartya (2009) *The Idea of Justice* (Cambridge, MA: Harvard University Press).

Serres, Michel (1991) *Le Tiers Instruit* (Paris: François Bourin).

Sessions, George (ed.) (1995a) *Deep Ecology for the 21st Century* (Boston: Shambhala).

Sessions, George (1995b) 'Postmodernism, Environmental Justice, and the Demise of the Ecology Movement?', *Wild Duck Review* 5.

Shaw, Sylvie and Andres Francis (eds) (2008) *Deep Blue: Critical Reflections on Nature, Religion and Water* (London: Equinox).

Shiva, Vandana (1989) *Staying Alive* (London: Zed Books).

Shiva, Vandana (1993) *Monocultures of the Mind: Biodiversity, Biotechnology and Agriculture* (London: Zed Books).

Shiva, Vandana (2005) *Earth Democracy: Justice, Sustainability, and Peace* (Cambridge, MA: South End Press).

Shklar, Judith N. (1984) *Ordinary Vices* (Cambridge, MA: Belknap Press).

Siegal, Charles (2008) *The Politics of Simple Living: A New Direction for Liberalism* (Berkeley: Preservation Institute).

Simms, Andrew (2007) *Tescopoly: How One Shop Came Out on Top and Why It Matters* (London: Constable and Robinson).

Singer, Peter (1977) *Animal Liberation* (London: Granada).

Singer, Peter (1981) *The Expanding Circle: Ethics and Sociology* (New York: Farrar, Strauss & Giroux).

Sivaraksa, Sulak (2005) *Conflict, Culture, Change. Engaged Buddhism in a Globalizing World* (Somerville, MA: Wisdom Publications).

Skinner, Quentin (1998) *Liberty Before Liberalism* (Cambridge: Cambridge University Press).

Smail, J. Kenneth (1997) 'Beyond Population Stabilization: The Case for Dramatically Reducing Global Human Numbers', *Politics and the Life Sciences* 16(2): 183–92.

Smil, Vaclav (1993) *Global Ecology: Environmental Change and Social Flexibility* (London: Routledge).

Smith, Barbara Herrnstein (1988) *Contingencies of Value: Alternative Perspectives for Critical Theory* (Cambridge, MA: Harvard University Press).

Smith, Barbara Herrnstein (1997) *Belief and Resistance: Dynamics of Contemporary Intellectual Controversy* (Cambridge, MA: Harvard University Press).

Smith, Kimberly (2003) *Wendell Berry and the Agrarian Tradition: A Common Grace* (Lawrence: University Press of Kansas).

Smith, Mark J. (1998) *Ecologism: Towards Ecological Citizenship* (Milton Keynes: Open University Press).

Snyder, Gary (1990) *The Practice of the Wild* (San Francisco: North Point).

Söderbaum, Peter (2008) *Understanding Sustainability Economics: Towards Pluralism in Economics* (London: Earthscan).

Solomon, M., A. S. Van Jaarsfeld, H. C. Biggs and M. H. Knight (2003) 'Conservation Targets for Viable Species Assemblages', *Biodiversity and Conservation* 12: 2435–41.

Soper, Kate (1995) *What is Nature? Culture, Politics and the Non-Human* (Oxford: Blackwell).

Sorrell, Roger (1988) *St Francis of Assisi and Nature. Tradition and Innovation in Western Christian Attitudes toward the Environment* (Oxford: Oxford University Press).

Spencer, Colin (1993) *The Heretic's Feast: A History of Vegetarianism* (London: Fourth Estate).

Speth, James Gustave (2004) *Red Sky at Morning: America and the Crisis of the Global Environment* (New Haven: Yale University Press).

Stanton, William (2004) *The Rapid Growth of Human Populations 1750–2000* (Brentwood, CA: Multi-Science Publishing Co).

Starhawk (2002) *Webs of Power: Notes from the Global Uprising* (Gabriola Island, BC: New Society).

Steinfeld, Henning, Pierre Gerber, T. D. Wassenaar and Vincent Castel (2006) *Livestock's Long Shadow: Environmental Issues and Options* (Rome: Food and Agriculture Organization of the UN).

Stengers, Isabelle (2011) 'Comparison as a Matter of Concern', *Common Knowledge* 17(1): 48–63.

Stevens, Val (2003) 'Does Anyone Have the Answer (to the question of what determines fertility rates)?' *The Jackdaw* (February).

Stone, Christopher (1987) *Earth and Other Ethics: The Case for Moral Pluralism* (New York: Harper and Row).

Stone, Christopher (1995) 'Moral Pluralism and the Course of Environmental Ethics', in Brennan (ed.).

Sullivan, Sian (2009/10) 'Green Capitalism, and the Cultural Poverty of Constructing Nature as Service Provider', *Radical Anthropology* 3: 18–27.

Sullivan, Sian (2010a) 'Ecosystem Service Commodities – A New Imperial Ecology?', *New Formations* 69: 111–28.

Sullivan, Sian (2010b) 'The Environmentality of 'Earth Incorporated': on Contemporary Primitive Accumulation and the Financialisation of Environmental Conservation'; http://www.worldecologyresearch.org/papers2010/Sullivan_financialisation_conservation.pdf.

Swanton, Christine (2004) *Virtue Ethics: A Pluralist View* (Oxford: Oxford University Press).

Sylvan, Richard and David Bennett (1994) *The Greening of Ethics: From Human Chauvinism to Deep-Green Theory* (Cambridge: White Horse Press).

Tam, Henry (1998) *Communitarianism: A New Agenda for Politics and Citizenship* (Basingstoke: Macmillan).

Taylor, Bron (ed.) (2005) *Encyclopedia of Nature and Religion* (New York: Continuum).

Taylor, Bron (2010) *Dark Green Religion. Nature, Spirituality and the Planetary Future* (Berkeley: University of California Press).

Taylor, Paul (1986) *Respect for Nature* (Princeton: Princeton University Press).

Tennekes, Hendrik (1990) 'A Sideways Look at Climate Change', *Weather* 45: 67–8.

Thayer Robert (2003) *LifePlace: Bioregional Thought and Practice* (Berkeley: University of California Press).

Thomas, Chris D. (2004) 'Extinction Risk from Climate Change', *Nature* 427 (8 January): 145–8.

Thomas, Keith (1983) *Man and the Natural World* (London: Allen Lane).

Thompson E. P. (1991) *Customs in Common* (London: The Merlin Press).

Thorley, Anthony and Celia M. Gunn (2008) *Sacred Sites: An Overview. A Report for the Gaia Foundation* (London: The Gaia Foundation).

Tokar, Brian (1997) *Earth for Sale: Reclaiming Ecology in the Age of Corporate Greenwash* (Boston: South End Press).

Toledo, Victor M. (2001) 'Indigenous Peoples and Biodiversity', in Simon A. Levin et al. (eds), *The Encyclopedia of Biodiversity* (San Diego: Academic Press).

Tolkien, J. R. R. (1988) [1964] 'On Fairy-Stories', in *Tree and Leaf* (London: Unwin Hyman).

Toulmin, Stephen (1990) *Cosmopolis: The Hidden Agenda of Modernity* (Chicago: University of Chicago Press).

Toulmin, Stephen (2010) *Return to Reason* (Cambridge, MA: Harvard University Press).

Trainer, Ted (1995) *The Conserver Society: Alternatives for Sustainability* (London: Zed Books).

Trainer, Ted (2007) *Renewable Energy Cannot Sustain a Consumer Society* (Basel: Springer).

Ted Trainer (2010) 'The Transition Towns Movement: Its Huge Significance and a Friendly Criticism'; http://www.culturechange.org/cms/content/view/605/65/.

Trefil, James (2004) *Human Nature: A Blueprint for Managing the Earth – by People, for People* (New York: Henry Holt and Co).

Tucker, Mary Evelyn and John Grim (eds) (1994) *Worldviews and Ecology: Religion, Philosophy, and the Environment* (Maryknoll, NY: Orbis).

Tucker, Mary Evelyn and Duncan Ryūken Williams (eds) (1997) *Buddhism and Ecology: The Interconnection of Dharma and Deeds* (Cambridge, MA: Harvard University Press).

Tucker, Mary Evelyn and John Berthrong (eds) (1998) *Confucianism and Ecology: The Interrelation of Heaven, Earth, and Humans* (Cambridge, MA: Harvard University Press).

UN Population Division (2002) *World Population Prospects: The 2002 Revision* (New York: UN).

UNEP (2002) *GEO [Global Environmental Outlook]-3: Past, Present and Future Perspectives* (London: UNEP).

Varela, Francisco J. (1992) *Ethical Know-How* (Stanford: Stanford University Press).

Vitousek, P. M., P. R. Erlich, A. H. Erlich and P. A. Mateson (1986) 'Human Appropriation of the Products of Photosynthesis', *BioScience* 36: 368–73.

Vitousek, Peter M. et al. (1997) 'Human Domination of Earth's Ecosystems', *Science* 277(5325): 494–9.

Viveiros de Castro, Eduardo (1998) 'Cosmological Deixsis and Amerindian Perspectivism', *Journal of the Royal Anthropological Institute* 4: 469–88; repr. in Michael Lambek (ed.), *A Reader in the Anthropology of Religion* (Oxford: Blackwell, 2002).

Viveiros de Castro, Eduardo (2004) 'Exchanging Perspectives. The Transformation of Objects into Subjects in Amerindian Cosmologies', *Common Knowledge* 10(3): 463–84.

Wackernagel, Mathis and William E. Rees (1996) *Our Ecological Footprint: Reducing Human Impact on the Earth* (Philadelphia: New Society Publishers).

Wackernagel, Mathis and William E. Rees (1997) 'Perceptual and Structural Barriers to Investing in Natural Capital: Economics from an Ecological Footprint Perspective', *Ecological Economics* 20(1): 3–24.

Walker, Rebecca L. (2007) 'The Good Life for Non-Human Animals: What Virtue Requires of Humans', in Rebecca L. Walker and Philip J. Ivanhoe (eds), *Working Virtue: Virtue Ethics and Contemporary Moral Problems* (Oxford: Clarendon Press).

Wardle, Tony (2010) 'Knight with a Drooping Lance', *Viva* 45: 32–3.

Warren, Karen J. (1993) 'The Power and Promise of Ecological Feminism', in Michael E. Zimmerman (ed.), *Environmental Philosophy: From Animal Rights to Radical Ecology* (Englewood Cliffs, NJ: Prentice-Hall).

Warren, Karen J. (1994) *Ecological Feminism* (New York: Routledge).

Weber, Max (1991) *From Max Weber: Essays in Sociology*, ed. H. H. Gerth and C. Wright Mills (London: Routledge).

Weber, Michel (2005) 'James's Non-Rationality and its Religious Extremum in the Light of the Concept of Pure Experience', in Jeremy Carrette (ed.), *William James and The Varieties of Religious Experience* (London: Routledge).

Weizacher, Ernst von and Amory Lovins (1998) *Factor Four: Doubling Wealth, Halving Resource Use*, rev. edn (London: Earthscan).

Wensveen, Louke van (2000) *Dirty Virtues: The Emergence of Ecological Virtue Ethics* (Amherst, NY: Humanity Books).

Wenz, Peter S. (2001) *Environmental Ethics Today* (Oxford: Oxford University Press).

Weston, Anthony (1994) *Back to Earth: Tomorrow's Environmentalism* (Philadelphia: Temple University Press).

Weston, Anthony (2004) 'Multicentrism: A Manifesto', *Environmental Ethics* 26 (1): 25–40.

White, Lynn, Jr. (1967) 'Historical Roots of Our Ecological Crisis', *Science* 155 (10 March): 1203–7.

Wiggins, David (2000) 'Nature, Respect for Nature, and the Human Scale of Values', *Proceedings of the Aristotelian Society* XCX: 1–32.

Wilkinson, Richard (1996) *Unhealthy Societies: The Afflictions of Inequality* (London: Routledge).

Wilkinson, Richard and Kate Pickett (2009) *The Spirit Level: Why More Equal Societies Almost Always Do Better* (London: Allen Lane).

Willey, David (2000) 'An Optimum World Population', *Medicine, Conflict and Survival* 16: 72–94.

Willey, David and Jack Parsons (2004) *The Vatican Body-Count: A Study of the Holy See's Share of Responsibility for Excess Mother, Child, and Other Sickness and Death* (Llantrisant: Population Policy Press).

Williams, Bernard (1993) *Ethics and the Limits of Philosophy* (London: Fontana Press).

Windfuhr, Michael and Jennie Jonsén (2005) *Food Sovereignty: Towards Democracy in Localized Food Systems* (Rugby: ITDG).

Wirzba, Norman (2003) 'Placing the Soul: An Agrarian Philosophical Principle', in Norman Wirzba (ed.), *The Essential Agrarian Reader: The Future of Culture, Community and the Land* (Lexington: University Press of Kentucky).

Witoszek, Nina and Andrew Brennan (eds) (1999) *Philosophical Dialogues: Arne Naess and the Progress of Ecophilosophy* (Lanham, MD: Rowman & Littlefield).

Wittgenstein, Ludwig (1953) *Philosophical Investigations*, 3rd edn, trans. G. E. M. Anscombe and R. Rhees (Oxford: Blackwell).

WRI (2000) *World Resources 2000–2001: People and Ecosystems: The Fraying Web of Life* (World Resources Institute); http://www.wri.org/wr 2000.

WWF (2008) Living Planet Report (Gland, Switzerland: WWF).

WWI (2011) *2011 State of the World* (Washington, DC: Worldwatch Institute).

Yablokov, Alexey, Vassily Nesterenko and Alexey Nesterenko (2010) *Chernobyl: Consequences of the Catastrophe for People and the Environment*

(Moscow: Center for Russian Environmental Policy and Minsk: Institute of Radiation Safety).

Youngquist, Walter (1999) 'The Post-Petroleum Paradigm and Population', *Population and Environment* 20(4).

Zimmerman, Michael E., J. Baird Callicott, George Sessions, Karen J. Warren and John Clark (eds) (2005) *Environmental Philosophy: From Animal Rights to Radical Ecology*, 4th edn (Upper Saddle River, NJ: Pearson Publishing).

Zwicky, Jan (1992) *Lyric Philosophy* (Toronto: University of Toronto Press).

Index